D1116057

JOSEF HADAR

Case Institute of Technology

Elementary
Theory of
Economic Behavior

ADDISON-WESLEY PUBLISHING COMPANY

READING, MASSACHUSETTS • PALO ALTO • LONDON • DON MILLS, ONTARIO

This book is in the

ADDISON-WESLEY SERIES

IN MANAGEMENT

SCIENCE AND ECONOMICS

PREFACE

This is a textbook for undergraduates (most graduate students will find it a waste of time). As such it assumes that the student has had little or no exposure to economic theory. Consequently, the text attempts to perform two functions:

1. To present the basic subject matter of intermediate microeconomics;
2. To introduce the student to the principles of economic theorizing.

Thus, while the material in this text is introductory in nature, its exposition is designed to meet the requirements of sound methodology. We have therefore paid special attention to the handling of technical terms and the development of logical arguments. Every concept, technical expression, and tool of analysis introduced in the text is clearly defined. Whenever possible, with due respect to the general level of the book, each definition is expressed in quantitative terms and/or illustrated graphically. The use and application of analytical concepts, and the implications which derive from such applications, are demonstrated directly in the context of the topic discussed. In general, the discussion proceeds at a measured pace, and quite frequently we have been unabashedly simple-minded in our attempt to leave no part of the subject matter unexplained. Whenever uncertainty about the clarity of the material arose, the reader was given the benefit of the doubt.

At the same time we have tried to give the text a formal character in order to introduce the student to the language and method of theoretical analysis. This means that occasionally the student is expected to cope with a moderate amount of abstract reasoning. However, in view of the introductory nature of the text, the use of mathematical tools has been kept to a minimum. Certain small sections are more technical than the rest of the text, but they may be omitted without jeopardizing a basic understanding of the substance of the text. These sections are marked by a triangle ▶. The technical preparation which the student may want to have at his disposal can be summarized as follows:

1. He should be able to perform addition, subtraction, multiplication, and division with real numbers.
2. He should be able to rank measurable quantities in the order of their size.
3. He should be familiar with the rudiments of the graphical technique.

In providing examples of the various topics discussed in the text we have made only limited use of concrete cases. This was done in order not to reinforce the unfortunate tendency shown by many students to look upon theoretical models as descriptions of the real world. On the other hand, there is no doubt that carefully chosen illustrations can be of considerable pedagogical value. It is felt, therefore, that the selection of real-world examples, and the timing of their discussion, ought to be determined at the instructor's discretion.

The book contains two principal parts: the first of these deals with the behavior of the firm, the second with the behavior of the consumer. As in the case of the hen and the egg, the question of precedence is not intuitively obvious, and its solution depends very much on one's point of view. The order of presentation adopted in this text is based on the belief that the basic ingredients of the theory of the firm are probably easier to digest than the more abstract concepts used in modern utility theory. However, each part is sufficiently self-contained to make a reversal in the order of presentation feasible. Each part contains the material found in most standard texts, as well as certain extensions of a more advanced nature. The last part of the text provides an introduction to welfare economics and general equilibrium analysis.

At the end of each chapter (except the Introduction) we have placed a set of exercises. For the most part these are of the type found in students' workbooks. Many of the exercises are broken into a number of small parts, each of which can be worked out independently without much effort. The objective of the simple design of these exercises is to entice the student into trying his hand at some of them; they provide an excellent means of reviewing the preceding chapter. Some instructors may even want to assign some of the exercises as homework, and in order to lighten the instructor's burden as much as possible, a set of answers to the exercises has been prepared.

It is only in exceptional cases that a textbook presents a substantial amount of original work. This book is no exception. The basic material in it reflects what by now has become the standard theory of microeconomics as it is found in the professional literature. It has its origins in the works of generations of economists who have contributed to its development and sustained its growth up to the present time, from Marshall to Marschak, from Slutsky to Stigler. However, because of the extensive diffusion which microtheory has undergone, no attempt has been made in this text to trace the various parts of the theory to their original authors. And to convince himself of the fact that this text contains only second-hand material, the reader is invited to consult the references provided at the end of each chapter.

Upon completion of a project such as this, one's thoughts naturally turn to one's former teachers. After all, it is the encouragement and guidance, direct as well as indirect, that the student receives from his teachers which to a great extent shape the student's determination to pursue a professional course, and eventually to venture into the hazardous field of publication. And for this his teachers deserve to receive the credit, or take the blame, as the case may be. The teachers in question in this instance are Professors Oswald H. Brownlee, Harvey C. Bunke, Robert W. Clower, Morton C. Grossman, Leonid Hurwicz, and David T. Lapkin, all of whom, I like to think, are due a great deal of credit.

More directly, I have benefited from the criticism made by a number of persons who were kind enough to read the manuscript. These include Professors Oswald H. Brownlee, Phoebus J. Dhrymes, Lehman B. Fletcher, and Dennis R. Starleaf; their comments and suggestions have resulted in an improved final manuscript. The fact that the manuscript has been transformed into a publishable book is due largely to the efforts of Addison-Wesley, and in particular to the care and circumspection exercised by the manuscript editors. Special praise must go to Addison-Wesley's outstanding art department for its execution of the illustrations; it may be added that the artists' work has not necessarily been made easier by the inadequate instructions given them by the author. Last, but not least, I am indebted to Mrs. Maxine A. Cords who gave generously of her time, and thereby was able to type the entire manuscript. And finally, the customary acknowledgement of familial assistance is in order: if I *had* a wife and kids to look after, this book would probably never have been written.

Cleveland, Ohio   J.H.
April 1966

CONTENTS

1 **Introduction**

1-1 The Subject Matter of the Book 1
1-2 The Question of Methodology 5

2 **The Cost of Production: Short Run**

2-1 Total Costs 10
2-2 Average and Marginal Costs 14
2-3 The Relationship between Total, Average, and Marginal
Costs 17

3 **The Efficiency of Production**

3-1 The Production Function 26
3-2 Efficient Input Combinations 34
3-3 Efficient Input Combinations and Cost Curves 37

4 **The Cost of Production: Long Run**

4-1 Long-run Average Cost 45
4-2 Long-run Total and Marginal Cost 48
4-3 Changes in Input Prices and Technology 49

5   **Short-Run Profit Maximization: Pure Competition**

5–1   The Nature of Pure Competition 53
5–2   The Optimal Level of Output 55
5–3   The Supply Curve of the Firm and the Market   . . . 62

6   **Long-Run Profit Maximization: Pure Competition**

6–1   The Optimal Level of Output and Size of Plant   . . . 69
6–2   Adjustment to Price Changes 71
6–3   Changes in Input Prices   77

7   **Profit Maximization: Pure Monopoly**

7–1   The Demand Function   84
7–2   The Optimal Level of Output and Price 90
7–3   Price Discrimination   96
7–4   A Comparison Between Pure Competition and Pure
      Monopoly   105
7–5   Regulated Monopolies 108

8   **Profit Maximization: Monopolistic Competition**

8–1   The Nature of Monopolistic Competition   122
8–2   The Optimal Level of Output and Price 124
8–3   Advertising 129
8–4   Oligopolistic Markets 138
8–5   A Comparison between Pure Competition,
      Pure Monopoly, and Monopolistic Competition   . . . 151

9   **The Demand for Factors of Production: Pure Competition**

9–1   The One-Input Case   160
9–2   The Two-Input Case   170
9–3   Monopoly in the Product Market   173
9–4   The Long Run 176
9–5   A Comparison Between the Competitor and the
      Monopolist   176

10   **The Demand for Factors of Production: Pure Monopsony**

10–1   The One-Input Case   181
10–2   The Two-Input Case   185
10–3   Price Discrimination   187
10–4   Bilateral Monopoly 189
10–5   Price Control   192

11   **Linear Profit Maximization**

    11–1 The Properties of Linear Processes 198
    11–2 Output Maximization 207
    11–3 Profit Maximization 213
    11–4 The Imputed Value of the Inputs 219

12   **The Demand for Consumer Goods**

    12–1 The Utility Function 228
    12–2 Utility Maximization 234

13   **Further Problems in Demand Theory**

    13–1 The Consumer as a Seller 250
    13–2 A Two-Period Model 257
    13–3 Behavior Under Uncertainty 263

14   **Welfare Economics**

    14–1 The Nature of Welfare Economics 278
    14–2 The Distribution Problem 281
    14–3 The Production Problem 286
    14–4 The Production-Distribution Plan 290
    14–5 Welfare and the Price Mechanism 297

15   **General Equilibrium**

    15–1 The Construction of the Model 308
    15–2 The Workings of the Model 313
    15–3 Concluding Remarks 320

    Index 327

In memory of my parents

1

INTRODUCTION

*To learn means
to learn how
to learn.*

ANONYMOUS PHILOSOPHER

1-1 THE SUBJECT MATTER OF THE BOOK

Every economy may be thought of as consisting of two species of economic units: **producing units** and **consuming units.** The first group is made up of those establishments in the economy which engage in the production of some commodity or service. The second group comprises all the units whose primary function is the consumption of the final products of the producing units, and may be roughly identified as the total of all the households in the economy.

The subject matter of this book deals with the behavior of a typical representative of each of these groups. Since the treatment of the material is meant to be fairly general, we shall be concerned only with what we believe to be the basic problems common to all units in each group, rather than with problems peculiar to one or the other specific unit. To this end we shall omit all factors which are only incidental to the analysis. Thus our producing unit could represent a wheat farmer, a steel company, an umbrella manufacturer, a gas station, a bowling alley, etc. Similarly, by consuming unit we may mean an individual consumer, an entire household, or any other group of individuals who act as one single person with respect to consumption decisions. However, a word of caution is in order. Since the analysis is rather elementary and simple, many questions will have to be left unanswered—in particular those concerning specific phases of the operation of a productive enterprise or the management of a household, as well as problems pertaining to particular types of producers or consumers. However, in spite of this, the reader will find that the material

1

may at times become more meaningful and comprehensible if he views it in the context of some simple but concrete example. Whenever he feels the need for an illustration from the real world, the reader should give free rein to his imagination and cover the analytical skeleton of the text with a colorful cloak of his own fancy. For convenience we shall usually refer to the producing unit as the "firm," to the household unit as the "consumer," and to the commodities and services in question as the "product" or "output."

The reader will more fully understand the subject matter of this text and the manner of its presentation if he bears in mind the motivation for this study. The purpose of this analysis may be said to be an attempt **to describe the behavior of a rational economic unit in its pursuit of a certain objective within the framework of its environment.** Of course, it is quite conceivable that not every firm or consumer acts as rationally as we assume in our analysis, either because of a lack of knowledge, or perhaps a lack of desire. It is, therefore, quite appropriate and often helpful to think of some of our findings as **a set of rules designed to instruct the decision maker in the pursuit of his objectives.**

The above statement of purpose also focuses on two crucial elements in the analysis: (a) the objective of the decision maker and (b) the environment in which he operates. The importance of these factors should be self-evident, because the behavior of an economic unit is determined by both its objective and its environment. It is, therefore, to be expected that any two units pursuing different objectives will follow different courses of action, even if they operate under identical environmental conditions. Likewise, differences in the behavior of economic units having identical objectives may be explained in terms of the particular environment in which each of them operates.

Thus our investigation and its conclusions depend directly on what we assume about both the objective and the environment of the decision maker, and if the analysis is to be conducted in a rigorous fashion, it is essential that these assumptions be specified in most explicit terms.

1–1.1 The decision maker's objectives

The assumptions about objectives should be stated immediately. With respect to the producing unit, it will be assumed throughout the text that the firm has one single objective: **to maximize its profits.** Leaving aside for the moment the question of the precise definition of profit, it is clear that the above assumption need not necessarily hold in every instance. Some producers, for example, may put less emphasis on profit maximization, and instead aim at capturing a large share of the market for their product. Others are perhaps mainly concerned with the rate of return on their investment, and still others may be primarily interested in the sheer size of their enterprise. Indeed, economists are by no means convinced that the assumption of profit maximization provides the best explanation for the behavior of business firms. An alternative approach, for example, suggests that the objective of a firm may consist of a number of target variables rather than just one. The firm's behavior can then be explained as an attempt to attain these targets in some order of priority. We shall, nevertheless, stick to the assumption of profit maximization, because the more sophisticated substitutes require the use of analytical tools with which the reader may not be familiar at this stage, and so long as the analysis is to be limited to firms which are assumed to follow one single objective, our choice seems quite reasonable.

Our approach to the behavior of the consumer is of a similar nature; that is, we assume that the consumer also pursues a single objective. Accordingly we take the view that the actions of the consumer can be rationalized in terms of his desire **to maximize his own satisfaction**. This assumption also raises a number of critical problems which the reader will be able to appreciate more fully after he has become familiar with the text. In any event, any criticism concerning the naiveté of our approach will be rejected on the ground that the conception of the consumer as a perfect hedonist is a good first approximation.

1–1.2   The decision maker's environment

The specification of the decision maker's environment is a task to which large parts of the following chapters are devoted. At this point a few general remarks will suffice. It is possible, and convenient, to think of the firm as operating in both **a technological environment** and an **economic environment.** The technological environment refers to the state of technology which prevails at the time the firm makes its production plan and the technical know-how to which it has access. We are not interested in this information from an engineering point of view, of course, but only in its economic interpretation. Consequently, the characteristics of the technological environment will be expressed in terms of the quantities of various factors of production which are required to achieve some desired level of output. The economic environment, on the other hand, describes the structure of the market in which the firm operates and the demand for its product. Here we are concerned with such matters as the number of firms in the market, the nature of the product produced by rival firms, and the strength of the demand for the product in question.

Now that some of the relevant concepts have been given a more concrete meaning, it may be helpful to restate the purpose of the analysis in more specific terms. With respect to producing units we can now say that our aim is **to describe the behavior of a rational firm which wishes to maximize its profit, subject to the conditions of the prevailing technology, the specifications of the**

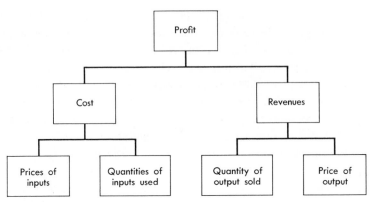

Figure 1–1

market structure, and the demand for its product. Figure 1–1 may further clarify the relationship between the firm's objective and environments, and their role in the analysis.

The firm's objective appears at the top of the pyramid, while the lower levels represent various factors which play a part in determining the level of profit which the firm will earn under various sets of circumstances. Thus the amount of profit depends first of all on the firm's cost and revenues, since profit, by definition, is the difference between the two. Cost and revenues in turn depend on a number of other factors, some of which can be controlled directly by the firm. Cost, as the diagram shows, depends on the quantities of inputs used, and on the prices which the firm has to pay for them. The quantities of inputs actually purchased by the firm will, of course, be determined by the level of output it wishes to produce, in conjunction with the prevailing state of technology, while the input prices may be considered to be part of the firm's economic environment. The firm's revenues depend on how much output it produces and sells, and on the price at which the output is sold. Both of these are influenced by the firm's economic environment.

Admittedly, the above diagram is highly simplified. It shows only definitional relationships, ignoring many other cause-and-effect relations which link the components into a complete system. These will be introduced later in the text. Here we merely wish to show some of the direct relations between the more important concepts toward which this analysis will be directed, and to lend additional emphasis to the fact that any action of the firm must always be analyzed and evaluated with reference both to the firm's objective and its environmental conditions.

The consumer also operates in two environments; one of these is a **psychological environment,** and the other an **economic environment.** The first of these represents the consumer's preference for the various goods and services which are available in the market. It may perhaps seem strange to refer to these subjective factors as part of the consumer's environment, since the consumer himself may change his pattern of preferences. However, this is also true about the technological environment of the firm, which can undergo various changes as a result of the firm's own research and development efforts. We think of technology and preferences as part of the environment (rather than, say, a decision variable) because our analysis is concerned with relatively short periods of time during which both technology and preferences can be considered constant. The consumer's economic environment, like that of the firm, describes the nature of the market in which he trades and the resources, or income, at his disposal.

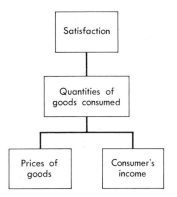

Figure 1–2

Some of the important variables involved in the analysis of the consumer's behavior are shown schematically in Fig. 1–2. The consumer's target variable is placed at the top. The level of satisfaction experienced by the consumer depends directly on the quantities of the various goods he consumes. These, in turn, are restricted by the prices of the goods, as well as by the income available to the consumer.

1–2 THE QUESTION OF METHODOLOGY

There is one additional point which the reader should fully understand before he embarks on the main part of the text. A great deal of the material is concerned with a discussion of the decision maker's environmental conditions and the extent to which these conditions determine his actions once he has chosen a certain objective. It must be emphasized at this point—and it cannot be overstressed—that in stating the various specifications of the environments in which an economic unit is said to operate, we **do not** attempt to

describe the real world; rather we paint an imaginary picture of it. In more technical terms, we build a **model** of the real world.

An economic model is a theoretical construct which represents certain aspects of an economic system, or parts thereof, **as they are conceived in the mind of the model builder.** A model is an assumption rather than an empirical fact. Model building is also selective in character; in building a model one chooses only a limited number of factors and relationships which appear to be important determinants of the phenomena under investigation. Consequently, a model is meant to simplify the real world, rather than to describe it in full.

The reason for dealing with these somewhat artificial representations of the economy instead of with true descriptions of it is simple: it would be an impossible task to describe the real world with the facilities presently available. This is so not only because the real world, at least as it appears to our minds, is an agglomeration of bewildering complexities, but also because, when researching in the realm of human affairs, we are often hampered in our endeavors to learn what the real world is like by the lack of opportunities to conduct adequately controlled experiments. Thus in our study of the behavior of the producing and the consuming units we use models of the economy as the best substitutes for a true description of the economic system.

Of course, the models which we use are not entirely a product of our imagination. As a result of our own observations and research we have accumulated a body of knowledge about the economy and the behavior of its components which provides us with both inspiration and direction in the construction of economic models. We believe that the models used in the study of the theory of the firm and consumer behavior, as well as those used in other areas of economic theory, are reasonably effective tools of analysis, and that they can be considered to be fairly good approximations of their counterparts in the real world. However, the fact should never be overlooked that even good models are only models, and therefore the conclusions which are derived from them cannot be regarded as empirical facts.

To really drive this point home—even at the risk of appearing tedious— let me tell you a short story.

> Once there was a king who was very fond of toys. To indulge his playful whims he kept among his servants a toymaker whose sole duty was to make new toys for his master, and to repair and maintain the old ones.
>
> One day a package arrived for the king, but it had been crushed and broken en route. It contained only fragments, and there was no way of identifying its sender. The king became very curious about the gift, because it appeared to him to be a most unusual toy. He summoned his toymaker immediately, and commanded him to restore it to its original state. The toymaker was granted three days in which to complete his task.

The king waited impatiently for his gift to be repaired, and when at the end of the third day the toymaker presented him with nothing but a sheaf of drawings, the king was very angry.

"Where is my toy?" he thundered. "What are all these pictures?"

"By your leave, Your Majesty," begged the toymaker. "I humbly ask your indulgence. Unfortunately the pieces were in such a poor state of repair that I was unable to reconstruct the original gift, which, I venture to speculate, must have been a toy of highly intricate design. Instead I have prepared these drawings, depicting a number of different toys which the broken pieces have suggested to me. For your edification, Your Majesty, each diagram is accompanied by a list of instructions explaining how the toy is to be operated, and what it is capable of performing under various circumstances."

When the toymaker had delivered his explanation the king's anger subsided somewhat, but his curiosity about the original toy was not yet satisfied.

"Tell me," he demanded of the toymaker, "which of these drawings represents the real toy? And if none of them does, which one bears the greatest resemblance to it?"

"Your Majesty," replied the toymaker, "the toy which can be put together from the broken pieces will have the greatest resemblance to the real toy. Of course, to construct such a toy will require a great amount of time and effort, but if you command me, I will set about the task immediately."

Whereupon the toymaker was ordered to begin work right away. The prospect of learning something about the unusual toy restored the king's good spirits, and the toymaker was saved from disgrace—at least for the time being.

So much for the story. In this text we play the part of the toymaker. We shall construct simple models representing certain aspects of the economy, embodying in them those features which our limited knowledge of the real world suggests to us. We shall analyze these models, and examine their properties. In other words, we shall make statements and predictions about events in the real world which would be true **if** our models were true descriptions of the real world. More specifically, we shall show how a rational economic unit would behave **if** it were trying to maximize profit or satisfaction, as the case may be, and **if** it operated under environmental conditions identical to the specification of our models. The main purpose of this text is not to describe the real world, but to develop a convenient method through which one can discover an explanation for certain observed phenomena. Essentially we wish to demonstrate how our ideas about various aspects of the economic system can be organized and processed to yield verifiable hypotheses.

Incidentally, what about building a real toy instead of just drawing blueprints? Toy building does, indeed, exist, not only in the above allegory, but also in real practice. It is concerned with the testing of theoretical models to determine how well they fit the pattern of events in the real world. The testing of economic models is a discipline by itself, and it usually requires highly advanced analytical techniques. In any case, model building precedes model testing, and the reader is well advised to acquire an adequate background in the former before embarking on a study of the latter.

1–2.1 Fasten your seat belt!

It was not the purpose of this brief digression on methodology to shock or confuse the reader unnecessarily, but we feel that before we take off, he should have some general idea of the nature of things to come. We believe that the preceding comments are not only important, but are also necessary for a complete understanding of what this book is all about. The reader should review this discussion from time to time as he proceeds with the rest of the text. Its purpose is to provide him with a sense of balance—to discourage the buildup of undue reverence for all the wonders he may believe economic theory to be capable of performing, and at the same time to forestall the frustration which is likely to set in as soon as he realizes its limitations.

SELECTED REFERENCES

FRIEDMAN, MILTON, "The Methodology of Positive Economics." *Essays in Positive Economics*, Chicago: The University of Chicago Press, 1953, pp. 3–43.

KOOPMANS, T. C., "The Construction of Economic Knowledge." *Three Essays on the State of Economic Science*, New York: McGraw-Hill, 1957, pp. 129–166.

LANGE, O., "The Scope and Method of Economics." *Review of Economic Studies* **13**, 1945–46, pp. 19–32.

NAGEL, E., "Assumptions in Economic Theory." *American Economic Review*, Papers and Proceedings **53**, 1963, pp. 211–219.

WOOTTON, B., "The Value of Scientific Method" in *Basic Issues of American Democracy*. New York: Appleton-Century-Crofts, 1956, pp. 469–475. (Excerpts from *Testament for Social Science*, New York: Norton, 1951.)

2

THE COST OF PRODUCTION: SHORT RUN

From Fig. 1–1 we can see that the firm's profit depends on two major factors—cost and revenues. Cost is determined by the amount of inputs used, and the prices of these inputs. It would be logical to begin the analysis at the bottom of the pyramid, perhaps with a discussion of how the firm chooses the combination of inputs to be used for any particular level of production. However, in order to start with a relatively easy topic, we shall begin instead with a discussion of various cost relationships. In the next chapter we shall consider the question of the determination of the proper input combination, and the relationship between the amounts of inputs used and the firm's cost.

In this text the concept of cost will refer for the most part to the money outlays which the firm makes in connection with its productive activities. However, if the firm happens to own some of the inputs which it uses in production, these inputs do not give rise to direct outlays, and their cost must be imputed in some appropriate fashion. Thus our concept of cost may refer to actual as well as imputed outlays. This concept is, therefore, akin to the notion of cost as it is used in ordinary accounting practices. We call attention to this because of the existence of a different concept of cost frequently employed by economists: the idea of **opportunity cost.** The latter is not concerned with direct money outlays, but with the value of the product which could have been produced with the resources currently employed in the production of another product. Suppose, for example, that cream may be used for making either cream cheese or whipped cream, and suppose also that it takes two pounds of cream, and nothing else, to produce one pound of cream cheese. The **direct cost** of one pound of cream cheese then is simply equal to the value of two pounds of cream, whereas the **opportunity cost** of one pound of cream cheese is equal to the value of that quantity of whipped cream which may be obtained by whipping up two pounds of cream. Except for a few isolated instances we shall not make use of the concept of opportunity cost in this text.

The reader should clearly understand at this point that our analysis is meaningful only with reference to a certain period of time (a day, a week, a year), but in general we shall not specify the time period or use the phrase "per period of time." Thus when we speak of the firm's profit, output, cost, we really mean profit per period of time, output per period of time, etc. However, all the variables will be measured with respect to the same period of time, whatever it may be.

2–1 TOTAL COSTS

The theory of the firm normally makes use of a number of different types of costs, all of which relate expenditures incurred by the firm to the respective level of output. This will become clear from the definitions which follow below.

Definition 2–1

TOTAL COST (TC) = the total money outlay for a given level of output.

This definition is self-explanatory. The concept of TC will become somewhat more meaningful when it is viewed as the sum of two components. These are, respectively, total fixed cost and total variable cost.

Definition 2–2

TOTAL FIXED COST (TFC) = the total money outlay on the **fixed inputs** used for a given level of output.

Fixed inputs are factors of production whose quantities cannot be varied during the time period underlying the analysis. Included in this category are factors which are purchased on a contractual basis for the entire period of time, or factors whose quantities can be changed only over a period of time which is longer than the one in question. Examples of fixed costs are rent for physical facilities such as land, buildings, and heavy machinery, interest on borrowed capital, security expenses (the watchman's salary), license fees, etc. It is customary to refer to the totality of all the fixed factors as the "size of the plant," because a change in the size of the firm's physical plant normally involves a change in the various fixed costs in the same direction. From the nature of the fixed inputs it follows that TFC is also fixed during the period of time in question. Furthermore—and this is important to remember—TFC does not vary with the level of output; i.e., it is independent of the level of output. Thus, for example, if the firm contracts to lease certain facilities for a period of one year at a specified rent, the cost of these facilities is entirely independent of the level of output that the firm chooses to produce in the same year. (There might, however, be instances in which the rent is determined on the basis of the rate of production. In that case rent is not a fixed, but a variable, cost.) Indeed, TFC may be defined as **any type of outlay which is independent of the level of output.**

It should be emphasized that factors of production cannot be classified as fixed or variable merely on the basis of their inherent characteristics; whether they are fixed or not in any particular case depends entirely on the length of the time period, and on certain institutional arrangements in the market in which they are sold (as in the case of rent mentioned above). Whenever it is assumed that the firm does have some fixed costs, the respective model represents an analysis of the firm's operations in the **short run.** Thus the crucial element in the definition of the short run is not the length of the time period as such, but the existence of fixed costs.

Definition 2–3

TOTAL VARIABLE COST (TVC) = the total money outlay on the **variable in-puts** used for a given level of output.

It hardly seems necessary to elaborate on this definition. All the inputs which are not fixed are variable, and hence those items of TC which are not included in TFC belong to TVC. If we use the above abbreviations as symbols representing the number of dollars of each respective type of cost, we can describe the relationship between these three concepts by the following algebraic equation:

$$TC = TFC + TVC. \tag{2–1}$$

Since each of the above types of cost is defined with reference to a certain level of output, changes in output will presumably change cost. Hence we think of cost as being dependent on output or, in more technical terms, as being a **function of output.** These functional relationships may best be explained with the help of a numerical example. Table 2–1 represents hypothetical cost relations of a firm for the output levels 0–10. A comparison of the first two columns shows that when the level of output increases, TC increases too, since output cannot be increased unless one increases the quantity of some of the inputs. We should add that it is assumed that input prices are constant, so that any increase in cost necessarily implies the use of more inputs. Column 3, on the other hand, has identical numbers in all its rows. That follows directly from the definition of TFC. In this example the firm pays $32 on its fixed inputs, regardless of whether it produces zero units of output, eight units, or any other amount. Finally, we see that the numbers in column 4 also increase with the level of output, reflecting the fact that in order to obtain higher levels of output, the firm must increase some of its variable inputs. Note that at the zero level of output the firm's total expenditures equal its TFC. Table 2–1 may also be used to verify the equation TC = TFC + TVC; in each row the number in column 2 is equal to the sum of the numbers in columns 3 and 4.

Units of output	TC in $	TFC in $	TVC in $
1	2	3	4
0	32	32	0
1	44	32	12
2	52	32	20
3	56	32	24
4	60	32	28
5	72	32	40
6	86	32	54
7	102	32	70
8	128	32	96
9	167	32	135
10	212	32	180

Table 2–1

Although tables of the type represented above are useful for illustrating the meaning of certain concepts, they are somewhat clumsy tools of analysis. We shall, therefore, carry out most of our investigation with the help of graphical representations of the various functional relationships. Figure 2–1 shows the graphs of the three cost relations discussed above. The vertical axis measures cost, the horizontal axis measures output. Because all costs are measured in dollars the vertical axis carries the label $. The letter X is used to denote the level of output. Unlike cost, or profit, output is always expressed in some appropriate physical unit of measurement. A few clarifying comments are now in order.

First, notice that Fig. 2–1 contains more information than does Table 2–1. The latter shows us the various total costs for only eleven selected levels of output, whereas in Fig. 2–1 we can read off the cost for a great many levels of output—an infinity of different levels of outputs, in fact. If the reader has ever translated a numerical table into graphical form he may recognize that the graphs of the three cost functions given in Table 2–1 consist of a collection of

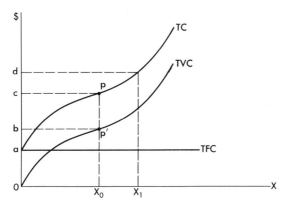

Figure 2–1

points, rather than continuous lines such as those in Fig. 2–1. When cost functions are represented as continuous lines, certain assumptions about the underlying technology are made implicitly. We shall state these assumptions explicitly. We assume in this case that the level of output is capable of continuous variations. Since any point on each of the cost curves is a well-defined point, we may choose any arbitrary point on any of the cost curves and associate with it a particular level of output and cost. For example, the arbitrary point p on the TC curve tells us that the total cost of producing X_0 units of output is equal to c dollars. (The various letter symbols on the two axes are used to denote numbers.) Thus X_0 may be any number greater than zero, and it is not restricted to one of the integers in column 1 of Table 2–1. Furthermore, since we are also entitled to choose another point on the TC curve, we could select a point which is arbitrarily close to point p, so that the output associated with the second point would be very close to X_0. The assumptions underlying continuous cost curves may, therefore, be summarized as follows:

(2A) There exists an infinity of output levels at which the firm may operate.

(2B) The level of output may be changed by infinitesimally small increments.

The above statements are derived directly from the fact that any continuous line segment has infinitely many points, and that we can always choose two distinct points on such a segment which are separated by an arbitrarily small distance. Of course, in many concrete situations it will be impossible to increase the level of output by an arbitrarily small amount, but only by discrete increments as in the example given in Table 2–1. However, the convenience gained by working with continuous curves far outweighs the cost of the distortions involved in making the above assumptions.

In spite of these discrepancies, Table 2–1 and Fig. 2–1 are consistent in many other respects. Table 2–1 shows, as has already been observed, that TC is an **increasing function** of output; i.e., whenever output is increased, TC increases as well. This property is also incorporated in the graphs of Fig. 2–1. For example, while the total cost of producing X_0 units of X is c dollars, that of producing X_1 is d dollars. Since $X_1 > X_0$, and d > c, the relationship between X and TC is as stipulated above (> means "is greater than," and < means "is less than"). As the reader can see from the shape of the TC curve, this result holds for any two points on that curve. Now how can this property (i.e., the fact that TC is an increasing function of X) be described in geometric terms? Observe that if you take any arbitrary point on the TC curve, say point p, and examine the shape of the curve in the region to the right of point p, you will find that the curve is sloping up and to the right. Curves, or straight lines, with this property are said to have a **positive slope.** Thus the fact that both the TC curve and the TVC curve are shown as curves with positive slopes implies that TC as well as TVC are increasing functions of X.

What about TFC? Geometrically a horizontal line has a slope which is equal to zero. A line like the one labeled TFC may also be referred to as a **constant function,** meaning that as X is increased, TFC remains constant. And that is precisely how the relationship between X and TFC has been defined.

Finally, we show that Fig. 2–1 is also consistent with the cost equation TC = TFC + TVC. Let us consider the level of output X_0. At that output TC equals c dollars, and TVC equals b dollars. Substituting these values into the equation we find that TFC equals c − b dollars. Now the number c − b may also be represented by the vertical distance between the points c and b on the vertical axis, or, since it forms the opposite side of a rectangle, by the vertical distance between the points p and p′. But the diagram also indicates that TFC is equal to a, and therefore the distance between p and p′ equals the distance on the vertical axis between the origin (the point labeled 0) and a. And since TFC is the same at any level of output, the vertical distance between the TC and TVC curves is the same at any level of output. It follows, therefore, that the shape of these two curves is identical. That is, if you were to move the TVC curve vertically upward by a distance equal to a, it would coincide with the TC curve. [By the way, we have not yet discussed the reason for the particular shape (other than the slope) given to these curves. This will be done later.]

2–2 AVERAGE AND MARGINAL COSTS

We shall now introduce another set of costs which are closely related to the three total cost concepts discussed so far. Instead of focusing on **total outlays** incurred by the firm, the concepts to be defined below (that is, the first three of them) have to do with **average outlays,** i.e., the cost of production **per unit of output.**

Definition 2–4

AVERAGE TOTAL COST (ATC) = the total money outlay per unit of output at a given level of output. ATC is defined as TC divided by the respective level of output; that is, ATC = TC/X.

Definition 2–5

AVERAGE FIXED COST (AFC) = the money outlay on the fixed inputs per unit of output at a given level of output. AFC is defined as TFC divided by the respective level of output; that is, AFC = TFC/X.

Definition 2–6

AVERAGE VARIABLE COST (AVC) = the money outlay on the variable inputs per unit of output at a given level of output. AVC is defined as TVC divided by the respective level of output; that is, AVC = TVC/X.

Definition 2–7

MARGINAL COST (MC) = the change in TC as the level of output is increased by one unit.

Note that like the total costs, the concepts just defined are expressed as functions of the level of output. Table 2–2 provides a numerical illustration of these relationships.

The first four columns are the same as Table 2–1. They have been reproduced here because columns 5–8 can be constructed directly from the information

X	TC in $	TFC in $	TVC in $	ATC in $	AFC in $	AVC in $	MC in $
1	2	3	4	5	6	7	8
0	32	32	0	—	—	—	
1	44	32	12	44	32	12	12
2	52	32	20	26	16	10	8
3	56	32	24	$18\frac{2}{3}$	$10\frac{2}{3}$	8	4
4	60	32	28	15	8	7	4
5	72	32	40	$14\frac{2}{5}$	$6\frac{2}{5}$	8	12
6	86	32	54	$14\frac{1}{3}$	$5\frac{1}{3}$	9	14
7	102	32	70	$14\frac{4}{7}$	$4\frac{4}{7}$	10	16
8	128	32	96	16	4	12	26
9	167	32	135	$18\frac{5}{9}$	$3\frac{5}{9}$	15	39
10	212	32	180	$21\frac{1}{5}$	$3\frac{1}{5}$	18	45

Table 2–2

given in columns 1–4. Thus for any row except the first, the following holds: the number in column 5 equals the number in column 2 divided by the number in column 1; the number in column 6 equals the number in column 3 divided by the number in column 1; the number in column 7 equals the number in column 4 divided by the number in column 1.   These relationships follow directly from the definitions given earlier. The first cells of columns 5–7 are left empty because average cost is not defined for a zero level of output.   To compute average cost for that output according to the stated definitions would involve division by zero—an operation which is not defined in the system of mathematics generally used.

Another useful relationship is the following equation:

$$\text{ATC} = \text{AFC} + \text{AVC}. \tag{2–2}$$

It is obtained directly by dividing both sides of the equation $\text{TC} = \text{TFC} + \text{TVC}$ by the respective level of output.   This may be verified by noting that each number in column 5 is equal to the sum of the numbers in columns 6 and 7 in the same row.   Column 8 is computed directly from the table.   Since MC is defined as the change in TC as X is increased by one unit, it can be computed immediately by taking the difference between the total outlays for the respective levels of output. For example, TC for two units of X is \$52, and for three units of X it is \$56. Therefore MC is equal to \$4 when the level of X is changed from 2 to 3. In Table 2–2 the value of MC always appears in the row belonging to the terminal level of output, i.e., the level **to** which (rather than **from** which) output is being increased. Note also that the increments in TVC for any increase in X by one unit are the same as the increments in TC for the same increase in X. Therefore it is also true that MC is equal to the change in TVC as X is increased by one unit.

The various average cost functions, as well as the marginal cost function, are represented graphically in Fig. 2–2. As in the case of the total cost functions, the graphs in Fig. 2–2 are generally consistent with the information given in columns 5–8 of Table 2–2. An inspection of columns 5, 7, and 8 reveals that the numbers in these columns (i.e., the value of the respective cost functions) read from the top downward, tend to decrease as the level of output is increased from zero, but that beyond a certain level—different for each of these functions—the respective costs increase with output. Consequently, the graphs of the ATC, AVC, and MC functions are U-shaped, with the bottom of each U at a different level of X. That is, at relatively small levels of output, ATC, AVC, and MC are **decreasing functions** of X, while at sufficiently high levels of X they are **increasing functions** of X. But AFC, as shown in Table 2–2 and Fig. 2–2, is always decreasing with increases in X. This follows from the simple fact that

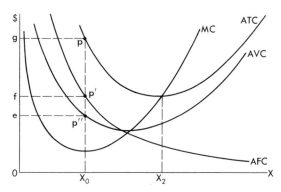

Figure 2–2

the values of AFC at successively higher levels of X are obtained by dividing a fixed number (TFC) by successively larger numbers.

The graphs in Fig. 2–2 also satisfy the equation ATC = AFC + AVC. For instance, at the level of output X_0, AFC equals f dollars, and AVC equals e dollars. Hence ATC equals f + e dollars. Thus g = f + e, or g − e = f, and so the vertical distance between the points p and p″ equals the vertical distance between the points p′ and X_0. In other words, at any level of output the vertical distance between the ATC and AVC curves equals the vertical distance between the AFC curve and the horizontal axis. And since AFC is a decreasing function of X, the ATC and AVC curves approach each other as X is increased.

2–3 THE RELATIONSHIP BETWEEN TOTAL, AVERAGE, AND MARGINAL COSTS

The reader should make sure at this point that he understands that the average cost functions do not introduce into the model any assumptions which are not implied by the total cost functions. This should be very clear since the average cost at any level of output (other than zero) is computed directly from the respective total cost. Therefore columns 5–7 of Table 2–2 should not be regarded as containing any information which cannot be obtained from columns 1–4; columns 5–7 simply represent the same information in different form.

The same is true about Figures 2–1 and 2–2. Therefore, a very close relationship exists between the graphs in each diagram. In fact, it is possible to make various statements (or draw conclusions) about average and marginal cost by using the information given in Fig. 2–1, and about total cost by using the information in Fig. 2–2. For convenience the TC curve is reproduced in Fig. 2–3. Suppose that we wish to compute ATC for the level of output X_0. By definition, ATC at X_0 (ATC_{X_0}) equals TC at X_0 (TC_{X_0}) divided by X_0; that is, $ATC_{X_0} = TC_{X_0}/X_0$. From Fig. 2–3 we see, therefore, that $ATC_{X_0} = h/X_0$, which, according to

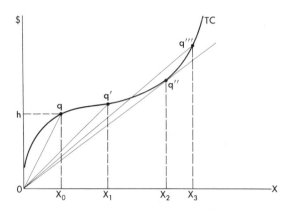

Figure 2-3

Fig. 2-2, is also equal to **g**. Now since the number h may also be represented by the vertical distance between the points **q** and X_0, and the number X_0 may be represented by the distance between the origin and the point X_0, the ratio h/X_0 is also equal to $\overline{X_0 q}/\overline{0X_0}$. The notation $\overline{X_0 q}$ **does not** mean the product of X_0 and **q** but rather the distance between the points X_0 and **q**. The same holds for $\overline{0X_0}$. Since the line segments $X_0 q$ and $0X_0$ form the height and base, respectively, of a right-angle triangle, the ratio $\overline{X_0 q}/\overline{0X_0}$ is also equal to the slope of the ray $0q$, that is, the slope of the straight line which goes through the origin and point **q**.*

The representation of **ATC** as the slope of a certain ray is particularly useful for the purpose of comparing the levels of **ATC** at different outputs. Thus since **ATC** at the output X_1 (ATC_{X_1}) is equal to the slope of the ray $0q'$, and since the slope of the ray $0q$ is greater than the slope of the ray $0q'$, it follows that $ATC_{X_0} > ATC_{X_1}$. (The slope of $0q$ is greater than that of $0q'$ because $0q$ is steeper than $0q'$.) We may, therefore, conclude that in the range between X_0 and X_1 the **ATC** curve in Fig. 2-2 is falling. Similarly, a comparison of the slopes of the rays $0q''$ and $0q'''$ in Fig. 2-3 reveals that $ATC_{X_2} < ATC_{X_3}$; hence in the range between X_2 and X_3 the **ATC** curve in Fig. 2-2 is rising. We have therefore shown that the "inverted S"-shaped **TC** curve in Fig. 2-3 is consistent with the U-shaped **ATC** curve in Fig. 2-2, and vice versa. We may employ the same method to verify the consistency between the shapes of the remaining total and average cost curves.

It remains to discuss the **MC** function. First we should remove a certain discrepancy between the definition of **MC** (Definition 2-7), and the representation of the **MC** function in Fig. 2-2. The latter implies (since the **MC** function

---

* The ratio $\overline{X_0 q}/\overline{0X_0}$ is also equal to the tangent of the angle formed by the ray $0q$ and the horizontal axis.

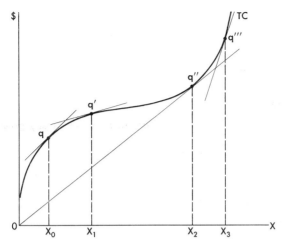

Figure 2–4

is shown as a continuous curve) that MC may be measured at any single level of output, whereas in Definition 2–7 (see p. 15) MC is associated with a given **pair** of outputs. We shall redefine the concept of MC in terms of its relationship to the TC curve. In the preceding discussion we have already implicitly introduced the definition of the slope of a straight line. This definition may be stated explicitly as follows. Drop perpendicular lines (one horizontal, the other vertical) from a point on the line whose slope you wish to measure, to construct a right-angle triangle which has as its hypotenuse a segment of the line in question. Then the slope is equal to the ratio of the height to the base of the triangle. (This ratio is sometimes referred to as "rise over run.") Actually, the slope is a concept which is generally defined with respect to a single point on a line, rather than as an over-all property, but since the slope of a straight line is the same at every point, it makes no difference at which point or segment the slope is measured.

Not so, however, with curves. A curve like the TC curve in Fig. 2–4, which has no straight segments, has a different slope at every point.* How, then, do we measure the slope of a curve at a given point, say point q on the TC curve in Fig. 2–4? By definition the slope of the TC curve at the point q is equal to the slope of a line tangent to the TC curve at q. A tangent line to the curve TC at q is a straight line passing through q, and lying completely on one side of the TC curve in a small neighborhood around q. This means essentially that a tangent line cannot (except for a special case) intersect the curve at the point of

---

* By "different" we are referring here, of course, to the algebraic, or numerical, value of the slope rather than merely its sign. We have already established that the TC curve has a *positive* slope throughout.

tangency. Thus the slope of the straight line going through point q in Fig. 2–4 defines the slope of the TC curve at that point. The same definition holds for any other point on the curve.

We are now ready to introduce the new definition.

Definition 2–8

MARGINAL COST (MC) = the slope of the TC curve at any given point.

Thus, for example, MC for the level of output X_0 (MC_{X_0}) is equal to the slope of the tangent line at point q in Fig. 2–4. A comparison of the values of MC at selected levels of output in Fig. 2–4 shows that

$$MC_{X_0} > MC_{X_1}, \qquad MC_{X_1} < MC_{X_2}, \qquad \text{and} \qquad MC_{X_2} < MC_{X_3}.$$

This, then, also confirms the consistency between the shape of the TC curve in Fig. 2–4 and the U-shaped MC curve in Fig. 2–2.

Next, let us ask the following question: "At what level of output does ATC reach its minimum?" Recall that ATC can be measured by the slope of a ray from the origin to the respective point on the TC curve (Fig. 2–3). Hence the smaller the slope of such a ray, the smaller the ATC. Our problem, therefore, consists of finding a ray from the origin to some point on the TC curve whose slope is smaller than that of any other ray from the origin to a point on the TC curve. Ray 0q″ in Fig. 2–3 satisfies this condition. Note that any ray with a slope smaller than that of 0q″ has no points in common with the TC curve, and hence has no relevance to the problem at hand. But note too that the ray 0q″ is tangent to the TC curve at the point q″, so that ATC at X_2 (ATC_{X_2}) equals MC at X_2 (MC_{X_2}). (See also Fig. 2–2.) We see further from the curvature of the TC curve that at points to the right of q″, say q‴, MC > ATC, since a tangent line at q‴ is steeper than the ray 0q‴, and the opposite holds for points left of q″. All this may be summarized in the following statements:

(2C) When ATC = MC, ATC is at a minimum, and vice versa.

(2D) When ATC > MC, ATC is falling, and vice versa.

(2E) When ATC < MC, ATC is rising, and vice versa.

We have also shown (Fig. 2–1) that the shape of the TVC curve is the same as that of the TC curve, which implies, among other things, that the slopes of these two curves at any given level of output are identical. (This result is equivalent to our earlier observation that the numbers in column 8 of Table 2–2 represent the change in TC as well as the change in TVC as X increases.) Consequently we can also state:

(2F) When AVC = MC, AVC is at a minimum, and vice versa.

(2G) When AVC > MC, AVC is falling, and vice versa.

(2H) When AVC < MC, AVC is rising, and vice versa.

And finally, since the intersection of the MC and AVC curves must occur to the left of the intersection of the MC and ATC curves, we also have

(2I) AVC attains its minimum at a level of output which is smaller than that at which ATC has its minimum.

Thus far we have shown how to make certain statements about average and marginal cost by using the information given in the total cost curves diagram. The opposite is also possible. For instance, the geometrical representation of TC_{X_0} in Fig. 2–2 is given by the area of the rectangle $0gpX_0$, since by definition $TC = ATC \cdot X$. Likewise, TVC_{X_0} is equal to the area of the rectangle $0ep''X_0$, and the difference between the two, that is, TFC_{X_0}, is equal to the area of the rectangle egpp'', or to the area of the rectangle $0fp'X_0$. Thus, since TFC is constant, all rectangles like $0fp'X_0$, that is, rectangles constructed by dropping perpendiculars from any point on the AFC curve to the two axes, have the same area. Therefore the AFC curve has the form of a rectangular hyperbola.

2–3.1 The shape of the ATC curve

Before concluding this discussion of cost curves we shall explain the reason for the particular curvature which the various curves are assumed to have. Let us consider the ATC curve. The U-shape of that curve is a characteristic description of the behavior of ATC in the short run, and it derives directly from the existence of fixed factors of production. We know that in order to increase its output in the short run the firm must increase some of its variable inputs, and in doing so it changes the proportion between the fixed and the variable inputs. At small levels of output, when the firm uses only relatively small quantities of variable inputs, the proportion of fixed inputs to variable inputs may be too high, so that the proportion of inputs can be improved by adding more variable inputs. This means that by increasing the variable inputs by some percentage, output will increase more than proportionally. For example, a firm which has at its disposal a large plant equipped with many heavy machines but employing a relatively small number of workers, may be able to double its output by increasing its labor force less than 100%. The reason for this increase in productivity is a purely technological phenomenon resulting from a better combination of labor and machines. So long as such a change in input proportion increases productivity, and all input prices remain constant, ATC will fall, because when output increases by more than the proportionate increase in variable inputs, it also increases by more than the proportionate increase in cost; hence at the increased level of output each unit of output carries a smaller share of total cost. Thus Fig. 2–2 tells us that when the firm produces X_2 units, it uses the best amounts of the variable inputs **relative to its fixed inputs,** and that at outputs other than X_2 the input combinations are such as to cause a decline in productivity.

However, it should be pointed out that even if output should increase by the same percentage as the increase in variable inputs, total cost would nevertheless increase by a smaller percentage because part of total cost is fixed. Thus if all inputs were fixed, the ATC curve would have the shape of the AFC curve which is always a decreasing function of X. If fixed and variable inputs exist, the shape of the ATC curve reflects the effects of both types of inputs. At relatively small levels of output it is falling as a result of the use of better proportions between the fixed and variable inputs, **and** the spreading of the fixed cost over a greater number of units; at somewhat higher levels of output the AVC curve rises, owing to a decline in productivity, but the ATC curve continues to fall because the decrease in AFC more than offsets the rise in AVC. But when output is pushed beyond X_2, the increase in AVC resulting from the use of excessive amounts of variable inputs is sufficiently large to bring about a change in the slope of the ATC curve in spite of the continuous fall in AFC.

This fully explains the shapes of the cost curves, because once the shape of the ATC curve is given, the shapes of the other curves follow directly from the definitional relationships.

SUMMARY

In this chapter we have begun to assemble our model. We chose a number of variables—the various types of cost—to serve as building blocks for our theoretical construction. These concepts were then carefully described with respect to their individual characteristics, as well as with respect to the relationships between them. The importance of this material should not be underrated, since a thorough familiarity with these tools will greatly facilitate the analysis which follows. The assumptions about the shapes of the cost curves can be interpreted as a description of certain aspects of the technological environment in which the firm is assumed to operate. This will be discussed further in the next chapter. We also made an assumption about the firm's economic environment when we assumed that the prices which the firm has to pay for the inputs are constant, i.e., that they are not affected by the quantities of inputs purchased by the firm.

SELECTED REFERENCES

McKenzie, L. W., "A Method for Drawing Marginal Curves." *Journal of Political Economy* **58,** 1950, pp. 434–435.

Robinson, J., *The Economics of Imperfect Competition.* London: Macmillan, 1933, Chapter 2.

Viner, J., "Cost Curves and Supply Curves." *Zeitschrift für Nationalökonomie* **3,** 1931, pp. 23–46. Reprinted in K. E. Boulding and G. J. Stigler (eds.), *Readings in Price Theory.* Chicago: Irwin, 1952, pp. 198–232.

EXERCISES

1. (a) Complete the cost table (Table E2–1) to make it consistent with the given values. (You may find it convenient to reproduce an enlarged table on a separate sheet of paper.)

   (b) If your cost table is correct it must show, among other things, that MC is equal to the difference between successive levels of TC, as well as the difference between successive values of TVC. Check this.

   (c) Plot the data from the completed table on two separate diagrams (preferably on graph paper). On one diagram plot the three total cost functions, and on the other the average cost functions and the marginal cost function. (The data in the table will give you only a number of points in your diagram; these should be connected by lines.)

   (d) Verify that your diagrams show the basic relationships between the various cost functions (as, for example, in Figs. 2–1 and 2–2 of the text).

   (e) Another important relationship, which will be used later in the text, is that MC is independent of TFC. This means that changes in TFC do not affect MC. To convince yourself of this fact do the following: (i) Change the value of TFC by adding some convenient (either positive or negative) number to the number in the TFC column. (ii) Adjust the numbers in the other columns which

X	TC	TFC	TVC	ATC	AFC	AVC	MC
0	24						
1						10	
2			18				
3							6
4				13			
5	55						
6			36				
7							6
8	74						
9						7	
10				$10\frac{2}{5}$			

Table E2–1

are affected by the change in **TFC**, that is, **TC**, **ATC**, and **AFC**. (iii) Note that the numbers in the **MC** column need not be adjusted since they still give the correct difference between successive values of **TC** and **TVC**.

X	TC	TFC	TVC	ATC	AFC	AVC	MC
0	20						
1			1				
2							3
3						4	
4				12			
5	75						
6						16	
7				$24\frac{6}{7}$			
8							86
9			360				
10	540						

Table E2–2

2. (a) Complete the cost table (Table E2–2) to make it consistent with the given numbers.
   (b) Plot the total cost functions for the range of output 0–10 on one diagram, and the average and marginal cost functions on another diagram.
   (c) Compare these diagrams with those of Exercise 1. Your graphs should show that some of the cost functions in this example have a different shape than those in Exercise 1. Those in Exercise 1, like the examples in the text, are of the more general variety, but it is conceivable that for some productive processes the cost functions may behave as shown in this exercise.

3. Figure E2–1 shows the three total cost curves. Complete the sentences given below.
   (a) The ATC of producing 10 units of X is equal to $_____.
   (b) The ATC of _____ units of X is the same as the ATC of 10 units of X.
   (c) The TC of producing 21 units of X is equal to $_____.
   (d) The ATC has its minimum at the output level _____, and is equal to $_____.
   (e) The MC of the output level 14 is equal to $_____.
   (f) The AVC of producing 10 units of X is equal to $_____.
   (g) The AFC of producing 21 units of X is $_____.
   (h) The AFC attains a minimum at _____ level of output.
   (i) AVC = AFC at the output level _____.
   (j) For all levels of output greater than _____, AVC > AFC.

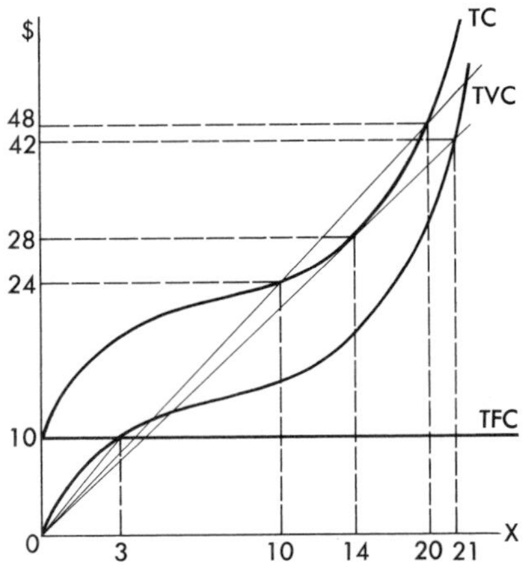

Figure E2–1

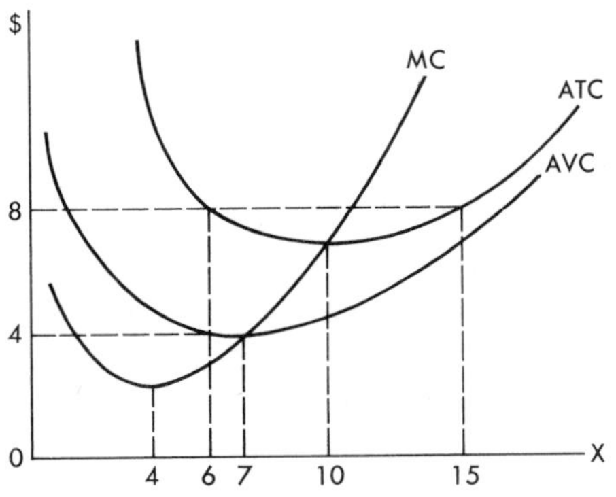

Figure E2–2

4. Figure E2–2 shows two average cost curves and the MC curve. Complete the sentences given below.
   (a) The TC of producing 15 units of X is equal to $_____.
   (b) The TFC of producing 15 units of X is equal to $_____.
   (c) The AVC of producing 15 units of X is equal to $_____.
   (d) At output level 7 AVC is (*greater, smaller*) than AFC.
   (e) At output level 7 TVC is (*greater, smaller*) than $24.
   (f) The flattest point on the TC function (i.e., the point at which the numerical value of the slope is at a minimum) occurs at the output level _____.
   (g) The slope of the TVC function at 7 units of output is (*greater, smaller*) than 4.
   (h) AVC is decreasing at all levels of output less than _____.
   (i) At the level of output at which ATC has its minimum, TC is greater than $_____, but less than $_____.
   (j) ATC, AVC, and MC are all increasing at output levels greater than _____.

3

THE EFFICIENCY OF PRODUCTION

This chapter deals with certain technological aspects of the firm's operation. The justification for studying this topic is twofold. As was pointed out in the Introduction, the essential function of a firm is to produce; hence a familiarity with some of the basic technological principles helps the reader to understand the firm's decision-making process as a whole. Of course, we are not dealing with engineering problems here, but with the economic aspects of the production technique, i.e., those which bear directly on the firm's cost position. In this chapter we shall establish a direct link between the firm's environments and its cost curves, and determine the conditions under which the firm achieves the highest degree of efficiency in its productive activities.

3-1 THE PRODUCTION FUNCTION

The production of most products involves processes that are technically quite complex, as well as specialized to meet the requirements of the particular product in question. But the making of any product can be viewed as the end result of a chain of activities which involves the combining and processing of certain inputs. The act of production may therefore be thought of as **a transformation of inputs into an output.** It is convenient to describe this transformation as a functional relationship in which output is considered a function of the inputs. Such a relationship is referred to as a **production function.** Using the mathematician's shorthand, we can express the production function in symbolic form by

$$X = f(Z^1, Z^2, \ldots, Z^n) \qquad (3-1)$$

where the Z's denote n inputs used in this particular production process. For any chosen quantities of the n inputs the production function gives us the **maximum** level of output that can be obtained under these circumstances.* Of course, the above equation indicates only that there exists **some** relationship between the output X and the n inputs, but it does not tell us the form which this relationship is assumed to have. This unspecified relationship is denoted here by the letter f. If the form of the function f is given, i.e., if the right-hand side of Eq. (3–1) is given in specific form, it is possible by the use of mathematical methods to thoroughly investigate the nature of this relationship.† Instead we shall discuss only certain general properties of production functions, and there will be no need to state the complete mathematical form of this function. We shall also simplify matters further, for reasons which will become obvious, by assuming that the production process to be considered uses only two variable inputs. Our immediate concern is with a production function of the form

$$X = g(L, M), \tag{3–2}$$

where L and M denote the two variable inputs. We are denoting this functional relationship by g since presumably it is a different relationship from that denoted by f. We have also omitted to denote the fixed inputs since the present analysis is concerned with the short run, and therefore the fixed inputs (i.e., the size of the plant) cannot, by definition, be changed during the period in question. For expository purposes it may be convenient to think of the inputs as labor and machine hours, respectively.

3–1.1 Total product curves

Let us first discuss the relationship between the output and one input, labor, for example. (It should be understood that the results are generally valid for relationships between X and any other input.) This relationship is depicted in Fig. 3–1, where the level of output is measured on the vertical axis, and that of the input on the horizontal axis. Both variables are measured in some physical units of measurement, for example, tons and man-hours, respectively. The curve in Fig. 3–1 shows the maximum levels of output X that can be obtained

---

* A slightly different, but equivalent way of defining the production function is to say that if we select a level of output and the quantities of n − 1 of the inputs, then the production function can be used to determine the *minimum* amount of the nth input necessary to obtain the desired level of output.

† A function may be said to be stated in a specific form if one is able to compute the value of X, once the values of the independent variables (the variables in parentheses) are given.

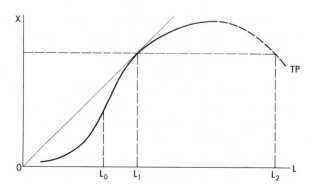

Figure 3–1

from using different amounts of L. Such a curve is referred to as the **total product** (TP) curve of L. Now since X depends not only on L but also on M, the TP curve is really an ambiguous relationship unless we make clear what happens to M when L is changed. We shall assume that M is fixed. This **does not** mean that M is a fixed factor, however; it only means that to describe accurately the meaning of the TP curve in Fig. 3–1 one must say that it shows the levels of X which can be obtained from various levels of L if M **is held constant.**

The TP curve has a positive slope, implying thereby that X is an increasing function of L. This is only partially correct, as it is generally assumed that for sufficiently large amounts of the input (any input, not only labor) the TP curve tends to slope downward. Thus beyond a certain point any additional increases in the input will **reduce** the level of output. This is explained by the fact that the application of excessive amounts of some input will hinder rather than assist the production process.

For example, increasing the number of workers along an automobile production line may increase the weekly output of automobiles if the use of the additional workers increases the speed at which the line moves. However, it is not difficult to see that the output of automobiles will decline if the firm increases the number of workers to a level which results in workers getting in each other's way. We have shown the negatively sloped segment as a dashed curve (and in the future will omit it altogether), because a rational producer will never operate in that unproductive range.

3–1.2 Average and marginal product curves

While the assumption about the slope of the TP curve has a considerable intuitive appeal, the properties of the production technique which are embodied in the curvature of the curve are less obvious, but perhaps more important. For the discussion of these properties we have drawn in Fig. 3–2 the **average**

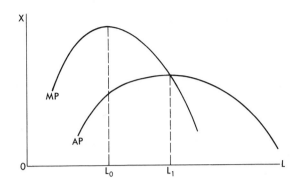

Figure 3–2

product (AP) curve and the **marginal product** (MP) curve of L. Average product means total product per unit of input, that is, AP $=$ TP$/$L, and marginal product means the change in TP as L is increased by one unit, or equivalently, the slope of the TP curve at a given point.

Note that the definitions of AP and MP are similar to those of ATC and MC. It follows, therefore, that so long as the TP curve is upward sloping the MP of the input is positive. The AP and MP curves are related to the TP curve in exactly the same way as the ATC and MC curves are related to the TC curve, and hence we shall not repeat here the demonstration of the consistency between Figs. 3–1 and 3–2. Note, however, that the TP curve is S-shaped (unlike the TC curve which has the shape of an inverted S); therefore the AP and MP curves have the shape of an inverted U. (See the relevant discussion in Chapter 2, and note also the auxiliary lines in Figs. 3–1 and 3–2.)

We learn the following from Figs. 3–1 and 3–2. As the amount of L is increased from some initial small level, i.e., a level less than L_0, output increases at an **increasing rate;** that is, the additions in output from successive increments in L increase. This is evident from the rising part of the MP curve. At the same time we also observe that the AP curve is rising. (The reason for the relationship between the AP and MP curves has already been established in Chapter 2. Replace ATC by AP, MC by MP, and "minimum" by "maximum" in statements 2C, 2D, and 2E.) As L is increased beyond L_0, output increases at a **decreasing rate,** as is shown by the fall in the MP curve, and beyond L_1 both MP and AP are falling. The reason for this particular behavior of the TP curve has been mentioned briefly in the discussion of the shape of the ATC curve (Section 2–3.1). It has to do with the fact that the performance of productive processes depends on the combinations of the various inputs used. An increase in one input, while the other inputs are held constant, may increase productivity if the level at which that input is being used is low relative to the level of the inputs which are held constant, or it may decrease it if it is being used in relative abundance. This decline in productivity which occurs when the amount of one input exceeds a certain level is generally referred to as the **Law of Diminishing Returns.** It is one of the few principles which economists have found to be worthy of the title "law" in spite (or perhaps because?) of the fact that it describes a purely technological phenomenon. However, there seems to be a lack of agreement with respect to the precise definition of the law: Some writers identify it as the falling part of the MP curve, others as the falling part of the AP curve. According to one definition diminishing returns set in when L is increased beyond L_0 in Fig. 3–2, while according to the other, returns are said to diminish only when L is used in amounts greater than L_1.

3–1.3   Shifts in total product curves

We have emphasized earlier that the TP curve in Fig. 3–1 is drawn on the assumption that the quantity of M is held constant. This assumption was made because we wanted to investigate the relationship between the level of output and variations in only one single input. But since the amount of M may actually be changed (provided it is not a fixed input), it is quite legitimate to ask whether the relationship between X and L is at all dependent on the level at which M is held constant. The answer to this question is generally in the affirmative.

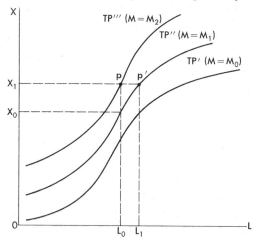

Figure 3–3

The effect of holding M constant at different levels is shown in Fig. 3–3. Each curve in Fig. 3–3 shows the relationship between X and L for a particular level of M as indicated by the respective labels. It is assumed that $M_0 < M_1 < M_2$.

The first point to observe is that all three curves have similar shapes. This means that the Law of Diminishing Returns holds regardless of the level of the constant inputs. Thus the only effect of changing the level of M (except for a possible effect on the **degree** of the curvature of the TP curve) is a shift in the **position** of the TP curve; an increase in M shifts the TP curve up, a decrease in M shifts it down. This is a reasonable result, and it is perfectly consistent with our previous assumption that TP curves have positive slopes (Fig. 3–1) or, equivalently, that the MP of each input is positive. An upward shift in the TP curve means that for any fixed level of L, output may be increased by increasing M, and vice versa. For example, if L is held constant at L_0, an increase in M from M_1 to M_2 increases output from X_0 to X_1. A similar result obtains for a decrease in M.

There is still more information to be extracted from Fig. 3–3. Compare the output and input combinations associated with points p and p', respectively. At p the firm uses L_0 units of L, and M_2 units of M; at p' it uses L_1 of L, and M_1 of M; and both input combinations yield the same level of output, X_1. Also note that at p' the firm uses **more** L than at p (since $L_1 > L_0$) but **less** M than at p (since $M_1 < M_2$). We have, therefore, obtained the following important results:

(3A) The firm may produce any given level of output by using either one of a number of different input combinations.

(3B) If the firm wishes to decrease the amount of one of the inputs used without changing the level of its output, it must increase the amount of some other input.

These results will serve as the basis for the determination of the conditions under which a given output is produced with maximum efficiency.

3–1.4 Isoquants

In Fig. 3–4 we present a graphical description of the results stated above. Here the axes are used to measure the quantities of the two inputs. The curve X_1 represents all the input combinations which are capable of producing X_1 units of X. Thus the input combinations associated with the points p and p' in Fig. 3–3 are represented in Fig. 3–4 by the distinct points, q and q', respectively, on the curve X_1. A curve such as X_1 is called an **isoquant** (meaning equal quantity). Observe that the isoquant X_1 fully agrees with the verbal statements made in the previous section. Since there are many different points on this isoquant, it correctly describes the content of statement 3A; indeed, we see that the firm's choice of input combinations for the level of output X_1 (or for any other level, for that matter) consists of an infinity of alternatives. It is, of course, assumed that each input, like the output X, may be varied continuously. The fact that the isoquant X_1 has a **negative** slope verifies statement 3B. This is so because a negative slope implies that when the firm moves from one point on the isoquant to another, it increases one input while decreasing the other.

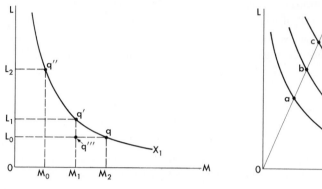

Figure 3–4   **Figure 3–5**

The curvature of the isoquant may be interpreted with reference to still another technological property of the production function. For simplicity let us assume that the difference between the amounts M_0 and M_1, and M_1 and M_2, is one unit, respectively. Then in moving from point q'' to point q' the firm is substituting $L_2 - L_1$ units of L by one unit of M, and in moving from q' to point q it is substituting $L_1 - L_0$ units of L by one unit of M. Clearly $L_2 - L_1 > L_1 - L_0$. This shows that the **ratio** at which factors are substituted along an isoquant depends on the levels of the factors at which the substitution takes place. For example, Fig. 3–4 shows that when L is used in relative abundance, and M is used relatively sparsely, as at point q'', or in other words, when the ratio L/M is relatively high, an increase in M by one unit makes it possible to reduce the amount of L by as much as $L_2 - L_1$, but when the ratio L/M diminishes, as at point q', one unit of M replaces only $L_1 - L_0$ units of L. Since the number of units of L which additional units of M are capable of substituting tends to diminish, this phenomenon is known as the **diminishing marginal rate of substitution.** Recall that the slope of a curve at a point is defined by the slope of the tangent line at that point. Therefore for small increases in M the slope of the isoquant is a fairly accurate measurement of the rate of substitution since, for example, the slope of a tangent line at point q' will be approximately equal to the slope of a straight line through the points q' and q which, of course, is equal to $(L_1 - L_0)/(M_2 - M_1)$, the ratio of substitution. For this reason the slope of the isoquant at any point is interpreted as the **marginal rate of substitution** (MRS) [sometimes also called the

marginal rate of technical substitution (MRTS)]. The word "marginal" is meant to draw attention to the fact that the substitution of factors takes place at the margin, i.e., for small increments of M.* It is because the slope of the isoquant decreases (i.e., becomes flatter) as the amount of M increases that this property is referred to as **diminishing** marginal rate of substitution.

We also see from Fig. 3–3 that when the firm uses L_0 units of L and M_1 units of M, its output is X_0 units of X. Therefore the output associated with point q''' in Fig. 3–4 is X_0. Since any level of output may be produced by an infinity of different input combinations (at least under the assumptions of this model), we may draw into Fig. 3–4 another isoquant which passes through the point q'''. Like isoquant X_1 it is a negatively sloped curve, and it lies entirely to the left and below isoquant X_1. This statement implies that no two isoquants can touch or intersect each other, because under the conditions of any given production technique any one input combination can produce only one particular level of output.† Or put differently, conditions under which a particular input combination gives rise to two different levels of output must be interpreted as involving two different production techniques. Thus a production function is **defined** by associating with each possible input combination **one single** level of output.‡ It is, of course, possible to draw in Fig. 3–4 as many isoquants as one may wish. By doing so one would obtain a family of convex, and non-intersecting curves, each one representing all possible input combinations capable of producing the level of output indicated by the label attached to the isoquant (Fig. 3–5). In each family the isoquants are ranked in the order of their outputs; that is, the farther an isoquant is from the origin, the higher its output. This, too, makes sense, since on any ray from the origin the input combinations on higher isoquants (such as the combinations represented by points a, b, and c) consist of larger quantities of inputs than those on lower isoquants. And when one uses more of **all** variable inputs, then, excluding the range in which the TP curves have a negative slope, output will always increase.

---

* Strictly speaking, MRS measures the rate of change of L *at a point* rather than with respect to finite increments in M, but this slight mathematical inaccuracy in no way affects the substantive meaning of the concept.
† Formally this statement says that the production function is single-valued.
‡ In real life it is quite possible to find that a given production process which uses a fixed input combination yields different levels of output at different points in time. Such deviations from the expected level of output may be due to random variations in factors which are either unknown or uncontrollable. The latter are ignored in our exposition.

3–2 EFFICIENT INPUT COMBINATIONS

We have now completed one part of what we set out to do in this chapter by describing certain basic technological principles which govern productive processes. The rest of the chapter is devoted to finding an answer to the following question: "What is the most efficient input combination for any given level of output?" At this point in the analysis we shall give the term "efficient" a well-defined meaning. In the context of this discussion "efficient" shall mean "least-cost," so that the question posed here really means "What is the least expensive method (i.e., input combination) for the production of a given level of X? We are asking this question because efficient production, as defined above, is a necessary condition for profit maximization.

3–2.1 Isocosts

First we shall restate an assumption about the firm's economic environment. The assumption is that at any moment of time the firm faces a set of fixed prices or equivalently, that the price which the firm has to pay for each input is independent of the amount of the respective input purchased by the firm. Suppose now that we wish to describe, or list, all the input combinations that the firm can purchase with a fixed number of dollars, say C_0. This is done in Fig. 3–6, which has the same axes as Fig. 3–5. Let P^L (also known as the wage rate) be the price of one unit of L, and P^M the price for the use of one unit of M. Any point in Fig. 3–6, exactly as in Fig. 3–5, represents some input combination. For instance, the point on the vertical axis labeled C_0/P^L is an input combination consisting of C_0/P^L units of L, and zero units of M. The latter point also lies on the straight line labeled C_0, and is referred to as the L-intercept of the line (the point at which the line C_0 intercepts the L-axis). Now if the firm were to expend C_0 dollars on L only, it would be able to purchase C_0/P^L units of L, and if it spent that sum on M only, it could purchase C_0/P^M units of M. In other words, the intercepts of the line C_0 represent two input combinations each of which costs C_0 dollars. These are only two of many such combinations. As it turns out, any point on the line C_0 represents an input combination whose cost is C_0 dollars. For this reason the line C_0 is called an **isocost** (meaning equal cost).* The isocost has a negative slope for a reason similar to that which explains the negative slope of isoquants; if the firm wishes to purchase more of one input without spending more money, it must reduce its purchase of some other input. The economic interpretation of the slope of the isocost is very

---

* In general we have $P^L \cdot L + P^M \cdot M = C_0$; that is, the total expenditure on both inputs is equal to C_0. The line C_0 in Fig. 3–6 is the graph of this equation.

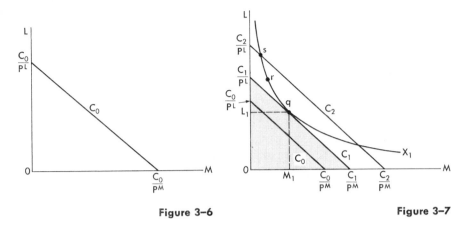

Figure 3–6   Figure 3–7

simple. By definition the slope of the line C_0 is equal to $\dfrac{C_0/P^L}{C_0/P^M}$ (height over base) $= P^M/P^L =$ the ratio of the input prices. It is because input prices are assumed to be constant that the isocost is represented by a line of constant slope.

If the firm wants to spend C_1 dollars on inputs, where $C_1 > C_0$, we can draw another isocost representing all input combinations that may be purchased with C_1 dollars. The isocost C_1 lies above and to the right of the line C_0, and since input prices are constant, it has the same slope as C_0. One may, therefore, draw a family of isocosts for any number of selected levels of outlays. Such a family consists of a set of parallel lines, and the isocosts in each family are ranked according to their outlays, such that the outlay increases with the distance of the isocost from the origin.

3–2.2 The condition for efficient production

We shall now determine the least-cost input combination for the output X_1 by making use of the information about the technological as well as the economic environment of the firm. This is done in Fig. 3–7, which shows the isoquant for the desired level of output X_1, and the isocosts for three levels of cost, $C_0, C_1,$ and C_2, and, of course, $C_0 < C_1 < C_2$. To find the least-cost input combination for output X_1 really means to find a point on the isoquant X_1 which costs less than any other input combination on that isoquant. Compare, for instance, the input combination at the points s and r, respectively. The combination at s costs C_2 dollars, and that at r costs less than C_2 dollars. The isocost which goes through point r has been omitted in order not to clutter the diagram unnecessarily, but it is obvious that the isocost through r lies below the line C_2, and hence it represents an outlay less than C_2 dollars. (Remember that we can draw an isocost, or an isoquant for that matter, through **any** point in that diagram.) The comparison of points s and r suggests that we can locate the least-cost input combination by traveling along the isoquant X_1 in a direction which implies passing from high-cost isocosts to low-cost isocosts until the lowest isocost is reached. In Fig. 3–7 the lowest isocost is reached at point q. This point is a point of tangency between isocost C_1 and isoquant X_1, hence it is the only point the two isolines have in common. Moreover, **any** point on isoquant X_1 other than q lies on a higher isocost, so that the line C_1 is the lowest isocost of those which either intersect or touch isoquant X_1. Therefore the pair (L_1, M_1) represents the least-cost input combination for the output X_1. It is true that input combinations on isocosts below line C_1, such as isocost C_0, cost less than C_1 dollars, but none of these is capable of producing X_1 units of X. Since at the point of tangency the slopes of isoquant X_1 and isocost C_1 are identical, we can formalize this condition for efficient production by the following statement:

(3C) In order to ensure maximum efficiency in the production of any given level of output, the firm must select an input combination for which it is true that the MRS = the ratio of input prices.

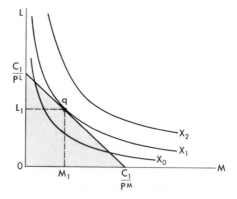

Figure 3–8

It is interesting to note that efficiency, which has been defined above in terms of the **minimization of cost of a given level of output,** may also be defined as the **maximization of output for a given level of money outlay.** Suppose we ask the following question: "What is the highest level of X the firm can produce with C_1 dollars?" We may obtain the answer to this question from Fig. 3–8, applying the same type of reasoning as in the preceding problem. In this case the process of finding the solution (i.e., the greatest output for C_1 dollars) may be described as traveling along the isocost C_1 until the highest isoquant is reached. This occurs at point q. Note that there exist isoquants of higher output such as isoquant X_2, but all input combinations on isoquants lying above the curve X_1 require an outlay which exceeds C_1 dollars. The fact that both problems have the same solution may be stated as follows:

(3D) The input combination which minimizes the cost of a given level of output X_1 also maximizes the output for a money outlay which equals the minimum cost of producing output X_1.

In other words, let C_1 be the cost of the input combination (L_1, M_1) which minimizes the cost of producing X_1 units of X. Then it is true that the maximum level of output that can be produced with C_1 dollars is X_1, and it is obtained by using the combination (L_1, M_1).

3–3   EFFICIENT INPUT COMBINATIONS AND COST CURVES

We shall now demonstrate a convenient method for studying the relationship between the firm's environmental conditions (technological as well as economic) and its cost curves. We shall do this by showing how we can use the process of finding the least-cost input combinations to generate the firm's total cost curves.

Part (a) of Fig. 3–9 shows the least-cost input combinations for the output levels X_1, X_2, and X_3. (Strictly speaking, the diagram shows only the relevant points of tangency.) Now each such point is associated with a pair of numbers (X, C) one of which indicates the level of output, the other the minimum cost of that output. Each of these points may be transferred into part (b) of Fig. 3–9 and represented there by a point whose coordinates are given by the respective pair (X, C). Thus point q in part (a) becomes point r in part (b),

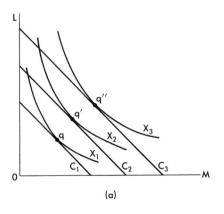
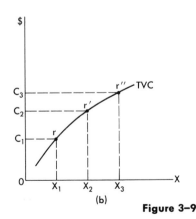

(a)   (b)

Figure 3–9

q' becomes r', and so on. It should be clear from the meaning of points q, q', and q'' that the points r, r', and r'' in part (b) of the diagram lie on the firm's TVC curve. If TFC is also given, it is possible to obtain points on the firm's TC curve by moving each point on the TVC curve upward by a vertical distance equal to the firm's TFC. It should be understood now that the cost curves developed in Chapter 2 should be regarded as **minimum** cost curves; that is, as functions which indicate the minimum cost of producing a given level of output.

3–3.1   Changes in input prices

Finally, let us investigate the effect of changes in input prices on the production of a given level of output. Let us suppose, first, that all input prices change in the same proportion; assume, for instance, that all prices double. Since a doubling of prices does not change the ratio P^M/P^L, the slope of the isocosts (which is equal to P^M/P^L) also remains unchanged. But if the price of every input is doubled, then it certainly follows that after the price change the outlay on any input combination is twice as large. Thus a doubling of all prices causes a doubling of the cost of all input combinations on every isocost. Hence part (a) of Fig. 3–9 should be adjusted by changing the labels on all isocosts accordingly —the lowest isocost in the diagram should be labeled $2C_1$, the next one $2C_2$, and so on. The reader may also think of this adjustment as a shift in the isocosts toward the origin by an amount which moves the intercepts of each isocost to points halfway between the origin and their initial position. Part (b) of the diagram should be adjusted by moving each point on the TVC function upward by a vertical distance equal to its initial distance from the horizontal axis, so that the value of TVC for each level of output is twice its initial value. Of course, any shift in TVC will also shift TC by the same amount.

When input prices do not change proportionately, the resulting effects are not quite as simple. Assume the following situation: the price of labor doubles, but the price of M remains constant. Since this price change decreases the ratio P^M/P^L by one-half, the isocosts which are consistent with the new set of prices have a slope half as steep as that of the initial isocosts. We also know the following: Since the price of M is not changed, the firm can still buy the same quantity of M as it could have bought with the same amount of money before the price change; on the other hand, after the price change any given number of dollars will purchase only half as many labor hours. With this information one can determine the slope and labels of the new isocosts.

Figure 3–10 shows a portion of part (a) of Fig. 3–9, and two isocosts which are consistent with the increased price of L. Since the firm can still purchase C_1/P^M units of M with C_1 dollars, the adjusted isocost for C_1 dollars has the

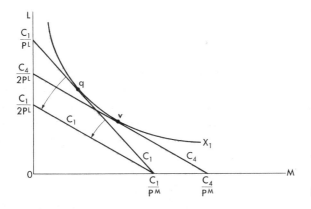

Figure 3–10

same M-intercept as the initial one, but its L-intercept is lower because C_1 dollars purchase only $C_1/2P^L$ hours of L after the price of L is doubled. Thus the adjustment of part (a) of the diagram due to doubling the price of L may be thought of as pivoting all the isocosts on their M-intercepts until each one intercepts the L-axis at a point halfway between the origin and its initial L-intercept. It is also evident from Fig. 3–10 that the input combination at point q is no longer the least-cost input combination for output X_1. The tangency between isoquant X_1 and the lowest isocost is now at point v which lies on isocost C_4. Since isocost C_4 lies above the adjusted isocost C_1, it follows that the cost of the input combination at v at the new prices is higher than the cost of the input combination at q at the initial prices. Hence it is also necessary to adjust part (b) of Fig. 3–9 by shifting the points on the TVC curve upward. This shift, however, is less than that which follows a doubling of all prices. Observe that the second example just examined has a dual effect on the least-cost input combination of output X_1: (a) it **raises the cost** of the least-cost input combination, and (b) it **changes its composition.** This latter change amounts to a substitution of machines for labor, which is not a surprising result in view of the fact that the price of labor has been raised relative to the price of machines.

We have discussed only two examples of price changes but they provide an adequate illustration of the technique for analyzing other possible cases.

SUMMARY

In this chapter we have further developed the description of our model. We discussed with considerable detail some basic technological principles which characterize productive processes. The discussion was focused first on the relationship between the level of output and variations in the quantity of one input. The most important property of this relationship was presented as the Law of Diminishing Returns.

The discussion then led to the introduction of isoquants and their properties, and we discovered further characteristics of the production function, especially the phenomenon known as diminishing marginal rate of substitution.

In connection with the firm's economic environment the concept of isocost was defined. We saw then how the two types of isolines are used for the determination of the most efficient method of production. A link was thus established between the firm's cost curves and its environmental conditions. In a sense this chapter demonstrates that the cost curves introduced in Chapter 2 are consistent with maximum efficiency in production. We also saw how the firm's cost curves change as a result of certain changes in the firm's environment (i.e., input prices) and the subsequent adjustment in the firm's choice of input combinations.

SELECTED REFERENCES

CARLSON, S., *A Study on the Pure Theory of Production*. London: King, 1939, Chapters 1 and 2.

CASSELS, J. M., "On the Law of Variable Proportions." *Explorations in Economics*, New York: McGraw-Hill, 1936, pp. 223–236. Reprinted in W. Fellner and B. F. Haley (eds.), *Readings in the Theory of Income Distribution*. Philadelphia: Blakiston, 1946, pp. 103–118.

FRISCH, R., *Theory of Production*. Chicago: Rand McNally, 1965, Chapters 1–4.

HICKS, J. R., *Value and Capital*. Oxford: Clarendon Press, 2nd ed., 1946, Chapter 7.

STIGLER, G. J., "Production and Distribution in the Short Run." *Journal of Political Economy* **47**, 1939, pp. 305–327. Reprinted in W. Fellner and B. F. Haley (eds.), *Readings in the Theory of Income Distribution*. Philadelphia: Blakiston, 1946, pp. 119–142.

STIGLER, G. J., *The Theory of Price*. New York: Macmillan, revised ed., 1952, Chapter 7.

EXERCISES

1. Figure E3–1 shows the TP function of input L. Complete the sentences given below.
   (a) Total output increases at an increasing rate at all levels of L less than _____.
   (b) The average product increases at all levels of L less than _____.
   (c) The marginal product reaches its maximum at _____ units of L.
   (d) The average product equals the marginal product at _____ units of L. At that point the average product attains its (*maximum*, *minimum*).
   (e) Marginal product is negative at all levels of L greater than _____.
   (f) Average product and marginal product are both increasing at levels of L less than _____, and are both decreasing at levels of L greater than _____.
   (g) The average product is greater than the marginal product at all levels of L greater than _____.

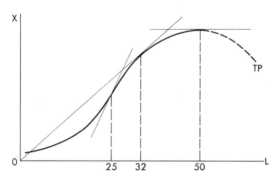

Figure E3–1

2. The curves in Fig. E3–2 represent isoquants. Complete the sentences given below.
   (a) Four units of L and 3 units of M yield _____ units of output (X).
   (b) Using 3 units of each input gives at least _____ units of X, but less than _____ units.

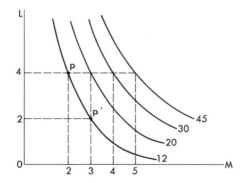

Figure E3–2

(c) The marginal rate of substitution between points p and p′ is approximately equal to _____.

(d) The marginal rate of substitution along any isoquant tends to increase as one increases the use of input _____.

(e) When input L is fixed at 4 units, the marginal product of M in the range 2–5 is (*increasing, decreasing, constant*).

(f) When production takes place at point p, the average product of input L is equal to _____, and that of input M equals _____.

(g) If "marginal product" in part (e) is replaced by "average product," then the last word in that sentence should be _____.

3. The line in Fig. E3–3 represents an isocost. Complete the sentences given below.

(a) If the price of one unit of M is $4, then the price of one unit of L is $_____.

(b) If the price of one unit of M is $4, then the value of the isocost (i.e., the number of dollars associated with the isocost) is equal to $_____.

(c) The input bundle consisting of 6 units of each input is represented by a point in the above diagram (*left of, right of, on*) the isocost.

(d) If the value of the isocost is $96, then the bundle consisting of 16 units of L, and 12 units of M costs $_____.

(e) An increase in the price of L will make the above isocost (*steeper, flatter*).

(f) A proportionate increase in the prices of both inputs will shift the isocost to the (*left, right*).

(g) An increase in the price of L which is accompanied by a decrease in the price of M will cause a rotation of the isocost around a point such as p in a (*clockwise, counterclockwise*) direction.

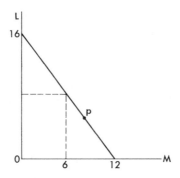

Figure E3–3

4. Figure E3–4 represents the isoquant for 25 units of X, and two isocosts. Complete the sentences given below.

(a) If the price of M is $\frac{3}{2}$ times the price of L, then the least-cost input combination of 25 units of X requires _____ units of L.

(b) If $C_0 = 90$, then the price of M is $_____.

(c) If the prices of both inputs increase by 50%, and $C_0 = 90$, then the maximum level of output that can be produced with $125 is (*less, greater*) than 25 units.

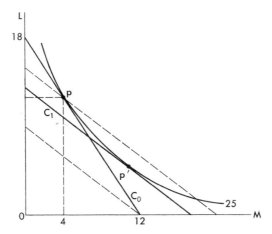

Figure E3–4

(d) If the price of L rises, the price of M remaining constant, then the least expensive method of producing 25 units of X requires (*an increase, a decrease, no change*) in the amount of input M used.

(e) Production will shift from point p to point p′ if input M becomes relatively (*more, less*) expensive than input L.

(f) If the initial price of L (i.e., that which makes p the optimal production point) is $2, and if a doubling of the price of L makes p′ the optimal production point, then C_1 (the value of the new isocost) is greater than $_____, but less than $_____. (The two dashed lines are parallel to isocost C_1.)

5. (a) Set up a diagram with the vertical axis labeled L, and the horizontal axis labeled M. Choose some convenient unit for the scales, and mark off on the L-axis the points 6, 9, 12, 15, 18, and 21, and on the M-axis the points 4, 6, 8, 10, 12, and 14.

(b) Draw six isocost lines into your diagram, the lowest one joining the points $L = 6, M = 4$.

(c) Assume that the price of one unit of L is $2. To each isocost attach the proper dollar figure.

(d) Draw into your diagram six isoquants, each one tangent to one of the isocosts. Attach some arbitrary label to each isoquant, indicating the respective levels of output. (But make sure that the level of output increases with the distance of the isoquant from the origin.)

(e) Set up a second diagram with the vertical axis labeled $, and the horizontal axis labeled X. On the basis of the information contained in your first diagram plot in the second diagram six points of the TVC function. Connect these points by line segments or a smooth curve, and label the graph TVC.

(f) Assume that both input prices increase by 50%. Adjust the labels of the isocosts accordingly. Draw into your second diagram the TVC function for the new set of prices, and label it TVC′.

4

THE COST OF PRODUCTION: LONG RUN

This chapter may be considered a continuation of Chapter 2, as it too deals with cost curves. However, the class of situations analyzed in this chapter is distinctly different from those discussed in Chapter 2, thus making it convenient as well as desirable to present the entire discussion of cost curves in two separate chapters. The material on the technological side of production is placed between the two, in Chapter 3, because it performs the dual function of explaining the shape of short-run cost curves and providing a helpful background for the analysis of long-run cost curves.

The long run is a period of time during which the firm can vary all its inputs. It is, therefore, distinguished from the short run by the absence of fixed inputs, and consequently the absence of fixed costs. As we pointed out in Chapter 2, it is customary to consider the size, or scale, of the firm's plant as the typical fixed input. The term "plant" in this context may be interpreted as including such items as land, structures, and heavy machinery. Thus long-run analysis deals with situations in which the firm may not only vary its output, but also move from one plant to another. A long-run cost curve is, therefore, a functional relationship between output and cost which shows the least cost of producing any given level of output under conditions which permit the firm to choose the most efficient combination of all its inputs, including, of course, the size of its plant. We are already familiar with the properties of short-run cost curves (i.e., cost curves for operating conditions under which the size of the firm's plant is fixed.) Consequently the analysis of long-run cost curves may be approached by investigating the effects of changing the firm's plant on the firm's short-run cost curves.

4–1 LONG-RUN AVERAGE COST

Figure 4–1 shows two short-run average total cost (SAC) curves for two different plants, Plant 1 and Plant 2, and it is assumed that Plant 2 is the larger of the two. A comparison of the firm's cost conditions for these two plants shows the following: For outputs less than X_0 the cost of production (average as well as total) is lower if the firm uses Plant 1; for outputs greater than X_0 Plant 2 has a lower production cost; the cost of producing X_0 units of X is the same for both plants. This result may be stated in another way by saying that for relatively small levels of output the smaller plant is more efficient, while for relatively high levels of output the larger plant operates at lower cost. It is not difficult to see why this should be so. At low levels of output Plant 2 uses a smaller percentage of its total capacity than does Plant 1. This could mean, for instance, that the machinery in Plant 2 is operated at less than the optimum rate, or is left partly idle. The same may be true about other production facilities. The reader should remember also that Plant 2 incurs a higher level of TFC, hence it takes a greater rate of output to attain a given level of AFC. On the other hand, at relatively high levels of output Plant 1 is at a disadvantage because of its limited facilities. Whereas Plant 2 provides larger space and a type of machinery which is geared to handle large volumes, Plant 1 is relatively crowded and operates under conditions which result in inefficient production at high levels of output.

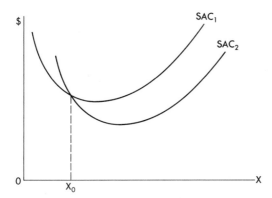

Figure 4–1

Since this relationship holds generally for any two different plants, the cost curves for any number of plants may be represented in a similar fashion. In Fig. 4–2 are shown the SAC curves for five different plants. Notice that the diagram is drawn in accordance with the principles just discussed. In addition, Fig. 4–2 depicts a property of long-run cost conditions not yet mentioned. It shows that as the size of the plant is increased from Plant 1 to Plant 2, and

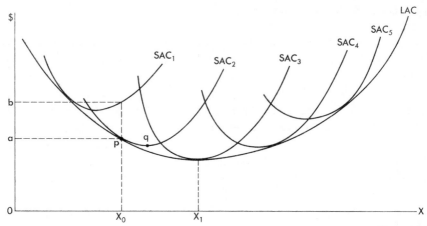

Figure 4–2

from Plant 2 to Plant 3, the minimum level of ATC for successively bigger plants decreases; but as the size of the plant is increased further, the minimum level of ATC for successive plants increases. Thus if we draw a curve which envelops, or supports, all the SAC curves from below, such as the curve labeled LAC in Fig. 4–2, we obtain a U-shaped curve. Notice that each SAC curve touches the LAC curve only once, and that at the touching point the respective curves are tangent to each other. If we were to draw still more SAC curves into Fig. 4–2, each of these would also form a point of tangency with the LAC curve. Indeed, if we assume that the size of the firm's plant can be varied continuously—an assumption which we have made with respect to the other variables—then there exists an infinity of SAC curves each of which is tangent to the LAC curve at some point. The LAC curve is nothing else but the locus of all these tangency points. In other words, **each point on the LAC curve is a tangency point between the LAC curve and some SAC curve.**

The economic meaning of the LAC curve can also be explained with reference to Fig. 4–2. Consider the arbitrary level of output X_0. In the long run the firm may produce X_0 by using one of many plants of differing sizes. In particular, Fig. 4–2 tells us that if the firm were to use Plant 1 the average cost of output X_0, that is, ATC_{X_0}, would be **b** dollars, whereas ATC_{X_0} for Plant 2 is only **a** dollars. Of course, the output X_0 may be produced with other plants as well, and the use of each of these plants will give rise to a different level of ATC_{X_0}. We cannot say exactly what the cost of production for each of these plants would be without drawing their respective SAC curves into the diagram, but we know that none of them is capable of producing X_0 for **a** dollars or less. This conclusion follows from the fact that none of the SAC curves lies below the LAC curve, and no SAC curve other than SAC_2 passes through point p. Hence each point on the LAC curve indicates the least long-run ATC for the respective level of output. For this reason it is referred to as the long-run average total cost curve, i.e., a relationship between cost and output which shows **the minimum ATC for any level of output when all inputs are variable.**

The reader should note, however, that except for one unique size of plant the tangency point between a given SAC curve and the LAC curve does **not** occur at the lowest point on the SAC curve. For example, the most efficient method of producing X_0 units of X in the long run is to use Plant 2, and operate at point p in Fig. 4–2. This point is obviously not the minimum point on SAC_2, since the latter is at point q. This is true at all levels of output except X_1. To produce X_1 units of X the firm should use Plant 3, in which case it is operating at the lowest point of both SAC_3 and LAC.

4–1.1 Returns to scale

We still have to explain the assumptions which give the LAC curve its U-shape. One might be tempted to explain the shape of the LAC curve with the help of the assumptions which give rise to U-shaped SAC curves, as, for instance, the Law of Diminishing Returns. To do so, however, would be formally incorrect because the latter refers only to those cases in which some inputs are fixed. The fact that LAC tends to fall in a certain range of output is primarily associated with certain economies which the firm may realize when it operates on a large scale. Larger plants usually make use of more specialized types of equipment, which permit the firm to introduce a higher degree of division of labor. Thus while in the short run decreases in cost (the downward sloping segment of SAC curves) are related to changes in the ratio of variable inputs to fixed inputs, the fall in LAC is due to the use of more specialized factors of production, and more efficient organization of the productive process in general. The latter phenomenon is referred to as **economies of scale.**

So much for the downward sloping part of the LAC curve. The fact that the LAC curve rises beyond a certain point indicates that the long-run average cost of production increases as output exceeds a certain level. While large-scale operations make it possible to introduce more intensive specialization into many phases of the productive process, certain factors of production have a tendency to become inefficient with increases in the size of the plant. These factors are the various managerial functions which are an integral part of any productive process. Thus when the firm's plant is enlarged beyond a certain size it ordinarily becomes necessary to employ more supervisors. The resultant increase in the firm's personnel raises the total cost of management, and in addition it lengthens the channels of communication between the men on the production line and top management. This makes for a more cumbersome managerial structure, and hence the overall efficiency of management declines. In sufficiently large plants such inefficiencies more than offset the economies of scale, thereby causing an increase in LAC. It may also be pointed out that when the scale of operation reaches large dimensions the firm may incur additional costs in connection with marketing and moving its output. This, too, contributes to the eventual rise in LAC. The inefficiencies which appear as a result of increasing the size of the plant beyond a certain limit are referred to as **diseconomies of scale.**

4–2 LONG-RUN TOTAL AND MARGINAL COST

Other long-run cost curves may, of course, easily be derived from the LAC curve. For instance, long-run total cost (LTC) can be computed by multiplying LAC by the respective level of output. (Remember that in the long run, by definition, there exist no fixed costs, hence all costs are variable costs.) We can also derive long-run marginal cost (LMC) (i.e., the increase in LTC as long-run output is increased by one unit), since it is related to LAC in exactly the same manner as short-run marginal cost (SMC) is related to SAC. Therefore, the shape and position of the LMC curve must be as shown in Fig. 4–3.

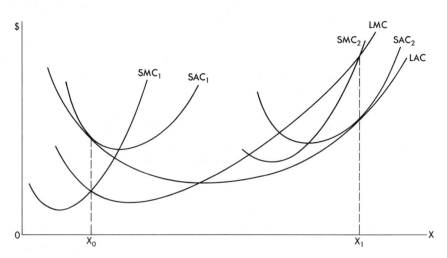

Figure 4–3

Figure 4–3 also shows an important relationship between the LAC curve and the various SMC curves. This relationship indicates that **at the level of output at which a particular SAC curve is tangent to the LAC curve, the respective SMC**

function intersects the LMC function. This proposition can be proved quite easily with the use of certain mathematical tools, or somewhat less easily by using a graphical technique. The proof is given in the section which follows.

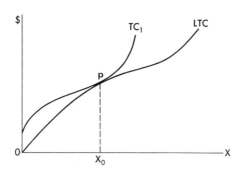

Figure 4–4

▶ **The relationship between LMC and SMC**

In Fig. 4–4 are represented the TC curve for Plant 1 and the LTC curve. From Fig. 4–3 we see that for outputs other than X_0, LAC $<$ SAC$_1$. Since LAC $<$ SAC$_1$ implies LTC $<$ TC$_1$, the LTC curve lies below the TC$_1$ curve at all levels of output except X_0. Since at X_0, LAC $=$ SAC$_1$, it follows that LTC $=$ TC$_1$ at X_0. Therefore the LTC curve is tangent to the TC$_1$ curve at point p in Fig. 4–4. Since at the point of tangency both curves have the same slope, it follows (recalling that MC is also defined as the slope of the respective TC curve at any point) that SMC$_1$ $=$ LMC at X_0.*

4–3   CHANGES IN INPUT PRICES AND TECHNOLOGY

At this point we should call the reader's attention to the fact that long-run cost curves, like short-run cost curves, are not necessarily fixed, and are apt to change from time to time. Remember that the cost curves in this analysis are derived from a given set of environmental conditions. In particular, we have assumed that there prevails a certain state of technology, the relevant properties of which are embodied in the production function. We have also assumed that from the firm's point of view input prices are fixed. We saw in Chapter 3 how changes in input prices cause shifts in the short-run cost curves, and so we may conveniently use the results obtained in Chapter 3 to determine the effects of changes in input prices on the long-run cost curves. For example,

---

* Note that LMC and SMC$_2$ in Fig. 4–3 are equal at *two* levels of output. That, however, does not contradict the proposition just proved; it simply means that the converse of the proposition in question is generally false.

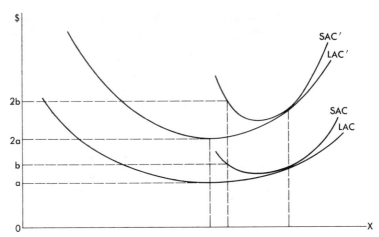

Figure 4–5

if all input prices double, then the cost of producing any given level of output doubles as well (Section 3–3). This example is illustrated in Fig. 4–5 which shows the LAC curve and the SAC curve for an arbitrary size of plant, and for an initial set of prices. When all input prices are doubled the curves shift to the positions shown by the curves LAC′ and SAC′, respectively. This price change produces a vertical shift of the entire cost structure, and it brings about a doubling of LAC and SAC at any level of output. When increases in input prices are not proportionate, it is impossible to determine the percentage increase in the cost of production unless further information is given. Furthermore, in that case the shift in the cost curves is not necessarily vertical, i.e., the minimum point on the various cost curves need not occur at the same level of output.

Cost curves may also shift in response to technological changes. For instance, a change in technology which lowers the input requirements for any level of output causes a downward shift in cost curves. This is so because a decrease in the quantity of an input used for a given level of output, like a fall in the price, reduces the cost of producing that output. In this text we shall not deal with technological changes, and consequently we shall limit the analysis to the behavior of the firm for a fixed state of technology.

SUMMARY

This chapter completes the main discussion of cost curves. We now have available two different sets of cost curves: one set for the description of cost conditions when the size of the firm's plant is fixed, the other for situations in which all inputs are variable. In this chapter we have focused our attention primarily on the relationship between these two sets of cost curves. In connection with long-run cost curves we have introduced the concepts of economies of scale and diseconomies of scale. We have also shown how the long-run cost structure changes as input prices change.

SELECTED REFERENCES

STIGLER, G. J., *The Theory of Price.* New York: Macmillan, revised ed., 1952, Chapter 8.

VINER, J., "Cost Curves and Supply Curves." *Zeitschrift für Nationalökonomie* **3,** 1931, pp. 23–46. Reprinted in K. E. Boulding and G. J. Stigler (eds.), *Readings in Price Theory.* Chicago: Irwin, 1952, pp. 198–232.

EXERCISES

1. Figure E4–1 shows a section of the firm's LAC curve, and the SAC curves for Plant 1 and Plant 2, respectively. Complete the sentences given below.
   (a) Plant 1 is more efficient than Plant 2 for all levels of output less than _____.
   (b) In order to produce 330 units of X the firm should use Plant _____.
   (c) SMC_1 and LMC (neither of which is shown on the diagram) intersect each other at the level of output _____.
   (d) In order to produce 230 units of X the firm should use (*either Plant 1 or Plant 2, a plant smaller than Plant 2, a plant larger than Plant 2*).
   (e) In the long run the minimum unit cost of producing 500 units of X is equal to $_____.

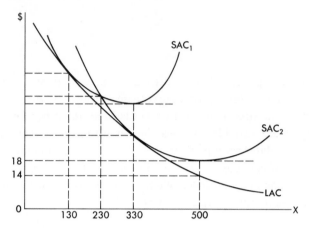

Figure E4–1

(f) If Plant 3 is the optimal plant for the production of 500 units of X, then SAC₃ (the SAC curve of Plant 3, not shown on the diagram) has its minimum point at (500 *units of* X, *less than* 500 *units of* X, *more than* 500 *units of* X).

2. Figure E4–2 shows a segment of the firm's LAC curve, a segment of its LMC curve, and the SAC curves of Plants 5 and 6, respectively.
   (a) Draw into the diagram the SMC₅ and SMC₆ functions.
   (b) At the output level 1200 (SMC₆ = SAC₆, SMC₆ < SAC₆, SMC₆ > SAC₆).
   (c) At output levels greater than 1200 (SMC₆ > LMC, SMC₆ < LMC).
   (d) The plant whose SAC curve has its minimum point at the output level 800, has a SMC curve which intersects LMC (*at* 800 *units of* X, *at more than* 800 *units of* X).
   (e) At the output 700 (SMC₅ > LAC, SMC₅ < LAC).
   (f) The plant which can produce 1000 units at a lower unit cost than any other plant has a SMC curve which intersects LMC at (1000 *units of* X, 1200 *units of* X, *more than* 1000 *units of* X).

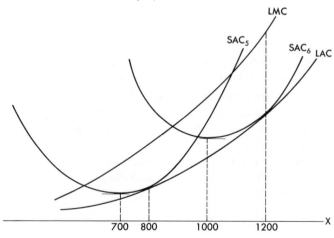

Figure E4–2

5

SHORT-RUN
PROFIT MAXIMIZATION:
PURE COMPETITION

5–1 THE NATURE OF PURE COMPETITION

Having completed the discussion of the firm's technological environment,
we turn now to a description of its economic environment. In subsequent
chapters we shall analyze the behavior of the firm under different environmental
conditions (or—to use a more familiar term—under different market conditions);
in this and the following chapter we are assuming a type of economic environment commonly referred to as **pure competition**. This type of market may be
identified by the following conditions:

(5A) The number of firms in the market

The number of firms in a purely competitive market is "very large." Now
this is obviously an ambiguous way of stating this condition; however, the
ambiguity cannot be removed simply by substituting a number for the phrase
in quotation marks. The important thing is not the number itself, but rather
whether it is sufficiently large to satisfy condition 5B.

(5B) The size of the firms in the market

The term "size" in this context really means "level of output," but since in
most cases there exists a direct correlation between the level of output of a
firm and its physical dimensions, "size" may also be interpreted here as "size
of plant." **In pure competition it is assumed that firms are "very small."** That

is, they are sufficiently small relative to the size of the industry as a whole (the totality of all firms taken together) so that changes in the level of output of any single firm (even as extreme a change as reducing output from its maximum level to zero, or vice versa) will have no appreciable effect on the market price of the output. It should now be clear why condition 5A is necessary to obtain condition 5B, and the meaning of "very large" as used in 5A should also be less ambiguous.

(5C) The product produced by the firms in the market

In pure competition firms are assumed to produce identical products. Even though we have dispensed with quotation marks this time, the pedant may insist that the meaning of "identical" in the preceding sentence is also ambiguous. It is indeed true that physical objects are rarely, if ever, exactly alike, and no such complete identity is required here. For the purpose of this analysis we shall tolerate differences between products which the consumer does not know about and those about which he is indifferent, and shall assume that two similar products are identical if consumers are willing to pay just as much for one product as for the other.*

(5D) The mobility of the firms

Under conditions of pure competition firms are free to leave or enter the market. This condition, however, plays a role only in the analysis of the long run. Remember that in the short run the firm's plant is fixed, hence it cannot be changed or abandoned. Of course, the firm can always opt to produce nothing at all, but in the short run it will still have to pay all fixed costs.

The above conditions are meant to describe some of the institutional characteristics of pure competition. In the formal analysis of the model we shall not refer to these conditions directly, but concentrate on the behavioral

---

* Even this is not a completely satisfactory definition, as it merely shifts the ambiguity from "identical" to "similar." We shall not try to define the term "similar" because it is unlikely that we would succeed without using terms which themselves will need to be defined in order to give "similar" an unambiguous meaning. This case may perhaps serve as a good example of the fact that good definitions are sometimes hard to come by. (For example, how would you define such familiar terms as "product," "market," or "industry"?) Quite often in attempting to provide suitable definitions one finds himself caught (as in the above example) in an infinite regression from which there seems to be no escape. In such instances the best course is *not* to define all the terms, especially if it can be assumed that the lack of precise definitions will not jeopardize the process of communication. In such cases the reader is kindly requested not to make things unnecessarily difficult by asking too many questions (definitions), but to use his intuition and imagination in place of formal definitions.

implications which follow from them. The most important of these are the following:

(5E) The firm in pure competition can sell all it is capable of producing at the going market price.

(5F) The firm in pure competition always sells its output at the going market price.

The first of these behavioral statements says that the firm can always count on selling even its greatest output at the going market price. This follows directly from condition 5B, according to which firms are assumed to be so small as to be unable to upset the market price through changes in the level of their output. Statement 5F says in effect that the firm does not set the price for its product, but sells its output, in whatever quantity it wishes, at the going market price. The explanation for this conformity to the market price can also be found in the institutional framework of pure competition. If the firm were to charge a price **higher** than the market price, it could expect to lose all its buyers, since the latter could obtain the identical product from the firm's competitors at the going market price. Such a course of action would obviously result in losses to the firm. On the other hand, there is also no reason why the firm should ever charge a price **lower** than the prevailing market price when, according to statement 5E, it can sell everything **at** the market price. Here, again, the firm would incur a loss if it deviated from the market price. It is the firm's acceptance of the going market price (behavioral implication 5F) which we shall incorporate explicitly into the model. Indeed, from a completely formal point of view, a market may be defined as purely competitive whenever all its firms behave according to 5F. It would have been possible, therefore, to start the discussion of pure competition by simply assuming statement 5F, dispensing with any justification for this assumption in terms of the institutional factors. We have gone into further detail in order to avoid unnecessary abstractness, and to make it easier to identify those markets in the real economy which satisfy, or approximate, the specifications of our model. With respect to the latter point it may be suggested that in most economies the agricultural sector comes closest to resembling a model of pure competition.

5–2 THE OPTIMAL LEVEL OF OUTPUT

We are now ready to tackle the first decision-making problem: How much of a certain product X should a purely competitive firm produce in order to maximize its profit? Earlier in the text it was indicated that profit is the dif-

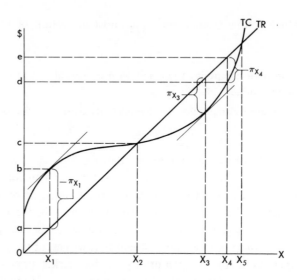

Figure 5–1

ference beteen total revenues and total cost. This definition may be stated conveniently by the equation

$$\pi = \text{TR} - \text{TC}, \tag{5–1}$$

where the Greek letter pi denotes total profit and TR stands for total revenues. The symbol TR represents the firm's total money receipts from a certain level of output, and may also be defined in terms of price and quantity; that is,

$$\text{TR} = \text{P} \cdot \text{X}, \tag{5–2}$$

where P denotes the unit price at which the output X is sold.

Since π is the difference between TR and TC (which we defined in Chapter 2), it is possible to obtain a graphical representation of profit by plotting the TR and TC functions on a suitable diagram (Fig. 5–1). The reader should be familiar by now with the TC curve; hence it requires no further comment at this point. With respect to the TR function the following may be observed. First, it has a positive slope, indicating that when output increases, TR increases too; in other words, as the firm sells more, its receipts increase. Second, the TR function goes through the origin, which means that at the zero level of output the firm's revenues are zero. Finally, it is evident that the TR function is **linear,** i.e., it is represented by a straight line. The latter follows from the fact that whenever X increases or decreases by one unit, TR increases or decreases by some constant amount, namely P, the price at which the output is sold.

Now the difference between TR and TC at any level of X is simply the vertical distance between the respective functions at that level of X. Thus, for instance, at the level of output X_4 the level of profit, π_{X_4}, equals $TR_{X_4} - TC_{X_4} = e - d$ dollars; at X_2 we have $\pi_{X_2} = c - c = 0$ dollars; and at X_1, $\pi_{X_1} = a - b$ dollars. From these observations we may derive the following conclusions:

(1) At levels of output less than X_2 and greater than X_5, profit is negative (for instance, at X_1, since $a < b$, therefore $a - b < 0$).
(2) At levels of output between X_2 and X_5 profit is positive.
(3) At the outputs X_2 and X_5 profit is zero.

Outputs like X_2 and X_5 are sometimes referred to as a **break-even points.**

The above stated conclusions simplify to some extent the determination of the optimal (profit-maximizing) level of output, since it can be inferred from them that the optimal output lies somewhere between X_2 and X_5. The problem may therefore be stated as finding a point on the X-axis between X_2 and X_5 at which the vertical distance between the TR and TC functions is greatest. Such a point is at X_3 at which the tangent line to the TC curve is parallel to (has the same slope as) the TR line. In other words, at the optimal level of output the slopes of the TR and TC functions are equal.

We shall now define the concept of **marginal revenue** in the same way we defined MC (Definition 2–8).

Definition 5–1

MARGINAL REVENUE (MR) = the slope of the TR function at any given point.

For discrete changes in output MR measures the change in TR as output is increased by one unit. Making use of the definitions of MC and MR, we can restate the condition for finding the optimal level of output in the following manner.

(5G) At the optimal level of output MC must be equal to MR.

A relevant question to raise at this point is whether statement 5G represents a complete and unambiguous rule capable of ensuring profit maximization. Imagine that you are employed as an adviser for profit maximization. Would you be doing a good job if you merely told the firm's manager: "Choose an output for which MC = MR"? The answer to this question is in the negative. Another look at Fig. 5–1 will show that there are **two** levels of output at which MC = MR, namely X_1 and X_3. Thus in the absence of additional instructions the firm could conceivably choose X_1 and believe that by doing so it is actually maximizing its profit. We know from the diagram, of course, that at X_1 profits are negative, so that X_1 cannot possibly be a profit-maximizing output. In fact, since at X_1 the vertical distance between the TR and TC functions in the

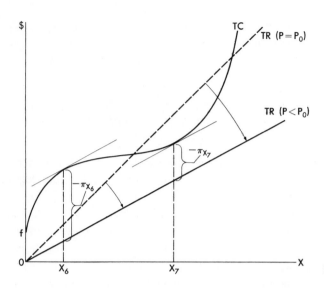

Figure 5–2

range of output $0–X_2$ is greatest, the choice of X_1 leads to **loss** maximization, or equivalently, to profit **minimization.*** It is, therefore, necessary to formulate an additional provision in order to make certain that the firm chooses an output which is consistent with its objective (rather than with the opposite of its objective). For this purpose we note that outputs X_1 and X_3 may be distinguished from each other on the basis of the shape of the slope of the TC curve in the neighborhood of these respective points. If output is increased past X_1 the slope of the TC curve becomes flatter, while beyond output X_3 it becomes steeper. This leads to the condition

(5H) At the optimal level of output MC must be increasing.

Of course, it may have occurred to the reader that we could have differentiated between outputs X_1 and X_3 on the basis of the fact that X_3 gives rise to positive profit, whereas X_1 yields negative profit. While this would be a correct procedure in the special situation depicted in Fig. 5–1, it may not be a satisfactory rule in general. This is so because if the price is sufficiently low, **both** minimum and maximum profit may be negative. Such a case is shown in Fig. 5–2, which assumes a price less than that implied by Fig. 5–1. The TR function of Fig. 5–1 is reproduced in Fig. 5–2 as a dashed line for comparative purposes. The optimal output is now X_7, and the maximum profit is negative.

---

* Strictly speaking, profit is minimized at X_1 for all levels of output between 0 and X_5. As output is increased beyond X_5 the level of profit falls indefinitely.

Note that in Fig. 5–2 the TR function has a smaller (flatter) slope, because when the price falls the revenues from any level of output decrease as well. As a matter of fact, since by definition $P = TR/X$ (Eq. 5–2), and since TR and X form the height and base, respectively, of the right-angle triangle of which the TR function forms the hypotenuse, it follows that the slope of the TR function equals P. (See definition of slope, Section 2–3.) But since by definition the slope of the TR function is equal to MR, we find that when the TR function is linear and goes through the origin, then $P = MR$.

Now the profit picture which emerges from Fig. 5–2 is, perhaps, a little disturbing; here is a situation in which a firm can only lose money. Not that we expect our model to have a built-in protection against losses, but we know that a firm cannot afford to lose money indefinitely, and if adverse financial conditions persist, it is bound sooner or later to disappear from the market. Remember, however, that in the **short run** a firm cannot simply leave the market, because it has fixed obligations (costs), so that short-run adjustments can only be made through variations in the level of output. Thus if X_7 is the optimal output for the situation depicted in Fig. 5–2, then our model may indeed yield negative profit. It should be quite clear from Fig. 5–2 that **any** level of output yields a loss. This can easily be seen from the fact that the TC function lies entirely above the TR function. Hence regardless of what the optimal output turns out to be in this case (it is, in fact, X_7), the firm is necessarily losing money. Thus the determination of the optimal level of output in Fig. 5–2 means finding a point on the X-axis for which the firm's loss is smallest. (This example aptly illustrates that **profit maximization** is equivalent to **loss minimization.**)

We may also note that there exists one particular level of output for which the profit can be computed quite easily—the zero level of output. Recall (Table 2–1) that when output is zero, $TC = TFC$ (since $TVC = 0$). Hence using the definition of profit (Eq. 5–1), we find from Fig. 5–2 that at $X = 0$, profit equals $-f$ dollars. What is the significance of this bit of information? It tells us that if for some reason the firm chooses an output which yields a profit less than $-f$ dollars, it is not maximizing profit. This is so because the firm can make a greater profit (smaller loss) by producing at the zero level of output, at which its profit is exactly $-f$ dollars. What we are really saying here is that **a firm need never lose an amount which is greater than its TFC.** If the firm **does** choose a level of output at which its loss is greater than TFC, then the firm's revenues are not sufficient even to cover the variable cost of the output in question. In that case the firm loses an amount which is equal to its **TFC plus** a portion of its **TVC.** To avoid such an unnecessary loss the firm should never choose an output from which the revenues are less than TVC. But this is equivalent to saying that the firm should never produce a positive output if AVC exceeds the price of the product. We have thus derived an additional rule which is designed to guide the firm in those cases in which the price is so low as to make all levels of output losing propositions. The rule says, in effect, that when the market price falls below the minimum value of the AVC function the firm should shut down; i.e., should produce zero units of X. Formally we say that:

(5I) At the optimal level of output (except when it is zero) the market price must not be less than AVC. Whenever the market price is less than AVC, the optimal output is zero.

▶ A more formal proof

The argument which leads to condition 5I above can also be presented in a slightly more formal manner. We want to make sure that profit is always greater than −TFC; that is, we require

$$TR - TC > -TFC.$$

Replacing TC by its two components (Eq. 2–1) we get

$$TR - TFC - TVC > -TFC.$$

Subtracting −TFC from both sides of the inequality we get

$$TR - TVC > 0,$$

and by adding TVC to both sides we have

$$TR > TVC.$$

If we now divide both sides of the last inequality by X we get

$$\frac{TR}{X} > \frac{TVC}{X},$$

and making use of the respective definitions we can state

$$P > AVC.$$

Therefore when $P > AVC$, then $\pi > -TFC$. Similarly, it can be shown that if $P < AVC$, then $\pi < -TFC$; and, of course, at the border line where $P = AVC$, we have $\pi = -TFC$.

When the price is greater than or equal to **AVC**, the firm should produce the output for which conditions 5G and 5H are satisfied even if the price is not high enough to cover **ATC**. If **P** > **AVC**, or equivalently, if **TR** > **TVC**, the firm is in a position to defray all its variable costs, and at least part of its fixed costs; and that is certainly better than not being able to pay any of the fixed cost (and hence incur a still greater loss) as is the case when the firm shuts down.

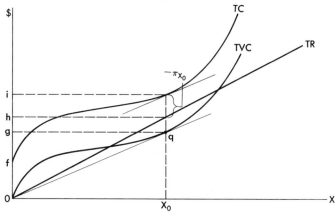

Figure 5–3

Figure 5–3 describes such a situation. The optimal output is X_0, since at this output all three conditions are satisfied. We see that **P** > **AVC**, since the slope of the **TR** function is greater than the slope of the ray 0q which represents **AVC** (Fig. 2–3). The firm's **TR** (h) is sufficient to cover all of **TVC** (g) and a portion (h − g) of **TFC** (i − g = f). The uncovered part of **TFC** (i − h) is equal to the firm's loss. When **P** = **AVC** it makes no difference, so far as profits are concerned, whether the firm shuts down or produces the output which satisfies conditions 5G and 5H; in either case the firm's loss is exactly equal to its **TFC**.

In summary, then, we can state the following rule for profit maximization:

In order to maximize its profit the firm should choose a level of output, call it $\overline{X}$, which satisfies either one of the conditions stated below. (AVC_{min} denotes the minimum value of the AVC function.)

(5J) If $P \geq AVC_{min}$, then the following must hold:

(1) $MC_{\overline{X}} = MR$;

(2) $MC_{\overline{X}}$ is increasing.

(5K) If $P < AVC_{min}$, then $\overline{X} = 0$.

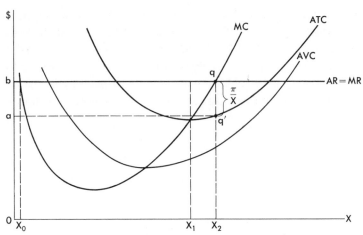

Figure 5–4

We shall now proceed to analyze the firm's decision-making process by the use of **average** (instead of total) cost and revenue curves. Figure 5–4 shows the familiar cost curves, and a horizontal line indicating that the going market price is **b** dollars. Here we are using the term **average revenue** (AR) (revenues per unit of output) instead of the more popular word "price." The horizontal line also shows that AR = MR, which was shown to be true for the type of TR function assumed in this model. The AR line is sometimes thought of as the firm's demand curve. This is a proper procedure, since the line shows the quantities of X that the firm can expect to sell at the going market price.

According to Fig. 5–4 both output levels X_0 and X_2 satisfy provision (1) of condition 5J, but only X_2 satisfies (1) and (2); hence X_2 is the optimal level of output. At that level of output the firm's **average profit** (profit per unit of output, also known as **mark-up**) is equal to **b** − **a** dollars, and total profit equals (**b** − **a**) · X_2 dollars. The latter is represented graphically by the area of the rectangle **abqq'**. Note that at output X_1, **average** profit is greater than at X_2; indeed, at X_1 average profit is at its maximum, because at that level of output the vertical distance between **AR** and **ATC** is greatest. This demonstrates that the maximization of **total** profit is in general not consistent with the maximization of **average** profit; i.e., each of these objectives may lead to a different course of action.

5–3   THE SUPPLY CURVE OF THE FIRM AND THE MARKET

It is now quite easy to see how changes in the market price affect the firm's choice of output. Figure 5–5 shows the optimal levels of output for four different levels of the market price. Thus when P = **d**, then $\overline{X}$ = X_3, and the

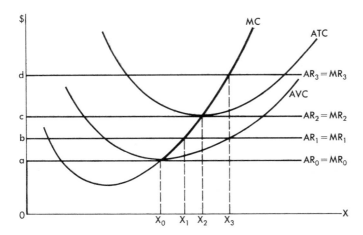

Figure 5–5

firm has a positive profit; when $P = c$, then $\bar{X} = X_2$ and $\pi = 0$; when $P = b$, then $\bar{X} = X_1$ and $\pi < 0$; when $P < a$, then $\bar{X} = 0$ and $\pi = -TFC$. That is, whenever $P \geq a$, the firm chooses that level of output which is vertically below the point on the MC curve which corresponds to the given market price; when $P < a$, it chooses $X = 0$. Thus the part of the MC curve at and above the line AR_0 and the segment of the vertical axis between the origin and a can be considered to constitute the firm's **supply function,** a relationship between price and quantity which indicates the quantity of the output which the firm will produce (supply) at any given market price.

In a sense, the supply curve provides a summary description of the function performed by the firm in its role as a seller, and that is precisely one of the main objectives of the theory of the firm. We shall go one step further and show how the behavior of individual firms determines the behavior of the market as a whole; after all, the total market output is nothing but the sum of the outputs of all the firms in the market. Consequently, a market supply curve can be derived directly by "summing" all the individual supply curves. This process is demonstrated in Fig. 5–6, which assumes—for expository purposes only—that there are only two firms in the market. The market supply curve S is obtained by adding the outputs of all firms for any given market price, and then plotting the resulting point in the market diagram. For example, when $P = P_0$, A's output is X_0 and B's output is X_2; therefore, market output, or market supply, is $X_0 + X_2$, and this yields point q in the market diagram of Fig. 5–6. Point q' is obtained in a similar fashion. The supply curve S is the locus of all points which have been obtained in this fashion. In the case of pure competition, of course, the summation is performed over a large number of firms.

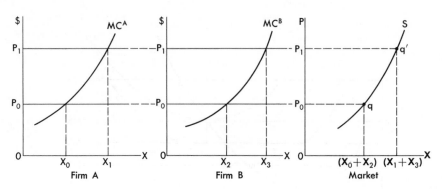

Figure 5–6

To complete this discussion of short-run profit maximization we should say a few words about the determination of, and changes in, the market price. The market price, at least in a purely competitive market, tends to settle at a level at which the quantity offered for sale equals the quantity which buyers wish to purchase; in other words, where supply equals demand. Thus for the condition depicted in Fig. 5–7 the market price is P_0. The curve labeled **D** is the market demand curve, which is a relationship between **P** and **X** showing the quantity of **X** demanded for any given level of the market price. (The derivation of demand curves will be discussed in Chapter 12.) Also shown is the position of a "representative" firm in the market. Figure 5–7 may be said to describe a short-run **equilibrium** position, a state of affairs in which certain quantities tend to remain constant over time.

In the above example every firm is in equilibrium because each one is producing its optimal level of output, and will continue to do so as long as all the relevant variables (prices and technology) remain constant. Since at the price

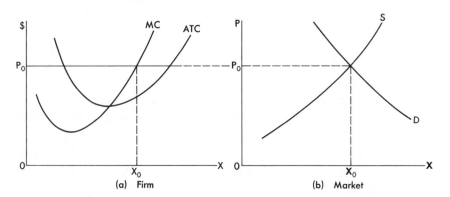

Figure 5–7

P_0 market demand and supply are both equal to X_0, the market price will also remain constant, and therefore the entire market is said to be in short-run equilibrium.

However, the equilibrium may be disturbed as a result of a shift in either the market supply or demand curve. When that happens the two curves will intersect at a different point in the diagram, and consequently may cause a change in the market price. This will, of course, also induce each firm in the market to make an appropriate adjustment in the level of its output. The causes and consequences of disturbances in the short-run equilibrium will be analyzed in greater detail in the next chapter.

SUMMARY

In the first part of this chapter we introduced a particular type of economic environment known as pure competition. This type of market was described in terms of its institutional characteristics, which then were shown to imply a certain behavioral pattern on the part of the firms in the market.

In the second part a typical decision problem was posed, and a method developed for finding the solution to the problem. Specifically, we explained how a firm in a purely competitive market chooses the level of its output to attain its objective of profit maximization. The decision-making process was summarized in the form of a set of simple rules. It was also shown how the firm's choice of output varies with changes in the market price, and how this relationship leads to the concept of the supply curve of the firm.

The chapter concludes with the derivation of the market supply curve and a brief mention of the concept of equilibrium.

SELECTED REFERENCES

GRUNBERG, E., "The Profit Maximization Assumption: Comment." *Oxford Economic Papers*, New Series **16**, 1964, pp. 286–290.

KOPLIN, H. T., "The Profit Maximization Assumption." *Oxford Economic Papers*, New Series **15**, 1963, pp. 130–139.

SIMON, H. A., "Theories of Decision-Making in Economics and Behavioral Science." *American Economic Review* **49,** 1959, pp. 253–283.

STIGLER, G. J., "Perfect Competition, Historically Contemplated." *Journal of Political Economy* **65,** 1957, pp. 1–17.

STIGLER, G. J., *The Theory of Price.* New York: Macmillan, revised ed., 1952, Chapter 10.

VINER, J., "Cost Curves and Supply Curves." *Zeitschrift für Nationalökonomie* **3,** 1931, pp. 23–46. Reprinted in K. E. Boulding and G. J. Stigler (eds.), *Readings in Price Theory.* Chicago: Irwin, 1952, pp. 198–232.

EXERCISES

1. Figure E5–1 shows the firm's TC function, and three different TR functions. Complete the sentences given below.

   (a) If the price is $10, the firm should produce (6 *units,* 8 *units,* 10 *units, between* 8 *and* 10 *units*).

   (b) When the price is $_____, the firm breaks even. Under these circumstances TR are allocated as follows: $_____ to pay for TFC, and $_____ for TVC.

   (c) If the price is $7.50, and the firm chooses to produce 8 units, its profit will be equal to $_____. Since the latter is (*less than* −TFC, *greater than* −TFC, *equal to* −TFC), it follows that (*the firm's choice is optimal, the firm's choice is not optimal*).

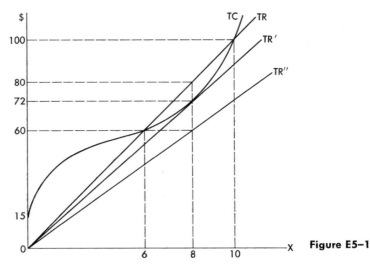

Figure E5–1

(d) It is impossible to determine the shut-down price because Fig. E5–1 gives no information about _____.

(e) When the price increases from $10 to $12, the firm's profit (*increases, decreases, changes in an indeterminate fashion*).

(f) If the firm's TFC increases by $8, the break-even price is ($10, *less than* $10, *more than* $10).

(g) From the cost table which you have completed in Exercise 1 of Chapter 2 determine the optimal levels of output for the prices $8 and $5, respectively.

(h) Assume that the cost conditions of a purely competitive firm are described by the completed cost table given in Exercise 2 of Chapter 2. What is the firm's shut-down price?

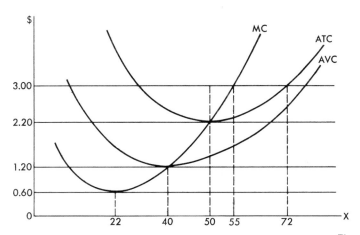

Figure E5–2

2. Figure E5–2 shows the firm's ATC, AVC, and MC functions, and a number of price lines. Complete the sentences given below.

(a) If the price is $3, the firm's maximum profit is equal to ($40, *between* $40 *and* $44, $44, *zero*), and the mark-up is ($0.80, *slightly less than* $0.80, *zero*).

(b) If the price is $3, and the firm wanted to maximize mark-up (rather than total profit), it should produce _____ units of X.

(c) The break-even price is $_____; at that price the firm's TVC equals ($48, $60, *between* $60 *and* $110, *between* $66 *and* $121).

(d) If the price is $_____, 50 units of X is the optimal level of output, regardless of whether the firm wishes to maximize average or total profit.

(e) The optimal level of output is zero whenever the price falls below $_____; in other words, under the cost conditions given in Fig. E5–2 the firm will never produce less than _____ units of X.

(f) Since MC does not depend on TFC [see Problem (e), Exercise 1 of Chapter 2], a change in TFC does not affect the MC (or the AVC) function. Assume that TFC increases by an amount which makes the ATC of 55 units of X equal to $3. Draw into Fig. E5–2 the new ATC function, and label it ATC'.

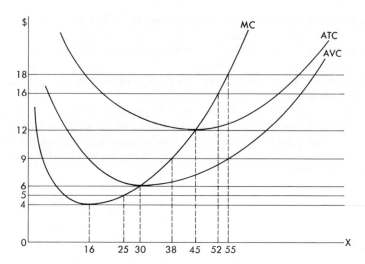

(g) Answer questions (a), (b), and (c) above under the new cost conditions.

(h) Verify that the answer to (e) above is not affected by the change in TFC.

3. Figure E5–3 shows various cost functions of a purely competitive firm, and a number of price lines. Assume that there are one thousand identical firms in the industry, i.e., assume that each of the one thousand firms has cost functions as shown in the above diagram.

(a) Prepare a diagram with the vertical axis labeled P, and the horizontal axis labeled X. Draw into this diagram the short-run market supply curve for the industry.

(b) Draw a market demand curve into your diagram so as to obtain a market equilibrium output of 55,000 units. Then the corresponding equilibrium market price is $_____.

(c) At the price mentioned in (b) above, each firm produces _____ units of X.

(d) Shift the market demand function in your diagram to the left so that at the new equilibrium price each firm will break even. At the break-even price the industry as a whole produces _____ units of X.

(e) Assume that there occurs a further decrease in demand, so that the market demand function shifts to the left once more. Suppose that the market demand function now occupies a position which indicates, among other things, that at the market price of $5 buyers will purchase a total quantity of 16,000 units of X. If the demand function is everywhere downward sloping, what will be the total market supply at the new equilibrium?

6

LONG-RUN
PROFIT MAXIMIZATION:
PURE COMPETITION

The decision problem to be considered in this chapter differs from short-run profit maximization in one respect essentially: In the short run, as was shown in Chapter 5, the firm's problem consists of choosing only the optimal level of output, whereas in the long run it involves choosing the optimal level of output **and** the optimal size of plant. This follows directly from the definitions of short run and long run. In the short run the size of the plant is fixed, and the firm's immediate objective is to choose a level of output which maximizes its profit **for the given plant**; in the long run the output is chosen under conditions in which all inputs are variable, so that the process of profit maximization also involves the selection of an optimal size of plant.

6–1 THE OPTIMAL LEVEL OF OUTPUT AND SIZE OF PLANT

The decision-making process may be analyzed with the help of long-run cost curves. These are graphed in Fig. 6–1, which also shows a set of short-run cost curves, as well as long-run average revenues (LAR) and long-run marginal revenue (LMR). Long-run average revenue may be interpreted as the market price which, according to the firm's expectations, will prevail in the long run. Therefore long-run total revenues (LTR) are equal to LAR · X, or P · X. Long-run marginal revenue bears the same relationship to LTR as (short-run) MR does to (short-run) TR.

In the determination of the optimal level of output we can make use of a set of conditions similar to those which govern profit maximization in the short

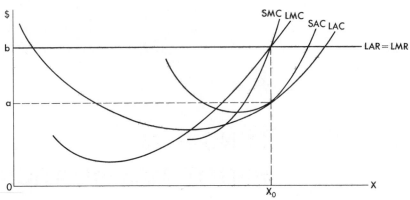

Figure 6–1

run. Using the notation appropriate for the long-run situation we can state
the following:

In order to maximize its profit in the long run the firm should choose a level of
output, call it $\overline{X}$, which satisfies either one of the conditions stated below.

(6A) If $P \geq LAC_{min}$, then the following must hold:

$$(1) \ LMC_{\overline{X}} = LMR;$$
$$(2) \ LMC_{\overline{X}} \text{ is increasing.}$$

(6B) If $P < LAC_{min}$, $\overline{X} = 0$.

In the above, LAC_{min} denotes the minimum value of the LAC function. These
conditions are virtually the same as the conditions for short-run profit maximization (5J and 5K), except that since in the long run all costs are variable,
the firm will not produce at all if the market price is less than the total cost
per unit. Thus in the short run a firm need never lose more than its TFC, but
in the long run, having no fixed obligations whatsoever, the firm can always
choose to avoid losses altogether by staying out of the market.

   In Fig. 6–1, X_0 is the optimal level of output since it fully satisfies condition
6A. Of course, long-run profit maximization presupposes that the firm is
free to select the least-cost input combination for any level of output, and, in
particular, to select the most suitable size of plant. In other words, the firm
will maximize long-run profit at the output X_0 only if the average cost of
producing X_0 is not greater than that indicated by the LAC curve—a dollars in
the above example. Now we know from Chapter 4 that there exists only one
size of plant for which the minimum average cost of producing X_0 is a dollars,

namely the plant whose SAC curve is tangent to the LAC curve at X_0 (Fig. 4–2). Therefore that particular plant, whose cost curves are shown in Fig. 6–1, is the one the firm should select in order to ensure long-run profit maximization at the output X_0.

Once the firm has selected and constructed a particular plant, it incurs the usual fixed costs associated with any given plant, and from that time on adjustments in the production plan in response to changes in environmental conditions must be viewed from both short-run and long-run perspectives. Of course, this point also raises the question as to what precisely is the relationship between short-run and long-run profit maximization. For example, suppose we were to erase the LAC and LMC curves from Fig. 6–1, and ask the following question: "What is the firm's optimal level of output, given the firm's plant as represented by the SAC and SMC curves, if the market price is b dollars?" The answer is clearly X_0, since that level of output satisfies condition 5J for short-run profit maximization.* From this observation we can conclude that **long-run profit maximization implies short-run profit maximization.** We can also say that the firm whose position is depicted in Fig. 6–1 is in long-run equilibrium (because its size of plant and output are optimal with respect to long-run profit maximization) **and** in short-run equilibrium (since X_0 is also optimal for the particular plant shown). Rephrasing the above statement we can say that **long-run equilibrium implies short-run equilibrium.** As we shall see shortly, the converse of these statements is generally false.

6–2   ADJUSTMENT TO PRICE CHANGES

6–2.1   Adjustment of a single firm

Suppose now that the long-run equilibrium of the firm is disturbed by a change in the long-run market price; let us assume it falls from b to c dollars, as shown in Fig. 6–2. Obviously, X_0 is no longer the optimal level of output. The conditions for long-run profit maximization indicate that when the long-run market price is c dollars, the optimal output is X_2 and the appropriate size of plant for that output is the one represented by the curves SAC_2 and SMC_2. But it must be remembered that to carry out long-run adjustments, such as switching plants, may require a considerable period of time; certainly more than is required for merely changing the level of output in a given plant. Hence it is unreasonable to assume that the firm can adjust instantaneously to

---

* It is assumed implicitly that the current market price is the same as the expected long-run price.

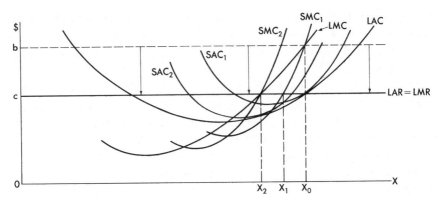

Figure 6–2

its new long-run equilibrium. Should the firm in the meantime produce X_2 with the current plant, Plant 1, or should it stay put at X_0? Rational behavior dictates that it should do neither. While making preparations for the construction and operation of Plant 2 the firm should continue operating Plant 1 in a manner consistent with short-run profit maximization. Accordingly, the firm should produce X_1 units of X, which is the optimal level of output for Plant 1 when the market price is **c** dollars. This solution is certainly not consistent with long-run profit maximization, but it is the best course of action the firm can follow during the period of time that it takes to adjust from the initial long-run equilibrium to the new one at X_2. Thus the adjustment to a long-run equilibrium may be viewed as proceeding in two steps: the first is a short-run, or transitory, adjustment which involves the selection of the optimal output for whatever plant the firm happens to operate; the second, made at a later point in time, is the switchover to the new size of plant, and a further change in output to the level which is consistent with long-run equilibrium. Note that the firm's position during the adjustment period (the production of X_1 with Plant 1) represents a short-run equilibrium which does not imply long-run equilibrium. (See the last two sentences in Section 6–1.)

6–2.2   Adjustment of the market

So far we have limited the discussion to short-run and long-run adjustments of a single firm. Since the market price is bound to change when all the firms adjust their output, we shall now view the process of adjusting to price changes from the perspective of the entire market. For this purpose the following assumptions will be made: When firms in any particular industry have positive profits, firms (owners of capital) in other industries earning less or no profit at

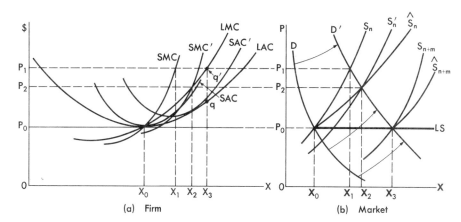

Figure 6–3

all are attracted to the more profitable industry. Moreover, in the long run such firms will actually abandon their current lines of activity and move into the more lucrative market. Similarly, firms which incur losses will in the long run leave the market altogether. The freedom of firms to move between industries is one of the characteristics of a purely competitive market (condition 5D).

It is most convenient to analyze the adjustment process by assuming an initial long-run equilibrium position. Such a position is depicted in Fig. 6–3, in which market supply S_n and demand D are equal at the initial price P_0. Each firm produces X_0 units of X, and market supply is $\mathbf{X}_0$. (Boldface letters will be used to denote market output.) Each firm operates the plant represented by the curves SAC and SMC. Since P = LAR, profit is zero, so that no firm will want to either leave or enter the market. Since firms in a purely competitive market produce identical products it is not too unreasonable to assume that they also have identical cost curves, so that part (a) of Fig. 6–3 can be taken to represent the position of every firm in the market. It also follows that if there are n firms in the market then $\mathbf{X}_0 = nX_0$, since the short-run market supply curve is obtained by "summing" the SMC curves of the n firms in the market (see Fig. 5–6). The subscripts attached to the labels of some curves in part (b) of Fig. 6–3 denote the number of firms in the market.

We shall now disturb the long-run equilibrium by assuming an increase in the demand for product X as shown by the shift of the market demand curve from position D to position D'. Equilibrium no longer obtains, since at the price P_0 quantity demanded exceeds quantity supplied (by $\mathbf{X}_3 - \mathbf{X}_0$ units). Such an increase in demand may be caused by a number of factors, such as an increase in the preference on the part of buyers for product X (sometimes referred to as a "change in tastes"), an increase in consumers' income, or an increase in the prices of products for which product X may be used as a substitute. This excess demand exerts an upward pressure on the market price, and as the price moves up each firm expands its output to maintain the equality between price and SMC. As soon as market supply has increased sufficiently to eliminate the excess demand, the price movement comes to a halt. In the above example this occurs when the price reaches the level P_1. At that price each firm produces X_1, and both market supply and market demand equal $X_1 = nX_1$. Note that the increase in quantity supplied ($X_1 - X_0$) is less than the amount of excess demand which prevailed at the initial price of P_0 ($X_3 - X_0$). In other words, in order to reduce excess demand to zero it is in general not necessary for quantity supplied to increase by the full amount of the excess demand, because quantity demanded declines as the price increases. There is no inconsistency between the assumption that the excess demand which disturbed the initial equilibrium was created by an increase in demand, and the subsequent decline in quantity demanded. An increase in demand refers to a desire to increase purchases **at a given price,** whereas the decline in quantity demanded from X_3 to X_1 represents a cut in purchases made **in response to an increase in the price.** In other words, a **change in demand** is represented by a **shift** in the demand curve, and a **change in quantity demanded** by a **movement along** the demand curve.

When the price settles at P_1 the market and every firm in it are in **short-run** equilibrium; each firm is maximizing short-run profit, and since market demand equals market supply, the price remains constant. Viewed from the **long-run** perspective, however, the situation appears to be unstable. Note that the firms in the market are not in long-run equilibrium. Long-run profit maximization requires that they produce X_3 units of X, and it also calls for an enlargement of the plant size. For the output X_3 the optimal plant is the one whose SAC curve is tangent to the LAC curve at point q, and whose SMC curve intersects the LMC curve at q'. (Neither of these curves is shown in Fig. 6–3.) Now, if the firms actually proceeded to make this adjustment, the new SMC curve of each firm would lie to the right of the SMC curve shown in part (a) of Fig. 6–3, and consequently the short-run supply curve S_n in part (b) of the diagram would also shift to the right. The position of the S_n curve associated with this adjustment is not shown in the diagram, but regardless of its exact location, we can be certain that such a shift results in a decrease in the market price. This in turn entails a readjustment of the size of plant and output in the opposite direction, because for prices lower than P_1 the output X_3 is too large.

This action-reaction type of process will go on until a position is reached in which each firm finds itself in long-run equilibrium, and market supply equals market demand. In Fig. 6–3 this situation obtains when the market price is

P_2. At that price each firm produces X_2 units of X, using the plant represented by the curves SAC′ and SMC′. The short-run market supply curve is shown by the curve labeled S'_n (obtained by "summing" the n SMC′ curves), and market supply and demand are equal at $X_2 = nX_2$. This solution can also be found by a slightly different method. If we "add" those segments of the n LMC curves which lie at and above the price line P_0, we obtain the curve labeled $\hat{S}_n$. (The parts of the LMC curves below P_0 are ignored because long-run profit maximization requires $P \geq LAC$.) Since long-run profit maximization requires that $P = LMC$, it follows that the intersection of the $\hat{S}_n$ and D′ curves yields a pair of values for P and X (P_2 and X_2) which is consistent with long-run profit maximization for each firm, as well as an equality between market supply and demand. Thus the $\hat{S}_n$ curve is a useful tool for identifying the position at which firms will attain their long-run equilibrium, but it does not by itself shed any light on the various stages through which each firm passes on its way to the equilibrium position. It is only by following the shifts of the short-run market supply curve that one obtains a more complete picture of how equilibrium is brought about by the interaction between the motive of profit maximization on the one hand, and the tendency of the price to eliminate excess demand in the market on the other.

Had we not made the assumption of interindustry mobility, i.e., had we assumed that the number of firms in the industry is fixed, then the intersection of the $\hat{S}_n$ and D′ curves would represent a long-run market equilibrium. It would represent a long-run equilibrium, since under these circumstances every firm in the market is in long-run equilibrium, and unless one of the market curves shifted due to a change in some exogenous factor, the market price would stay at P_2. Mobility of firms, however, cannot be assumed away in a purely competitive market, **and in spite of the fact that every firm in the market is in long-run equilibrium, the market as a whole is not.*** We may refer to this situation as **quasi long-run market equilibrium,** and the $\hat{S}_n$ curve may accordingly be called **quasi long-run market supply curve.**

6–2.3   Entry of new firms

The disequilibrating factor in the above situation is the existence of profit. Under the assumption made earlier (beginning of preceding subsection) profit attracts firms into the market, and thus the number of firms in the market grows. To simplify the analysis, the firms which enter into the market are

---

* Do you remember the section on the "fallacy of composition" in the introductory chapter of Samuelson's *Economics*?

assumed to have the same cost curves as the firms already in the market. As the new firms start to produce, the total quantity of X supplied to the market increases, and hence the short-run supply curve shifts once more to the right. The magnitude of the shift depends, of course, on the increase in the number of firms, but unless the increase is sufficiently large to completely eliminate the profit, the influx of firms into the market continues. It is quite clear from Fig. 6–3 that firms make a profit so long as the price remains above P_0. Consequently, the elimination of profit requires an increase in the number of firms such that the short-run market supply curve is shifted to the position shown by the curve S_{n+m}. In this example it is assumed that the number of firms has increased by m, that is, from n to $n + m$. Each firm now produces X_0 units of X, using the plant whose SAC curve is tangent to the lowest point on the LAC curve. Total output is $X_3 = (n + m) \cdot X_0$. Note that each firm produces the same output as it did at the initial equilibrium, but market output is greater because there are more firms in the market. The intersection of the S_{n+m} and D′ curves represents a long-run market equilibrium; every firm in the market is in long-run equilibrium, and since profit is zero, the number of firms in the market will remain unchanged, as will the market price. The line joining the two long-run equilibrium points is the long-run market supply curve (LS).

In the foregoing discussion we demonstrated through a particular example how the market, when out of equilibrium, moves to a new long-run equilibrium position. The main purpose of this analysis was to bring into play the various factors which impinge on the adjustment process, and to describe their role in moving the market toward equilibrium. By no means did we intend to analyze this process in all its details, since such a task would require further assumptions about the nature of the technical environment of a purely competitive market. For instance, none of the assumptions which we made in this model imply anything about the **sequence** in which the different events take place. We assumed, for the sake of simplicity only, that the process may be viewed as consisting of a number of discrete phases, and that during the first two phases the number of firms in the market remains constant. This approach presupposes that it takes less time for a firm to switch plants in a given market than it does to switch from one market to another. Perhaps there is no general justification for such an assumption, but for the purpose of the present analysis it is not really necessary to make any assumption at all about these aspects of the adjustment process. We are more interested here in the conditions which guarantee the maintenance of long-run market equilibrium than in the manner in which it is reached. It would, in fact, be more realistic to assume that the pertinent factors begin to exert their effects as soon as the initial equilibrium is disturbed, so that the market may very well reach the new long-run equilibrium position without ever getting to the intermediary stage which we called quasi long-run market equilibrium. The partitioning of the adjustment process into conceptually different phases is merely a convenient method by which one can identify the different forces which provide the adjustment with its motive power, and thus obtain a clearer picture of the cause-and-effect relationships underlying this process.

6–3 CHANGES IN INPUT PRICES

The adjustment to long-run market equilibrium also depends on certain assumptions about the economic environment which so far have not been spelled out. In the example shown in Fig. 6–3 it has been implicitly assumed that the cost structure of the firms does not change as the market moves from one long-run equilibrium to another. Under certain circumstances this need not be the case. In the above example, for instance, total output at the new equilibrium is greater than at the initial point, which means that the industry as a whole is now using a greater quantity of factors of production than at the initial equilibrium. If the increased demand for these factors causes an increase in their prices, then the production cost of each firm increases as well. (For a discussion of the effect of changes in input prices on the cost structure, see Sections 3–3 and 4–3.) Since higher input prices raise production cost regardless of the size of the plant which the firm uses, the impact of this increase in prices can be depicted by an upward shift in the LAC curve of every firm. When this is the case the analysis of the adjustment process must be slightly modified.

In Fig. 6–4 initial equilibrium prevails under conditions identical to those assumed in Fig. 6–3; that is, the price level is P_0, each firm produces X_0 units

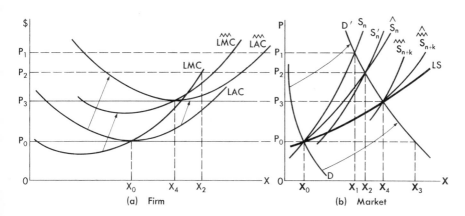

(a) Firm

(b) Market

Figure 6–4

of X, and market supply and demand equal X_0. (SAC and SMC curves are omitted for graphical clarity.) As in the first example, we shall assume that the adjustment consists of a number of discrete phases. We also assume again that demand increases to D', so that the market price rises at first to P_1. In the first phase of the process each firm in the market makes a short-run adjustment by increasing its output to maximize short-run profit. The new output of each firm is not shown in the diagram, but the corresponding market output is X_1. In the second phase firms make their long-run adjustment by switching to larger plants, and at the end of this phase quasi long-run market equilibrium is established with market price P_2, and outputs X_2 and X_2 for the firm and market, respectively. In the third phase the existence of profit attracts new firms into the market. It is in this phase that the present example differs from the first one. As in the first example this phase is characterized by a fall in the market price due to a further increase in market supply, but in addition there now occurs an upward shift in every firm's long-run cost curves to the position indicated by the curves $\widehat{LAC}$ and $\widehat{LMC}$. The significance of this shift from the point of view of the adjustment process lies in the fact that in order to eliminate the profit the market price need not be pushed all the way back to P_0; instead, the new long-run market equilibrium is now attained when the price reaches P_3. In this new position each firm produces X_4 units of X with the plant whose SAC curve is tangent to the $\widehat{LAC}$ curve at its lowest point. The summation (over all firms) of the SMC curves belonging to the latter SAC curve yields the short-run market supply curve labeled $\widehat{S}_{n+k}$. The curve labeled $\widehat{S}_{n+k}$, the quasi long-run market supply curve, is obtained by "summing" the $\widehat{LMC}$ curves of all the firms in the market. Market supply and demand equal $X_4 = (n + k) \cdot X_4$. Since $X_4 < X_3$ and $X_4 > X_0$, it follows that $k < m$. In other words, compared with the new long-run equilibrium in the first example (Fig. 6–3), the new long-run equilibrium in the second example (Fig. 6–4) is characterized by a smaller market output (since $X_4 < X_3$), which means that in moving from the initial equilibrium (at X_0) to the new equilibrium (at X_4) market output increases less than in the first example. At the same time we observe that each firm produces a higher level of output (since $X_4 > X_0$), so that it will take a smaller number of firms to produce the smaller output X_4.

Summarized formally, in the first example $n + m$ identical firms produce the total output X_3, that is,

$$(n + m) \cdot X_0 = X_3,$$

and in the second example $n + k$ identical firms produce the total output X_4, that is

$$(n + k) \cdot X_4 = X_4.$$

Since $X_3 > X_4$, we have $(n + m) \cdot X_0 > (n + k) \cdot X_4$. But since $X_4 > X_0$, the last inequality can hold only if $(n + m) > (n + k)$, and therefore $m > k$.

It should be pointed out, however, that the relationship between the number of firms in the two cases may not always be as determinate as in the above example. For instance, had we shifted the LAC curve upward and to the **left** [instead of to the right as in part (a) of Fig. 6–4], so that its lowest point occurred at an output less than X_0, then the number of firms at the new equilibrium might have been either smaller than, the same as, or greater than, in the first case. This follows from the fact that under such circumstances the output of each firm is **less** than X_0. That is, if $X_4 < X_0$, then the inequality $(n + m) \cdot X_0 > (n + k) \cdot X_4$ may hold for either $m > k$, $m < k$, or $m = k$. The exact nature of the shift of the LAC curve depends on the relative increases in the prices of the various factors of production, and the proportions in which the factors are used in the productive process. However, the most important aspect of the increase in production cost is the fact that the new equilibrium obtains at a higher price than that which prevails at the initial equilibrium, and hence the long-run market supply curve (LS) has a positive slope. An industry in which the LAC curves rise as new firms enter the market (Fig. 6–4) is called an **increasing-cost** industry, while the first example (Fig. 6–3) is known as a **constant-cost** industry.*

Finally, there is the case of a **decreasing-cost** industry. This case is shown in Fig. 6–5. At the initial equilibrium the price is P_0. In the first phase demand increases to D' and price to P_1; market output increases to X_1. In the second phase quasi long-run market equilibrium is established with the price of P_2, and outputs X_2 and X_2 for the firm and market, respectively. In the third phase new firms enter the market, and the subsequent increase in output lowers the market price. Now the crucial feature of the present example is the assumption that higher demand for the factors of production **lowers** their prices. This could happen if the factors of production are themselves produced under conditions of decreasing cost. Thus in the third phase of the adjustment process there occurs a **downward** shift in the cost structure to the position shown by the curves labeled $\widetilde{\text{LAC}}$ and $\widetilde{\text{LMC}}$. When the new short-run market supply curve reaches the position shown by $\widetilde{S}_{n+r}$, profit is completely eliminated, and a new

---

* Strictly speaking, it might be no less plausible to argue that factor prices start to rise in either the first or the second phase of the adjustment process. If the supply of factors is relatively inelastic, then the increase in output due to the adjustments made by the firms in the first two phases may lead to higher input prices before new firms start to enter the market. In fact, if factor prices increase sufficiently in the first two phases, the adjustment to long-run market equilibrium may require *no change* in the numbers of the firms, or, for that matter, may *reduce* the number of firms. That is, for a sufficiently large increase in input prices we may have $k = 0$ or $k < 0$.

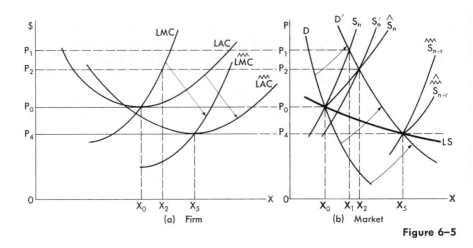

Figure 6–5

long-run market equilibrium is established; the price is P_4, and market output equals $X_5 = (n + r) \cdot X_5$. The long-run market supply curve is negatively sloped. Since firms now produce more than X_0, the number of firms in the market may be smaller than, the same as, or greater than, in either of the preceding examples. But here again the indeterminacy of the number of firms is the direct result of the arbitrary manner in which the LAC curve has been shifted.

SUMMARY

   This concludes the basic analysis of profit maximization under conditions of pure competition. Although this chapter has mainly been addressed to the problem of long-run profit maximization, it has demonstrated that the two time dimensions can be treated in an integrated fashion. In the early part we carried out the analysis from the point of view of a single firm. We saw how long-run equilibrium is reached by a two-stage adjustment process: In the first stage the firm makes a transitory adjustment in its output; in the second it adjusts both output and scale of plant in conformity with the conditions for long-run profit maximization.

   Later we saw how the market as a whole served as the frame of reference, which brought into play the assumption about interindustry mobility. Relative to this we assumed that the movement of firms is determined by the presence or absence of profit. In the adjustment toward long-run market equilibrium we identified three different phases: In the first two the existing firms in the market reach their long-run equilibrium, and in the last phase market equilibrium is established as a result of the elimination of profit. The working of the adjustment process was demonstrated with three different examples, showing thereby that industries may be classified on the basis of the behavior of their long-run supply curve.

SELECTED REFERENCES

GABOR, A., and I. F. PEARCE, "A New Approach to the Theory of the Firm." *Oxford Economic Papers*, New Series **4,** 1952, pp. 252–265.

STIGLER, G. J., *The Theory of Price*. New York: Macmillan, revised ed., 1952, Chapter 10.

VINER, J., "Cost Curves and Supply Curves." *Zeitschrift für Nationalökonomie* **3,** 1931, pp. 23–46. Reprinted in K. E. Boulding and G. J. Stigler (eds.), *Readings in Price Theory*. Chicago: Irwin, 1952, pp. 198–232.

EXERCISES

1. Figure E6–1 shows the firm's LAC function and the SAC curves for Plants 1 and 2, respectively. Complete the sentences given below.
   (a) If the long-run price is $15, a producer wishing to enter the market for X who faces technological conditions such as those shown in the above diagram should build (*Plant 2, a plant smaller than Plant 2*). His long-run output should be (720 *units*, 890 *units*, *less than* 890 units).
   (b) Assuming that the producer in (a) above has chosen the optimal plant and output, and that after a certain lapse of time the long-run price drops to $12, then the producer must make the following adjustments: *Short-run adjustment:* (i) cut output to 720 units, (ii) cut output to 820 units, (iii) produce the output at which SMC = $12, (iv) leave output unchanged. *Long-run adjustment:* (i) switch to Plant 1 and produce 500 units, (ii) switch to Plant 1 and produce

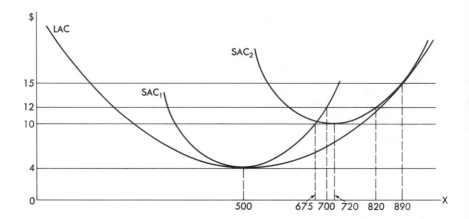

700 units, (iii) switch to a plant smaller than Plant 2 and produce the output at which LMC = $12, (iv) switch to a plant smaller than Plant 2 and produce the output which minimizes the ATC of the new plant.

(c) Assume that all the firms in the market have identical cost curves. Then if the price of X is $10, and every firm produces 720 units using Plant 2, then the *market* is in (*short-run equilibrium, short-run disequilibrium, long-run equilibrium*).

(d) Under the conditions described in (c) above, the following is likely to happen: (i) new firms will enter the market, (ii) some firms will leave the market, (iii) firms will switch to smaller plants, (iv) the situation will remain unchanged.

(e) If the price is $10, and every firm produces 500 units using Plant 1, then the *market* is in (*short-run equilibrium, long-run equilibrium, disequilibrium*).

(f) Under the conditions described in (e) above the following is likely to happen: (i) each firm will continue to produce 500 units, (ii) producers will increase output to 675 units, (iii) new firms will be attracted to the market, (iv) firms will switch to smaller plants.

(g) The situation described in (e) above would be a long-run equilibrium if the long-run market price were $_____.

2. Part (a) of Fig. E6–2 depicts the cost conditions of a representative firm. There are 1000 identical firms in the market, and the relevant market relationships are shown in part (b) of the diagram. Initially the market is in long-run equilibrium at the market price of $5. Complete the sentences given below.

(a) Market demand for product X increases as shown by the shift of the demand function from D to D′ in part (b) of the diagram. Consequently the market price is pushed up to $10, and each firm responds by increasing its output accordingly. When the market regains its short-run equilibrium, industry (market) output is equal to _____ units (approximately). Label the relevant point on the X-axis in part (b).

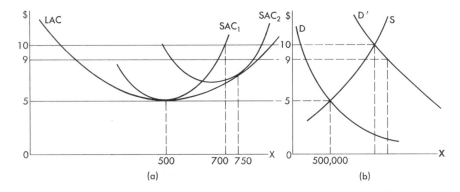

Figure E6–2

(b) In the next phase of the adjustment process firms move into bigger plants, and increase their output further. This will lower the market price. Let us assume that when the market price is $9 each firm attains long-run equilibrium (LMC = $9), with Plant 2 operated at the output level 750. Draw into part (b) the new short-run market supply curve, and the quasi long-run market supply curve. Indicate the new level of the market output.

(c) Every firm is now in long-run equilibrium, but the market is not yet in long-run equilibrium because of the existence of excess profit. As new firms begin to enter the market, and market output is increased further, the market price falls below $9. The market will be in long-run equilibrium only when all excess profits are wiped out.

(d) If the industry in question is a constant-cost industry, the long-run market equilibrium will be reestablished at the market price of $_____. Each firm will then use Plant _____, and produce _____ units of X. The number of firms in the market will be (1000, *greater than* 1000, *less than* 1000). Draw into part (b) the long-run market supply curve.

(e) If the industry is an increasing-cost industry, long-run market equilibrium is reestablished at the market price between $_____ and $_____. This is the result of the (*upward, downward*) shift in every firm's cost curves caused by the (*rise, fall*) in input prices. The output of each firm is (500, *less than* 500, *more than* 500, *either less than or more than or equal to* 500), and market output is more than _____. Draw into part (b) the long-run market supply curve for this case.

(f) If the industry is a decreasing-cost industry, the entry of new firms causes every firm's cost curves to shift (*upward, downward*), and the long-run market supply curve has a (*positive, negative*) slope. Consequently, the new long-run market equilibrium price is less than $_____.

7

PROFIT MAXIMIZATION: PURE MONOPOLY

If pure competition represents the most competitive type of market, then pure monopoly represents the opposite. Pure monopoly is defined as a market in which there exists only one single seller of the product in question, so that the monopolist faces no competition at all. Like pure competition, it is a rare phenomenon. In spite of the rarity of pure monopoly it is useful to study the workings of this type of market since it helps to gain an understanding of the behavior of firms in situations which approximate a pure monopoly. Perhaps the best example of this class of producers are the public utility companies. From the viewpoint of our analysis the most important feature of a purely monopolistic market is the pricing practice of the monopolist. He does not follow any given market price, but formulates a policy of his own. Obviously, since he is the only seller in the market, the monopolist must decide himself at which price to offer his product for sale. Hence the behavioral implications of the purely competitive market structure (statements 5E and 5F) no longer apply. Unlike firms under pure competition, whose decision-making problem consists of selecting a level of output for a given market price, the monopolist must choose a level of output **and** a price. However, as we shall see shortly, to do so means making only one choice: choosing the optimal level of output implies choosing the optimal price, and vice versa.

7-1 THE DEMAND FUNCTION

In his decision making the monopolist must take into account what the market will buy at various prices; more formally, the monopolist must make his choice of output and price with reference to the **market demand function.**

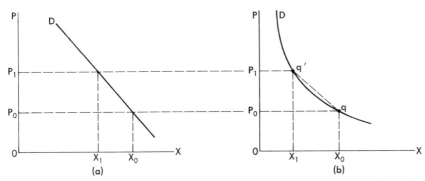

Figure 7–1

It is in order, therefore, to precede the analysis of the monopolist's decision process with a discussion of the relevant properties of demand functions. A demand function, as we have seen, is a relationship between price and output which indicates the amount of the product that buyers are willing to purchase at various levels of the price. It is normally assumed that the relationship between these two variables is an inverse one, which means that the graph of the demand function has a negative slope. Demand functions are frequently described by a property called **elasticity.** Essentially it is a measurement of the sensitivity of the quantity demanded to changes in the price. Like marginal cost and marginal revenue, elasticity may be defined for a discrete change in output—**arc** elasticity, or at a single point—**point** elasticity. We shall define and illustrate these two concepts respectively.

Definition 7–1

$$\text{Arc elasticity} = \frac{\text{percentage change in quantity demanded}}{\text{percentage change in price}}.$$

It is to be understood of course that the change in quantity mentioned in the numerator of the above ratio is associated with the change in price appearing in the denominator. In other words, arc elasticity may be thought of as the percentage change in quantity demanded resulting from a change of one percent in price. Symbolically we can write

$$E = \frac{\Delta X/X}{\Delta P/P} = \frac{\Delta X}{\Delta P} \frac{P}{X}, \tag{7–1}$$

where E is arc elasticity, and the Greek letter delta (Δ) stands for the phrase "change in." The measurement of elasticity is illustrated in Fig. 7–1 for a linear and nonlinear demand function, respectively. At the price P_0, quantity demanded equals X_0, and at P_1, it equals X_1; hence

$$\frac{\Delta X}{\Delta P} = \frac{(X_0 - X_1)}{(P_0 - P_1)}.$$

This expression represents the ratio of the **absolute** changes in quantity and price, respectively. Note that $\Delta X/\Delta P$ equals the reciprocal of the slope of the demand function in part (a) of Fig. 7–1, and also the reciprocal of the slope of the line joining the points q and q' on the demand function in part (b) of the diagram. Now to obtain the **percentage** changes in quantity and price as required by the definition of elasticity, the above expression must be multiplied by the ratio P/X. Unfortunately, however, the definition is somewhat ambiguous in that it fails to specify what values of P and X are to be used in the formula. We could, for instance, use either the initial values P_0 and X_0, or the terminal values P_1 and X_1. Since $P_0/X_0 < P_1/X_1$, it is clear that each of these methods yields a different value of elasticity. One could also compromise, so to speak, and use some average of the two such as

$$\frac{(P_0 + P_1)}{2} \quad \text{and} \quad \frac{(X_0 + X_1)}{2}.$$

Note also that the smaller the change in price (and hence the smaller the change in quantity demanded), the smaller the difference between the ratios P_0/X_0 and P_1/X_1, and hence the smaller the difference between the values of elasticity obtained under each interpretation of P/X. To minimize these differences arc elasticity should be used only for relatively small changes in price and quantity.

As the change in price (ΔP) approaches zero, arc elasticity becomes point elasticity. The latter is a more useful definition of elasticity since it does not give rise to any ambiguity. We define:

Definition 7–2

Point elasticity $= e = \dfrac{1}{\text{slope of the demand function}} \dfrac{P}{X}.$

This definition is straightforward since all three quantities involved in the formula are measured at one single point on the demand function. The only ambiguity that could possibly arise in the context of this discussion has to do with the definition of the demand function itself. It is customary in demand analysis to think of price as the independent variable, and of quantity demanded as the dependent variable. In this text, in deference to what appears to be the prevailing practice, the axes of the diagrams are labeled **as though** quantity demanded were the independent variable. Therefore the demand schedules in our diagrams really represent **inverse** demand functions, and thus their slopes are equal to the reciprocal of the slopes of the ordinary demand functions. Since the slope at point q in Fig. 7–2 is equal to $-P_0/(X_1 - X_0)$ (or $-\overline{OP_0}/\overline{X_0X_1}$ in terms of line segments), the elasticity of the ordinary demand function at q is equal to

$$- \frac{(X_1 - X_0)}{P_0} \frac{P_0}{X_0} = - \frac{(X_1 - X_0)}{X_0}.$$

It should be pointed out that the method for measuring the slope of a line, or curve, explained in Section 2–3 yields the **absolute** value of the slope. For **negatively** sloped relationships, like those in Fig. 7–2, the absolute value obtained must be multiplied by -1 if we wish to obtain the **algebraic** value of the slope. It is clear that the elasticity of downward sloping demand functions is always negative, and since demand functions are generally assumed to be of that type, we often ignore the minus sign and express elasticity in absolute magnitudes.

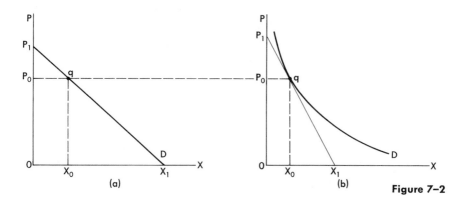

(a)   (b)   **Figure 7–2**

The reader may observe that for the linear demand function in part (a) of Fig. 7–2 the elasticity (in absolute value) at q is also equal to the ratio $\overline{qX_1}/\overline{P_1q}$, where the numerator and the denominator of this ratio represent the lengths of the line segments between the respective points on the demand function. This is so because

$$\frac{X_1 - X_0}{X_0} = \frac{\overline{X_0X_1}}{\overline{OX_0}} = \frac{\overline{qX_1}}{\overline{P_1q}}$$

by the laws of similar triangles. Furthermore, it is also easy to see that at outputs less than X_0 the elasticity is greater than at X_0, and vice versa; that is, if you think of point q as moving upward on the demand curve, then it is obvious

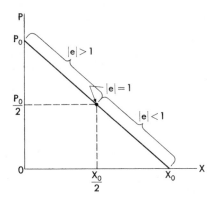

Figure 7–3

that the segment qX_1 increases, while the segment P_1q decreases, and hence $\overline{qX_1}/\overline{P_1q}$ necessarily increases. The opposite holds for downward movements on the demand function. It is convenient to identify the segments of the demand function according to their elasticity as shown in Fig. 7–3. At the "midpoint" of the demand function, $|e|$, the absolute value of point elasticity, is equal to one. Above it, it is greater than one, and below it less than one. At points at which $|e| > 1$, the demand function is said to be **elastic;** at points at which $|e| < 1$, the demand function is said to be **inelastic;** at $|e| = 1$ the demand function is **unit-elastic** (or of **unitary elasticity**).

When it comes to nonlinear demand functions the situation is quite different. It is, of course, true that the elasticity at any particular point on such a function can be measured in the manner explained above, i.e., by the ratio of the appropriate segments of the line tangent to the point in question, but one cannot generalize about the elasticity at other points on the demand function. For example, it is not necessarily true that the elasticity at points above q on the demand function in part (b) of Fig. 7–2 is greater than that at q; nor, for that matter, is the elasticity at these points necessarily smaller than at q. Thus, whereas a linear demand function has a different elasticity at every point, a nonlinear demand function can be **isoelastic** (having the same elasticity at every point). A particular function of the latter type is a demand function whose graph has the form of a rectangular hyperbola, and which is unit-elastic at every point.

7–1.1   The relationship between elasticity and marginal revenue

It is convenient at this point to discuss the relationship between the demand function and the marginal revenue (MR) function. The formal aspect of this relationship has already been analyzed in Chapter 2, where it was established that when ATC is falling, ATC > MC. Since the relationship between TR, AR,

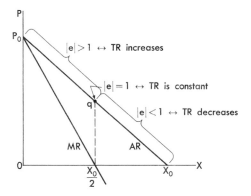

Figure 7–4

and MR is (from the mathematical point of view) identical to the relationship between TC, AC, and MC, we can conclude that the MR function must lie below the AR function (provided, of course, that AR is a decreasing function of X). This, incidentally, also makes economic sense: in order to increase his sales by one unit the monopolist must lower his price by some amount, say from P_0 to P_1, and so MR, the change in TR, is equal to the receipts from the last unit sold, P_1, **minus** a loss in revenues, since all units except the last sell for less than they sold for before the price reduction. Thus MR $<$ P. It can be shown that the exact relationship between MR and P is given by the equation

$$MR = P\left(1 - \frac{1}{|e|}\right). \tag{7–2}$$

If the demand function is linear, the location of the MR function is extremely simple: it is a straight line* which has the same P-intercept as the AR function, and it intercepts the X-axis halfway between the origin and the X-intercept of the demand function. It follows that the output at which the MR function crosses the X-axis, $X_0/2$ in Fig. 7–4, lies vertically below the point (q) which bisects the demand curve. We thus obtain the following relationships between $|e|$ and MR:

> When $|e| = 1$, MR $= 0$, and vice versa.
> When $|e| > 1$, MR > 0, and vice versa.
> When $|e| < 1$, MR < 0, and vice versa.

These relationships can also be verified by Eq. (7–2). Furthermore, recalling that MR is the change in TR, the above relationships can be stated in the following

---

* The converse is not necessarily true; if the MR function is linear the AR function may be nonlinear.

equivalent version:

When $|e| = 1$,   TR   is constant, and vice versa.
When $|e| > 1$,   TR   increases, and vice versa.
When $|e| < 1$,   TR   decreases, and vice versa.

The reader should remember that in this context the change in TR, that is, MR, is always measured with respect to an **increase** in output, and hence is always associated with a **decrease** in price.

When the demand function is nonlinear the construction of the MR function is, in general, more difficult, and requires more specific information about the demand function. However, so long as the demand function is downward sloping it lies entirely above the MR function (except at $X = 0$).

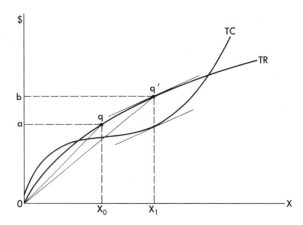

Figure 7–5

7–2 THE OPTIMAL LEVEL OF OUTPUT AND PRICE

The mechanics of the monopolist's decision-making process may be described with the same analytical tools employed in the preceding chapter. First let us look at total cost and total revenue functions which are shown in Fig. 7–5. This diagram is similar to Fig. 5–1 except that the monopolist's TR function is in general not a straight line. Since demand functions are normally downward sloping the monopolist must lower his price in order to increase his sales. For example, AR at output X_0 is equal to $\overline{qX_0}/\overline{0X_0}$ = the slope of the ray 0q, and TR equals a dollars, but in order to sell X_1 and increase his TR to b dollars, the monopolist must reduce his price to

$$\frac{\overline{q'X_1}}{\overline{0X_1}} = \text{the slope of the ray } 0q'.$$

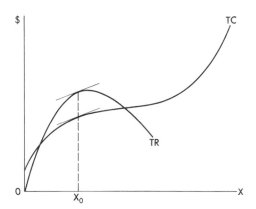

Figure 7–6

[See Section 2–3 for the relationship between the total cost (revenue) curve and average cost (revenue) curve.]

According to Fig. 7–5 the monopolist maximizes his profit with output X_1 at which the slopes of the TC and TR functions are equal, i.e., where MC = MR, and where MC is increasing. This is in line with the conditions for profit maximization as they were defined for a firm in a purely competitive market (conditions 5J and 5K.) These rules, however, require a slight modification in order to become applicable to all the environmental conditions in which a pure monopoly might find itself. We shall explain the reason for this with the aid of Fig. 7–6.

Under the conditions depicted in Fig. 7–6 the optimal level of output is X_0, since this is the output at which the vertical distance between the TR and TC functions is greatest. At the same time it can be seen that at X_0, MC is decreasing. However, since the vertical distance between the TR and TC functions diminishes as output is increased beyond X_0, it is clear that MR, the slope of the TR function, decreases faster than MC (that is, it decreases more than MC does for a given increase in X). To put it differently, since a decrease can be thought of as a negative increase, it is also correct to say that at X_0, MC **increases faster than MR.** This condition is perfectly consistent with provision (2) of condition 5J, since if MR is constant, as it is under conditions of pure competition, MC will be increasing faster than MR whenever MC is increasing at all.

The modified rules for profit maximization apply to all firms regardless of the type of market they operate in. But the differences between one market and another warrant a slightly different formulation of these rules. Since a firm in pure competition makes its choice of output on the basis of the going market price, the first step in **its** decision-making process is to compare that price with AVC_{min} in order to determine whether 5J or 5K is applicable. A

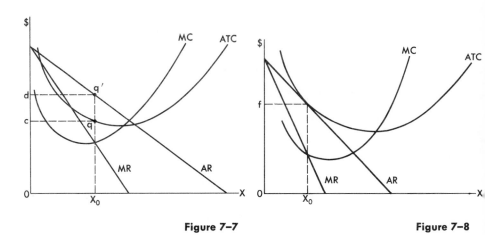

Figure 7–7   Figure 7–8

monopolist, on the other hand, chooses his price and output simultaneously, and hence the comparison between P and AVC comes at a later stage in the decision process. For a pure monopoly the rules for profit maximization are more appropriately stated as follows:

In order to maximize his profit the monopolist should choose a level of output, call it $\overline{X}$, for which the following conditions hold. ($P_{\overline{X}}$ denotes the price which the demand function associates with the output $\overline{X}$.)

(7A) $MC_{\overline{X}} = MR_{\overline{X}}$;

(7B) $MC_{\overline{X}}$ increases faster than $MR_{\overline{X}}$;

(7C) $P_{\overline{X}} \geq AVC_{\overline{X}}$.

If conditions 7A and 7B hold, but 7C fails to hold, then $\overline{X} = 0$.

We now carry out the analysis with average cost and revenue curves. These are shown in Fig. 7–7. For convenience the demand (AR) function is assumed to be linear. The optimal level of output is X_0, and the price charged by the monopolist is d dollars. TR can be identified as the area of the rectangle $0dq'X_0$, TC as the area of $0cqX_0$, and profit as the area of $cdq'q$.

Like firms in pure competition, the monopolist may find himself in a position in which he just breaks even. Such a case is depicted in Fig. 7–8. The monopolist sells output X_0 at f dollars per unit, TR = TC, and profit equals zero. The reader should realize that the tangency between the ATC and AR functions is the only "fabricated" aspect of this example, whereas the fact that MC = MR at the same level of output (X_0) follows as a logical implication. It is cer-

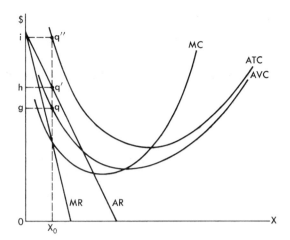

Figure 7–9

tainly easy to see that X_0 is the optimal level of output, since at any level of X other than X_0 the ATC function lies **above** the AR function, which means that the selection of an output level different from X_0 results in negative profits. As for the formal proof of this result, we have already proved a similar proposition when it was shown that SMC = LMC at the level of output at which SAC is tangent to LAC (Section 4–2). In both cases the result derives from the fact that the relevant average curves have identical slopes at the price and output in question.

Figure 7–9 shows the monopolist in a still less fortunate position; at the optimal rate of output he is actually losing money, but since his price (h) is still higher than AVC (g), he continues to produce. His loss is represented by the area hiq″q′ which is less than TFC, the area of giq″q. Note also that at X_0, MC is not increasing, but it decreases at a lower rate than MR.

We may also observe that in each of the examples presented above the monopolist operates at levels of output at which the demand function is elastic. Since MC is always positive, and since at the optimal level of output MC = MR (except when X = 0), MR is also positive at that output; therefore $|e| > 1$ (Section 7–1.1). Since linear demand functions always have an elastic segment,* they serve as convenient models for the analysis of monopolistic behavior. Of course, many nonlinear demand functions are just as convenient to work with, but there are some functions which are capable of causing a considerable amount of trouble.

---

* An exception is the special case of a *perfectly inelastic* demand function, i.e., one for which $|e| = 0$ at every point.

▶ A problem with no solution

Consider the demand function which is of the form of a rectangular hyperbola. We know that all rectangles constructed "underneath" the curve of that hyperbola are of equal area. Thus, for example, the areas of $0P_0q'X_0$ and of $0P_1qX_1$ in part (b) of Fig. 7–10 are identical, or $P_0 \cdot X_0 = P_1 \cdot X_1$ which is the same thing. Such a demand function implies that the total expenditures made by all buyers on product X is constant, i.e., total revenues are the same (b dollars in this case) at every price. In other words, the demand function in part (b) of Fig. 7–10 is unit-elastic at every point, which also explains why the TR function in part (a) of the diagram is a horizontal line. Furthermore, since the slope of a horizontal line is zero, $MR = 0$ at every point; that is, the MR function coincides with the X-axis in part (b) of the diagram.

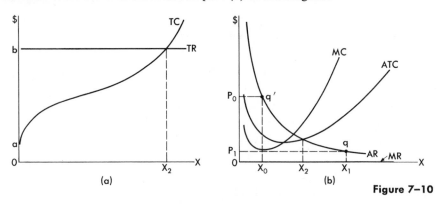

(a)   (b)

Figure 7–10

Imagine now a monopolist who is confronted with a demand function of the type shown in Fig. 7–10. It is evident that his decision-making problem is an extremely difficult one since the rule for profit maximization does not seem to provide him with a solution: there exists no level of output at which $MC = MR$, and the rule does not specify what one ought to do when condition 7A fails to hold. Let us take another look at part (a) of Fig. 7–10. It is clear that at outputs greater than X_2 the monopolist incurs a loss, while at outputs less than X_2 he makes a profit. In fact, since TR is constant, the monopolist can increase his profit by cutting his cost. In this special case, then, profit maximization is identical with **cost minimization.** Total cost is, of course, minimized at $X = 0$ at which $TC = TFC = a$. That level of output, however, has to be ruled out, since at $X = 0$ we also have $TR = 0$. Recall that the rectangular hyperbola does not touch the $-axis, but approaches it asymptotically, hence the demand function is not defined at $X = 0$. This means, in a sense, that no price is too high for this market; one can always sell **some** quantity of X at **any** price (which is not true in the case of a linear demand function). But if the monopolist does not offer any quantity for sale, his receipts are necessarily zero. Therefore the TR line in part (a) of Fig. 7–10 does not intercept the $-axis, but stops short of point b.

The implication of all this is that in order to maximize his profit the monopolist should produce the smallest positive output possible. If the product in question is produced only in discrete units, the smallest output is one unit. Our continuous cost curves, however, imply that product X is perfectly divisible. In that case there exists no smallest positive level of output; to put it differently, for any positive level of output chosen, regardless of how small, one can always find a smaller output. And so we are forced to conclude that under these circumstances **it is impossible to choose an optimal level of output.**

To what extent a unit-elastic demand function is of empirical relevance remains to be determined by empirical research. The main purpose of the analysis of this special example is to draw the reader's attention to the fact that it is possible, in the context of a theoretical framework, to pose meaningful problems which turn out **to have no solutions.** No wonder our rule for profit maximization was of so little help in this case!

7–2.1   Long-run profit maximization

So far we have implicitly dealt with short-run profit maximization. In the long run the monopolist, like firms in pure competition, is free to vary the size of his plant. The choice of the optimal long-run output is, therefore, made on the basis of long-run cost and demand conditions. We can, without further ado, write down the conditions for long-run profit maximization.

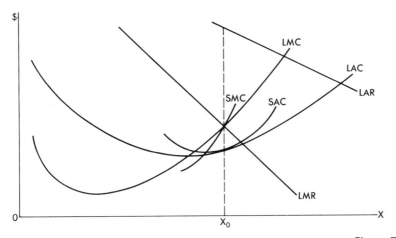

Figure 7–11

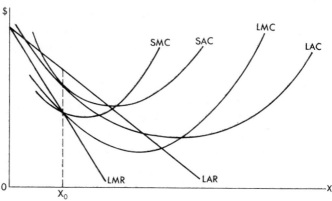

Figure 7–12

In order to maximize his profit in the long run the monopolist should choose a level of output, call it $\bar{X}$, for which the following conditions hold.

(7D) $LMC_{\bar{X}} = LMR_{\bar{X}}$;

(7E) $LMC_{\bar{X}}$ increases faster than $LMR_{\bar{X}}$;

(7F) $P_{\bar{X}} \geq LAC_{\bar{X}}$.

If conditions 7D and 7E hold, but 7F fails to hold, then $\bar{X} = 0$.

An example of long-run profit maximization is shown in Fig. 7–11, in which X_0 is the optimal level of output, and the monopolist uses the plant whose ATC curve is shown by the curve labeled SAC. LAR represents the monopolist's expectation about the long-run market demand. It should also be pointed out that since the monopolist is the only firm in the market, **firm equilibrium** and **market equilibrium** are one and the same. This also means that the monopolist, unlike firms in pure competition, need not operate at the lowest point of his LAC curve when the market is in long-run equilibrium. As a matter of fact, he may even operate on the **downward** sloping segment of his LAC curve as Fig. 7–12 shows.

7–3 PRICE DISCRIMINATION

At the beginning of this chapter we defined pure monopoly as a market with only one seller. Under certain conditions the monopolist may be the only seller not only in one, but in several markets. We are not referring here to a monopolist who produces a diversified line of products, but to a monopolist who produces a single product X, and who treats the total market for X **as**

though it consisted of a number of separate markets. Sometimes, in fact, such a situation may be quite real, as in the case of a monopolist who sells in the domestic as well as in the foreign market. In other instances the separation may be only functional, resulting from the fact that the product may be purchased for different uses, such as electricity for industry and for home use.

For the purpose of our analysis we shall say that the monopolist faces a number of different markets if the buyers in each submarket can be represented by a separate demand function. Under these circumstances the monopolist's price and output are determined by making explicit use of the demand functions of the different submarkets instead of the demand function of the total market. This procedure may be justified by the following argument. For simplicity let us assume that the monopolist is able to distinguish between two different markets, i.e., he can sell his product to two groups of buyers, each of which has its own distinct demand function. And suppose, temporarily, that the monopolist has a fixed output which he can just sell at the price of P_0 dollars. At that price the first market takes some quantity of X, say X_0^1, and the second market takes X_0^2. Now if MR in Market 1, MR^1, is different from MR^2, say $MR^1 > MR^2$, then the monopolist will find it profitable to increase his sales in Market 1 by lowering his price to buyers in that market, and to decrease sales in Market 2 by the same amount by raising his price in that market accordingly. Then, since $MR^1 > MR^2$, the increase in the monopolist's revenues from the increase in sales in Market 1 is greater than the loss in revenues due to the contraction in sales in Market 2, so that on the whole the monopolist's revenues, and profit, are increased. This suggests, therefore, that so long as MR^1 is different from MR^2, a redistribution of sales between the markets is profitable, and that only when $MR^1 = MR^2$ can sales be said to be distributed optimally.

Before formalizing the decision process of a discriminating monopolist we should point out that the mere existence of groups with different demand functions is not in itself a sufficient condition for the implementation of a discriminatory price policy. Price discrimination requires that the different markets be **effectively separated** from each other. This separation is necessary in order to prevent the transfer of goods from one market to another. If such a separation does not exist, then buyers in the market with the lower price are in a position to set aside a part of their purchases for resale in the other market at a price somewhat below that charged by the monopolist, and thus make a profit on the sale. Consequently, buyers in the high-price market will turn away from the monopolist and make their purchases from the buyers in the low-price market. This will necessarily lead to a loss of the monopolist's profit, rather than an increase in it. The separation between the markets need not, of course, be a geographical one; for instance, lack of information about the price differential on the part of the buyers in each market constitutes an effective separation, and a high degree of perishability of the product makes intermarket transactions equally unlikely.

▶ Optimal prices for a fixed level of output

We shall first demonstrate formally the validity of the argument just presented concerning the equality of the MR's in the different markets. In Fig. 7–13 are shown the AR and MR functions of two markets, Market 1 and Market 2. The quantity demanded in Market 1 is measured from the origin to the **left**. Suppose that the monopolist does not discriminate between the two markets, and charges the price P_0. At that price buyers in Market 1 demand X_0^1 units of X, and those in Market 2 demand X_0^2. TR^1 is equal to $P_0 \cdot X_0^1$, or to the area of the rectangle $X_0^1 e P_0 0$. Now we have already established that when the AR function is linear, the MR function bisects the segment between the origin and the X-intercept of the AR function (Fig. 7–4). Consequently it follows that MR^1 also bisects the line segment $e P_0$, so that $\overline{ec} = \overline{cP_0}$, and therefore the triangles bec and cdP_0 are congruent (identical). Thus TR^1 may also be represented by the area of the polygon $X_0^1 bd0$. Similarly, TR^2 may be represented by the area of $0uqX_0^2$.

We shall now show that by charging different prices in the two markets the monopolist is able to sell the same total output of X ($X_0^1 + X_0^2$), and collect a greater amount of revenues. Since the total output (and hence total cost) is held constant, an increase in revenues in this case means an increase in profit, We proceed as follows: A line is drawn through point b parallel to the X-axis.

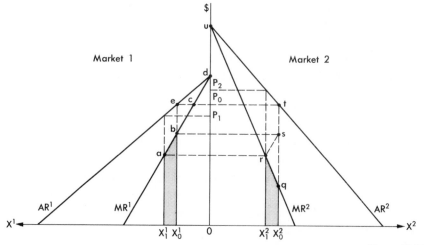

Figure 7–13

intercepting the line qt at s. Since the line segment bs is of the same length as the segment $X_0^1 X_0^2$, $\overline{bs}$ also represents total output. Next, a line is drawn through point s parallel to the MR^1 function, intercepting MR^2 at r; and through r a line is drawn parallel to the X-axis, intercepting MR^1 at a. Since absr is a parallelogram, $\overline{ar} = \overline{bs}$. The points on the X-axis vertically below points a and r, respectively, that is X_1^1 and X_1^2, indicate the optimal distribution of sales. This distribution is optimal since at these levels of output the condition $MR^1 = MR^2$ holds. Note also that total output is constant; that is, $X_0^1 + X_0^2 = X_1^1 + X_1^2$ (since $\overline{ar} = \overline{bs}$). The prices are, of course, read off the respective demand functions: P_1 in Market 1, and P_2 in Market 2.

To conclude this demonstration we must show that the revenues from the second distribution of sales are greater than those from the first distribution; i.e., we must show that $(P_1 \cdot X_1^1 + P_2 \cdot X_1^2) > (P_0 \cdot X_0^1 + P_0 \cdot X_0^2)$. TR^1 is now represented by the area of $X_1^1 ad0$, and TR^2 by the area of $0urX_1^2$. Therefore total revenues from the second distribution may be represented by the area which represents total revenues from the first distribution $(X_0^1 bd0 + 0uqX_0^2)$, **minus** the shaded area $X_0^2 rqX_0^2$ (revenues lost in Market 2), **plus** the shaded area $X_1^1 abX_0^1$ (revenues gained in Market 1). It is clear that the bases of the shaded polygons are the same (since $\overline{X_1^1 X_0^1} = \overline{X_1^2 X_0^2}$), and therefore the area $X_1^2 rqX_0^2$ is smaller than the area $X_1^1 abX_0^1$, which proves that total revenues from the second distribution are greater than those from the initial distribution.

7–3.1 Optimal prices and levels of output

While the above demonstration has illustrated the determination of the optimal distribution of a **given** level of total output, we have not yet explained how the level of total output itself is chosen. To do this we turn to Fig. 7–14. In addition to the revenue functions of the two submarkets, Fig. 7–14 also shows the demand function of the **total** market. If the demand functions for each of the submarkets are given, the total market demand function can be constructed by a process of "horizontal summation," of the type illustrated in Fig. 5–6. This yields the kinked market demand function consisting of the segment uz and the line labeled AR. A similar "summation" of MR^1 and MR^2 yields the segment ut, and the line labeled MR. However, the latter is **not** the marginal revenue function of the total market demand function. The marginal revenue function of the kinked market demand function consists of two separate pieces: the segment uv, and the segment of the line labeled MR below point w. Although these two functions happen to coincide in part, they represent different concepts, and are used for different purposes. As we shall illustrate below, when the monopolist follows a nondiscriminatory pricing

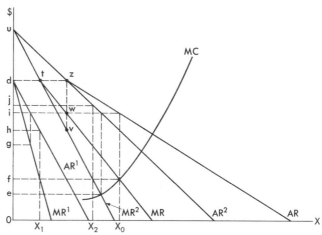

Figure 7–14

policy he makes use of the marginal revenue function of the total market demand function, and when he plans to set a different price in each submarket then the "summation" of the individual MR functions is the function to be considered. Note also that the segment uz is common to both AR^2 and AR, and ut is common to both MR^2 and MR.

If we look for a moment only at the total market, then given the MC function as shown in Fig. 7–14, it is clear (from the rule for profit maximization) that the monopolist's optimal level of output is X_0, and his price is i dollars. This is so because in this range the line MR also happens to be the marginal revenue function of the total market demand function. However, if we take explicit account of the two submarkets, then we can see that the monopolist should set a different price in each market. This is so because if the price in each market were set at i, $MR^1(g)$ would be greater than $MR^2(e)$. The monopolist maximizes profit by selling X_1 units in Market 1 at h dollars per unit, and X_2 units in Market 2 at j dollars per unit. At these levels of output $MR^1 = MR^2 = MR = MC = f$, and it follows from the way the MR function is constructed that $X_1 + X_2 = X_0$.

7–3.2   The shut-down condition

It should be pointed out that in the preceding discussion we implicitly assumed that the monopolist's profit is sufficiently high to justify any production at all; i.e., we assumed that his profit is greater than $-TFC$. We know, of course, that the monopolist's profit need never be less than $-TFC$, since he can always shut down and thereby lose just his TFC. What we wish to do now is to formulate a rule which will specify the conditions under which a discriminating monopolist will shut down rather than continue to produce.

The reader will recall that in the absence of discrimination, production (in the short run) takes place so long as the price is not less than AVC (condition 7C). This rule is obviously not applicable to the case on hand since under conditions of discrimination we are dealing with **two** (or more) prices instead of just one. The problem can nevertheless be solved quite easily by working with total, rather than average, quantities. In Section 5–2 we saw that the firm's profit is greater than $-$ TFC whenever TR $>$ TVC. Now in the example shown in Fig. 7–14

$$TR = TR^1 + TR^2 = hX_1 + jX_2.$$

Therefore the condition TR $>$ TVC can be stated as $(hX_1 + jX_2) >$ TVC. If we now divide both sides of this inequality by total output we get

$$\frac{(hX_1 + jX_2)}{X_0} > \frac{TVC}{X_0}, \quad \text{or} \quad \frac{(hX_1 + jX_2)}{X_0} > AVC.$$

The left-hand side of this inequality is a **price index** in which the weights consist of the shares of total output sold in the respective market. It should also be clear that this weighted AR is **greater** than the price at which the output X_0 is sold if no discrimination takes place. In other words,

$$\frac{(hX_1 + jX_2)}{X_0} > i.$$

This follows because we know that the monopolist's profit is greater under discrimination than in the absence of the latter, and since total output and total cost are the same (output being constant at X_0), it follows that discrimination necessarily results in a higher level of total revenues; that is, $hX_1 + jX_2 > iX_0$, and so

$$\frac{(hX_1 + jX_2)}{X_0} > i.$$

Thus if the AVC function lies entirely above the AR function it **does not** follow that the discriminating monopolist should shut down (as would be the case with the nondiscriminating monopolist), because AVC may still be less than the weighted AR which is the relevant quantity to consider here.

It is possible to compute the weighted AR for any given level of total output under the assumption that discrimination is exercised, and provided that sales are distributed between the two markets such that $MR^1 = MR^2 = MR$. Thus

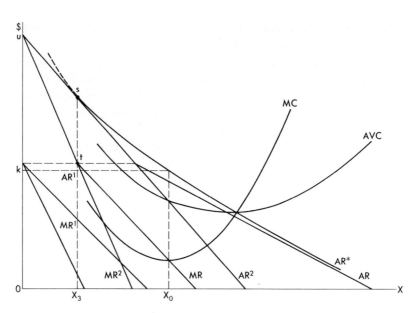

Figure 7–15

there exists a functional relationship between total output and the weighted AR. The latter is plotted in Fig. 7–15 and labeled AR*. It is tangent to AR^2 at X_3, and at outputs greater than X_3 its slope is always flatter than the slope of AR^2, and steeper than the slope of AR. If the AVC function lies entirely above the AR* function, the monopolist will shut down, but production will take place so long as some part of the AVC lies below or on the AR* function. For the purpose of determining the levels of total output, cost, revenues, and profit, one can think of the discriminating monopolist's environment **as though** it were made up of one single market whose demand function consists of the segment us and the curve AR*, and whose marginal revenue function consists of the segment ut and the line MR. The latter may be denoted by MR*. Thus in the example shown in Fig. 7–15 the monopolist produces X_0 units of X, and $TR = kX_0$, k being the weighted AR. (The prices and quantities in each sub-market are not shown.) It may also be pointed out that if the MC function intersects MR* at an output level less than X_3, then the entire output is sold in Market 2. To put it differently, discrimination is feasible so long as the optimal level of output is greater than X_3; otherwise the output is sold in Market 2 and discrimination does not exist.†

---

† If the market demand functions are not linear, then MR* may not coincide with MR for outputs greater than X_3. Under such circumstances price discrimination results not only in different prices, but may also bring about a change in *total* output.

7–3.3   The rule for profit maximization

We can now summarize the discussion on price discrimination by stating the following rule for profit maximization under conditions of price discrimination.

In order to maximize his profit the discriminating monopolist should choose levels of output for each market, call them $\bar{X}^1$ and $\bar{X}^2$, for which the following conditions hold.

(7G) $MR^1_{\bar{X}^1} = MR^2_{\bar{X}^2} = MC_{(\bar{X}^1 + \bar{X}^2)}$;

(7H) $MC_{(\bar{X}^1 + \bar{X}^2)}$ increases faster than $MR^1_{\bar{X}^1}$;

$MC_{(\bar{X}^1 + \bar{X}^2)}$ increases faster than $MR^1_{\bar{X}^2}$;

(7I) $\dfrac{P_{\bar{X}^1} \cdot \bar{X}^1 + P_{\bar{X}^2} \cdot \bar{X}^2}{\bar{X}^1 + \bar{X}^2} \geq AVC_{(\bar{X}^1 + \bar{X}^2)}$.

If conditions 7G and 7H hold, but 7I fails to hold, then $\bar{X}^1 = \bar{X}^2 = 0$.

▶ **Two special cases**

Two concluding remarks may be made at this point. Since profit maximization requires $MR^1_{\bar{X}^1} = MR^2_{\bar{X}^2}$, then by virtue of the equation $MR = P(1 - 1/|e|)$ (Eq. 7–2) we can write

$$P_{\bar{X}^1} \cdot \left(1 - \frac{1}{|e_1|}\right) = P_{\bar{X}^2} \cdot \left(1 - \frac{1}{|e_2|}\right), \qquad (7\text{–}3a)$$

or equivalently

$$\frac{P_{\bar{X}^1}}{P_{\bar{X}^2}} = \frac{(1 - 1/|e_2|)}{(1 - 1/|e_1|)}, \qquad (7\text{–}3b)$$

where e_1 denotes the point elasticity of AR^1 at the point $\bar{X}^1$, and a similar interpretation attaches to e_2. These equations indicate that the price is higher in the market which has the lower elasticity (in absolute value) at the output in question, and vice versa. Furthermore, if the elasticities are the same in each market, the prices are also the same, and hence no discrimination takes place. But this latter statement is not necessarily true if the elasticities at the optimal levels of output are unitary. (If both elasticities are equal to one, equation (7–3b) makes no sense, i.e., is undefined, since it involves a division by zero.) Therefore, it may happen that the monopolist will choose to discriminate **even though the elasticities are the same in each market.** Such a situation may occur when the total cost of production is fixed, as in the case of inventories whose cost of production can be considered to be historically given. In that

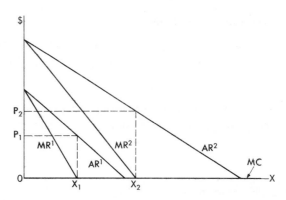

Figure 7–16

event the monopolist maximizes profits by **maximizing revenues** from the sale of the inventories. Since $MC = 0$ (TFC being constant), the optimal levels of sales are those at which the market demand functions are unit-elastic, i.e., at the levels of output at which $MR^1 = MR^2 = 0$. This will, in general, require a different price in each market as illustrated in Fig. 7–16.

We pointed out earlier, that there is no point in practicing discrimination if the elasticities at the optimal levels of output in each market are identical (but different from unity). A special case which satisfies these conditions is that of identical demand curves in each market. It is not the only case, however, which precludes discrimination. If the demand functions have different slopes but identical P-intercepts, discrimination does not occur (not even if $MC = 0$). The reason for this is explained with the help of Fig. 7–17.

Suppose that MC intersects MR at a dollars. Then the optimal distribution of sales requires levels of output for each market such that $MR^1 = MR^2 = a$, that is, X_1 in Market 1, and X_2 in Market 2. Now we know that MR^1 bisects the line segment ac, so that from the properties of similar triangles it also follows that the line bg bisects the line segment ci, and the line fg bisects the

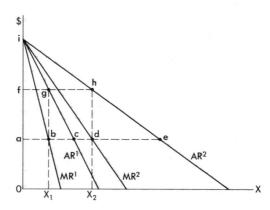

Figure 7–17

line segment ai. Similarly with respect to Market 2, we know that MR^2 bisects the line segment ae, therefore dh bisects ei, and the horizontal line through point h must bisect the segment ai, and hence must intersect it at f. Thus the monopolist charges f dollars in each market. It can also be shown, incidentally, that under the circumstances depicted in Fig. 7–17 (linear demand functions with identical P-intercepts), the proportions of total output sold in each market are the same regardless of the price at which the output is sold.

7–4   A COMPARISON BETWEEN PURE COMPETITION AND PURE MONOPOLY

Before introducing any new material it may be convenient to pause and attempt to draw a comparison between the operation of a firm in pure competition on the one hand, and a pure monopolist on the other. We wish to focus in this comparison on the performance of the firm, or the whole industry, with respect to its level of output and price. We should state at the outset that such a comparison is a task fraught with great difficulties, and certain aspects of it become meaningful only under quite restrictive assumptions. The main source of difficulty lies in the fact that in pure competition we are dealing with a large number of firms, whereas in the case of monopoly there exists only one single firm.

7–4.1   The level of output

Of considerable interest in this comparison is the size of the total output produced under each of the different market structures. More specifically, the following question might be asked: "What would happen to the level of total output if a purely competitive industry were monopolized, assuming constant demand conditions?" As we shall see, the answer is ambiguous because the question is not specific enough. Assuming that market demand and supply functions are as shown in Fig. 7–18 (S being the short-run market supply function), the output under pure competition is X_0. Now if the industry is monopolized, **and the monopolist continues to operate the plants taken over from the firms of the competitive industry,** then total output falls. Under such

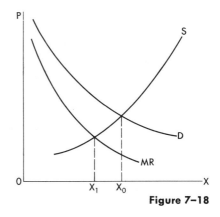

Figure 7–18

conditions profit maximization requires that the monopolist equate MR of the total output with MC in each plant.* Since the (short-run) market supply curve in pure competition is a "summed" MC curve (see Figs. 5–6 and 5–7), the monopolist's output is X_1, at which MC of every plant equals MR of total output. It is this example which often gives rise to the charge that monopolies restrict their outputs. The example of monopolizing a competitive industry is, of course, highly hypothetical, but under such conditions it would be equally reasonable to assume that the monopolist, rather than continue to operate a number of very small plants, will consolidate his operations in one, or perhaps a few relatively large plants. What the monopolist's cost conditions would be under these circumstances one cannot say *a priori*, but it is certainly not unlikely that such reorganization will result in greater efficiency since it will permit the adoption of a technology suitable for large-scale operations. Further savings may be realized from a reduction in input prices which the monopolist may be able to obtain through improved purchasing techniques. If all the reductions in cost are sufficiently large, the monopolist's output may exceed X_0. This is so because the increases in efficiency will shift the monopolist's MC curve (the S curve) to the right. The main point of this discussion, however, is to underscore the fact that the result of the comparison is indeterminate except under the assumption that the monopolist continues to operate the facilities of the competitive industry. A comparison of the prices produces similar results: if the monopolist continues to operate the plants of the competitive industry the market price will be higher than under competitive conditions, but in the absence of this assumption the comparison yields no conclusive evidence.

7–4.2 The level of profit

A second point of interest in this comparative study is the existence or absence of profits. With respect to this question it is necessary to explicitly distinguish between the short run and the long run. Once this distinction is made the answer is quite straightforward: in the short run, competitive firms as well as monopolies may earn a profit; in the long run (i.e., in long-run market equilibrium) firms in pure competition earn no profit, while monopolies may or may not do so. Textbooks usually display the monopolist's cost and demand functions in a manner which indicates the existence of monopoly profit, but such practice is probably the result of a graphical habit. Certainly there is

---

* From the mathematical point of view this problem is similar to that of a discriminating monopolist who equates MC of the total output with MR in each market (condition 7G).

nothing in the structure of the monopolist's model which suggests that he will always reap a positive profit in either the short or the long run, and break-even situations, such as shown in Fig. 7–8, are theoretically just as likely.

7–4.3   The relationship between price and marginal cost

The third aspect of the firm's operation to be compared here is a question about which we can make a very definite statement, but the economic interpretation of the proposition is not so obvious as in the preceding questions. The problem has to do with the relationship between price and marginal cost, and the following can be stated:

(7J) A firm in pure competition always operates at an output at which P = MC.

(7K) A monopolist always operates at an output at which P > MC.

Naturally, every firm operates at a level of output at which MR = MC, but since the market demand curve has a negative slope, at the monopolist's output we have P > MR, and hence P > MC.*

We should point out at this time that the greater part of this text is meant to deal exclusively with **positive** economics. This means that we are primarily concerned with the analysis of cause-and-effect type relationships, but are not prepared to make statements such as "This situation is good, and that situation is bad," or, "This market structure is better than the other." The latter belong in the realm of **normative** economics for which we have set Chapter 14 aside. However, since the relationship between price and marginal cost plays an important role in the normative evaluation of different market structures, we shall discuss this question briefly in the present context.

The fact that under conditions of monopoly price exceeds marginal cost, gives rise to a certain criticism of the monopolist's performance. The argument is based on the following propositions:

(a) The price of a commodity can be regarded as a measure of the (minimum) amount of satisfaction which the last unit of the commodity sold brings to those who purchase that commodity. (This proposition may be justified on the grounds that if the last unit of the commodity was not worth at least as much as its price, it could not sell at that price.)

(b) The optimal allocation of resources requires that the ratio of price to marginal cost be the same in each industry.

---

* This is obviously not the case if the market demand curve is *perfectly elastic*, i.e., horizontal. Since the latter is highly unlikely, we have excluded it altogether.

Let us illustrate the argument with the following example. Let us suppose that two industries, one competitive and one a monopoly, operate at levels of output at which the marginal cost in each industry is equal to one dollar; that is, $MC_c = MC_m = 1$. (The subscripts refer to the type of industry.) Now in the competitive industry we also have $P_c = MC_c = 1$, and thus $P_c/MC_c = 1$. The monopolist, equating MC_m with a falling MR_m function, charges a price which is higher than MC_m, say three dollars, so that

$$\frac{P_m}{MC_m} = 3 > \frac{P_c}{MC_c}.$$

Now suppose that the competitive industry were to cut its output by one unit, and that the resources thus saved (worth one dollar) were shifted to the monopolist to increase **his** output by one unit. The result of such a reallocation of resources would decrease the satisfaction of buyers in the competitive industry by one dollar, and increase the satisfaction of buyers in the monopolistic market by three dollars, and hence the net result is an increase of satisfaction in the two markets taken together. It should be quite clear that once the ratio P/MC is the same in all industries, total satisfaction cannot increase any further by a reallocation of resources between industries. Thus in an economy in which some industries are competitive and some are monopolies, the latter may be said to produce a level of output which is inconsistent with an optimal distribution of resources.*

As a matter of fact, in connection with this discrepancy between P and MC, it would be meaningful to say that the monopolist restricts his output, without, however, making any reference whatsoever to the **actual** level of output. The monopolist may be said to produce a restricted output in the sense that if he chose (or were forced) to produce an output at which $P = MC$, his output would be larger than that which he produces by equating MR with MC.

7–5 REGULATED MONOPOLIES

In the foregoing discussion we compared, on a theoretical basis, the performance of purely competitive firms with pure monopolies. Various points were raised which under certain circumstances could suggest that the performance of monopolies is not necessarily in the best interest of social welfare.

---

* Note that this argument may not apply to an economy in which *all* industries are monopolies.

The extent to which these theoretical conclusions provide a sound base for the formulation of a public policy toward monopolies should be determined by empirical research, but the fact remains that real-life monopolies are almost invariably restricted in their actions by some form of public regulations. It is in order, therefore, to incorporate into the theory of monopoly an analysis of the effects of such statutory restrictions. In this text we shall examine two means of regulating a monopoly: price control and taxation.

7–5.1 Price control

By price control we essentially mean the imposition of a **price ceiling** on the monopolist. Normally, if the control is to be effective, the price ceiling is set **below** the price which the monopolist charges in the absence of any control. For example, in the case shown in Fig. 7–19 the uncontrolled price charged by the monopolist is P_0. Therefore the price ceiling could possibly be set at P_1, the level at which $MC = AR$. The imposition of a price ceiling has the effect of placing the monopolist (at least up to a point) in a position in which his decision-making process is identical with that of a firm in pure competition. Since for outputs between zero and X_1 (in Fig. 7–19) the monopolist cannot charge more than P_1, and since he has no reason to charge less than that, his price can be considered as given in that range of output. Hence, like the firm in pure competition, the line P_1q is the monopolist's price line, as well as his MR function. For outputs greater than X_1 the ceiling may be considered to be ineffective since even if the ceiling were removed, the monopolist would never

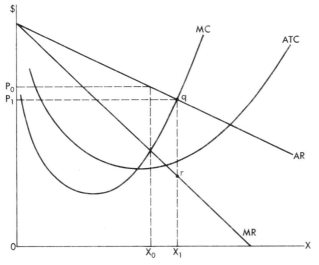

Figure 7–19

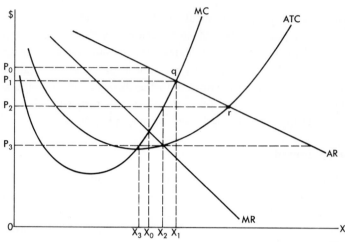

Figure 7-20

charge more than P_1. In the latter range, therefore, the monopolist works with those segments of the **AR** and **MR** functions which lie to the right of (below) points **q** and **r**, respectively. The monopolist's effective demand function consists, therefore, of the segments P_1q, and the segment of the **AR** function below point **q**; the corresponding **MR** function consists of the segment P_1q, and the segment of the original **MR** function below point **r**. Consequently, with the ceiling at P_1, the monopolist produces output X_1 at which **MC** = **MR** = P_1.

It is clear that by placing the ceiling at the level at which **MC** = **AR**, the monopolist is forced to increase his output, and lower his price. He is, in fact, producing that level of output which is consistent with the optimal allocation of resources, since he is forced to produce the output for which P = **MC**. (See discussion in Section 7-4.3.) At the same time we would also expect a change in the monopolist's profit. At first glance it appears as though the nature of this change were indeterminate; it seems that **average** profit (AR − ATC) has diminished, whereas the level of output has increased. However, the solution is quite determinate after all, and for once we need not even invoke the laws of geometry in order to give an unqualified answer to this question. If the monopolist is a profit maximizer, as, indeed, we do assume, then his profit after the imposition of the price ceiling **must be less** than what it is at his initial position (P_0, X_0), **since if that were not the case the monopolist would have chosen to produce output X_1 in the first place.**

It has been shown in the above example that the imposition of a price ceiling which is lower than the uncontrolled price has the effect of increasing the monopolist's output. It does not follow, however, that the monopolist's output increases **whenever** the price ceiling is lowered. Figure 7–20 illustrates a number of possible effects. The initial price and output are P_0 and X_0, respectively. When the price ceiling is set at P_1 the monopolist's MR function in the range relevant to the ceiling is given by the line segment P_1q, and output is X_1. (Price ceilings between P_0 and P_1 have been omitted to prevent cluttering. The reader, however, should be able to verify that for price ceilings between P_0 and P_1 the monopolist's output is found vertically below the intersection of the relevant price line with the AR function.) If the ceiling is lowered to P_2, P_2r becomes the monopolist's MR function in the relevant range, and his output falls to X_2. If the ceiling is set at P_3, the monopolist's output is X_3, which is **less** than his initial (uncontrolled) output. We can see, therefore, that the highest level of output is forthcoming when the ceiling is set at the level for which MC = AR.

Ceilings below P_1, however, give rise to another problem. For example, if the ceiling is set at P_2 the monopolist's output, X_2, is less than the quantity demanded by the market at that price. Since the monopolist cannot legally charge more than P_2, the excess demand prevailing in the market at that price may encourage the development of a "black" market for the monopolist's product, with the result that consumers will be paying a price higher than the ceiling. To avoid the consequences of such a state of affairs, price ceilings below P_1 must be accompanied by some form of rationing. But to the extent that the desired objective of the imposition of a price ceiling is to bring about an **increase** in the monopolist's output, the ceiling should in any case never be set below P_1.

Some of the conclusions which have just been stated require further qualification because the example in Fig. 7–20 is not sufficiently general for the analysis in question; the fact that it is limited to levels of output at which ATC is rising puts this example into a special class. When in the relevant range ATC is falling, the situation is somewhat different, as is shown in Fig. 7–21. Under these circumstances it is no longer possible to set the ceiling at the point where MC = AR since that price is less than ATC, in which case the monopolist may not produce at all. Higher price ceilings, however, are feasible. Suppose the price is set at P_1; then the MR function consists of the segment P_1q, and the segment of the original MR function below point r. Now according to the diagram MC = MR at output X_3, but since at that output MC is falling while MR is constant, condition 7B of the rule for profit maximization is violated. Hence X_3 must be ruled out as the optimal level of output. This, of course, leaves us in a somewhat awkward position, since at no other level of output is it true that MC = MR. The reason for this is the fact that as a result of the

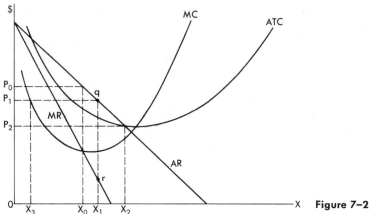

Figure 7–21

price ceiling the MR function is discontinuous at output X_1 (i.e., it has a gap between the points q and r.) As it turns out, the monopolist should produce output X_1 for the following reasons. For an output slightly smaller than X_1, where MC < MR, profit can be increased by increasing the level of output by a small amount. Alternatively, at an output slightly higher than X_1, where MC > MR, it is profitable to decrease output somewhat; therefore X_1 must be the most profitable output.*

When the price ceiling is set at P_2 the monopolist produces X_2. This is quite easy to verify, since at that price X_2 is the only output at which the monopolist does not incur a loss; X_2 is also the largest output which under these circumstances can be elicited from the monopolist by means of price control.

7–5.2 Taxation

A second method by which a monopolist may be regulated is by means of taxation. In the context of the present analysis we shall distinguish between two types of taxes: a **fixed** tax, and a **variable** tax. This terminology has been chosen in order to emphasize the similarity of these taxes to the concepts of fixed and variable cost. Thus a fixed tax, sometimes referred to as a "lump-sum" tax, is a charge levied on the monopolist, the magnitude of which is **independent of the monopolist's level of output.** A license fee is a typical example

---

* Note that even at X_1, MC $\neq$ MR. Thus even though X_1 is the optimal level of output, not all the conditions for profit maximization are satisfied. This is so because our rules are designed only for "smooth" (kinkless) demand functions, and continuous MR functions (MR functions without "holes").

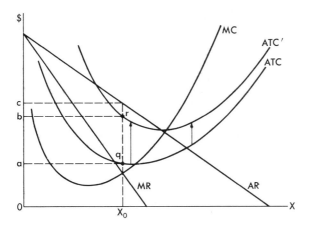

Figure 7–22

of such a tax. The effect on the monopolist's cost conditions of imposing a fixed tax is identical to the effect of an increase in his TFC. In terms of Fig. 2–1, this effect can be shown by an upward shift of the TFC function. At the same time the TC function also shifts upward, since it has the same $-intercept as TFC. And since the vertical distance between the TC and TVC functions is the same at each level of output, the shape of the new (raised) TC function, and hence its slope, is exactly the same as that of the initial one. This means, therefore, that **changes in TFC have no effect on** MC.

The ultimate effect of the fixed tax in terms of average and marginal functions is shown in Fig. 7–22. Before the tax the monopolist produces X_0, and he charges c dollars per unit. After the imposition of the tax the ATC function moves up to the position shown by the curve labeled ATC'. Since MC is not affected by the tax, ATC' has its lowest point at a higher level of output than that at which ATC has its minimum. The vertical distance between ATC and ATC' is the fixed tax per unit of output. Total tax being fixed, tax per unit diminishes with output, hence ATC and ATC' approach each other as output increases. Since there is no change in either MC or MR, the monopolist's output and price are the same as before the tax. The sole effect, then, of the tax is a diminution of the monopolist's profit by an amount represented by the area of the rectangle abrq, which, of course, is exactly equal to the amount of the tax collected from the monopolist. From this example we can also see that if the monopolist were required to pay a **fixed share of his profit** in the form of a tax, the effect would be the same as in the case of a fixed tax: a decrease in the monopolist's profit, but no change in his price or output. This is so because profit after tax is maximized at the output which maximizes profit before the tax. That is, the maximization of gross profit (profit before the tax) leads to the same solution as the maximization of net profit (profit after the tax).

A variable tax, on the other hand, is one which does change with the level of output. Excise taxes, such as the taxes on cigarettes, gasoline, alcoholic beverages, etc., are variable taxes; an excise tax is a fixed levy **per unit of output,** hence **total** tax payments increase with output. The effect of an excise tax takes the form of an increase in ATC. The monopolist's reactions to this change are shown in Fig. 7–23. The pre-tax price and output are c and X_0, respectively. When the excise tax is imposed, the ATC curve moves vertically upward by a distance ($\overline{rq}$) which is equal to the tax (per unit). Therefore the minimum point on both ATC and ATC′ occurs at the same level of output. At the same time MC also moves up by the vertical distance $\overline{rq}$ to the position shown by MC′. As a result of the shift in MC the monopolist cuts back his output to X_1, and raises his price to d.

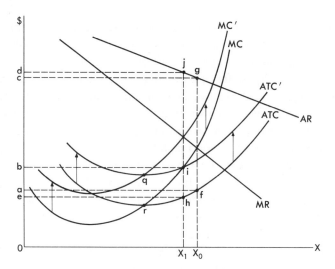

Figure 7–23

When taxation leads to an increase in the price of the taxed commodity the tax is said to be **shifted.** Whatever this term may connote, it is clear that the higher price puts an extra financial load on the buyers of that commodity. What is less obvious, however, is whether the monopolist actually escapes the tax burden by "shifting" the tax. This question can be answered by referring to Fig. 7–23. The monopolist's profit before the tax is represented by the area of the rectangle acgf, and his profit after the tax by the area of bdji. The amount of tax paid is ebih. Now, had the monopolist produced output X_1 before the imposition of the tax, his profit would have been less than his profit at X_0, since the latter is the profit-maximizing output in the absence of a tax. In other words, the area acgf is greater than the area edjh. But the latter represents the sum of the monopolist's profit after the tax (bdji), plus the amount of tax paid (ebih). This means that **the monopolist's net profit after the imposition of the tax is smaller than his net profit before the imposition of the tax by an amount greater than the tax payment.** Not only does the monopolist fail to escape the tax burden, he actually suffers a net loss the magnitude of which exceeds the tax payments!

7–5.3   The effectiveness of monopoly regulation

We may briefly summarize the discussion of monopoly regulation by first pointing out the differences between the two methods of control: price control (if applied properly) leads to an increase in output, a decrease in price, and a decline in monopoly profit; taxation always reduces monopoly profit, and in the case of a variable tax it also leads to a lower output and a higher price.

It should be pointed out that under certain circumstances the necessity of controlling the monopolist may be obviated by the monopolist's voluntary deviation from the profit-maximizing price and output. This may happen as a result of an attempt on the part of the monopolist to maintain his monopoly position over the long run. To accomplish this objective the monopolist will adopt a strategy which will discourage, and hopefully prevent, the entry of competing firms into the industry.* One such strategy is to operate at a less elastic point on the demand function, such as points q or r in Fig. 7–20. Such a move is based on the following reasoning: A firm which might attempt to enter the market of the monopolist will presumably be faced with a higher cost structure than that facing the monopolist, simply because the new firm will not have had an opportunity to develop as efficient a technique. By setting the price sufficiently low the monopolist may effectively eliminate any incentive a prospective producer might have to enter the market in question; since the new producer will have to set his price at about the same level at which the monopolist is selling, he may find that he is unable, given his cost structure, to make a profit at that low price.

The extent to which the imposition of a particular form of control is effective depends, of course, directly on the desired objective. Let us look at the three following aspects.

Level of Output. As we have shown in Section 7–4.1, the theoretical comparison of the competitive and monopolistic levels of output may not yield a determinate answer; and even if the answer were unambiguous, it might be of little help in formulating a public policy toward monopolies (as it might be

---

* Of course, in the case of public utilities the entry of new firms is regulated by law.

unfeasible, politically or otherwise, to break up a monopoly and convert it into a competitive industry). A regulatory agency may, nevertheless, have good reason to be concerned about the output produced by the monopolist. This is particularly relevant in the case of public utility companies. The production of a satisfactory level of output may possibly be assured by means of a price ceiling, as the preceding analysis has shown. The larger output will at the same time be sold at a lower price, which may also be considered to have socially desirable implications. But it must be remembered that the imposition of a price ceiling also affects the monopolist's profit position, and that effect normally cannot be ignored. In particular, if the monopolist breaks even at the uncontrolled level of output, the imposition of a price ceiling will lead to losses, and it will be necessary to subsidize the monopolist in order to have him produce the desired level of output over the long run. If the monopolist does make a profit, the decrease in the price of his output, as well as the increase in the level of production, may reduce his profits to a level which will prevent him from providing the kind of service the public may desire, because he may be deprived of sufficient funds to replace worn-out machinery and to introduce technological innovations. The question of the adequacy of the monopolist's profit is discussed further in the section which follows.

Level of Profit. Both means of control discussed in this chapter cause a fall in the monopolist's profit; indeed, a lump-sum tax reduces the monopolist's profit without affecting the level of output and the price. The monopolist's level of profit may be the object of public regulation if, in the eyes of the regulatory agency, it seems excessive in relation to the profit earned in other industries. In that case it may be considered desirable to tax away a part of the monopolist's profit and channel it to other sectors in the economy. In such a case the taxing of a monopolist is a method of effecting a redistribution of income.

But what precisely is the proper amount of profit which the monopolist should be allowed to earn? This is a question for which it is not easy to find an answer. Certainly the monopolist should be allowed enough profit to ensure his economic viability. This means, as mentioned earlier, that he should be able to maintain and improve his stock of capital, and also, as is often argued, to accumulate a certain reserve with which to finance the future growth and expansion of the enterprise. Also the monopolist's operations must yield an adequate rate of return on the invested capital, because if the rate of return falls below that which can be earned in other industries, the owners of the capital (either the shareholders, or the monopolist himself, if he is the sole owner) are likely to shift their investment into other industries. But while these criteria may serve as broad guidelines in the formulation of a general policy toward regulated monopolies, it should be quite clear that the mere adoption of these criteria does not provide the quantitative information necessary to prescribe and implement specific rules of control.

The relationship between price and marginal cost. If the regulatory agency is concerned with the allocation of resources from the point of view of social welfare, it may wish to induce the monopolist to operate at a level of output at which P = MC. (See the discussion in Section 7–4.3.) Under certain conditions this may be accomplished through price control, as is shown in Figs. 7–19 and 7–20, while in other cases it may not be attainable at all without subsidizing the monopolist, as Fig. 7–21 illustrates.

Rarely, if ever, will a regulatory agency be concerned with only one of these aspects. To the extent that two or more of the factors mentioned above are of public interest, it is up to the agency (i.e., society) to determine the relative importance of each, and to assign proper priorities to them. The regulatory agency will then have to choose a means and degree of control, or a combination of different methods, to bring about conditions which satisfy the desired objectives as closely as possible.

SUMMARY

This chapter has been devoted to the behavior of a firm which is the only seller in a particular market. The basic difference between the decision-making process of such a firm and one in pure competition is that the monopolist does not take the market price as given, but forms a pricing policy of his own. Therefore he works directly with the market demand function. In connection with demand functions we introduced the concept of elasticity, which is used frequently for the purpose of describing and comparing different demand functions.

Using the same tools employed for firms in pure competition, we analyzed the process of profit maximization by the monopolist. We saw that the monopolist follows a set of rules which, except for a slight generalization, are identical to those developed for purely competitive firms. But we also saw in a particular example that under certain special circumstances the rules for profit maximization may fail to produce an optimal production plan, because none exists.

We then took up a unique aspect of monopolistic behavior which applies when the monopolist can sell his product to a number of effectively separated groups of buyers. Under these circumstances profit maximization may induce the monopolist to charge a different price in each market for the identical product. This practice, which is known as price discrimination, permits the monopolist to earn a greater profit than he could earn by nondiscriminatory pricing.

A comparison of the models of the competitive firm and monopoly showed that a clear-cut distinction between the two types of markets does not exist on all points investigated. Thus the output of the competitive industry can be said to be larger than that of the monopolist only when we make quite strong assumptions, whereas in the absence of these assumptions the comparison is inconclusive. With respect to profits, no essential distinction between the two models exists. In the short run, either model may, but need not, show profits; in the long run, profits in the competitive industry tend to be wiped out, whereas the monopolist's long-run profit position is indeterminate. The only definite distinction between the two models revealed by the comparison is the differential between price and marginal cost which characterizes the monopolist's output. The significance of this lies in the fact that if some industries in the economy are competitive, monopoly output is not consistent with the optimal distribution of resources.

Finally, we analyzed the effects of subjecting the monopolist to public regulation. We demonstrated how price control can be used to increase monopoly output, and at the same time lower the price to consumers. The effects of taxation, on the other hand, either leave monopoly output unchanged, or decrease it. In the latter case the price rises. Under either method of control the monopolist experiences a net loss in profits.

SELECTED REFERENCES

BOULDING, K. E., "In Defense of Monopoly." *Quarterly Journal of Economics* **59**, 1945, pp. 524–542.

HARBERGER, A. C., "Monopoly and Resource Allocation." *American Economic Review*, Papers and Proceedings **44**, 1954, pp. 77–87.

ROBINSON, J., *The Economics of Imperfect Competition.* London: Macmillan, 1933, Chapters 3–5 and 11–16.

EXERCISES

1. Figure E7–1 shows a monopolist's **AR** and **MR** functions. Complete the sentences given below.
   (a) At output levels greater than 4 the demand for product **X** is (*elastic, inelastic*).
   (b) If the monopolist sets the price at $2, his **TR** will be (*less than $12, more than $12*).
   (c) **MR** is equal to $4.50 at the output level _____.
   (d) The point elasticity of the demand for **X** at the output level 2 is equal to _____.
   (e) The slope of the **MR** function is equal to _____.
   (f) If the monopolist's **TC** is constant (**MC** = 0), then his optimal level of output is _____ units of **X**.
   (g) If the monopolist's **MC** is positive at all levels of output, he will never produce more than _____ units per period of time.
   (h) The highest level of **TR** the monopolist can possibly collect in any period of time is equal to $_____.

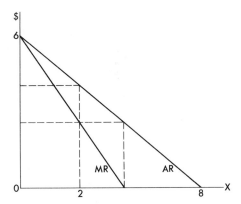

Figure E7–1

2. The operator of a hamburger stand discovered that by lowering the price of his product from 15c to 12c his weekly sales increased from 800 to 1100 hamburgers. What is the arc elasticity of the demand for the operator's hamburgers in the range 12–15 cents?
3. If the absolute value of the elasticity of the demand for a certain product in the neighborhood of $5 is equal to 2, what is the percentage change in price which will bring about a 10% increase in sales?
4. Figure E7–2 shows the monopolist's cost and revenue functions. Complete the sentences given below.
   (a) At the optimal level of output the monopolist's profit is ($240, *less than* $240, *more than* $240).
   (b) If his **TFC** increases by $48, the monopolist will (*raise his price by* $1, *lower his price by* $1, *leave his price unchanged*). Consequently, his profit will (*increase by* $48, *decrease by* $48, *remain unchanged*).

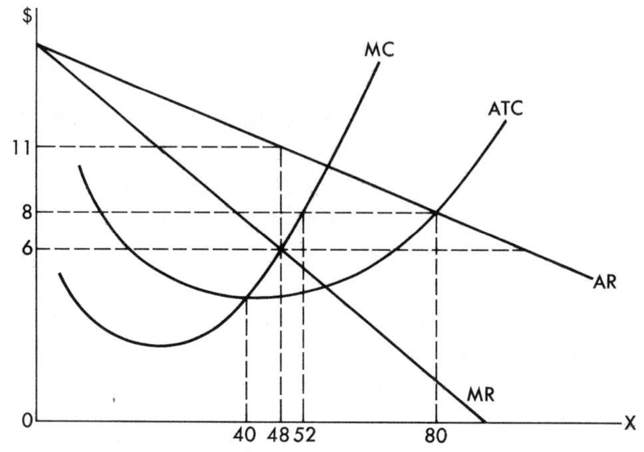

Figure E7–2

(c) The imposition of a $2 excise tax on each unit of output will bring about an upward shift of (*the* ATC *function, the* MC *function, both the* ATC *and the* MC *function*). The monopolist will react to the imposition of the tax by (*cutting his output, increasing his output, leaving his output unchanged*), and (*raising his price, reducing his price, leaving his price unchanged*). After the adjustment is completed the monopolist will produce a level of output at which MR is (*equal to* $6, *equal to* $8, *between* $6 *and* $8, *greater than* $8).

(d) If the monopolist is regulated by means of a price ceiling, and the ceiling is set at $8, the monopolist will produce (40 *units*, 52 *units*, 80 *units*, *between* 52 *and* 80 *units*).

(e) If the price ceiling is set at $_____, the monopolist will produce just as much as he would produce in the absence of the ceiling. In that case the sole effect of the price ceiling is to reduce the monopolist's profit by _____ dollars.

(f) In order to induce the monopolist to produce as large an output as possible, the price ceiling should be set (*at* $11, *at* $8, *between* $11 *and* $8, *between* $8 *and* $6).

(g) An increase in demand which causes an upward shift of the monopolist's demand function by a vertical distance of $2 will lead to (*an increase, a decrease*) in output by (4 *units, less than* 4 *units, more than* 4 *units*).

5. A monopolist is confronted with two separate markets for product X. The demand of each market can be described as follows:

   Market 1

   (i) When the price is $12, quantity demanded is zero.

   (ii) Whenever the price drops (rises) by $3, quantity demanded increases (decreases) by 2 units.

   Market 2

   (i) When the price is $16, quantity demanded is zero.

(ii) Whenever the price drops (rises) by $1, quantity demanded increases (decreases) by 1 unit.

(a) Draw the AR and MR functions for each of the two markets, all on one suitably scaled diagram.

(b) Construct (on the same diagram) the monopolist's *total* market demand function, and the corresponding MR function.

(c) Assume that the monopolist faces a constant cost function, i.e., assume that ATC = MC = $6 at all levels of output. Superimpose the MC (= AC) function on the above diagram.

(d) Determine the monopolist's price and output, on the assumption that he chooses not to price discriminately. How much is he selling in each market? What is his profit?

(e) Determine the monopolist's prices and outputs if he chooses to engage in discrimination. What is his profit?

(f) Compute the demand elasticities at the two respective points on the two market demand functions at which the monopolist is selling when he adopts a discriminatory pricing policy [your answer to (e) above]. Verify that the market in which the monopolist charges a higher price has the lower of the two elasticities at the points in question.

8

PROFIT MAXIMIZATION:
MONOPOLISTIC COMPETITION

Between the two extremes of pure competition and pure monopoly lie a variety of different types of markets which are generally referred to as **monopolistic competition.** As the name suggests, these markets combine monopolistic and competitive features. Models of firms operating under conditions of monopolistic competition probably give a more faithful representation of real-life markets than either the purely competitive or the purely monopolistic models, but for precisely the same reason their analytical framework is not quite so neat and self-sufficient. By its very nature, monopolistic competition introduces a great number of new elements into the economic environment of the firm, thus giving rise to a proliferation of possible theoretical constructs. In this chapter we do not intend to investigate the behavior of the firm under all conceivable sets of circumstances which fit into the broad framework of monopolistic competition; instead we shall examine a number of fairly general cases in order to illustrate the most characteristic aspects of such markets.

8–1 THE NATURE OF MONOPOLISTIC COMPETITION

The competitive element of monopolistic competition arises from the fact that such a market may consist of a large number of firms. Of course, so far as the definition of monopolistic competition is concerned, the number of firms need not be very large, since any type of market which is neither purely competitive nor a pure monopoly belongs in this class. For instance, a market with two firms, known as a **duopoly,** is a special kind of monopolistic competition, as is a market with a few firms, usually called an **oligopoly.** The point, however, is that markets with a great number of firms are not excluded from this classification, and in those markets which include many firms the degree of competition may be quite high.

Even if the number of firms in the market is fairly large, the firms do not act in quite the same manner as purely competitive firms, because unlike the situation which obtains in pure competition, each firm produces a somewhat different product. This brings us once again face to face with the vexing problem of how to define such terms as "product" and "market." (See the discussion in Section 5–1.) When we talk about a "market" or "industry" in the discussion of monopolistic competition, we mean a number of firms all of which produce the same **type of commodity,** and the latter serves as the common denominator by which the market may be identified.

However, the product of a firm is usually quite different from that of any other firm, which gives rise to the distinction between different **brands** of a certain commodity. Such characteristics as shape, materials, color, scent, packaging, etc., are the source of the most obvious differences. Sometimes the elements of product differentiation may manifest themselves in the circumstances under which the product is sold rather than in its physical properties. Thus such factors as availability of credit, delivery, location of retail outlet, and other related services must also be considered factors by which one product may be differentiated from another.

A monopolistically competitive market can be thought of as a collection of firms producing a variety of products which are different from one another, but which at the same time are close substitutes for one another. It does not matter at all whether the differences between one product and another are **real;** what matters is that these differences should be **apparent** to the buyer. This, of course, is a sword which cuts both ways: It means, for example, that if Product A possesses a characteristic which makes it qualitatively or quantitatively different from Product B, but of which the buyer is not aware, then for the purpose of market analysis the two products should be considered identical. It is true, therefore, that it is as wasteful to improve a product without alerting the buyer to the change as it is lucrative to make a product appear superior to another when in fact there has been no change which would render it so.

It should be evident from the description of monopolistic competition that firms in this market follow a decision-making process different from that of firms in pure competition. It cannot be argued, for instance, that a monopolistic competitor is not justified in formulating his own pricing policy, because he **can** increase his sales by cutting his price, and he need **not** lose all his sales by pricing above competitors' prices. It is true, however, that the firm can expect pronounced reactions when it changes its price relative to those of its competitors, because of the availability of close substitutes in the market. If it were to undercut its competitors, the firm would probably experience a marked increase in sales at the expense of its relatively high-priced competitors; if it were to raise its price above competitors' prices, the firm could expect a large drop in its sales, with only the more loyal buyers remaining among its customers. The monopolistic competitor thus faces a downward-sloping demand function, which, however, can in general be assumed to have a relatively flat slope.

8–2 THE OPTIMAL LEVEL OF OUTPUT AND PRICE

Given its demand function, the firm chooses its output by the same decision rule as that used by the monopolist. For example, under the conditions depicted in Fig. 8–1 the firm's output is X_0, and it charges P_0 dollars per unit. This is in accordance with the rules for profit maximization for firms facing a downward sloping demand function (conditions 7A through 7C). But here the similarity to pure monopoly ends. The first thing we must note is that the demand function facing a typical firm in monopolistic competition is **not** the market demand function. Strictly speaking, there exists no market demand function in monopolistic competition because every firm produces a different brand of the commodity, and it makes little sense to lump them all together. The firm's demand function is, therefore, a brand demand function.*

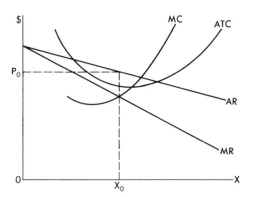

Figure 8–1

8–2.1 The interdependence of demand functions

If the demand for each brand were completely unrelated to that for any other, the theory of monopolistic competition would be identical to that of

---

* In certain special models to be presented later in this chapter we shall remove the assumption of product differentiation.

pure monopoly; each monopolistic competitor would have a complete monopoly over his own brand. This, however, is not the case. Since all the different brands in the market are close substitutes, the demand functions of all the firms are interdependent. This means that the quantity of output that each firm can sell depends not only on the price of its own product, but also on the prices (and hence quantities sold) of the other brands. The firm's demand function is, therefore, a relationship between the quantity demanded and the prices of all other products in the market.

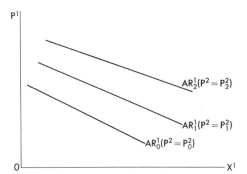

Figure 8–2

    To clarify, let us consider the following example. Assume for simplicity that there are only two firms in a certain market, Firm 1 and Firm 2. In that case the quantity that each firm can sell depends on its own as well as its competitor's price. Thus the demand function in this example is a relationship among three variables (one quantity and two prices), which unfortunately makes the graphical presentation of the entire demand relation somewhat more difficult.* Figure 8–2 shows a partial picture of the demand conditions facing Firm 1. The lowest of the three lines, AR_0^1, is the demand function of Firm 1 when Firm 2 charges P_0^2 for **its** product. Thus if Firm 2 does in fact set its price at P_0^2, Firm 1 chooses its optimal output in relation to AR_0^1 and the MR function that belongs to it (not shown). But now suppose that Firm 2 raises its price to P_1^2, that is, $P_1^2 > P_0^2$. This will cause the demand function of Firm 1 to shift to the position shown by AR_1^1. When Firm 2 raises its price then, assuming that all demand functions are downward sloping and that everything else remains constant, the sales of Firm 1 will increase. Since the products of the two firms are substitutes (rather than complements), some of the buyers who reduced or completely discontinued their purchases from Firm 2 following the rise in P^2

---

* Typically a demand function also depends on the consumers' incomes and tastes, but we are not concerned with these variables in this analysis.

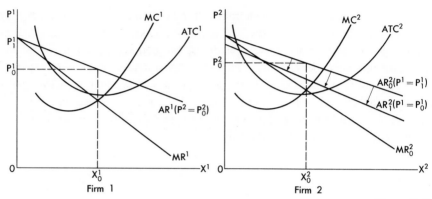

Figure 8–3

are likely to switch to Firm 1. Firm 1 is now in a position to sell the same amount as before, but at a higher price, or to sell a greater quantity at the same price. If Firm 2 raises its price further, say to P_2^2, the demand function of Firm 1 moves further upward, as shown by AR_2^1. In general, therefore, each firm faces a family of demand functions, one for each price charged by its competitor.

The extent to which firms in such a market are interdependent should now be obvious. If Firm 2 changes its price, the demand function of Firm 1 shifts, which will induce Firm 1 to adjust its price and output. But when Firm 1 makes that adjustment, the demand function of Firm 2 shifts as well. This in turn will warrant a readjustment in the price and output of Firm 2, and so on, back and forth. The process may conceivably go on indefinitely, but under certain stabilizing conditions this sequence of successive adjustments will gradually move each firm to a position in which it will no longer be profitable to make any further adjustment. At that point every demand function will

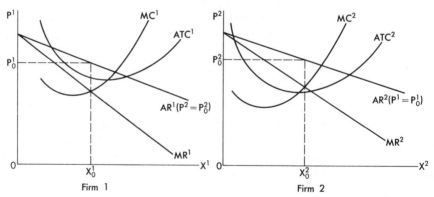

Figure 8–4

stay put, and the market will be in equilibrium. These states of affairs are illustrated in Figs. 8–3 and 8–4.

8–2.2 Short-run market equilibrium

In Fig. 8–3 Firm 1 maximizes profit with price P_0^1 and output X_0^1. As the diagram indicates, the pair of values P_0^1 and X_0^1 belong to that demand function which corresponds to the price currently charged by Firm 2, P_0^2. Thus Firm 1 cannot improve its position by changing either price or output; its profit is maximized so long as Firm 2 charges P_0^2. On the other hand, Firm 2 produces an output which yields a level of profit that would be a maximum if its demand function were in the position shown by AR_0^2. However, the latter does **not** correctly describe the current demand for the firm's product, since Firm 1 is charging a price less than P_1^1. It may be assumed here that Firm 1 had charged the price P_1^1 at some previous point in time, and that Firm 2 has not yet realized that a change in the price of Firm 1 has been effected. As soon as the reduction in the price of Firm 1 makes itself felt in the market (probably through a decline in the sales of Firm 2), Firm 2 will adjust its production plan by choosing a new optimal price–output combination from the demand function AR_1^2. The adjustment by Firm 2 will in due time cause Firm 1 to readjust its price and output, and it is thus obvious that the situation depicted in Fig. 8–3 is not consistent with market equilibrium.

Figure 8–4, on the other hand, shows the market in a state of short-run equilibrium. Each firm maximizes profit with respect to the "correct" demand function, and hence neither firm can gain by moving from its position.

8–2.3 Long-run equilibrium

In the long run the monopolistic competitor, like the pure competitor and the monopolist, is able to make adjustments in the size of his plant. In doing so he follows essentially the same rules for long-run profit maximization as the monopolist, and like the latter he may operate on any segment of his LAC curve (Fig. 7–11 and Fig. 7–12).

In the case of monopoly, however, firm equilibrium and market equilibrium represent identical situations, but under conditions of monopolistic competition the two types of equilibria have a different meaning. In fact, the nature of market equilibrium and the adjustment toward it in a monopolistically competitive market strongly resemble the conditions prevailing in a purely competitive industry. The basic assumption about long-run market adjustment is that the presence of profit in the industry brings about an influx of capital and resources, and thus an increase in the number of firms in the market. Therefore, underlying the discussion of short-run market equilibrium is the assumption that the number of firms is fixed, while the adjustment to long-run equilibrium allows for the entry of new firms. As the new firms place their products on the market, the demand functions of the old firms shift to the left. The reason for this is quite simple: Total sales of all brands in the market at any given set of prices is limited to some fixed quantity. When a new firm enters the market, it must attract buyers from the old firms in order to sell anything at all. It is true that under some circumstances the appearance of the new firm may increase the demand for the commodity as a whole, since it may draw into the market buyers who previously had not purchased this product at all, nor considered doing so. Although the attraction of new buyers is a distinct possibility, the importance of this effect in quantitative terms is probably not very great, and it is therefore plausible to assume that the entrance of a new firm into the market causes a fall in the level of sales of the old firms.

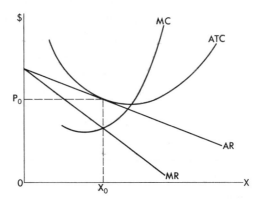

Figure 8–5

As every firm's demand function shifts to the left, the levels of profits shrink. Since this process continues so long as some firms earn a profit, the market cannot be in long-run equilibrium unless all profits are wiped out. The position of a typical firm when long-run equilibrium prevails is shown in Fig. 8–5. The optimal level of output is X_0, and both price and ATC equal P_0, so that profit is zero. It should also be pointed out that if the adjustment toward long-run equilibrium involves substantial changes in the demand for factors of production, the prices of the latter are likely to rise or fall, depending on the nature of the change in demand for these factors, and the conditions under which they are supplied. Thus the long-run ATC curve of a typical firm (not shown in Fig. 8–5) may either rise or fall during the adjustment process, but this does not affect the condition for long-run market equilibrium which requires the elimination of all profits.

8–3 ADVERTISING

A characteristic feature of the behavior of a firm in monopolistic competition, especially in markets in which a few firms compete directly with each other, is its activity in sales promotion and advertising. Since these two fields are merely different methods of achieving identical objectives, we shall for simplicity refer to all these activities as advertising. The basic purpose of advertising is to attract to the firm as great a number of customers as possible. By advertising, a firm attempts to emphasize the distinctive qualities of its product and to persuade buyers to believe in its superiority. Advertising is a form of product differentiation, and an important weapon of competition. From the analytical point of view advertising is meant to shift the firm's demand function as far to the right as possible. It is clear that advertising is one of the factors which contrasts the behavior of the firm in monopolistic competition with that of the purely competitive firm on the one hand, and the purely monopolistic one on the other. The purely competitive firm cannot gain by advertising, since its product is identical with that of other firms in the market, and it can always sell its entire output at the going market price without engaging in any promotional efforts. The purely monopolistic firm does not need to advertise, as it is the only seller in the market, and thus faces no competition whatsoever.* It is true, however, that certain types of advertising are a manifestation of competition between **industries** rather than firms. Such advertising is aimed at persuading the consumer to use a certain general type of product instead of some other: for example, to travel by air instead of by rail or bus; to use gas instead of electricity; to drink milk instead of coffee. But since inter-industry advertising is quantitatively less important than intra-industry advertising, and since it is essentially a form of collective behavior on the part of the industry rather than a typical decision problem of a single firm, we shall not be concerned with it in our discussion.

8–3.1 The direct effects of advertising

To understand the direct effects of advertising, let us look at Fig. 8–6. For simplicity, assume that initially, i.e., before any advertising is undertaken, the firm is in a break-even position; it produces X_0, and its price is P_0. Suppose that the firm decides to spend some fixed amount, say A_0 dollars, on advertising.

---

* Pure monopolies may sometimes engage in "advertising" with the explicit purpose of creating a favorable image in the mind of the public. Such public relations acts constitute, among other things, an attempt to forestall regulations which might jeopardize the monopolist's position in the market, and thus may be considered to be consistent with (very) long-run profit maximization.

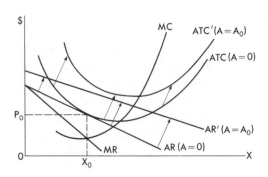

Figure 8–6

The immediate effect of that action is to raise the firm's total cost by A_0, and hence to raise its ATC curve to the position shown by ATC'. (Recall that an increase in cost which is independent of the level of output does not affect MC, so that the lowest point on ATC' must lie to the right of the lowest point on ATC. See Fig. 7–22 and discussion in Section 7–5.2.) The second effect (and it may indeed take some time for this effect to assert itself) is an increase in the demand for the firm's product, i.e., a shift of the demand function to the position AR'. The notation in parentheses which is part of the label of each demand function serves to remind us that the firm's demand function depends on the level of its advertising, and the label also indicates the specific amount of advertising expenditures for which the respective demand function is drawn. [The position of the demand function also depends on the prices charged by competitors (Fig. 8–2), but these are assumed to remain constant in this particular example.]

We should point out that to make things reasonably simple we do not explicitly distinguish between different advertising media; instead we consider only the **total money outlay** for advertising. It is assumed, of course, that funds allocated to advertising are always distributed among the various media in the most efficient manner. This means, from the analogy with the choice of the optimal input combination for a productive process (Fig. 3–7), that the distribution of funds must be such as to satisfy the equality between the MRS and the price ratio of any pair of media.

Now it is clear from Fig. 8–6 that, although the advertising program of the firm has been effective in shifting the firm's demand function to the right, the increase in demand represented by that shift is not sufficient to enable the firm to recover the funds put into the venture, let alone reap a profit from the operation. The new MR function is omitted from the diagram, but it is obvious that, whatever level of output the firm chooses, it is bound to incur a loss, and hence its position will be worse than it was in the absence of advertising. An advertising campaign, to be successful, must therefore bring about a **sufficiently**

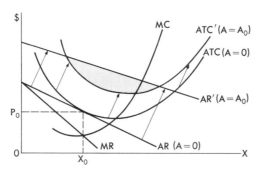

Figure 8–7

large increase in demand. An example of such a case is shown in Fig. 8–7. Since the new demand function, **AR′**, lies partly above **ATC′**, there exist levels of output which yield positive levels of profit, and this situation, compared with the initial break-even position, represents an improvement in the firm's rate of profit.

8–3.2 The optimal level of advertising

At this point we should naturally ask the following question: If A_0 dollars spent on advertising increase profit from zero to some positive amount (as assumed in the example in Fig. 8–7), what would be the change in profit if the firm were to spend a little more than A_0, or perhaps a little less? In other words, if advertising, at least in some limited range, is an effective means of increasing profit, what is the **optimal** advertising outlay? This question is, of course, just one facet of the firm's overall optimization problem; once advertising is introduced explicitly into the model, the firm has to make a choice of price, output, and advertising expenditures.

Since these three variables are directly related to one another through their effect on the firm's profit, the choice is usually made simultaneously, but it is somewhat cumbersome to depict the method for finding the solution to this problem with two-dimensional diagrams. Common sense, however, suggests the following principle for the determination of the optimal level of advertising outlays: If an additional dollar spent on advertising increases net revenues (i.e., profit exclusive of advertising expenditures) by more than one dollar, advertising outlays should be increased because the contribution of advertising to net revenues is greater than the cost of advertising. But if an additional dollar spent on advertising increases net revenues by less than one dollar, advertising outlays should be contracted because the contribution of advertising to net revenues is less than the cost of advertising.

It should be understood, of course, that the effect of advertising expenditures on profit presumes the proper variations in output, price, and cost. Thus the

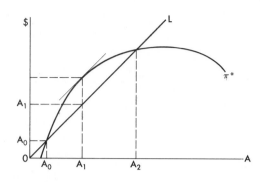

Figure 8-8

link between advertising and net revenues may be described as follows: The amount of advertising expenditure determines the position of the firm's demand function; given the demand function, one can find (by applying the rules for profit maximization) the optimal price and output; and given these factors, one can compute TC, TR, and net revenues. If advertising expenditures are changed, all the other variables mentioned above will in general also change, and hence a new level of net revenues must be computed in the manner just outlined. This functional relationship between advertising expenditures and net revenues is shown in Fig. 8–8. The horizontal axis measures advertising expenditures, and the vertical axis net revenues, π^*. Both axes, therefore, have a dollar scale. The concept of net revenues introduced here may be formally defined as

$$\pi^* = \text{TR} - \text{TC},$$

so that
$$\pi = \pi^* - \text{A} \qquad (8\text{--}1)$$

$$= \text{TR} - \text{TC} - \text{A}.$$

(See Eq. 5–1.) It is assumed in Fig. 8–8 that net revenues are an increasing function of A for relatively low levels of A, and a decreasing function of A for relatively high levels of A. This assumption can be justified on two grounds. First, we have already seen that the relationship between net revenues (i.e., profit) and output is of this general form. Figure 7–5, for example, indicates that as output is increased beyond some relatively small level, profit changes from negative to positive; it then increases further and reaches its maximum, after which it declines, finally turning negative again. Second, it is reasonable to assume that the effectiveness of additional dollars expended on advertising tapers off beyond a certain point, so that the additional sales generated by marginal advertising dollars diminish. Hence the two effects reinforce each other, resulting in a relationship between π^* and A shown by the curve in Fig. 8–8.

The straight line L drawn through the origin is designed to facilitate the interpretation of the diagram. The line bisects the angle between the two axes, and hence it has the property that every point on it is equidistant from either axis. The line L can be thought of as projecting the A-axis onto the $-axis, so that with the help of L the level of advertising expenditures can be read off the $-axis. Now profit, which is the difference between net revenues and advertising expenditures [see Eq. (8–1) above], is represented by the vertical distance between the π^* function and the line L. For example, at levels of A below A_0 advertising expenditures exceed net revenues, since π^* lies below L. In this range, therefore, profit is negative. At A_0, π^* intersects L, which means $\pi^* = A$, so that $\pi = 0$. Between A_0 and A_2, π^* lies above L, hence $\pi > 0$, and beyond A_2, $\pi < 0$. By now the problem should be recognized as a familiar one, because analytically it is the same as that of finding the optimal level of output in models without advertising. (See Fig. 7–5 and discussion in Section 7–2, or, if need be, go back to Fig. 5–1 and its relevant explanation.) Profit is maximized at the level of A at which the vertical distance between π^* and L (in the proper range) is greatest. That, of course, occurs at A_1, at which the slope of the π^* function is equal to the slope of line L. But a straight line which forms a 45° angle with the horizontal axis has a slope equal to unity, hence at the optimal level of A the slope of the π^* function is equal to one. Now the slope of the π^* function may be interpreted (in line with the interpretation of the slope of the TR function, Definition 5–1) as **marginal net revenue,** i.e., the change in net revenues as advertising expenditures are increased by one unit. Therefore, at the optimal level of advertising, marginal net revenue is equal to one. This confirms our earlier conclusion that, so long as the increment in net revenue is greater than the incremental change in advertising expenditures, the latter should be increased, and conversely. When the last dollar expended on advertising increases net revenues by just one dollar, profit cannot be increased by changing the level of advertising outlay.

8–3.3 Secondary effects

Thus far we have considered only the immediate effects of advertising on the firm's own demand and profit, but have ignored the effects on the firm's competitors, and the possible repercussions from these secondary effects. Let us now consider these factors.

If the advertising campaign of one firm is effective and results in an increased demand for its product, then at the same time the demand for the products of the competing firms must diminish. As soon as the rival firms become aware of the loss in their sales, they can be expected to try to win back their lost

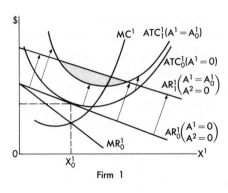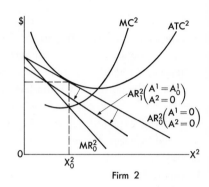

Firm 1   Firm 2

Figure 8–9

customers, or at least to try to retain those they still have, by stepping up their own advertising. To the extent that this counter-advertising is effective, it will offset some of the gains made by the first firm, and the latter may be induced to readjust its advertising outlays in order to neutralize the actions of its competitors as much as possible. When this readjustment is made, another round of new adjustments on the part of the competing firms gets under way, and the entire process just described repeats itself. It is important to realize here that advertising is one of the principal methods by which a firm attempts to capture the market-share of its competitors, and hence any move on the part of one firm designed to maneuver itself toward a more favorable position in relation to its competitors is bound to invite retaliatory reactions. A meaningful analysis of the full effects of advertising must, therefore, be carried out from the broader perspective of the competitive struggle in which the firms in monopolistic competition are engaged. We shall now formalize this analysis with a graphical illustration.

For simplicity we assume again that there are only two firms, that in the initial position there is no advertising, and that profits are zero. As the labels in Fig. 8–9 indicate, the position of the firm's demand function depends on the level of its own, as well as its competitor's, level of advertising. (Prices are again excluded from the analysis, since here we wish to focus only on advertising.) Initially, when there is no advertising, the relevant demand functions are given by AR_0^1 and AR_0^2, and the levels of output are X_0^1 and X_0^2, respectively. Let us now assume that Firm 1 begins to advertise at a rate of A_0^1 dollars per period of time. The immediate effects of this action on Firm 1 are a rise in ATC^1 to ATC_1^1, and a shift in the demand function to AR_1^1. Firm 1 now adjusts its output and price, and although these adjustments are not indicated on the diagram, it is clear that the firm's demand function has shifted far enough to enable the firm to make a positive profit. The effect on Firm 2 is a decrease in demand, as shown by the shift of its demand function toward the left to the

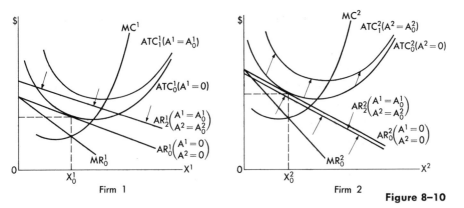

Figure 8–10

position AR_1^2. The shifts in the two demand functions indicate that through its advertising campaign Firm 1 succeeded in attracting some customers from Firm 2, and thus placed itself in a more favorable position.

Naturally, this is not the end of the story. Firm 2 can now be expected to make an attempt to recover its loss by initiating an advertising campaign of its own. Suppose that the amount Firm 2 decides to spend on advertising is A_0^2 dollars, which we shall assume is a sum approximately equal to the amount spent by Firm 1, A_0^1. The results of this move are shown in Fig. 8–10. The ATC of Firm 2 has risen to ATC_1^2, and its demand function to AR_2^2. Firm 2 has thus managed to improve its position in the market, but its present demand function is still to the left of its original position. The effect on Firm 1 is a shift to the left of the demand function as shown by AR_2^1, reflecting the loss of those customers who were sufficiently vulnerable to the advertising of Firm 2, and who consequently switched products. The assumptions about the **magnitude** in the shifts of the demand functions are, of course, arbitrary, since the impact of advertising on demand depends on the relative effectiveness of each firm's advertising efforts, and our model, in its present form, can provide no *a priori* information about this. If, however, the two firms are more or less "alike" in terms of size, product, location, etc., it is reasonable to assume that the effectiveness of each dollar spent on advertising is roughly equal for each firm. Thus the general conclusion is that when all firms engage in advertising at the same time, total sales by the industry are not significantly different from what they would be if no advertising took place at all.

8–3.4 What price advertising?

If the change in total sales is negligible, what can one say about the net effect of advertising on the firms in the market? The most important effect is, of course, the increase in every firm's ATC. As Fig. 8–10 shows, following the introduction of advertising ATC is higher than AR for both firms, and hence whatever the final optimal level of output might be, each firm incurs a loss. This result is obviously due to the special assumption that each firm started from a break-even position, but the point is that regardless of the initial profit position, reciprocal advertising generally leads to a reduction, and perhaps a complete elimination, of the representative firm's profit.

This conclusion immediately raises the question of why firms engage in advertising. More specifically, one may at this point ask the following questions.

(1) Why should a firm voluntarily embark on a course of action which brings about a deterioration in its financial position?

(2) In the face of the above results, how valid is the assumption of profit maximization? Or to put it more strongly, since profit maximization has been assumed throughout the discussion, is our model logically consistent?

The answers to these questions reveal some significant behavioral characteristics of firms operating under conditions of monopolistic competition. It should be obvious that if the firms in the market were to merge, or to agree to operate under a unified management, they would realize that their best strategy would be not to advertise at all, or, perhaps, to spend only a negligible amount on advertising. Since total sales of the industry are not significantly affected by advertising, the elimination of these expenditures would represent an act of saving, and hence an increase in profit. When the industry operates as one single firm it is behaving like a pure monopoly which, of course, maximizes profit by completely refraining from advertising.

But if the relationship between the firms is governed by competition rather than cooperation, the situation is totally different. Since a firm can usually improve its profit position by increasing its share of the market, the temptation to advertise is strong. The firm must, of course, anticipate a reciprocal effort on the part of its competitors, but it may nevertheless decide to go ahead with its advertising program for two reasons: (a) The firm may believe that there will be a considerable time lag between the initiation of its own advertising campaign and the retaliatory reactions of its competitors. If this time lag does materialize, it will provide the firm with at least a temporary gain in market share. (b) The firm may have faith in the superiority of its own product strong enough to make it anticipate an increase in its own share of the market in spite of competitive advertising by rival firms. It seems inevitable, therefore, that at one time or another some firms will find themselves in a position in which advertising will appear to be a profitable plan of action. And as soon as one firm makes the first move, the chain-reaction type of adjustment process is set in motion. This is clear from Fig. 8–9. If Firm 2 fails to counter-advertise, it will be condemning itself to an inferior position in the market. After the first round of the battle, the distribution of sales among the firms may be slightly different from what it used to be (due to differences in the relative effectiveness of advertising), but it is certain that every firm will be faced with higher costs.

This situation is far from being an equilibrium, and worse is yet to come. The firms are now in a position in which the temptation to "jump the gun" on competitors represents a considerable force. In fact, the present state of affairs is even less stable than the initial one, since the reduction in profits due to the first round of the advertising campaign has put every firm in a financial squeeze. Thus every potential opportunity to capture a few more percentage points of market share may be viewed by the firms as a highly tantalizing prize, the winning of which may justify a considerable amount of pecuniary exertion. Advertising sprees which are even more intense are therefore likely to follow, and may continue until the firms reach the point of financial exhaustion. It should also be pointed out that the likelihood of **reductions** in advertising expenditures is very small, except for temporary reductions. A voluntary cutback in one's outlay for advertising amounts to a surrender of one's market share (or part of it), and thus invites disaster. It is therefore obvious that the competitive struggle has a built-in bias for higher, rather than lower, advertising expenditures.

We are thus faced with the following seemingly paradoxical situation: Although the total elimination of advertising is the only way by which all the firms in the market could improve their financial position, competitive advertising by each firm is a prerequisite for individual profit maximization, and the only course of action which guarantees the firm's economic survival in the face of the competition to which it is subjected. It seems, therefore, that in their reliance on advertising as a means of consolidating their market position the firms are plainly the victims of a vicious circle. The analogy to a **circle** is particularly apt, because of the circular, and never-ending, adjustment process which advertising sets in motion, and it is justly described as **vicious** because it robs the firms of their profit, while at the same time breeding a waste of resources which, if it were not for advertising, could perform a socially useful function.*

---

* One must, of course, exclude from the above analysis the expenditures on informational (as opposed to persuasional) advertising. Since the magnitude of the latter is negligible, it has been omitted from this analysis.

8–4 OLIGOPOLISTIC MARKETS

We now turn our attention to some special forms of monopolistic competition. In Section 8–1 we pointed to the great variety of models which may exist within the framework of monopolistic competition. The purpose of the few examples to be presented here is to analyze in some detail several typical patterns of competition which may develop in certain markets, but these cases are by no means meant to present an exhaustive list. We shall examine markets which are classified as oligopoly, i.e., markets with a relatively small number of firms. In every example the number of firms has been chosen to make possible the use of relatively simple geometrical tools in carrying out the exposition.

Oligopolistic markets are characterized by a high degree of interdependence between the firms, because the actions of any one firm have a direct and pronounced effect on, and are in turn influenced by, the actions of its competitors in the market. We have already seen that this interdependence is characteristic of monopolistic competition in general, but when the number of firms is relatively small the high degree of interdependence creates conditions which produce quite unique rules of behavior. We shall now examine some of these.

8–4.1 Price Leadership

When the market consists of one or two large firms and a somewhat greater number of relatively small firms, the latter may find it convenient to relinquish their option to form a price policy of their own, and accept the price set by the dominant firm as the market price. The small firms thereby consider themselves as operating in a purely competitive environment. It is then up to the leading firm to set a price which will clear the market and maximize its profit at the same time.

The method by which this is done is illustrated in Fig. 8–11. It is assumed that the competitive fringe (the small firms which follow the leadership of the dominant firm) consists of two firms whose MC functions are shown in parts (a) and (b), respectively. The horizontal "summation" of these MC functions yields the short-run supply curve of the fringe S in part (c). Implicit in this analysis is the assumption of a homogeneous product, so that it is meaningful to represent the total market demand by one single function, as shown by line D in part (c). Now if the firms in the competitive fringe are permitted to sell their entire output at any given price, the share of the leading firm is obtained by subtracting the output of the small firms (Firm 1 and Firm 2 in the present example) from the market demand function. In other words, the quantity that the leader can sell at any given price is represented by the horizontal distance between the functions D and S in part (c). This relationship between the

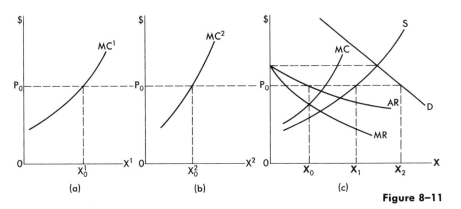

Figure 8–11

horizontal distance and price is given by the curve labeled **AR**, which is the demand function facing the leading firm under these conditions. For example, at the price P_0 market demand is $\mathbf{X}_2$, and the supply of the fringe is

$$\mathbf{X}_1 \,(= \mathbf{X}_0^1 + \mathbf{X}_0^2),$$

hence the quantity that the leader can sell at that price is equal to $\mathbf{X}_2 - \mathbf{X}_1 = \mathbf{X}_0$. (Note also that the intersection of **S** and **AR** bisects the horizontal distance between the \$-axis and the function **D**.) The best price the leader can choose is, of course, that which maximizes his profit. Suppose, for instance, that the rising part of the leader's **MC** function intersects his **MR** function at the output $\mathbf{X}_0$, as shown in part (c); then the price is set at P_0, and the outputs are $\mathbf{X}_0^1$, $\mathbf{X}_0^2$, and $\mathbf{X}_0$ for the three firms, respectively.

8–4.2 The kinked demand curve

When the firms in a given market are about the same size, price leadership may not be feasible. Being more or less evenly matched, all the firms may be anxious to retain the freedom to adjust to changes in environmental conditions as they see fit. In fact, because of the small number of firms, each firm may formulate for itself rules of behavior derived directly from its expectations about the reactions of its rivals under all possible circumstances. But before we proceed with the discussion of such a case, we shall introduce an additional analytical tool.

In Section 8–2.1 we discussed the close relationship between the demand functions of the firms in the market. For the purpose of the analysis which follows, we shall present a more detailed illustration of this interdependence. Assume that there are two firms in the market, each producing a differentiated

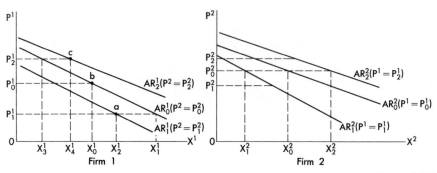

Figure 8–12

product. At the initial equilibrium Firm 1 faces the demand function AR_0^1 (Fig. 8–12), and Firm 2 faces AR_0^2. The equilibrium outputs and prices are X_0^1, X_0^2, P_0^1, and P_0^2, respectively. Suppose now that Firm 1 lowers its price to P_1^1. According to AR_0^1, if Firm 2 keeps its price fixed at P_0^2, the level of sales of Firm 1 increases to X_1^1. But the decrease in the price of Firm 1 from P_0^1 to P_1^1 shifts the demand function of Firm 2 to the left, to position AR_1^2 (Fig. 8–2), so that Firm 1 will be able to sell output X_1^1 only if Firm 2 reduces its output to X_1^2, which is the output it can sell at the price P_0^2. Normally, however, under these circumstances, Firm 2 will attempt to minimize the loss which the reduction in the price of Firm 1 imposes on it, and rather than maintain its initial price P_0^2, Firm 2 is likely to respond to the situation with a price cut of its own, say to P_1^2. This countermove shifts the demand function of Firm 1 to position AR_1^1, so that at the price P_1^1 Firm 1 sells only X_2^1 units.

The same reasoning can be applied to price increases. If Firm 1 raises its price from P_0^1 to P_2^1, it will thereby decrease its sales to X_3^1 if Firm 2 increases its output to X_2^2, thus holding its price constant at P_0^2. However, Firm 2 will be able to increase its profit by raising its price, and assuming that the optimal price with the demand function AR_2^2 is P_2^2, the sales of Firm 1 will level off at X_4^1.

If we generate infinitely many points like a, b, and c (in Fig. 8–12) by the method just described, then the locus of those points may be represented by the line ar in Fig. 8–13. The demand functions of Firm 1 (as well as those of Firm 2) in Fig. 8–12 may be referred to as **partial** demand functions, since each

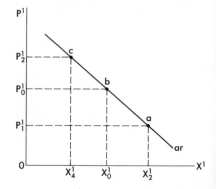

Figure 8–13

such function indicates the quantities that the firm can sell at various prices **if competitors keep their prices fixed.** The line ar in Fig. 8–13, on the other hand, may be referred to as the **effective** demand function, since it shows the firm's demand conditions after allowing for optimal counteradjustments in the prices of rival firms. An effective demand function can be derived for each firm in the market.

We now return to the main theme of the discussion. The particular model to be presented here is based on the following behavioral assumption: Starting from any given equilibrium position, each firm assumes that if it chooses to raise its price, its competitors will **not** change their prices; whereas if it chooses to lower its price, competitors **will** adjust by lowering their own prices. This model may seem to depart from our description of the general model of monopolistic competition, in which it is assumed that firms always react to moves by their competitors which affect their own demand conditions. However, the difference between this and the other models is perhaps more subtle than may appear at first sight. Note that this model **does not** assume that competitors actually refrain from reacting to price increases initiated by the representative firm. The model merely assumes that the representative firm adopts certain rules of behavior which are based on its own belief that its competitors will not react to price increases. Such behavior is not inconsistent with our earlier assumptions about decision-making in monopolistic competition, since in these models the participating firms need not know exactly how their rivals will act under all possible conditions. Essentially we have here an example of behavior under conditions of uncertainty, in which the decision maker possesses only partial information about the true state of his environment. As a result, his views of the system he operates in may be different from reality.

For the formal analysis of this model we turn to Fig. 8–14. The line AR represents one of the firm's partial demand functions, and the line ar the firm's effective demand function with respect to the initial position P_0, X_0. Since the

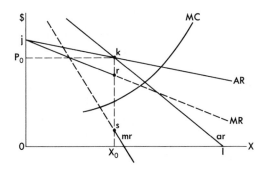

Figure 8–14

firm assumes that its competitors will not react if it raises its price above P_0, it views its true demand conditions for prices above P_0 as consisting of the segment of its partial demand function AR to the left of point k. On the other hand, the firm expects that price cuts will engender a reaction, and consequently for prices below P_0 expected sales are given by the segment of the effective demand function ar below point k. Thus the firm believes that its true demand function for the entire range of feasible prices is made up of the kinked demand function jkl. The marginal revenue function associated with the latter consists of two segments: In the range of output in which AR applies, i.e., from zero to X_0, the marginal revenue function consists of the corresponding segment of the MR function, namely jr; for outputs beyond X_0 it consists of the appropriate segment of the mr function, i.e., the portion of mr below s. The mr function has the same relationship to ar as MR has to AR.

In order to determine the optimal rate of output, we shall introduce the MC function. (ATC and AVC are omitted to maintain the clarity of the diagram.) If the MC function takes the position shown in Fig. 8–14, then the optimal output is X_0, and the price is P_0. The choice of the level of output at which MC intersects the discontinuity in the MR function (the vertical gap between points r and s) has already been justified in connection with the discussion of monopoly regulation (Fig. 7–21). Briefly, the argument is that at outputs less than X_0, MR $>$ MC, while at outputs greater than X_0, mr $<$ MC, hence X_0 is the optimal output. Thus in the above model the optimal output and price can always be identified as the coordinates of the point at which the firm's demand function is kinked.

If all the firms in the market, or at least most of them, behave as described in the above model, prices will generally tend to be quite rigid, and fluctuate less than in other markets, because for relatively small changes in its environmental conditions, the firm will not find it profitable to adjust its price. Suppose, for example, that the firm experiences a small change in its ATC, due perhaps to a change in variable input prices. As the ATC function shifts, so does the MC function. But so long as the MC function passes through some point on the line segment between points r and s in Fig. 8–14, both P_0 and X_0 continue to be the firm's optimal combination of price and output.

The price may also remain unaffected by a change in demand conditions. Suppose the demand for the firm's product increases so that its partial demand function shifts to the position shown by AR′ in Fig. 8–15. Such a shift can be the result of an autonomous increase in consumers' preference for the firm's brand of the product, or perhaps the effect of adjustments in price made by some of the firm's competitors. In any case, the functions AR and ar are no longer relevant. Under the new demand conditions, if the firm continues to

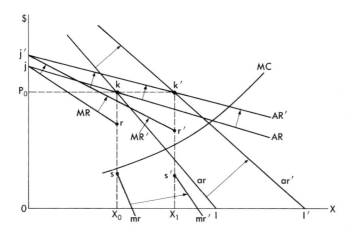

Figure 8–15

charge P_0, it can sell X_1 units of X, and for prices higher than P_0 its potential sales are indicated by the partial demand function AR′. If the firm chooses to lower its price below P_0, it expects its competitors to follow suit, so that expected sales must be read off the effective demand function. Thus the firm's new effective demand function ar′ goes through the point k′, and the firm's entire effective demand function consists of j′k′l′. The new marginal revenue function consists of the segment j′r′ and the portion of mr′ below point s′. If the firm's MC function passes through the discontinuity of the new marginal revenue function, as is assumed in Fig. 8–15, then the firm continues to charge the price P_0, but output is increased to X_1. The example just illustrated also indicates that the flatter the slope of the MC function, the smaller the likelihood that a given change in demand will induce the firm to change its price.

8–4.3   Cartels

From the preceding examples of monopolistically competitive markets it should be evident that markets of this type are characterized by two conspicuous features: (a) the interdependence among the firms, and (b) the uncertainty under which the decision maker operates. Some degree of uncertainty also prevails, of course, in purely competitive markets, as well as under conditions of pure monopoly, but in no market does it play such a critical role in the decision-making process as in monopolistic competition, especially in the oligopolistic markets. And both these features are detrimental to profit maximization. This has already been demonstrated (in Section 8–3.4) with the case of retaliatory advertising, in which profits are likely to be destroyed as a result of the promotional race into which the firms are plunged. The special conditions

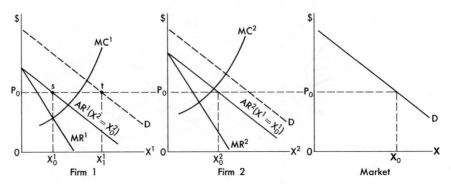

Figure 8–16

of oligopoly may also impinge on the costs of the firm in a less direct manner. Because of the strong and close interrelationship between the firms they may find it necessary to spend considerable sums of money on market research, in order to obtain information about demand conditions and the pricing and advertising strategies adopted by rival firms.   But while the conditions of oligopoly impose an extra burden on each firm, at the same time they provide the incentive for their own elimination. The heavy toll of the competitive contest may very well induce the firms in a given market to join in some form of collusion, and to operate their enterprises as one single unit. By doing so they are able to remove, or at least alleviate, both the competitiveness and some of the uncertainty with which they are confronted, and thus may be able to bring about a considerable improvement in their overall profit position. We shall examine the effects of collusion under a number of different conditions.

Homogeneous Products. In the first example let us assume that the industry produces a homogeneous product, and that there are two firms in the market. Under these conditions total market demand can be represented by one single function, while each firm faces a partial demand function whose location depends on the quantity sold by the other firm. These relationships are shown in Fig. 8–16. The line D is the market demand function, which also appears as a dashed line in the diagrams of the individual firms. Each firm is faced with a partial demand function which indicates potential sales at various prices **if the output of the other firm is constant.** Thus we assume that the current price is P_0, and the levels of output are X_0^1 and X_0^2, respectively. (It is assumed that average cost is sufficiently low to justify production.)   Industry output is $X_0^1 + X_0^2 = X_0$. The demand function of Firm 1, AR^1, is a line which has the same slope as the market demand function D, but which is displaced from the function D by a horizontal distance equal to X_0^2. For example, the distance between points s and t equals $X_1^1 - X_0^1 = X_0^2$. The function AR^1 indicates the

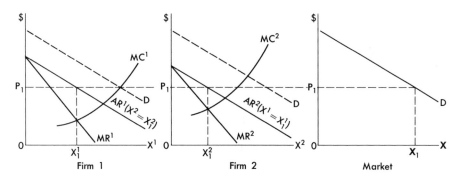

Figure 8–17

levels of output Firm 1 can sell at various prices if Firm 2 produces X_0^2. The same general relationship exists between AR^2 and D, except that the horizontal distance between these two functions is equal to the output of Firm 1, that is, X_0^1. Note that the market demand function D is **not** a horizontal summation of the functions AR^1 and AR^2, except along the horizontal line which indicates the current price.

According to Fig. 8–16 Firm 1 is in equilibrium, since given the output X_0^2 of Firm 2, its profit is maximized. Firm 2, on the other hand, is not in equilibrium, because at its current level of output $MC^2 > MR^2$. Firm 2 can therefore be expected to contract its output, and by doing so it will also disturb the equilibrium of Firm 1. Market equilibrium requires that each firm maximize its own profit at the current market price, given the output of its rival. Such a situation is depicted in Fig. 8–17.

When Firm 1 and Firm 2 agree to join in collusion they take it upon themselves to operate as a pure monopolist. This will in general make it possible for the two firms to increase their combined profit, so that if the profit is distributed "properly" (i.e., so that no firm receives less than it can earn in the absence of collusion), each firm can benefit from the arrangement. The reason for the potential increase in profit is not difficult to detect. Suppose, for example, that Firm 1 were to produce one unit more, and Firm 2 one unit less, than their respective equilibrium outputs. This would leave total output, and hence total revenues for the industry, unchanged. But since $MC^1 < MC^2$ at the equilibrium outputs (see Fig. 8–17), the increase in cost incurred by Firm 1 is less than the savings in cost realized by Firm 2, so that total cost for the industry is reduced, and that, of course, means an increase in industry profit. Thus through collusion industry profit may be increased, because such arrangement makes it possible to allocate the resources used by the industry in a more efficient manner. The optimal allocation occurs when the MC of each firm is

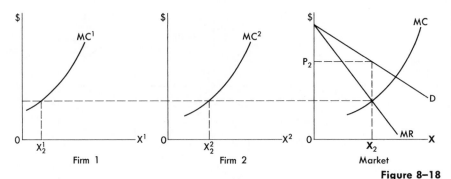

Figure 8–18

equal to the MR of the industry output. This problem is, of course, analytically identical to that of a multi-plant monopolist who determines his output by equating the MC of each plant with the MR of his total output (Section 7–4.1 and footnote).

The determination of the optimal level of output is illustrated in Fig. 8–18. Here MC is the horizontal summation of MC^1 and MC^2; hence the intersection of MC and MR indicates the level of marginal cost at which $MC^1 = MC^2 = MR$. The optimal levels of output are, therefore, X_2^1 and X_2^2, respectively, and the price is P_2.

▶ **A technical digression**

It is of some interest to examine more closely the position of a representative firm under this arrangement. For this purpose we have, in Fig. 8–19, super-imposed the relevant market functions on those of the representative firm. Here D, MR, and MC are the functions shown in the market diagram of Fig. 8–18; MC′ is the marginal cost function of the representative firm, and AR′ and MR′ its partial demand and marginal revenue functions, respectively. Industry output is X_2, the firm's output is X_0, and the price is P_2. As has been pointed

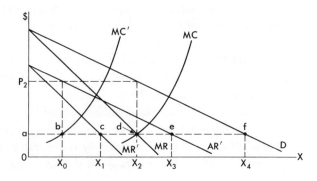

Figure 8–19

out earlier, the horizontal distance between the market demand function and that of the representative firm measures the total level of output produced by the other firms in the market. In other words, the length of the line segment $ef(=X_4 - X_3)$ equals the segment $bd(= X_2 - X_0)$. Now we know that the MR function of a linear demand function bisects the horizontal line segment between the \$-axis and the demand function (Section 7–1.1), so that $\overline{ad} = \overline{df}$, or equivalently, $X_2 = X_4/2$. Likewise, we have $\overline{ac} = \overline{ce}$, and $X_1 = X_3/2$. The first equation which we obtained above can be written as

$$X_4 - X_3 = X_2 - X_0, \tag{8–2}$$

which may be rearranged to yield

$$X_3 = X_4 - X_2 + X_0. \tag{8–3}$$

Since $X_4 = 2X_2$, substituting in the last equation gives

$$X_3 = X_0 + X_2. \tag{8–4}$$

Finally, since $X_1 = X_3/2$, substituting once more yields

$$X_1 = \frac{X_0 + X_2}{2}. \tag{8–5}$$

The purpose of this exercise is to prove that the MR′ function bisects the line segment bd, from which it follows that at the output X_0, MR′ > MC′. This means that the representative firm can increase the profit from its operation by lowering its price somewhat, and selling a higher output. The firm would thereby be able to augment whatever share of the total profit it receives in accordance with the collusion agreement. Of course, this will work only if all the other firms keep their outputs fixed; if this condition is not fulfilled, then AR′ and MR′ will shift to the left, thus wiping out the potential gain which the representative firm can reap from undercutting the collusion price. To put it differently, cheating (in the sense of departing from the collusion price) pays, provided one's competitors abide by the agreement. If the number of firms in the market is relatively large, the enforcement of the collusion agreement may prove to be quite difficult, and firms may therefore be encouraged to break away from it. This suggests that cartels with a large membership are inherently unstable.

Differentiated Products. If the firms produce a differentiated product, collusion may be equally profitable. The analysis of this case differs from the preceding one, since under conditions of product differentiation we can no longer use a market demand function. When there is no collusion, market equilibrium is of the type discussed earlier (Fig. 8–4); that is, each firm maximizes its profit, given the prices of all competing firms. However, when the firms associate to form a cartel, the objective is to maximize profit for the cartel as a whole, and consequently the determination of the optimal levels of output for each member firm proceeds along lines slightly different from those followed by each firm under normal circumstances. The rules for profit maximization tell us that, when firms operate independently, their decisions as to the level of output are governed by changes in their cost of production (MC) and by changes in their revenues (MR). This general principle also applies to the cartel as a whole, but it requires a redefinition of marginal revenue. If the output of, say, Firm 1 is increased by one unit (by lowering the price of that firm's product), there will be a change in the revenues obtained from the sale of Product 1, and in addition there will be a change in the sales from all other products, and hence a change in the revenues from all other products.

This effect operates, of course, regardless of whether the firms act independently or as a cartel, but whereas under conditions of individual profit maximization the secondary effects play no role in the decision-making process of each firm, profit maximization for the cartel as a whole requires that these effects be accounted for explicitly. The optimal output for each firm in the cartel must satisfy the condition that marginal cost of the output be equal to **total** marginal revenue. For example, in a two-firm cartel the optimal output for Firm 1 must satisfy the condition

$$MC^1 = MR_1^1 + MR_1^2, \tag{8–6}$$

where MR_1^1 denotes the change in revenues from the sales of Product 1 as the output of Product 1 is increased by one unit, and MR_1^2 denotes the change in revenues from the sales of Product 2 due to the increase in the sales of Product 1. Now when the sales of Product 1 are increased, the price of Product 1 is decreased, which in turn causes a decrease in the demand for Product 2. (See the discussion on the derivation of the effective demand curve at the beginning of Section 8–4.2.) This implies that MR_1^2 is negative. If we use the notation MR_1 and MR_2 for total marginal revenue of Product 1 and Product 2, respectively, we can write

$$MR_1 = MR_1^1 + MR_1^2 \quad \text{and} \quad MR_2 = MR_2^1 + MR_2^2, \tag{8–7}$$

and total profit for the cartel is maximized only if $MC^1 = MR_1$ and $MC^2 = MR_2$.

Figure 8–20 depicts the revenue and cost conditions of Firm 1, and also the total marginal revenue function of Product 1. When there is no collusion Firm 1 produces X_0^1, at which its own marginal cost and marginal revenue are equal.

Under collusion the output is reduced to X_1^1, and the price is raised to P_1^1. The vertical distance between MR_1 and MR_1^1 measures the absolute value of MR_1^2. Thus at the optimal level of output MR_1^2 equals $a - b$. It can also be observed that at X_1^1, $MR_1^1 > MC^1$, which again gives the firm an incentive to violate the collusion agreement by increasing its output to X_0^1.

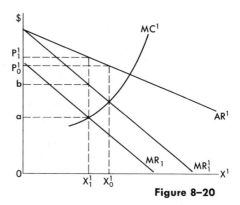

Figure 8–20

8–4.4 Market-Sharing

Homogeneous Products. Certain cartel agreements may be drawn up in terms of market shares for the member firms. In the narrow sense of the term, such arrangements are not necessarily consistent with short-run profit maximization, because the allocation of market shares to the participating firms is not governed by the marginal changes in cost and revenues. Market-sharing agreements may nevertheless be justified on purely pecuniary grounds, inasmuch as they prevent or reduce losses due to advertising, price wars, and other costly maneuvers in which the firm is likely to engage in the absence of a collective agreement. If the industry produces a homogeneous product, then the agreement specifies the market shares for each firm, as well as the market price of the product. Let us refer once more to Fig. 8–18; if the market price is set at P_2, and the shares are different from the outputs X_2^1 and X_2^2, respectively, then short-run profit for the cartel as a whole is not maximized.

Collusion involving fixed market shares may also be the result of a leader–follower type relationship. Suppose that there are two firms in the market, and that Firm 2 agrees always to sell one-third of the total output of a homogeneous product. In this case Firm 1, the leader, chooses its output to maximize its profit with respect to a demand function which represents two-thirds of the total market demand. In Fig. 8–21 the line D represents the market demand function, and the other functions represent the revenue and cost functions of Firm 1. The function AR^1 is drawn in a manner such that at any price the horizontal distance between the $-axis and AR^1 is two-thirds of the horizontal distance between the $-axis and D. Under these conditions Firm 1 maximizes its profit at the output X_0, and the market price is P_0. Industry output is X_1, so that Firm 2 sells $X_1 - X_0$, which, of course, is equal to $X_1/3$.

Differentiated Products. If the firms produce differentiated products the analysis requires some modifications. For this purpose we first derive the

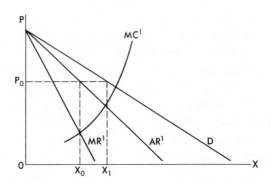

Figure 8–21

leader's total demand function. It is assumed again that Firm 2 is willing to take one-third of the total market, which in the case of differentiated products simply means to sell one-half as many units as Firm 1 sells of **its** product. In the initial equilibrium (as shown in Fig. 8–22), Firm 1 sells X_0^1 units of Product 1, and Firm 2 sells X_0^2 units of Product 2. By assumption, $X_0^2 = (X_0^1 + X_0^2)/3$, or equivalently, $X_0^2 = X_0^1/2$. Initially the firms face the partial demand functions AR_0^1 and AR_0^2, respectively. The latter are relationships between quantity demanded and price, assuming that the **quantity** (rather than the price) of the other commodity is held fixed.

Let us now suppose that Firm 1 intends to increase its sales to X_1^1. According to the function AR_0^1, the firm must then lower its price to P_1^1. But as the output of Firm 1 increases to X_1^1, the partial demand function of Firm 2 shifts leftward to position AR_1^2. Since Firm 2 wishes to maintain one-third of total sales, it lowers its price to P_1^2, in order to sell X_1^2 units of X^2, assuming $X_1^2 = X_1^1/2$. The increase in the output of Firm 2 will, in turn, shift the partial demand function of Firm 1 to the position shown by AR_1^1, and hence, in order to sell the output X_1^1, Firm 1 must lower its price to P_2^1.

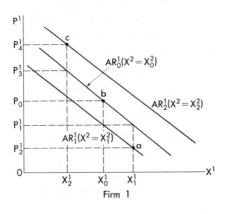

Firm 1

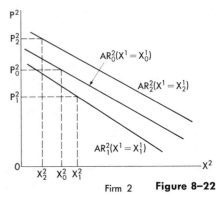

Firm 2   **Figure 8–22**

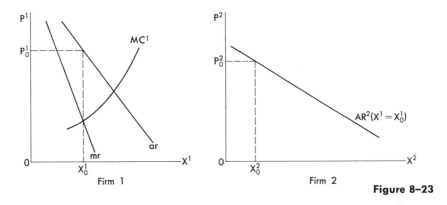

Firm 1   Firm 2

Figure 8–23

A similar process can be generated for decreases in output. If Firm 1 decreases its output from X_0^1 to X_2^1, AR_2 shifts to AR_2^2, so that in order to cut its output to $X_2^2 = X_2^1/2$, Firm 2 raises its price to P_2^2. The reduction in the output of Firm 2 shifts the demand function of Firm 1 to AR_2^1, which means that to keep its sales at the level X_2^1 Firm 1 must raise its price to P_4^1. Consequently the points **a**, **b**, and **c** in the diagram of Firm 1 lie on the latter's effective demand function. The reader should realize that the effective demand function of which three points were derived in Fig. 8–22 is a slightly different relationship from the effective demand function derived in Figs. 8–12 and 8–13. The latter shows the firm's effective demand conditions under the assumption that competing firms react to **maximize their profit,** whereas the effective demand function discussed in the above example assumes that rival firms react to **maintain a fixed share of total sales.**

In order to determine its optimal choice of output and price Firm 1 applies the rules for profit maximization, using for this purpose the effective demand function and its related marginal revenue function. These are shown in Fig. 8–23. Firm 1 maximizes profit with output X_0^1 and price P_0^1. Given the leader's output X_0^1, Firm 2 faces the partial demand function AR^2, and in order to sell the output $X_0^2 = X_0^1/2$, it charges the price P_0^2.

8–5   A COMPARISON BETWEEN PURE COMPETITION, PURE MONOPOLY, AND MONOPOLISTIC COMPETITION

Finally, let us briefly compare the performances of firms in monopolistic competition and those in other types of markets. As in the comparison between pure competition and monopoly (Section 7–4), the objects of the present comparison are **the size of the output, the existence of profit,** and **the divergence between price and marginal cost.**

With respect to the size of the output, the results are in general as ambiguous as in the comparison between pure competition and monopoly. Furthermore, if product differentiation exists, the lack of a satisfactory definition of industry output makes a meaningful comparison more difficult than a comparison without product differentiation. If the industry produces a homogeneous product, the comparison of its output with the output of firms in a purely competitive market is inconclusive because one can generally assume that cost conditions would be different in the two kinds of industry. If the industry is monopolized the result is just as ambiguous, even if we assume that the monopolist continues to operate the existing plants of the monopolistically competitive firms. Under these conditions the monopolist produces the same output that the industry would produce under a collusion agreement, and it may be smaller than, greater than, or the same as the output of the industry when all firms act independently. If the industry produces differentiated products the comparison makes little sense. For example, if such an industry is monopolized, the monopolist may find it profitable to produce more of one particular brand and less of another, but it is meaningless to make any statement about industry output as a whole.

The profit position of a firm in monopolistic competition is similar to that of a competitive firm. In the short run, as in other market structures, the firm may make a profit. In the long run, on the other hand, profits are wiped out through the influx of new firms. It must, however, be pointed out that under certain circumstances which are likely to prevail in oligopolistic markets, the industry may be able to block the entry of new firms into the market. In that case the firms may maintain their profits even in the long run.

With respect to the relationship between P and MC, the performance of the firm in monopolistic competition is the same as that of the monopolist; like the latter, the monopolistic competitor always operates at a level of output at which P > MC. The desirability of monopolistically competitive industries, from the viewpoint of social welfare, may therefore be questioned on the basis of the same arguments that could be advanced as a critique of the monopolist's performance. But because the demand function of a firm in monopolistic competition has a relatively flat slope, the divergence between P and MC may be of smaller magnitude than that which characterizes the operation of a monopolist.

SUMMARY

This chapter has dealt with the broad class of markets commonly known as monopolistic competition. Of the different types of market structures identified in economic theory, monopolistic competition is the most general, and one can, indeed, think of both pure competition and pure monopoly as special cases of it. Monopolistically competitive markets combine competitive as well as monopolistic elements. Because of product differentiation, firms normally face downward sloping demand functions, and they are therefore in a position to formulate their own pricing policy. At the same time, however, the demand functions of the firms are interdependent, since in any given market the products of any one firm are close substitutes for the products of another.

A typical firm in a monopolistically competitive market is constantly engaged in warfare with its competitors. The intensity of the competitive struggle among the firms is normally greater when there are few firms in the market, except, of course, when the number of firms is reduced to one (pure monopoly) and competition disappears altogether. One of the principal weapons in this contest is promotional activity designed to capture for the firm as many buyers (actual and potential) as possible. Since by and large advertising efforts by competing firms tend to neutralize one another, their main effect is to increase the general cost level in the industry, and thereby reduce profits.

The conditions under which the race for market shares is waged may place considerable strain, both financial and psychological, on the competitors, who may under certain conditions agree to turn competition into cooperation by forming a cartel. Such an association can be rationalized from the point of view of profit maximization, not only because it obviates the necessity for large advertising outlays, but also because it may bring about a more efficient use of resources. Sometimes, however, collusion arrangements are less than perfect, and may involve looser forms of association, such as market-sharing. One of the weaknesses of cartels (aside from the possibility of their being illegal) is that firms may find it individually profitable to act in contravention of the provisions of the agreement, and if such a practice is widespread it may very well lead to the disintegration of the cartel.

When it comes to decision-making, the most typical aspect of monopolistic competition is the fact that each firm in the market operates in the company of competitors who are affected by, and are likely to respond to, the actions taken by the firm. It is, therefore, incumbent on the decision maker to formulate explicit hypotheses about the behavior of his rivals, and to derive his own rules of behavior from them. Because of the great number of variations which may be found in this pattern of interrelationships, the theory of monopolistic competition gives rise to an abundance of different models. The small sample of such models presented in this chapter was designed primarily to illustrate how we can formulate problems in monopolistic competition, and the use we can make of various analytical tools in analyzing such models.

SELECTED REFERENCES

BAUMOL, W. J., "On the Theory of Oligopoly." *Economica*, New Series **25**, 1958, pp. 187–198.

BAUMOL, W. J., and R. E. QUANDT, "Rules of Thumb and Optimally Imperfect Decisions." *American Economic Review* **54**, 1964, pp. 23–46.

CHAMBERLIN, E. H., *The Theory of Monopolistic Competition*. Cambridge: Harvard University Press, 1950, 6th ed., Chapters 4, 5, 6, and 7.

CLARK, J. M., "Toward a Concept of Workable Competition." *American Economic Review* **30**, 1940, pp. 241–256.

ENCARNACIÓN, J., "Constraints and the Firm's Utility Function." *Review of Economic Studies* **31**, 1964, pp. 113–120.

HALL, R. L., and C. J. HITCH, "Price Theory and Business Behavior." *Oxford Economic Papers* **2**, 1939, pp. 12–45.

MARGOLIS, J., "The Analysis of the Firm: Rationalism, Conventionalism, and Behaviorism." *Journal of Business* **31**, 1958, pp. 187–199.

ROBINSON, J., *The Economics of Imperfect Competition*. London: Macmillan, 1933, Chapter 27.

ROTHSCHILD, K. W., "Price Theory and Oligopoly." *Economic Journal* **57**, 1947, pp. 299–320. Reprinted in K. E. Boulding and G. J. Stigler (eds.), *Readings in Price Theory*. Chicago: Irwin, 1952, pp. 440–464.

STIGLER, G. J., "The Kinky Oligopoly Demand Curve and Rigid Prices." *Journal of Political Economy* **55**, 1947, pp. 432–449. Reprinted in K. E. Boulding and G. J. Stigler (eds.), *Readings in Price Theory*. Chicago: Irwin, 1952, pp. 410–439.

SWEEZY, P. M., "Demand under Conditions of Oligopoly." *Journal of Political Economy* **47**, 1939, pp. 568–573. Reprinted in K. E. Boulding and G. J. Stigler (eds.), *Readings in Price Theory*. Chicago: Irwin, 1952, pp. 404–409.

EXERCISES

1. Suppose that a certain commodity is produced by two firms of more or less equal size: Firm 1 produces Brand X, and Firm 2 produces Brand Y. Figure E8–1 shows the cost and revenue curves of Firm 1. Complete the sentences given below.

 (a) If Firm 2 charges $7 for its product and advertising expenditures are $130 and $170, respectively, then Firm 1 will sell _____ units at $_____ per unit.

 (b) If Firm 2 lowers its price to $4, Firm 1 will respond by (*cutting its own price to $4 and leaving output unchanged, increasing its output, decreasing its output*).

 (c) If Firm 2 reduces its advertising expenditures to $130, the AR function of Firm 1 will (*shift up, shift down*). Consequently, Firm 1 will react by (*increasing its output, decreasing its output*).

 (d) If Firm 1 increases its advertising outlay to $200, it can expect the following changes: (i) an upward shift in both AR and ATC, (ii) a downward shift in both AR and ATC, (iii) an increase in ATC, but no change in AR, (iv) an increase in AR, but no change in ATC.

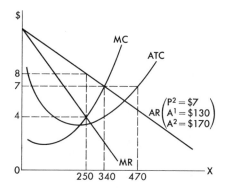

Figure E8–1

 (e) Since an increase in advertising outlay may be regarded as an increase in TFC (inasmuch as the level of advertising is independent of the level of output), such an increase will probably be accompanied by (*an increase, a decrease*) in quantity produced.

 (f) If Firm 2 lowers its price, Firm 1 can retaliate by (*raising its price, reducing its advertising, increasing its advertising*).

 (g) If the market is open to the entry of new firms, it cannot be in equilibrium unless excess profits are zero. Draw into Fig. E8–1 the AR and MR functions of Firm 1, assuming that the market is in long-run equilibrium. Indicate the firm's output and price, and also the level of output at which MC = MR.

2. A certain product X is produced in a market which has the following structure: One relatively large firm is accepted as a price leader, while all other firms take

the leader's price as given. There exists no product differentiation. The market relations are given by the following specifications:

Total market demand

(i) When the price is $20, quantity demanded is zero.

(ii) Whenever the price falls (rises) by $4, quantity demanded increases (decreases) by 5 units.

Market supply of the competitive fringe

(i) When the price is $4, quantity supplied is zero.

(ii) Whenever the price rises (falls) by $4, quantity supplied increases (decreases) by 5 units.

(a) Draw the above-mentioned demand and supply functions on one diagram, and label them D and S, respectively.

(b) Construct (on the same diagram) the AR and MR functions of the price leader.

(c) Assume that the upward sloping segment of the leader's MC function intersects his MR function at the output level 10. (i) What price will the leader set for product X? (ii) What are the quantities supplied by the leader and the competitive fringe, respectively?

(d) Answer (c) above, assuming MC and MR intersect at output level 5.

3. A firm which operates in an oligopolistic market faces the following linear partial demand function for product X: The $-intercept is 16 and the numerical value of its slope is $\frac{1}{4}$.

(a) Draw the firm's partial AR and MR functions on a suitably scaled diagram. The firm's cost conditions can be described by a linear MC function with a $-intercept at 8 and a slope of $\frac{1}{2}$.

(b) Draw the firm's MC function into your diagram. The firm's initial output is 8 units. Check whether your diagram is consistent with this statement.

(c) The firm's profit is ($16, *less than* $16, *more than* $16). Since in an oligopolistic market the demand functions of the firms in the market are interrelated, a change in the price of one firm will usually bring about counter-adjustments by all other firms. Each firm, therefore, is confronted with an effective demand function which incorporates these adjustments. For the firm in this problem the effective demand function, given the firm's initial position, is a linear function with the $-intercept at 22, and a slope whose magnitude is one.

(d) Draw into your diagram the firm's effective demand function and the corresponding MR function. (Use different labels, or a different color, to distinguish the partial from the effective revienue functons.) Verify that the effective demand function intersects the partial demand function at the output level 8. The firm believes that its rivals will always match price cuts, but that they will not react to price increases.

(e) If the firm experiences a decrease in variable cost which causes MC to fall by $4 at every level of output, then the firm will react by (i) increasing output, (ii) decreasing output, (iii) cutting the price, (iv) leaving price and output unchanged.

(f) If the firm experiences a decrease in TFC, then it will react by (i) increasing output, (ii) decreasing output, (iii) cutting the price, (iv) leaving price and output unchanged.

(g) If the firm changes its view about the behavior of its rivals, and believes that rivals will match all price changes (including price increases), then it will (i) cut its price and increase output, (ii) raise its price and lower output, (iii) cut output and leave the price unchanged, (iv) leave both price and output unchanged.

4. A certain market consists of two firms each of which produces a differentiated product. The two firms agree to form a cartel and to operate their firms under a unified management. Figure E8–2 shows, respectively, the AR and MC functions of the two firms, and the partial and total MR functions. Complete the sentences given below.

(a) In order to maximize its profit the cartel should assign Firm 1 to sell _____ units of X^1 at $_____ per unit, and Firm 2 to sell _____ units of X^2 at $_____ per unit.

(b) If Firm 1 were to increase its output by one (infinitesimally small) unit beyond the optimal level [your answer to part (a)], then the revenues of the cartel would increase by $_____. This amount is obtained as follows: The (*increase, decrease*) in sales of product X^1 (*increases, decreases*) total revenues by $_____, and the (*increase, decrease*) in sales of product X^2 (*increases, decreases*) total revenues by $_____.

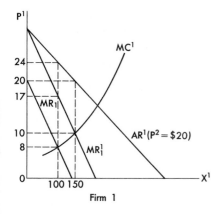

Firm 1

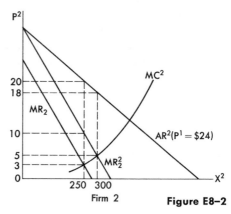

Firm 2

Figure E8–2

(c) The arrangement described in part (a) provides each firm with an incentive to deviate from the prescribed production plan. Thus in order to increase its own profit, Firm 1 would be tempted to (*increase, decrease*) its output to _____ units.

(d) If Firm 1 did, in fact, change its output as in part (c), the AR function of Firm 2, AR^2, would shift to the (*left, right*), and consequently the profit of Firm 2 would (*increase, decrease*).

(e) When the firms deviate from the cartel agreement, and choose levels of output which maximize their own profit, the sum of their individual profits is (*greater than, less than, the same as*) the profit of the cartel if the agreement is not violated.

5. A market in which all firms produce a homogeneous product consists of a leading firm and a number of followers. The latter agree to sell a certain share of the total market at the price set by the leader. The market demand function is represented by a linear function with the $-intercept at 16, and a slope of $\frac{1}{2}$ (in absolute value). The leader's technology is described by a constant cost function according to which ATC = MC = $4 at all levels of output.

(a) Plot the market demand function.

(b) Plot the leader's cost function and his AR and MR functions, assuming that the followers agree to sell one-fourth of the total output.

(c) Determine the price and output of the leader. What is the leader's profit? What is the total market output?

(d) Assume now that the number of followers increases, and that they demand (and get) one-half of the market. Draw (on the same diagram) the leader's AR and MR functions under this assumption, and label them AR′ and MR′, respectively.

(e) Determine the price and output of the leader. What is the total market output?

(f) Assume that the leader drives his followers out of the market (or buys them off) without thereby causing a change in his cost conditions. What is his price and output?

(g) Linear demand functions with the same $-intercept have the same (point) elasticity at points which represent the same price. Confirm this statement by measuring the elasticity of the leader's demand (AR) function at the points at which he sells in the three cases given in (c), (e), and (f) above.

9

THE DEMAND FOR
FACTORS OF PRODUCTION:
PURE COMPETITION

In Chapters 5 through 8 we have discussed the decision-making process of the firm under a number of different forms of market structures. While we have presented a fairly comprehensive treatment of the various types of environmental conditions in which a firm is likely to find itself, the exposition of the material has been somewhat one-sided in one respect: We have emphasized the firm's choice of **output,** and, whenever appropriate, its choice of price. In other words, we have been concerned with the producer in his role as a **seller.** While it is true that the sale of his final output may well be considered to be the producer's *raison d'être*, the production of the output itself is impossible without the use of certain inputs. Since these must normally be acquired by purchase, part of the producer's function is to act as a **buyer.** It is this aspect of the firm's behavior which forms the subject matter of Chapters 9 and 10.

To clarify the relationship between the material to be presented in this chapter and that which has preceded it, we should point out that in some sense the discussion in the present chapter may be thought of as a repetition. This is so because the analysis here, like that which has preceded it, is designed to provide an answer to the following basic question: What actions would (or should) the firm take under a particular set of circumstances in order to maximize its profit? In earlier chapters we have answered this question by showing how profit maximization leads to a particular choice of output and price, but we have made no explicit reference to the amounts of inputs used in the production of the optimal level of output. In this chapter we intend to show how profit maximization governs the firm's demand for inputs, while the (optimal) level of output associated with the optimal choice of inputs will be of no special concern. From the formal point of view the two approaches are merely different ways of solving an identical problem, each one emphasizing one particular facet of the firm's operation.

9–1   THE ONE-INPUT CASE

9–1.1   The revenue product and input cost functions

We shall limit this analysis to cases in which the representative firm is one of many firms purchasing the same input. Let us begin with a fairly simple short-run example and assume that the productive process requires only one variable input. There may, of course, be a number of fixed inputs, but since they are fixed they have no important effect on the analysis, and hence need not be considered directly. The first point of interest in this analysis is the relationship between the variable input and the firm's total revenues. We wish to find out how revenues vary when the firm uses different levels of the variable input (i.e., when it produces different levels of output), given the levels of its fixed inputs. Since revenues are the receipts from sales, it is obvious that the relationship between the variable input and revenues depends directly on the relationship between the variable input and output, i.e., on the **total product** function (Section 3–1.1). The relationship between these two functions is shown in Fig. 9–1, in which **TP** is the familiar total product function, indicating the amounts of output X obtained by using different levels of the variable input L, holding all other inputs constant. (See Figs. 3–1 and 3–3.) The curve labeled **TRP** is the relationship between input L and total revenues, which will be referred to as the **total revenue product** function of L. The terminology (and notation)

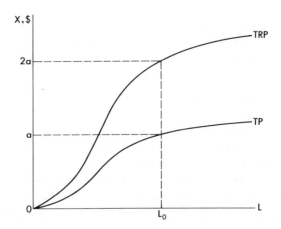

Figure 9–1

chosen here is designed (a) to point out that this function is **not** the same as the
TR function (which is a relationship between **output (X)** and total revenue) and
(b) to suggest that, conceptually at least, one can collapse the intermediary
link between the input and total revenues by simply ignoring the physical
output X, and think of total revenues as the "product" produced by the input.
In our exposition, however, we do not always suppress the level of output because we wish to emphasize the fact that the amount of revenue associated with
any given level of input depends directly on the level of output produced by
the input. In fact, by definition,

$$\text{TRP} = \text{TP} \cdot \text{P}^X, \tag{9-1}$$

where P^X denotes the price of the output. This relationship is clearly shown in
Fig. 9–1. If we assume that the firm sells its output in a purely competitive
market, and that the market price for product X is \$2, then at any given level
of L the vertical distance between the abscissa and the TRP function is twice
the distance between the abscissa and the TP function. For example, if the firm
uses L_0 units of L, it produces (and sells) a units of X, and receives $2a$ dollars
in revenue. Note that the numbers on the vertical scale represent units of X
when they are associated with points on the TP function, and dollars when
associated with the TRP function. Note also that if the price of X is \$1, the
TRP function coincides with the TP function.

The interpretation of the slopes of these functions is straightforward: The
slope of the TP function is the **marginal product (MP)** of L, with which we are
familiar from Chapter 3; the slope of the TRP function represents the **marginal
revenue product (MRP)** [sometimes referred to as the **value of the marginal
product (VMP)**], which measures the change in TRP due to a small change in L.
Since TP and TRP are so closely related (see Eq. 9–1), it is not surprising to
find that there exists just as close a relationship between their slopes. After
all, the contribution to total revenue made by the last unit of L (that is, MRP)
depends directly on the increase in output associated with the last unit of L.
In fact, it is simply equal to the marginal increase in output (MP) multiplied by
the price of the output (P^X). In symbols we can write

$$\text{MRP} = \text{MP} \cdot \text{P}^X. \tag{9-2}$$

To further clarify the relationship between these concepts, let us look at the
numerical example in Table 9–1, which is self-explanatory. Note that the
numbers conform to the general shape of the functions represented in Fig. 9–1.
The reader can also verify the definitions of TRP and MRP. Thus the numbers
in column 4 (TRP) are equal to the numbers in column 2 (TP) in the correspond-

ing row, multiplied by the price of the output (P^X), which is $2 in the example given above. The numbers in column 5 (MRP) are equal to the numbers in column 3 (MP) in the corresponding row, multiplied by the price of the output (P^X). And from the definitions of MP and MRP it follows, of course, that the numbers in columns 3 and 5 indicate the differences between successive numbers in columns 2 and 4, respectively. (For further explanation concerning the derivation of the numbers in columns 3 and 5, consult the discussion in Section 2–2 and Table 2–2.)

L	TP in units of X	MP in units of X	TRP in $ $P^X = \$2$	MRP in $
1	2	3	4	5
0	0		0	
1	1	1	2	2
2	3	2	6	4
3	6	3	12	6
4	10	4	20	8
5	15	5	30	10
6	22	7	44	14
7	28	6	56	12
8	32	4	64	8
9	34	2	68	4
10	35	1	70	2

Table 9–1

The total cost associated with various levels of L, given the amounts of fixed inputs, is referred to as the **total input cost** (TIC) function. Here again it should be pointed out that this relationship is **not** the familiar TC function. The definitions of the two concepts are, however, strikingly similar. We define

$$TIC = TVIC + TFC, \tag{9–3}$$

where TVIC denotes **total variable input cost,** and TFC is the familiar **total fixed cost** which appears also in the definition of TC (Eq. 2–1). The quantity TVIC is simply the cost of the variable input, and since it is assumed that the input is purchased under competitive conditions, we have

$$TVIC = P^L \cdot L, \tag{9–4}$$

where P^L denotes the price of L.

The TIC function is shown in Fig. 9–2. The $-intercept of the TIC function (b) represents the cost of the fixed inputs. The fact that TIC is a straight line

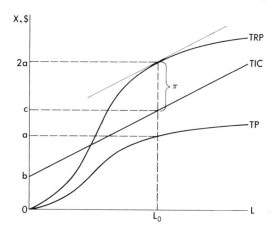

Figure 9–2

implies that the price of L is independent of the amount of L used (purchased). The latter is, of course, implied by the assumption of perfect competition among buyers of input L, so that at any moment of time each buyer regards the going price of L as given. The nature of competition among buyers is, of course, very similar to the concept of competition as applied to sellers, insofar as we assume that the quantity of the input purchased by any one buyer is so small as to have only a negligible effect on the input price.

9–1.2   The optimal level of input

Total profit is still defined as the difference between revenues and cost, so that in terms of the new notation introduced in this chapter we can write

$$\pi = \text{TRP} - \text{TIC}. \tag{9–5}$$

In Fig. 9–2, total profit may be identified as the vertical distance between TRP and TIC at any level of L. It is obvious, therefore (from Fig. 5–1, and related discussion), that profit is maximized with the level of input L_0 at which the slopes of TRP and TIC are equal. When the firm uses L_0 units of L, its output is equal to a units of X, TRP is $2a$ dollars, TIC is c dollars, and total profit is $2a - c$ dollars. The slope of the TIC function measures **marginal input cost** (MIC), i.e., the change in TIC as the level of L is increased by a small amount, which in the case of competition among buyers is simply equal to the price of the input. Thus at the optimal level of input we must have MIC = MRP.

▶ The relationship between optimal level of output and optimal level of input

It may be in order, at this point, to validate and elaborate on our earlier assertion that from the formal point of view this analysis may be regarded as an alternative method of solving the very same problem (i.e., the attainment of profit maximization) which Chapters 5 through 8 dealt with. We shall do so by showing that the rule which emerges from the present analysis is equivalent to the rule derived in the earlier chapters; that is, we shall demonstrate that

the condition MIC = MRP is equivalent to the condition MC = MR.

First we restate the relation between MRP and MP,

$$MRP = MP \cdot P^X. \tag{9-6}$$

Now MP can be broken down into two components, and may be represented as the ratio of the increments in output and input, respectively; that is,

$$MP = \frac{\Delta X}{\Delta L}. \tag{9-7}$$

If we let $\Delta X = 1$, and define ΔL as that increment in L which yields an increase in X of one unit, then we have

$$MP = \frac{1}{\Delta L}. \tag{9-8}$$

Next we observe that MC may be computed in the following way: In order to increase the output X by one unit, L must be increased by ΔL, hence the change in total cost as output is increased by one unit (that is, MC) is equal to the necessary increase in L multiplied by the price of L. Symbolically

$$MC = P^L \cdot \Delta L. \tag{9-9}$$

Now the optimal amount of input must satisfy the following condition:

$$MIC = MRP. \tag{9-10}$$

But in a competitive market MIC equals P^L, so that the condition for profit maximization can be stated as

$$P^L = MRP. \tag{9-11}$$

Substituting for MRP from Eq. (9–6), we have

$$P^L = MP \cdot P^X, \tag{9-12}$$

and substituting for MP from (9–8) yields

$$P^L = P^X/\Delta L. \tag{9-13}$$

If we multiply both sides of the above equation by ΔL, we get

$$P^L \cdot \Delta L = P^X, \tag{9-14}$$

and in view of Eq. (9–9) we can write

$$MC = P^X. \tag{9-15}$$

Since competition among sellers implies $MR = P^X$, substituting in the above equation gives

$$MC = MR, \tag{9-16}$$

which is what we intended to show.

9–1.3 Changes in input prices

Let us now return to the main theme of the discussion. Since we have already explained how the firm chooses the optimal level of the variable input, it should be quite easy to see how this choice is affected by a change in the price of the input. If, for instance, the price of the input rises, the firm might be confronted with a situation such as that depicted in Fig. 9–3. The TIC function for the initial price (as shown in Fig. 9–2) is reproduced as a dashed line. Since the firm has to equate P^L and MRP, the increase in price induces the firm to use a level of L at which MRP is greater than at L_0. The optimal level of L is therefore L_1, at which the slopes of the TIC and TRP functions are equal. In fact, since TIC is tangent to TRP at L_1, it follows that at that level of L, TIC = TRP, and hence $\pi = 0$. This is, therefore, a break-even point. If the price of L rises further, it is obvious that the firm will incur a net loss. It will be remembered, however, that in the short run the firm continues to produce so long as its losses are less than its TFC, but shuts down as soon as it loses more than its

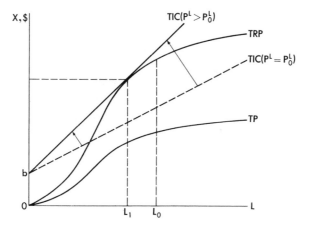

Figure 9–3

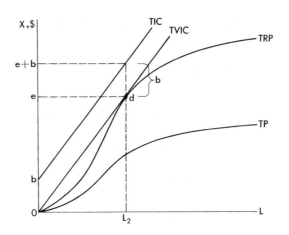

Figure 9–4

TFC (Section 5–2). We are thus led to ask: What is the highest price the firm would be willing to pay for input L before being forced to shut down? This question is answered with the help of Fig. 9–4.

The price of L is now so high that **TIC** lies entirely above **TRP**. However, P^L and **MRP** are equal at L_2. This is so because the **TVIC** function, which is parallel to **TIC**, is tangent to **TRP** at L_2. Hence at L_2 the slopes of these three functions are equal. We also observe that at L_2, **TRP** = e and **TIC** = e + b, hence $\pi = e - (e + b) = -b$. In other words, profit equals $-$**TFC**. The situation in Fig. 9–4, therefore, represents the shut-down point.

We now introduce the concept of **average revenue product** (**ARP**), which refers to the revenue product per unit of L. Formally we define it as

$$\text{ARP} = \frac{\text{TRP}}{\text{L}}. \tag{9–17}$$

(Compare with the definition of **AP**, Section 3–1.2.) Now the value of **ARP** at any level of L is measured by the slope of the ray from the origin to the appropriate point on the **TRP** function. (See Fig. 2–3 and relevant explanations.) For example, at L_2 the value of **ARP** is equal to the slope of **TVIC**, that is, the ratio $\overline{L_2 d}/\overline{0L_2}$. Furthermore, it is also clear that at L_2, **ARP** attains its maximum, since **TVIC** is the steepest ray from the origin which touches **TRP**. All this leads to the following conclusion: The firm will purchase a positive amount of the variable input (and produce a positive level of output) so long as the price of the input is less than, or equal to, the maximum value of **ARP**. If the price of the input exceeds the maximum value of **ARP**, the firm's demand for the input (and its level of output) falls to zero.*

---

* It can be shown that the condition $P^L > \text{ARP}_{max}$ is equivalent to the condition $P^X < \text{AVC}_{min}$.

9–1.4   The rule for profit maximization

The discussion up to this point may be summarized by stating the formal rule for profit maximization.

In order to maximize its profit the firm should choose a level of input L, call it $\hat{L}$, which satisfies either one of the conditions stated below.

(9A) If $P^L \leq ARP_{max}$, then the following must hold:

$$(1)\ MIC = MRP_{\hat{L}};$$
$$(2)\ MRP_{\hat{L}}\ \text{is decreasing.}$$

(9B) If $P^L > ARP_{max}$, then $\hat{L} = 0$.

In our discussion we have not, as the reader may have realized, dwelled on the reason for provision (2) of condition 9A in the above rule. However, an examination of Fig. 9–2 and a review of the justification for requiring MC to be increasing when choosing the optimal level of output (Fig. 5–2 and related discussion) should provide the reader with the answer.

9–1.5   The input demand function

The main results of this analysis can also be illustrated with the use of a different set of curves, as shown in Fig. 9–5. The shape of the ARP and MRP functions follows directly from the shape of the TRP function. (To refresh your memory, examine the relationship between Figs. 3–1 and 3–2.) The choice of the optimal level of L is made by finding the point on the MRP function at which the value of MRP is equal to the price of L. For instance, if the going price of L is equal to d dollars, the optimal level of L is L_0. The level of revenues (that is, TRP) associated with the optimal level of L is represented by the area of the rectangle $0ehL_0$. Since the price of L is really the same as **average variable input**

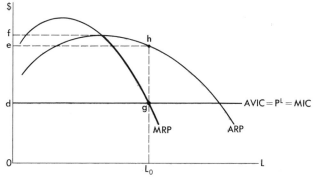

Figure 9–5

cost (AVIC), and by definition

$$AVIC = \frac{TVIC}{L},\qquad(9\text{–}18)$$

it follows that the area of $0dgL_0$ represents TVIC. Furthermore, the area of **dehg** represents "gross" profit, i.e., profit exclusive of fixed cost. It is also clear from the diagram that as the price of L falls, the firm increases its purchase of L, and when it rises, the amount of L purchased is decreased. But as we saw earlier, the firm ceases to produce altogether if the price of L exceeds ARP (condition 9B), and hence at prices of L above f the firm does not purchase any amount of L. Thus the portion of the MRP function below the ARP function constitutes the firm's **partial** demand function for the input L.

The above demand function is referred to as **partial,** inasmuch as it does not take into account possible repercussions from the output market following changes in the quantity of input purchased. So far we have assumed that the price of the output is constant. That this assumption bears directly on the analysis is immediately obvious from Eq. (9–2), which indicates that MRP depends directly on P^X. This means, in effect, that the firm faces a whole family of MRP functions—one function for each possible value of P^X.

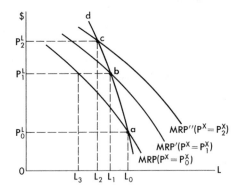

Figure 9–6

Figure 9–6 shows a few members of such a family. It is assumed that

$$P_0^X < P_1^X < P_2^X.$$

Here we see that an increase in P^X shifts the MRP function to the right. The reason for this is that when P^X increases, the value of MRP at any level of L also increases. If changes in input prices are closely associated with changes in output prices, more than just one MRP function may be relevant to the firm's adjustment. Suppose, for example, that initially the prices are P_0^L and P_0^X, respectively; then the firm uses L_0 units of L. Let us assume that the price of L increases to P_1^L. Then, if P^X remains at P_0^X, the firm cuts its use of L to L_3. But since a reduction in L also implies a lower level of output, it may be reasonable to assume that the fall in output (which, when summed over all the firms producing output X, may be considerable) will in turn bring about an increase in the price of the output. The increase in P^X then shifts the MRP function to the right, so that the firm will react again by increasing its use of L accordingly. When these adjustments work themselves out, the final situation may be as depicted in Fig. 9–6; that is, $P^L = P_1^L$, $P^X = P_1^X$, and $L = L_1$. Similarly, if the price of L rises to P_2^L, P^X may finally rise to P_2^X, and L may fall to L_2. A curve which constitutes the locus of all such points as a, b, and c in Fig. 9–6 may be referred to as the **effective** demand function for input L. Of course, if one wants to assume that the price of the output remains constant, then the demand function consists only of the one relevant MRP function.

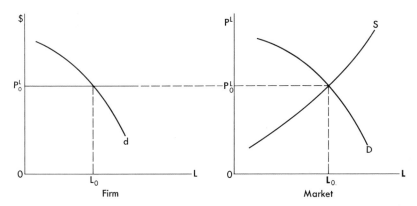

Figure 9–7

To obtain the **market** demand function for L one simply "sums" the demand functions of all the firms in the market. (See Section 5–3 with respect to the "summation" procedure.) This summation may be applied to either the partial or the effective demand functions, depending on the nature of the analysis for which the market demand function is needed. But it must be remembered that if one sums the partial demand functions, then the market demand function consists of a family of curves, each curve referring to a particular level of the product price. The market demand function and the market supply function determine the price of L, as well as the total amount of L employed. Figure 9–7 depicts the market in an equilibrium position. The curves D and S represent the market demand and supply functions, respectively. The market price is P_0^L, at which the representative firm employs L_0 units of L, while the entire market takes L_0 units.

9-2 THE TWO-INPUT CASE

Our next task is to generalize the analysis to cases in which the firm uses more than one variable input. In our discussion we shall use the case of two variable inputs, which is sufficiently general to illustrate most of the problems one encounters when there is more than one variable input. Rather than starting from the very beginning (which would involve a partial repetition of the preceding discussion), let us start with the following proposition: Each variable input should be employed at a level at which its price is equal to its MRP. This is, of course, what we have established in the preceding analysis for the one-input case, and now we are simply saying that this condition should hold for every variable input, regardless of the number of inputs used. This means, for example, that if the MRP of one input is greater than the price of that input, then the firm can increase its profit by using more of that input, while leaving the amounts of other inputs constant. It is only when each input is used at a level at which its MRP equals its price that the firm maximizes its profit.

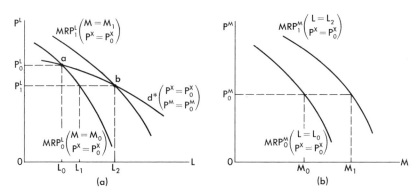

Figure 9-8

What makes the analysis of the two-input case somewhat more complicated is the fact that in general the two MRP's are interrelated. This interrelationship is illustrated in Fig. 9-8. The two inputs are L (labor) and M (machines), and their MRP functions are shown in parts (a) and (b), respectively. The notation in parentheses tells us that the MRP function of each input depends on the amount of the other input used, as well as on the price of the output. Initially the input prices are P_0^L and P_0^M, and the quantities are L_0 and M_0, respectively. Now assume that the price of P^L falls to P_1^L. Then, according to the diagram, the firm will find it profitable to increase the use of L from L_0 to L_1. While this is correct, it is not all there is to it. Because of the interrelationship mentioned above, we find that in general a change in the quantity of L used causes a shift in the MRP function of M; here it is assumed that MRP^M moves to the right. Such a shift means that the marginal product of M at any level of M increases as more of L is being used. This is, of course, a purely technological phenomenon, and in this particular example we might say that the relationship between the two inputs is **complementary,** in the sense that higher amounts of one input tend to increase the marginal productivity of the other. This is roughly equivalent to saying that the two inputs "help" each other in the productive process. Whether this is the most prevalent relationship between inputs is, of course, a question which must be settled by empirical investigation. Certainly, from the theoretical point of view we have no *a priori* reasons to rule out other possibilities. Thus if the inputs are technologically **independent,** the MRP functions do not shift at all following a change in the level of any one input, whereas if inputs are **substitutes** for each other, the increased use of one input shifts the MRP functions of other inputs to the left.

In our example, then, the higher level of L causes MRP to shift to the right, as a result of which the firm increases its use of M as well. This, however, will in turn shift MRP^L to the right, so that L_1 is no longer the optimal rate of L. It will, therefore, be necessary to adjust the amounts of L and M until the price of each input is equal to the appropriate value of MRP. After the final adjustment is made, the firm uses L_2 units of L and M_1 units of M.

9–2.1 The shut-down condition

Another slight complication arises with respect to the determination of the shut-down point. For convenience, we shall establish this result with a number of simple algebraic operations. Essentially, what needs to be done is to compare total revenues with total variable cost. The firm will shut down if

$$TVIC > TRP \tag{9–19}$$

or if

$$P^L \cdot L + P^M \cdot M > TRP. \tag{9–20}$$

If we divide both sides of the last inequality by one of the inputs, say L, we get

$$P^L + \frac{P^M \cdot M}{L} > ARP^L. \tag{9–21}$$

Comparing this condition with the corresponding condition for the one-input case (condition 9B) we may observe that, as in the one-input case, the firm will shut down whenever the price of some input exceeds the ARP of that input. For example, if $P^L > ARP^L$, then condition (9–21) holds, and the firm shuts down. But condition (9–21) also implies that the firm may have to shut down even if the price of some input is smaller than the ARP of that input. Thus if $P^L < ARP^L$, condition (9–21) may still hold if the term $(P^M \cdot M)/L$ is sufficiently large.

9–2.2 The rule for profit maximization

We can now state the rule for profit maximization, which takes the following form:

In order to maximize its profit the firm should choose levels of inputs L and M, call them $\bar{L}$ and $\bar{M}$, for which the following conditions hold:

$$(9C) \quad \begin{cases} MIC^L = MRP^L_{\bar{L},\bar{M}}; \\ MIC^M = MRP^M_{\bar{L},\bar{M}}; \end{cases}$$

$$(9D) \quad \begin{cases} MRP^L_{\bar{L},\bar{M}} \text{ is decreasing}; \\ MRP^M_{\bar{L},\bar{M}} \text{ is decreasing}; \end{cases}$$

$$(9E) \quad P^L \cdot \bar{L} + P^M \cdot \bar{M} \leq TRP_{\bar{L},\bar{M}}.$$

If conditions 9C and 9D hold, but 9E fails to hold, then $\bar{L} = \bar{M} = 0$.

It may be in order to restate our convention with respect to notation. Superscripts identify the product or input, as the case may be, while subscripts refer to the point at which the respective function is to be evaluated. For example, the notation $MRP^L_{\bar{L},\bar{M}}$ is designed to indicate that the marginal revenue product of L depends not only on the level of L used, but also on how much M is used. This means, of course, that the optimal levels of L and M must be determined simultaneously.

9–2.3 The input demand functions

Referring once more to Fig. 9–8, we see that the curve drawn through points a and b in part (a) of the diagram represents the firm's **partial** demand function for L; it shows the quantities of L which the firm demands at various levels of P^L, assuming that the amount of input M used is adjusted at the same time, so that the equality $P^M = MRP^M$ is always maintained, for some fixed P^M. Therefore, the two-input case differs from the one-input case, in that the partial demand function (the curve d* in Fig. 9–8) depends on the price of the output **and** the price of the other input.

The **effective** demand function in the two-input case can be derived in exactly the same way as in the one-input case. A graphical presentation of the effective

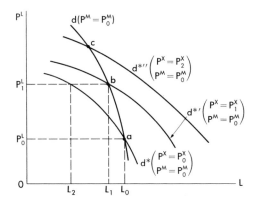

Figure 9–9

demand function for L is given in Fig. 9–9, but we omit any further discussion concerning its derivation, assuming that the reader, by referring to Fig. 9–6, and the explanation pertinent to it, will be able to reconstruct this exercise by himself. It should, however, be pointed out that the effective demand function for L depends on the price of M, and the effective demand function for M (which can be derived in a similar fashion) depends on P^L. Market demand functions can now be obtained for each input by "summing" either the partial or the effective demand functions of all firms in each market. This procedure is also identical to that demonstrated for the one-input case (Fig. 9–7), the only difference being that the market demand function for each input depends on the prices of all other inputs.

9–3 MONOPOLY IN THE PRODUCT MARKET

We now apply the analysis to a situation in which it is assumed that the firm sells its product under monopolistic conditions; for simplicity the seller is assumed to be a pure monopolist. The assumption about competition in the factor market, however, is retained. The assumption about the existence of monopoly in the product market requires certain modifications in the analysis, since unlike the competitive firm, the monopolist does not consider the price of the output as given.

9–3.1   The revenue product functions

Starting with the one-input case, we present in Fig. 9–10 the relevant revenue and cost functions. This diagram differs from the one describing the competitive case (Fig. 9–2) in that the graph of the TRP function has a different shape. Although the definition of TRP remains unaltered, that is, $TRP = TP \cdot P^X$, the value of TRP changes as L is changed, not only because TP varies with L, but also

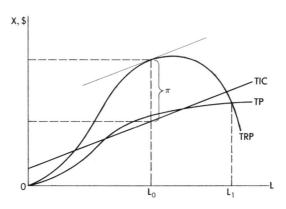

Figure 9–10

because different levels of L call for different prices of the output. If the monopolist faces a downward sloping demand function, he must lower the price of his output in order to sell more of it. Thus as L is increased, and a higher level of output produced, the price of the output falls, so that the value of each unit of output of successive units of L diminishes. It is, therefore, no longer true (as in the competitive case) that the vertical distance from the horizontal axis to the **TRP** function is some fixed multiple of the distance from the horizontal axis to the **TP** function; instead, the ratio of these distances becomes steadily smaller as L increases. It can be pointed out, as Fig. 9–10 indicates, that (a) for levels of L less than L_1, $P^X > 1$, (b) at L_1, $P^X = 1$, and (c) for levels of L beyond L_1, $P^X < 1$.

Let us also note that the slope of the **TRP** function, that is, **MRP**, is no longer equal to the marginal product multiplied by the price of the output (Eq. 9–2). We know that when the seller faces a downward sloping demand curve, the contribution to total revenues of the last unit of output is not equal to the price of the output, but to marginal revenue. Therefore, the contribution to total revenues of the last unit of the variable input is equal to the marginal product of the input times the contribution of the marginal product to total revenues, i.e., marginal revenue. In symbols, we have

$$MRP = MP \cdot MR. \tag{9–22}$$

Table 9–2 sheds more light on these relationships. Here we assume the same technological environment which underlies the example in Table 9–1, but instead of taking the output price as fixed, we assume that output price falls as output increases. The **MR** is computed by taking the increment in **TRP** and dividing it by the increment in output, i.e., the numbers in column 7 are equal to the numbers in column 6 divided by the numbers in column 3 in the corresponding row.

L	TP in units of X	MP in units of X	Px in $	TRP in $	MRP in $	MR in $
1	2	3	4	5	6	7
0	0		$5\frac{1}{2}$	0		
1	1	1	5	5	5	5
2	3	2	$4\frac{1}{2}$	$13\frac{1}{2}$	$8\frac{1}{2}$	$4\frac{1}{4}$
3	6	3	4	24	$10\frac{1}{2}$	$3\frac{1}{2}$
4	10	4	$3\frac{1}{2}$	35	11	$2\frac{3}{4}$
5	15	5	3	45	10	2
6	22	7	$2\frac{1}{2}$	55	10	$1\frac{3}{7}$
7	28	6	2	56	1	$\frac{1}{6}$
8	32	4	$1\frac{1}{2}$	48	-8	-2
9	34	2	1	34	-14	-7
10	35	1	$\frac{1}{2}$	$17\frac{1}{2}$	$-16\frac{1}{2}$	$-16\frac{1}{2}$

Table 9–2

The optimal level of L in Fig. 9–10 is found in the usual manner, i.e., at L_0, at which the slopes of TIC and TRP are equal. In fact, the rule for profit maximization is the same as for the competitive case (conditions 9A and 9B), and hence is not restated here.

9–3.2   The input demand function

Given an identical production function, and therefore an identical TP function, the MRP function of the monopolist
is steeper (in its falling range) than that
of the competitor, since as L increases
both MP and MR fall. In general, however, the MRP function's shape and relationship to the ARP function are of the
same form as the competitor's MRP function, as shown in Fig. 9–11. Of course,
since the monopolist's MRP function
already accounts for the change in
price which is necessary in order to sell

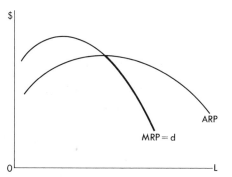

Figure 9–11

the greater output produced by higher levels of L, the monopolist's MRP function (below ARP) can be taken as his **effective** demand function for the input.
The construction of the market demand function proceeds as explained earlier
(Fig. 9–7): One simply "sums" the effective demand functions of all the firms
which purchase the input in question.

9–3.3 Two variable inputs

If the productive process requires more than one variable input, the monopolist must take into consideration the interrelationship between the inputs. Changes in the price of one variable input will therefore require a change in the other inputs as well. The effects of a change in P^L in a two-input case are shown in Fig. 9–12. The diagram is presented without any further explanation, since any comment would be merely a repetition of the discussion pertaining to Fig. 9–8. It should, however, be observed that the curve joining points a and b in part (a) of the diagram (curve d) represents the monopolist's **effective** demand function for L, and unlike the function d* in Fig. 9–8, it accounts for the appropriate changes in the price of the output. The effective demand function of each input does, however, depend on the price of the other input. The rule for profit maximization is the same as that given in Section 9–2.2.

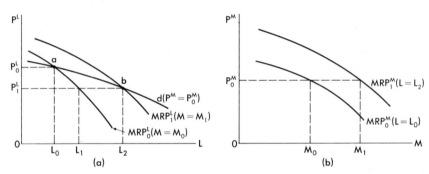

Figure 9–12

9–4 THE LONG RUN

Since all the examples discussed so far in this chapter have included some fixed inputs, they were obviously concerned with short-run situations. In the long run all inputs, including the size of the plant, are variable. The analysis of the long run is, therefore, identical to the multi-input case with zero fixed inputs. For instance, Figs. 9–4 and 9–10 can be modified to represent long-run situations simply by shifting the TIC function vertically downward until its intercept coincides with the origin (since in the long run TIC = TVIC). None of the other diagrams require any alterations, and Section 9–2.2 also applies to the long run.

9–5 A COMPARISON BETWEEN THE COMPETITOR AND THE MONOPOLIST

A final comment on the comparative performances of the monopolist and the competitor. This question was discussed in Chapter 7, where it was pointed out that since the monopolist, unlike the competitor, always chooses an output for which $P^X > MC$ (condition 7K), the monopolist, in some sense, produces a "restricted" output (end of Section 7–4.3). Since the present analysis makes no direct reference to the firm's MC, the difference between monopoly and competition must be given a slightly different interpretation.

We have seen that in either case the price of the input is equated with the MRP of the input, but whereas under competition MRP equals the MP of the input times the **price of the product,** in the case of monopoly MRP is equal to the MP of the input times the **marginal revenue of the product.** This difference may be interpreted as follows: When competition prevails among sellers, each variable input is paid the market value of its marginal product (that is, $MP \cdot P^X$); whereas if sellers are monopolists, inputs are paid less than the market value of their marginal product (since $MR < P^X$). It can easily be shown that this is inconsistent with an optimal allocation of resources.

Suppose that the market price for input L is P_0^L, and that each seller sells its product at the price P_0^X. Then we have for the competitor

$$P_0^L = MP_c^L \cdot P_0^X,$$ (9–23)

and for the monopolist

$$P_0^L = MP_m^L \cdot MR.$$ (9–24)

The subscript attached to MP^L denotes the type of industry. It is obvious that since $P_0^X > MR$, then $MP_m^L > MP_c^L$. This means that the monopolist operates at a level at which the marginal product of L is higher than it is in the competitive industry. Now if one unit of L were shifted from the competitive industry to the monopolistic one, then, since $MP_m^L > MP_c^L$, the increase in the monopolist's output is greater than the decrease in the output of the competitive industry. Since at the margin the two products sell for the same price, the reallocation yields a net increase in welfare, given the assumption (made in Section 7–4.3) that the market price can be taken as a measure of the subjective value of the last unit sold for the purchaser of the good in question.

SUMMARY

This chapter has approached profit maximization from the point of view of the firm's demand for inputs, rather than its choice of output; it has examined the decision-making process of a producer in his role of buyer rather than seller. Throughout the chapter we have assumed that competition prevails among buyers of inputs.

We have emphasized that rather than posing a new problem, the analysis in this chapter has provided an alternative method for solving the same general type of question to which answers were provided in preceding chapters. The equivalence of the two methods was demonstrated more formally by showing that the decision rules derived by the two methods imply and are implied by each other.

The analysis of the various cases was developed in such a way as to show how profit maximization generates the firm's demand functions for factors of production, which, in turn, are the bases for constructing market demand functions. This was done for the one-input, as well as the multi-input, case.

In the second part of the chapter the analysis was modified to fit situations of mixed environments, i.e., cases in which the firm purchases inputs under competitive conditions, yet occupies the position of a monopolist with respect to the sale of its output. Finally, we presented an alternative interpretation of the proposition that monopolists tend to produce a "restricted" output.

SELECTED REFERENCES

HIRSCHLEIFER, J., "An Exposition of the Equilibrium of the Firm: Symmetry Between Product and Factor Analyses." *Economica*, New Series **29**, 1962, pp. 263–268.

ROBINSON, J., *The Economics of Imperfect Competition*. London: Macmillan, 1933, Chapter 21.

EXERCISES

1. Figure E9–1 shows product, revenue product, and input cost functions of a purely competitive firm. The firm produces product X which, in the short run, requires one variable input; i.e., input L. Complete the sentences given below.
   (a) The current market price of product X is $_____.
   (b) The MRP of 5 units of L is equal to $_____, and the MP at that level of L equals _____.
   (c) When the price of L is $10, the firm purchases _____ units of L, and produces _____ units of X. Under these conditions it earns a profit of $_____.

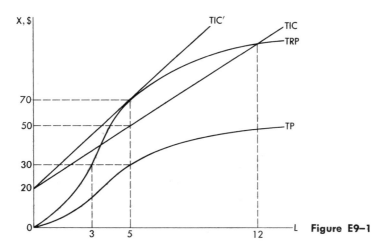

Figure E9-1

(d) When the firm uses 3 units of L, the ARP of L is equal to $_____, and output equals _____ units.

(e) When the price of L is $6, the firm uses (5, 12, *between 5 and 12*) units of L, and its profit is ($20, *less than $20, more than $20*).

(f) The shut-down price of L is ($10, *less than $10, greater than $10*).

(g) If the prices of X and L are both equal to $1, then the firm will (*shut down, continue to produce*), and its profit will be ($−20, $0, *more than $0*).

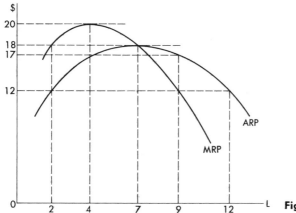

Figure E9-2

2. Figure E9-2 shows the revenue product functions of a purely competitive firm using the variable input L and a number of fixed inputs. Complete the sentences given below.

(a) If the price of L is $12, the firm purchases _____ units of L. Its profit will be ($45, *less than $45, more than $45*).

(b) If the price of product X is $2, and the firm uses 7 units of L, then its output is equal to _____ units.

(c) When the price of X rises (*the* ARP *function shifts upward, the* MRP *function shifts upward, both* ARP *and* MRP *shift upward*). Thus, given the price of L, an increase in the price of X leads to (*an increase, a decrease, no change*) in the use of L.

(d) The shut-down price of L is $_____.

(e) If the firm's TFC is $30, the break-even price of L is (*less than* $12, $12, *between* $12 *and* $18, $18).

(f) If the price of X is $1, then the MP of 2 units of L is _____.

L	TP in units of X	MP in units of X	p^X in $	TRP in $	MRP in $	ARP in $	MR in $
0	0						
1	2						
2		4					
3			19		105		
4				340			
5						87	
6	38						
7		6			9		
8			10				
9				475			
10					$-3\frac{1}{4}$		

Table E9–1

3. Table E9–1 is designed to show various product and revenue functions of a monopolist, i.e., a firm which *sells* in a monopolistic market. It faces a market demand function having the following specifications: (i) When the price is $22, quantity demanded is zero. (ii) Whenever the price falls (rises) by one dollar, quantity demanded increases (decreases) by 4 units.

(a) Complete Table E9–1 to make it consistent with the inserted values. Make sure that the equation MRP = MP · MR holds.

(b) How many units of L will the firm purchase if the price of L is $43? What is its profit?

(c) What are the answers to (b) above if the price of L is (i) $90? (ii) $5?

10

THE DEMAND FOR
FACTORS OF PRODUCTION:
PURE MONOPSONY

This chapter is a continuation of Chapter 9. Here, as there, we wish to construct the firm's demand for factors of production, but here we shall assume a different type of economic environment. Chapter 9 dealt with firms grouped into two classes according to their behavior as sellers; i.e., competitors and monopolists. With respect to their role as buyers, however, all firms were assumed to operate under conditions of competition. Consequently, in their decision-making the firms were assumed to take **input prices** as given. In the present chapter we shall consider situations in which the firm is the sole buyer of the input. A market which consists of a single buyer is called **pure monopsony.** The reader should realize that input markets may in general be classified in a fashion similar to the way product markets are classified. Thus one can speak about **oligopsony**—a market with few buyers—as well as **monopsonistic competition**—a market with a large number of buyers who purchase related, but differentiated, inputs. Because the analysis of these different cases is very much like that of the corresponding structures in product markets, we shall confine the discussion in this chapter to markets with only one buyer.

10–1 THE ONE-INPUT CASE

When a firm purchases the entire quantity of an input in a certain market, it must in general expect the price of the input to vary with the quantity purchased. The relationship between price and quantity sold depends, of course, on the conditions under which the input is produced, or supplied, and is represented by the supply function of the input, which, like a product supply function, is normally an increasing function. This means that if the firm wishes to increase its purchases of the input, it will have to pay a higher price per unit of input, and the opposite holds for decreases in purchases. It follows, therefore, that total input cost is no longer a linear function.

10–1.1   The input cost function

The input cost curves are shown in Fig. 10–1, where it is also assumed that the firm **sells** in a competitive market, and that it uses only one variable input. The TP curve is omitted. The curvature of the cost curves implies that the price of L increases with the level of L. For instance, at the level L_0 the price of L (that is, AVIC) is equal to the slope of the ray 0e (that is, the ratio $\overline{eL_0}/\overline{0L_0}$). At higher levels of L the slope of the ray from the origin to the appropriate point on the TVIC function is greater than at L_0. Thus at L_1 the price of L is represented by the slope of the ray 0f which is obviously steeper than that of the ray 0e. The optimal level of L is L_0, at which the slopes of the TIC and TRP functions are equal. At that level of the input we have TVIC = c, TIC = c + b, TRP = d, and $\pi = d - (c + b)$.

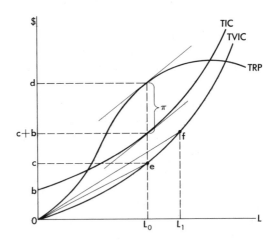

Figure 10–1

When the supply function of the input shifts, the TVIC and TIC functions rotate around their intercepts. For instance, a shift which amounts to a decrease in supply (i.e., a shift to the left) means that the firm has to pay a higher price for any given amount of L. Therefore TVIC and TIC are higher for any level of output, so that in this case TVIC and TIC rotate counterclockwise. Of course, if such rotation causes TVIC to lie entirely above TRP, the firm will not produce at all. The break-even situation occurs when at the optimal level of L, TVIC = TRP, as is illustrated in Fig. 10–2.

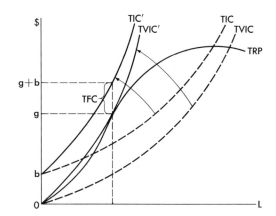

Figure 10–2

10–1.2 The rule for profit maximization

It thus seems that, except for the curvature of the **TVIC** and **TIC** functions, the description of the monopsonist's decision-making process is identical to that of a firm which purchases its inputs under competitive conditions. We can, therefore, summarize this process in the form of a maximization rule like the one stated in conditions 9A and 9B. Almost, that is. There exists a slight difference between the two cases which is illustrated in Fig. 10–3. The optimal level of **L** in that example is L_0, at which the slopes of **TIC** and **TRP** are equal. It is not true, however, that at that point the slope of **TRP** (that is, MRP) is decreasing. The diagram shows that as **L** is increased slightly beyond L_0, the slopes of both functions increase, but it is equally evident that **TIC** is rising faster than **TRP**. Thus at the optimal level of input **MRP** may increase, but it must do so at a lower rate than **MIC** (the slope of **TIC**). Hence the maximization

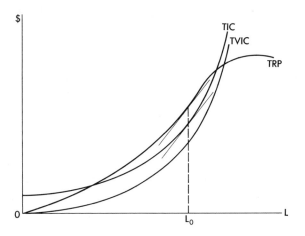

Figure 10–3

rule reads as follows:

> In order to maximize his profit the monopsonist should choose a level of input L, call it $\bar{L}$, for which the following conditions hold.
>
> (10A) $MIC_{\bar{L}} = MRP_{\bar{L}}$;
>
> (10B) $MIC_{\bar{L}}$ increases faster than $MRP_{\bar{L}}$;
>
> (10C) $AVIC_{\bar{L}} \leq ARP_{\bar{L}}$.
>
> If conditions 10A and 10B hold, but 10C fails to hold, then $\bar{L} = 0$.

The above rule is more general than that given in Chapter 9, and applies to both monopsony and competition.

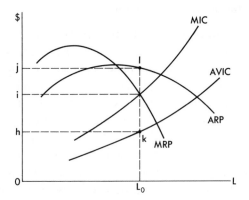

Figure 10–4

Next, in Fig. 10–4, we present the analysis with the help of average and marginal functions. The curve labeled **AVIC** is the market supply function of L; it shows the prices the buyer has to pay for various quantities of L. From the point of view of the monopsonist it represents his **AVIC** function, since the price of the input is equal to the cost per unit of L incurred by the buyer. The curve **MIC** shows the monopsonist's marginal outlays for additional units of L, and it is related to **AVIC** in the way which characterizes the relationship between any marginal and average curves. (See Section 2–3.) At the optimal level of input, L_0, we observe the following: **TRP** is represented by the area $0jlL_0$, **TVIC** is represented by the area $0hkL_0$, and "gross" profit (profit before fixed cost) by the area $hjlk$.

It must be remembered that the quantity of L purchased by the monopsonist represents the entire market demand for that input, and hence there exist no market demand functions as such, as in the case of competitive buyers. However, the quantity of L demanded by the monopsonist under any given supply conditions depends also on the price of the **output,** since the latter determines the position of the firm's MRP function. (See Fig. 9–6.)

10–1.3   A comparison between the competitor and the monopsonist

In the preceding chapter we made a comparison between the performances of the monopolist and the pure competitor from the point of view of the optimal allocation of resources (Section 9–5). A similar comparison can be made between a monopsonist and a firm which purchases inputs under competitive conditions. For simplicity, we shall use a one-input example, and assume that both firms sell an identical product in a purely competitive market. Then, for the firm which purchases its input competitively, we have

$$P^L = MP_c^L \cdot P^X \tag{10–1}$$

where P^L and P^X are the market input and output prices, respectively, and the subscript which is attached to MP^L identifies the type of industry. Now the monopsonist also chooses his level of output so that $MIC^L = MRP^L$, but the price he pays for the input is less than MRP. For example, Fig. 10–4 shows that at the optimal level of L, L_0, the price of the input is h dollars, while MRP is equal to i dollars. If we assume that the monopsonist happens to purchase a level of L for which he pays the same price as the competitor, that is, P^L, then we have for the monopsonist

$$P^L < MP_m^L \cdot P^X. \tag{10–2}$$

It follows, therefore [comparing Eq. (10–1) with inequality (10–2)], that $MP_m^L > MP_c^L$, and hence it can be shown that a reallocation of some amount of the input from the competitive firm to the monopsonist results in an increase in welfare (see explanation in Section 9–5). Thus a misallocation of resources may occur as a result of the existence of either monopoly or monopsony.

10–2   THE TWO–INPUT CASE

When there is more than one variable input, the monopsonist equates MIC with MRP for each input. But since in general the MRP functions of the various inputs are interrelated, the choice of inputs must be made simultaneously, to assure that MIC is equated with the correct MRP function. The optimal choice for a two-input case is shown in Fig. 10–5. The optimal quantities demanded are L_0 and M_0, respectively. It has also been assumed in the above example that the supply functions of the two inputs are independent of each other; if, say, a shift takes place in the supply curve of L, thus shifting the $AVIC^L$ func-

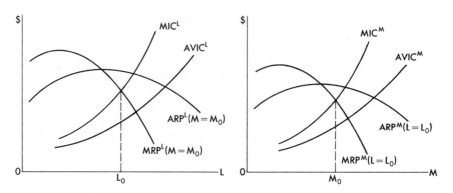

Figure 10–5

tion, this in itself will not affect the position of the supply function of M, that is, $AVIC^M$. This assumption has been made to simplify the analysis, but it certainly need not always be so, especially if the inputs are supplied by the same seller. It may also be pointed out that the present analysis requires no material alteration if the reader wishes to assume that the producer is a monopsonist with respect to one input, and a competitor with respect to another. In that case, one of his $AVIC$ functions has a positive slope, like those in Fig. 10–5, while the other is a horizontal line as shown in Fig. 9–5. The two-input case is summarized in the following maximization rule:

In order to maximize his profit the monopsonist should choose levels of inputs L and M, call them $\bar{L}$ and $\bar{M}$, for which the following conditions hold.

$$(10D) \quad \begin{cases} MIC^L_{\bar{L}} = MRP^L_{\bar{L},\bar{M}}; \\ MIC^M_{\bar{M}} = MRP^M_{\bar{L},\bar{M}}; \end{cases}$$

$$(10E) \quad \begin{cases} MIC^L_{\bar{L}} \text{ increases faster than } MRP^L_{\bar{L},\bar{M}}; \\ MIC^M_{\bar{M}} \text{ increases faster than } MRP^M_{\bar{L},\bar{M}}; \end{cases}$$

$(10F) \quad AVIC^L_{\bar{L}} \cdot \bar{L} + AVIC^M_{\bar{M}} \cdot \bar{M} \leq TRP_{\bar{L},\bar{M}}.$

If conditions 10D and 10E hold, but 10F fails to hold, then $\bar{L} = \bar{M} = 0$.

Although we assumed at the beginning of the chapter that the monopsonist sells his output under competitive conditions, the above rule applies equally well to a monopsonist who is the only seller in the product market. If the monopsonist is a monopolist so far as his output is concerned, then the analysis is affected only with respect to the shape of the producer's MRP function, (see Section 9–3.2), but this modification in no way undermines the validity of the above optimality rule.

10–3 PRICE DISCRIMINATION

The reader may recall that in the discussion of decision-making under conditions of pure monopoly (Chapter 7) it was shown that when the monopolist sells in two separate markets, he may under certain circumstances set a different price in each market for the identical product. A similar situation may arise when a monopsonist purchases an identical input in two separate markets. For the purpose of explaining such behavior we may think for a moment of the amounts of the input purchased in each market as different inputs. Then we know (from the rule for profit maximization just stated) that the amounts of each input used must be such as to satisfy the condition MIC = MRP for each input. Now if the inputs supplied by the two markets are in fact identical, then it follows that they have identical MRP functions. If so, the monopsonist will allocate his purchases between the two markets in such a way as to equate the MIC of the quantity purchased in each market. The problem is illustrated in Fig. 10–6.

Quantities of L from Market 1 are measured from the origin **to the left,** and those from Market 2 are measured in the customary fashion. To simplify the exposition it is assumed that the input supply functions, and hence the MIC functions, are linear. We assume that the monopsonist wishes to purchase a total quantity of input L equal to $L_0^1 + L_0^2$. This amount can be bought for **b** dollars per unit, at which price Market 1 supplies L_0^1 units and Market 2 supplies L_0^2 units. However, if the monopsonist distributes his purchases in this fashion, we find that $MIC^1 = d < MIC^2 = f$. In this case he can increase his profit

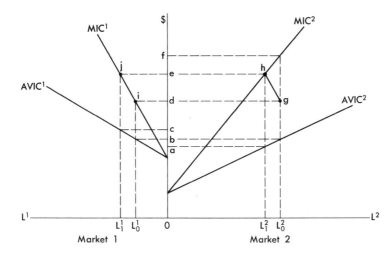

Figure 10–6

from the same total amount of input by a slight reallocation of his purchases. The optimal purchase distribution can be found as follows: Through point **g** (where the segment gL_0^2 represents MIC^1 at the level L_0^1, that is, $\overline{gL_0^2} = \overline{iL_0^1}$) a line is drawn parallel to MIC^1 to intercept MIC^2 at **h**. Since ijhg is a parallelogram, it follows that the segments ig and jh, respectively, are of equal length. Hence the quantity $L_1^1 + L_1^2$ equals the quantity $L_0^1 + L_0^2$. In order to purchase the amounts L_1^1 and L_1^2, the monopsonist pays **c** dollars in Market 1 and **a** dollars in Market 2, and $MIC^1 = MIC^2 = $ **e**. Such a reallocation enables the monopsonist to obtain the same total amount of L (and hence the same level of output) at a lower total cost. Symbolically this means $(L_0^1 + L_0^2) \cdot b > L_1^1 \cdot c + L_1^2 \cdot a$. The proof of this last statement (which the reader may want to furnish himself) follows along lines similar to those used in the proof of the rationality of price discrimination in product markets (Fig. 7–13 and explanatory material).

10–3.1 Optimal prices and levels of inputs

To determine the optimal total amount of the input as well as the allocation of purchases between the two markets, the supply functions of the two markets are drawn on one diagram, as shown in Fig. 10–7. The "summation" of the average and marginal cost functions of the two markets are given by the AVIC and MIC functions, respectively. Thus the total market supply function of L consists of the segment ze and the line labeled AVIC; the marginal input cost

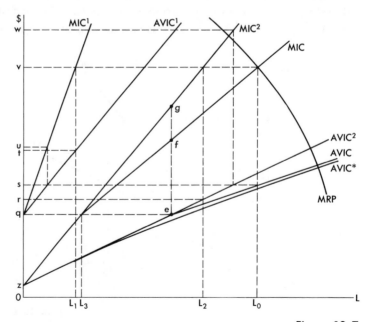

Figure 10–7

function of the total market supply function (which is slightly different from the "summation" of MIC^1 and MIC^2) consists of the segment zg and the segment of the line labeled MIC to the right of point f. (See the discussion in Section 7–3.1.) If the monopsonist were to regard the two markets as one, he would choose the amount L_0 (at which $MIC = MRP$), and pay s dollars per unit. But at that price the MIC's in the two markets are not equal, since

$$MIC^1 = u < MIC^2 = w.$$

To maximize his profit the monopsonist should allocate his purchases to satisfy the condition $MRP = MIC^1 = MIC^2$. The latter is satisfied at $MIC = MRP = v$. Therefore the monopsonist purchases L_1 units in Market 1 at t dollars per unit, and L_2 in Market 2 at r dollars per unit. The function AVIC* shows the average cost of the monopsonist's total purchases if he practices discrimination; it is the counterpart of the AR* function in Fig. 7–15. The discriminating monopsonist may, therefore, be thought of as facing one single input market, the supply function of which is given by AVIC*. It should also be clear that if MRP intersects MIC at a level of input less than L_3, then the entire quantity is purchased in Market 2.

The maximization rule for the discriminating monopsonist can be stated as follows:

In order to maximize his profit the discriminating monopsonist should choose levels of input from each market, call them L^1 and L^2, for which the following conditions hold.

(10G) $MIC^1_{L^1} = MIC^2_{L^2} = MRP_{(L^1+L^2)};$

(10H) $\begin{cases} MIC^1_{L^1} \text{ increases faster than } MRP_{(L^1+L^2)}; \\ MIC^2_{L^2} \text{ increases faster than } MRP_{(L^1+L^2)}; \end{cases}$

(10I) $AVIC^1_{L^1} \cdot L^1 + AVIC^2_{L^2} \cdot L^2 \leq TRP_{(L^1+L^2)}.$

If conditions 10G and 10H hold, but 10I fails to hold, then $L^1 = L^2 = 0$.

10–4   BILATERAL MONOPOLY

In our discussion we have covered so far the four main types of buyer-seller combinations in which a firm may find itself: In Chapter 9 the firm was assumed to purchase inputs under competitive conditions, while selling its output either as a competitor or as a monopolist; in the present chapter we have been examining monopsonistic buying, and both competitive and monopolistic selling. There remains one special case which deserves our attention: a situation in which a monopsonist purchases its input from a monopolist. Such a case is known as **bilateral monopoly.** It differs from the examples discussed hitherto in that each side of the market is represented by one single party. Under these circumstances the operation of the market is reduced to a direct confrontation between buyer and seller, and the price is established as a result of bilateral bargaining. In spite of this, bilateral monopoly can still be fitted into the analytical framework we have developed, inasmuch as both buyer and seller are assumed to be motivated in their bargaining by the desire to maximize profit.

10–4.1   The monopsonist's point of view

Let us first assume that the monopsonist has complete information about the cost conditions under which the monopolist operates; in other words, the monopsonist possesses the information shown in Fig. 10–8. These functions are labeled ATC and MC (rather than AVIC and MIC) because from the point of view of the monopolist, commodity L is an output, not an input. Thus ATC simply shows the total unit cost of producing various levels of L, and MC shows the increment to the monopolist's total cost of additional units of L. Now the best bargain which the monopsonist can possibly obtain from the monopolist without driving the latter out of business is to pay a price for L so low as to leave the monopolist no profit. This would be the case if he could purchase various amounts of L at cost value; or put differently, if he could force the monopolist to behave as though ATC were his supply function.

10–4.2   The monopolist's point of view

The monopolist, however, is in a similar position in his relation to the monopsonist. He is assumed to have information about the contribution of various amounts of L to the revenues of the monopsonist, so that his view of the

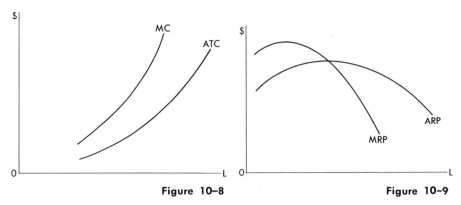

Figure 10–8   Figure 10–9

monopsonist's position is as shown in Fig. 10–9. The monopolist's best bargain is to charge a price which exacts the entire revenue product of each unit of L sold, i.e., to force the monopsonist to behave as if ARP were his demand function.

10–4.3 The solution

It is obviously impossible for both buyer and seller to obtain their best bargain at the same time, since their objectives, so far as the price is concerned, are in direct conflict. The situation is described in Fig. 10–10. If the monopsonist could have it his way, he would be in a position to purchase various quantities of L at prices indicated by ATC. In this case ATC is his AVIC, MC becomes his MIC function, and he chooses to purchase L_0 units of L at a dollars a unit. If, on the other hand, the monopolist prevails, he faces demand conditions as shown by the ARP function, while MRP becomes his MR function. He therefore chooses to sell L_0 units at b dollars a unit. It is thus clear that the confrontation between monopsonist and monopolist leads to a common choice of quantity to be exchanged (L_0) but the price at which the transaction takes place cannot be determined by the analysis. What we can say is that the price must fall somewhere between a and b dollars, but its exact level depends on the relative bargaining skill of the two transactors. The model, however, provides no information about this aspect of the problem.

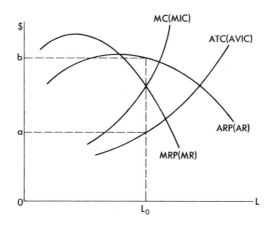

Figure 10–10

It is interesting to note that if the buyer and/or seller departed from his strategy of trying to drive the hardest bargain, the quantity exchanged would be smaller than L_0. Suppose that the monopolist were to behave like a competitor in the sense that he would take any bid from the monopsonist as a given price, and in response offer a quantity for sale which, at the stated price, maximized his profit. In that case the monopolist's MC function is also his supply function,

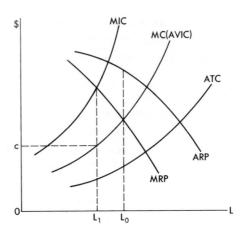

Figure 10–11

which indicates the price the monopsonist must pay for various amounts of L. Therefore MC becomes the monopsonist's AVIC function, while his MIC function lies above the monopolist's MC function, as shown in Fig. 10–11. The monopsonist now chooses L_1 as his optimal level, which he purchases at c dollars per unit. A similar result obtains if the monopsonist chooses to act like a competitor, or if both do so.*

10–5 PRICE CONTROL

In Chapter 7 it was shown how price control can be applied to regulate the actions of a monopolist. A similar application may arise in monopsonistic markets. When it comes to regulating a monopsonist, price control takes the form of a **price floor.** The purpose of the floor is to guarantee the seller of the input a minimum price for his product, and hence is normally set at a level which is higher than what the monopsonist pays in the absence of any control. The effect of the imposition of a price floor is shown with the aid of Fig. 10–12.

The monopsonist faces the supply curve AVIC, and hence in the absence of control he purchases L_0 units of L at a dollars per unit. Suppose that the price floor is set at b dollars. Then for levels of L between zero and L_1 the monopsonist takes the price of L as given. For levels of L greater than L_1 he must pay higher prices, as indicated by the AVIC function; hence in that range the price floor has no effect on the monopsonist's behavior. The monopsonist, therefore, faces a supply function consisting of the segments bq and the portion of AVIC above q, while his MIC function consists of the segment bq and the portion of

---

* Bilateral monopoly may also arise in a market for a final good when the good is sold by a single seller and purchased by a single consumer.

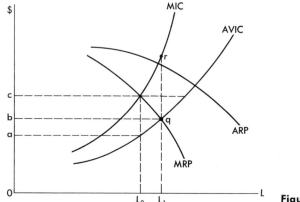

Figure 10–12

MIC above point **r**.   Under these circumstances the monopsonist chooses L_1 as his optimal level of L, since at that point MIC = MRP.   If the floor is set between **a** and **b**, the monopsonist purchases an amount between L_0 and L_1, and MRP crosses the discontinuity in the MIC function. (See discussion of the effects of a price ceiling, Section 7–5.1.)   If the floor is set between **b** and **c**, the monopsonist again chooses an amount between L_0 and L_1, while for floors above **c** the amounts purchased are less than what the monopsonist purchases in the absence of any control, that is, L_0.   It is, therefore, clear that the monopsonist purchases the largest amount of L when the floor is set at **b** dollars.   It may also be pointed out that for price floors above **b** the amount of L offered for sale exceeds quantity demanded.   As in the similar case of an excessively low price ceiling in a product market (Section 7–5.1), such a situation may bring about the emergence of a "black" market.   In the present example the excess supply is likely to induce sellers to offer their output at a price below the legal floor, in which case the objective of the imposition of the price floor is defeated.

SUMMARY

This chapter concludes the discussion on the demand for factors of production.   It has been devoted to markets in which the entire supply of input is purchased by one single buyer.   The analysis has made use of the same tools as Chapter 9, but in general the results have been different.   In particular, this chapter has shown that the monopsonist, unlike the competitive buyer, always purchases a quantity of the input at which MRP exceeds the price which he is paying. It was shown that, like the divergence between price and marginal cost which characterizes monopoly output, a divergence between MRP and input price results in a less-than-optimal allocation of resources.

The monopsonist, like the monopolist, may have occasion to practice price discrimination. This amounts to paying different prices for the identical input, and it requires, as in price discrimination in product markets, that the various markets be effectively separated. When the monopsonist is confronted in the market with a single seller, the normal market mechanism breaks down, and it is replaced by a process of bilateral bargaining. The model used in the text for this case indicates that, while the outcome with respect to the quantity to be exchanged can be determined, the price level remains uncertain.

Finally, it was shown how a monopsonist may be regulated by means of price control. The effects of such control are usually to raise the price in the market, and if the price floor is not set at an excessively high level, such price control may also increase the amount of the input purchased.

SELECTED REFERENCES

FELLNER, W., "Prices and Wages under Bilateral Monopoly." *Quarterly Journal of Economics* **61**, 1947, pp. 503–532.

FOLDES, L., "A Determinate Model of Bilateral Monopoly." *Economica*, New Series **31**, 1964, pp. 117–131.

ROBINSON, J., *The Economics of Imperfect Competition*. London: Macmillan, 1933, Chapters 18 and 19.

EXERCISES

1. Figure E10–1 shows the TIC and TRP functions of a firm which is the only buyer of input L, but which sells its output X under purely competitive conditions. Complete the sentences given below.
   (a) When the monopsonist purchases 30 units of L he pays $_____ per unit. In that case his profit equals $_____.

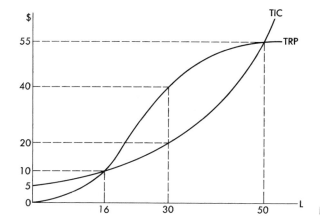

Figure E10-1

(b) The break-even level of L is _____. At that level the price of L is $_____.

(c) The optimal level of L is between _____ and _____ units.

(d) A decrease in the supply of L will cause (*an upward shift in* TIC, *a downward shift in* TIC, *an upward shift in* TRP).

(e) When the monopsonist is in a position in which he finds it necessary to shut down, (TIC *and* TRP *are tangent to each other*, TIC *lies entirely above* TRP, *his profit is zero*).

(f) When the price of product X falls, the monopsonist's demand for L (*increases, decreases, remains unchanged*). This also causes (*an increase, a decrease, no change*) in profit.

(g) When TFC falls, the monopsonist's demand for L (*increases, decreases, remains unchanged*). This also causes (*an increase, a decrease, no change*) in profit.

2. Figure E10–2 shows the revenue and cost curves of a monopsonist who sells his product X in a competitive market. Complete the sentences on page 196.

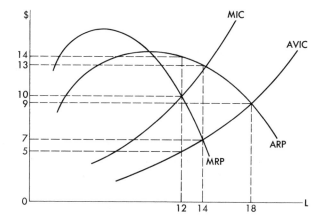

Figure E10-2

(a) The optimal level of L is _____, and the monopsonist's profit is less than $_____.

(b) At the optimal level of production the monopsonist pays to each unit of the input an amount (*greater than, smaller than, equal to*) the contribution of the last unit of input purchased to the monopsonist's revenues. At the same time it is correct to say that the return to each unit of the input is (*greater than, smaller than, equal to*) the average contribution of each unit of the input to the monopsonist's revenues.

(c) If the above firm were one of many buyers in the market for L rather than a monopsonist, then the answers to (b) above would be: (i) (first sentence) _____, (ii) (second sentence) _____.

(d) If the price of X falls, the monopsonist will (*increase, decrease*) his purchases of L, and at the same time will pay a (*higher, lower*) price per unit of the input.

(e) If the monopsonist is restricted in his actions by a form of price control which does not permit him to pay less than $7 per unit of L, then he will purchase a quantity of L which is (*greater than, smaller than, the same as*) the quantity he purchases in the absence of any price control.

(f) If the price floor is set at $9, the monopsonist purchases (18, *between* 12 *and* 14, *less than* 12) units of L.

(g) The effect of the imposition of an excise tax on each unit of product X can be shown in Fig. E10–2 by (*an upward shift in* ARP *and* MRP, *a downward shift in* ARP *and* MRP, *a downward shift in* AVIC *and* MIC). Thus the effect of the tax is to (*increase, decrease*) the production of X.

(h) Suppose that the monopsonist uses two variable inputs: L and M. Then if the two inputs are *substitutes* as far as technology is concerned, a decrease in the supply of M will induce the monopsonist to use (*more, less*) of M, and consequently the MRP function of input L will shift (*upward, downward*).

3. A monopsonist has the choice of purchasing input L in two separate markets. The conditions under which the input is supplied in each market are as follows. *Market* 1: (i) The supply function of L has a $-intercept at $12. (ii) The slope of the supply function equals one. *Market* 2: (i) The supply function of L has a $-intercept at $4. (ii) Same as (ii) for Market 1.

(a) Plot on one diagram the AVIC and MIC functions for each market, and label them accordingly. (It is a good idea to use a different color for each market.)

(b) Construct (on the same diagram) the total supply function of L facing the monopsonist, and the corresponding MIC function.

Assume that at 18 units of L, MRP = $26 (and that at that level of L, ARP > MRP).

(c) What is the monopsonist's total demand for L if he considers both markets as one? How much is he purchasing in each market, and at what price?

(d) What is the (numerical) difference between MIC^1 and MIC^2 under the conditions stated in (c) above?

(e) On the basis of your answer to (d) above, in what direction would the monopsonist redistribute his purchases if he decided to adopt a discriminatory policy?

(f) Determine the quantity of L which the monopsonist should purchase in each
market, and the prices he should pay, if he wants to practice discrimination?

(g) Since price discrimination calls for equating the MIC in each market with
MRP, the return to every unit of L purchased under conditions of discrimination
is equal to its marginal contribution to the monopsonist's revenues. This
last statement is generally (*true, false*).

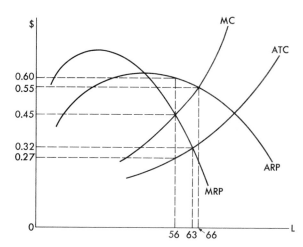

Figure E10–3

4. The functions ATC and MC in Fig. E10–3 represent the cost conditions under which
a monopolist produces the product L. The ARP and MRP are the revenue functions
of a monopsonist who uses L as an input in his production process. Complete
the sentences given below.

(a) When the seller and the buyer get together to bargain about the terms of trade,
the monopolist will aim at selling _____ units of L at $_____ per unit.

(b) The monopsonist, on the other hand, will attempt to pay no more than
$_____ per unit, at which price he would want to purchase _____ units.

(c) Although Fig. E10–3 does not provide enough information for one to be able
to derive a conclusive solution, it is clear that the accepted price will lie between
$_____ and $_____. The amount of L exchanged will be _____ units.

(d) Suppose that the monopsonist (not realizing that he is the only buyer in the
market) acts like a competitor, and takes the price quoted by the monopolist
as given. Then the _____ function can be considered to be the monopsonist's
demand function.

(e) Draw into Fig. E10–3 the MR function which the monopolist is facing under
the conditions stated in (d) above. Indicate on the axes the price and the
quantity exchanged, respectively.

11

LINEAR
PROFIT MAXIMIZATION

While in most of the preceding chapters we have described the decision-making process of the firm under a variety of different economic environments (i.e., market structures), in the present chapter we shall consider a special type of technological environment, and the way in which it affects the firm's production plans. The nature of the technology assumed in this chapter, and the extent to which it departs from the kind of environment assumed in the earlier chapters, will become clear as the discussion gets under way. It may be pointed out, however, that the type of conditions which characterize this unique technology are frequently found in decision problems other than those arising in the theory of the firm. Problems which are subject to such conditions are solved by a special technique known as **linear programming** (so called because the relationships involved are linear).

11-1 THE PROPERTIES OF LINEAR PROCESSES

The analysis of problems which require the use of linear programming normally centers around the concept of a **process** (sometimes also referred to as an **activity**). A process is simply a specific method of carrying out some productive activity. In the context of the standard problems of the theory of the firm, a process refers to the quantities of inputs required to produce one unit of some output.

Figure 11-1 depicts a process for a productive activity using two inputs. The inputs are measured along the axes, and the ray 0A represents the process. The output is measured along the ray, starting at the origin. For example, if

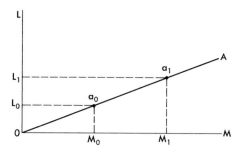

Figure 11–1

we denote the output by X, then according to the diagram it takes M_0 units of M and L_0 units of L to produce a_0 units of X. (Note that, although the diagram is two-dimensional, it handles three variables—two inputs and one output. The quantities of the output are denoted by a_0 and a_1, rather than, say, X_0 and X_1, in order to identify the process used.) The points on the process ray are also referred to as the **levels** of the process. Therefore we can say that in order to operate process A at the level a_0, the firm needs L_0 and M_0 units of the two inputs, respectively. A similar statement can be made with respect to the level a_1, and, indeed, any other point on the ray 0A. Thus every level of the process involves a particular level of output, and a particular set of quantities of inputs.

It is obvious, of course, that the higher the level of the output, the greater the amount of each input required. However, there is one property which all the levels of the process (except the zero level, i.e., the origin) have in common, and that is the fact that the **ratio** at which the inputs are used in the process is the same at all positive levels of output. This should be clear from Fig. 11–1. For example, at the level a_0 the input ratio is L_0/M_0, which can also be represented by the ratio of the segments $\overline{a_0M_0}/\overline{0M_0}$. The latter, however, is simply equal to the slope of the process ray. Similarly, at a_1 the input ratio is $L_1/M_1 = \overline{a_1M_1}/\overline{0M_1}$, which is also equal to the slope of the ray 0A. This proves that at any point on the ray 0A (except the origin) the ratio of the inputs used is equal to the slope of the ray, and hence they are all equal. Indeed, it is quite proper to **define** a process as a method of production in which all inputs are used in fixed proportions at all positive levels of output. It is because of this proportionality between the inputs that the graphical presentation of a process is a straight line through the origin.

11–1.1 The proportionality between inputs and output

A second important characteristic of these linear processes is the proportionality between the inputs and the output, which means that if all inputs are multiplied by some common factor, then the level of output will be multiplied by the same factor. Referring again to Fig. 11–1, let us suppose that initially the firm operates at the level a_0, and it decides to double its inputs. Then if $M_1 = 2M_0$ and $L_1 = 2L_0$, it follows that $a_1 = 2a_0$. (Note that if we assume that $M_1 = 2M_0$, we are no longer free to attach just any value to L_1, because by virtue of the definition of a process, L_1 **must** be equal to $2L_0$. Geometrically, since L_1/M_1 is equal to the slope of the ray 0A, and since the latter is also equal to L_0/M_0, then if $M_1 = 2M_0$, it necessarily follows that $L_1 = 2L_0$.)

This proportionality relation considerably simplifies the description of a process. For example, process A is completely described by **one point,** say a_0. To generate the entire process, or as much of it as is desired, we proceed in two steps: First we draw a line from the origin through point a_0 to obtain the process ray, such as 0A in Fig. 11-1. (Remember that a straight line is fully determined by two points. In the above example the two points are the origin and a_0.) The second step is to construct the proper output scale on the process ray. But from the proportionality relationship between the inputs and the output, it follows that the levels of output at different points on the process ray are proportional to their distances from the origin. For example, if $a_1 = 2a_0$, as shown above, then, by the law of similar triangles, it follows that the segment $0a_1$ is twice as long as the segment $0a_0$. Other points can be calibrated in the same way. For instance, to locate the level of output $a_0/3$, one simply measures off one-third of the distance between the origin and point a_0.

A process can also be described in nongeometrical terms. One such presentation consists of a triplet of numbers, as in Table 11-1. The first row of the

		X	L	M
1	(a_0)	80	50	20
2	(a_1)	160	100	40
3		120	75	30
4		40	25	10

Table 11-1

table contains the three numbers which describe point a_0—the level of the output and the levels of the inputs, respectively. Because of the proportionality between the inputs and the output, other points may be obtained by multiplying the numbers in row 1 by a suitable factor. For example, the numbers which define point a_1 are obtained by multiplying each number in row 1 by two. The numbers in the third row (obtained by multiplying row 1 by 1.5, or multiplying row 2 by 0.75) represent a point on ray 0A in Fig. 11-1 halfway between points a_0 and a_1, while those in the last row (obtained by multiplying row 1 by 0.5, or row 2 by 0.25, or row 3 by $\frac{1}{3}$) represent a point halfway between the origin and point a_0.

11–1.2   The relationship between different processes

While in any one process inputs are used in only one set of fixed proportions, a great many products can be produced by combining inputs in more than one ratio. In other words, the technological environment of the producer may consist of more than just one process. Figure 11–2 illustrates a set of two different processes, **A** and **B**. Since the slope of the ray 0B is steeper than that of the ray 0A, it is clear that the ratio of **L** to **M** which defines process **B** is greater than that of process **A**. For example, in order to absorb M_0 units of **M**, process **A** requires L_0 units of **L**, but process **B** requires a greater amount of **L**, namely L_1. If, for example, L and M stand for labor and machines, respectively, we could say that process **B** is more labor-intensive than process **A**, or conversely, that process **A** is more machine-intensive than process **B**.

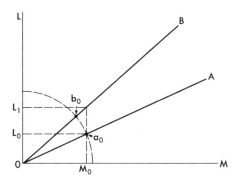

Figure 11–2

The general properties which characterize linear processes (i.e., fixed input proportions) and the proportionality between inputs and output hold, of course, for all processes. But one property which different processes need not necessarily have in common is the output scale. What this means is that points on different processes which are equidistant from the origin (i.e., lie on a circle centered at the origin), such as points a_0 and b_0 in Fig. 11–2, need not (although they may) represent the same quantity of output. Thus, although all processes share the same input scales, each has its own output scale.

11–1.3   Isoquants

It is generally possible, however, to find levels on each process ray which represent equal levels of output. In Fig. 11–3, it is assumed that levels a_1 and b_1 represent an equal amount of output **X**. A straight line connecting such points, such as the line segment a_1b_1, is called an **isoquant.** We have already encountered isoquants in Chapter 3, but because of the unique properties of linear processes, the isoquants of linear processes do not have quite the same

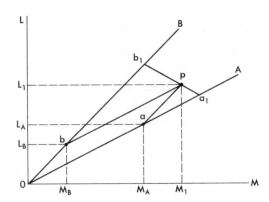

Figure 11–3

meaning as those derived from the more general type of production relation. A line such as a_1b_1 is said to be an isoquant in the sense that any arbitrary point on a_1b_1 represents a **combination of processes A and B** which produces a quantity of X equal to a_1 ($=b_1$).

Take the arbitrary point **p** on isoquant a_1b_1. Now the existence of point **p** does **not** mean that there exists a third process which can be described by a ray from the origin through point **p**, because by assumption the firm is faced with only processes A and B. In other words, it is assumed in the above example that the technology to which the firm has access admits of only two input mixes—the input ratios as given by the slopes of rays 0A and 0B, respectively, but not the input mix which is represented by the coordinates of point **p**. Point **p** simply represents two levels of activities, a certain level of process A and a certain level of process B, the combined output of which yields a_1 units of X. These levels can be found by drawing two lines through point **p**—one parallel to ray 0A, intercepting 0B at **b**, and one parallel to 0B, intercepting 0A at **a**. Thus the statement made above can be stated symbolically as follows: $a + b = a_1$, or equivalently, $a + b = b_1$. The proof of this is quite simple, although it is omitted here; it makes use of the basic properties of linear processes, as well as the fact that the triangles $0b_1a_1$ and apa_1 (or bb_1p) are similar triangles.

The coordinates of point **p**, L_1 and M_1, also play a role in the analysis; they represent the total input requirement of the two inputs, respectively, for the particular process combination associated with point **p**. In the example given in Fig. 11–3, for instance, the requirements for input M are M_A for process A operated at the level **a**, and M_B for process B operated at the level **b**. Similarly, we can see that the requirements for L are L_A and L_B for the two processes, respectively, and that the coordinates of **p** indicate the total requirements for each of them. Symbolically we have: $M_1 = M_A + B_B$ and $L_1 = L_A + L_B$. These equations can also be proved by direct reference to Fig. 11–3, using the law of similar triangles.

The properties of point **p** as stated above carry over to other points on the isoquant; indeed, **every** point on the isoquant can be given a similar interpretation. (Note, for example, that everything which has been said about point **p** holds, although trivially, for the points a_1 and b_1, which also belong to the isoquant.) Since there are infinitely many points on the isoquant, we can conclude that even though the firm can operate only two technically distinct processes, it has in fact a choice of infinitely many **process combinations** to choose from. Of course, the firm may be able to produce its output by using one of several (i.e., more than two) processes, but a basic feature of problems involving linear processes is the assumption that the number of processes available at any time is **finite.**

11–1.4   Linear processes and the "traditional" environment

At this point it may be instructive to try to compare the nature of the technological environment underlying linear processes with the "traditional" environment of the type described in Chapter 3. For this purpose we have drawn, in Fig. 11–4, a traditional isoquant of the kind shown in Fig. 3–4 and three processes: **A**, **B**, and **C**. For simplicity we assume that the isoquant cuts the three process rays at points of equal output; more precisely, it is assumed that $X_0 = a = b = c$. Now, if the linear technology prevails, then the firm can combine the inputs **L** and **M** in only three ratios, as indicated by the slopes of the three process rays, respectively. Hence in order to produce X_0 units of **X** the firm could choose to operate process **A** at the level a, process **B** at the level b, process **C** at the level c, or combinations of any two processes of which, as was mentioned earlier, there exist infinitely many. Under the conditions of the traditional technology, on the other hand, the output X_0 can be produced by all input combinations which are represented by a point on the isoquant.

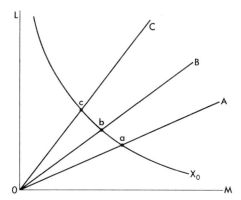

Figure 11–4

Furthermore, each point on the isoquant represents a **unique** input ratio. This is to say, if one selects any two distinct points on the isoquant, and then draws rays from the origin to these points, the two rays must have different slopes. Now, since there are infinitely many points on each isoquant, it follows that the firm can combine inputs in infinitely many ratios. Since a process can be identified with a unique input ratio we could think of the traditional technology as one in which the firm can choose from among infinitely many processes. The linear technology, in which the firm can operate only a finite number of processes, can therefore be considered a special case of the more general traditional technology, and we see also that as the number of available processes increases, the conditions of the linear technology approximate those which characterize the traditional technology.

However, one property of linear processes not normally found to hold in the traditional technology is the proportionality between the inputs and the output. When the firm faces a technology which is not of the linear type, it normally operates in a range in which an increase in all inputs by a certain percentage yields an increase in output by a smaller percentage. One reason for the development of the linear programming technique was the fact that the traditional method for solving problems of profit maximization fails to work under the conditions of linear processes.

11–1.5   Isoquants and inferior processes and process combinations

Returning now to the discussion of isoquants in the linear technology, suppose that we wish to find a second isoquant, say for the level of output a_2. Assuming that the isoquant for output a_1 is given, and that we have already located the point a_2 on the ray 0A, as shown in Fig. 11–5, then the rest, i.e., the locating of point b_2, is quite easy. We remember that the various levels on each process ray are proportional to their distances from the origin (Section 11–1.1). This

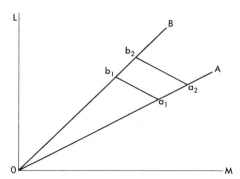

Figure 11–5

means that

$$\frac{a_2}{a_1} = \frac{\overline{Oa_2}}{\overline{Oa_1}}, \tag{11–1}$$

where the left-hand side of the equation is the ratio of the two levels, and the right-hand side is the ratio of their respective distances from the origin. Similarly, for process **B** we can state

$$\frac{b_2}{b_1} = \frac{\overline{Ob_2}}{\overline{Ob_1}}. \tag{11–2}$$

Now since $b_2 = a_2$, and $b_1 = a_1$, it follows (from Eqs. 11–1 and 11–2) that

$$\frac{\overline{Oa_2}}{\overline{Oa_1}} = \frac{\overline{Ob_2}}{\overline{Ob_1}}. \tag{11–3}$$

And now we make use once more of the law of similar triangles. The relevant triangles in this case are Ob_1a_1 and Ob_2a_2. The latter, according to Eq. (11–3), are similar triangles, from which it follows that the lines a_1b_1 and a_2b_2 are parallel. Thus we have shown that in the linear technology isoquants are represented by a set of parallel lines.

Next we extend our example somewhat (Fig. 11–6) by considering a case with three different processes and a number of selected isoquants. For any level of (positive) output there exist as many isoquants as there are pairs of distinct processes; in the following example there are three isoquants for each level of output. For the level of output a, the isoquants are the line segments ab, bc, and ac. This means, in fact, that the level of output in question

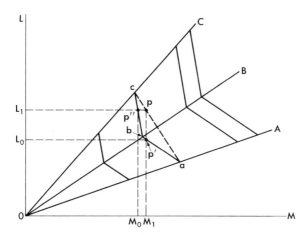

Figure 11–6

(that is, $a = b = c$) can be produced by any one of the following methods:

        (a) by using only process A;
        (b) by using only process B;
        (c) by using only process C;
        (d) by using some combination of processes A and B;
        (e) by using some combination of processes B and C;
        (f) by using some combination of processes A and C.

Inferior process combination.   The reader may have noted the fact that the isoquant between processes A and C is shown as a dashed line. This has been done in order to set it apart from the other two isoquants. Consider, for instance, points p and p'. Since each of these points is located on an isoquant for output a, each represents a particular process combination which yields a units of X. These combinations are not shown in the diagram, but we know that point p represents a combination of processes A and C, and p' represents a combination of processes A and B. Furthermore, recalling that the coordinates of points on an isoquant represent the total input requirements for the particular process combination (Fig. 11–3 and related discussion), it is clear that the combination associated with point p uses "more" inputs than the combination associated with point p'. Specifically, while both combinations use M_1 units of M, the combination of processes A and C requires more units of L, i.e., L_1 instead of L_0. It is, therefore, obvious that regardless of any other considerations that might affect the firm's choice of process combination, to use the combination associated with the point p would be wasteful, because by using instead the combination associated with point p' the firm can obtain the same level of output with a smaller quantity of L.

A similar comparison of points p and p'' shows that, by choosing the combination of processes B and C associated with point p'', the firm can produce a units of X with the same amount of L as that used by the combination associated with point p, that is, L_1, but only M_0 units of M instead of M_1. Also, combinations of processes A and B represented by points on the isoquant ab above point p', as well as combinations of processes B and C represented by points on the isoquant bc below point p'', yield a units of X with smaller amounts of **both** inputs as compared with the amounts used by the combination represented by point p.

Comparisons of this type can, of course, be made with every point on the isoquant ac, and each case produces similar conclusions. These can be stated as follows: **For each combination of processes A and C represented by a point on isoquant ac except the points a and c there exists at least one combination of either processes A and B or processes B and C which yields the same level of**

output with "fewer" inputs. In other words, combinations of processes A and B or B and C are more efficient than those involving processes A and C. In these circumstances process combinations involving processes A and C are said to be **inferior.** Since in the context of economic problems (i.e., problems involving scarcity of resources) a more efficient solution is always preferred to a less efficient one, isoquants representing inferior process combinations can be excluded from the analysis.

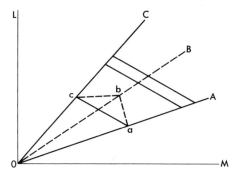

Figure 11–7

Inferior processes. Next, consider a somewhat different set of processes and isoquants, as shown in Fig. 11–7. As in the previous example, for each level of output one can draw three isoquants. Applying again the argument made in the preceding paragraph, we shall find that all combinations of processes A and B, as well as those involving processes B and C, are inferior. That is, the combinations of processes A and C are more efficient than any other combination. But if inferior combinations are never chosen, then it follows that process B will never be used (as only combinations of processes A and C are noninferior). In that case process B is said to be **inferior,** and like inferior process combination, it can be excluded from the analysis.

11–2 OUTPUT MAXIMIZATION

We are now ready to pose and analyze a typical decision problem. Let us take the problem of output maximization under certain financial restrictions. This problem has already been discussed once before in the context of a traditional environment (Section 3–2.2). In such a problem one seeks to determine the highest level of output that the firm can produce when its funds for inputs are limited. We assume the availability of four processes, as shown in Fig. 11–8. Note that none of the processes or process combinations shown in the diagram are inferior. That is, isoquants representing inferior process combinations are omitted, and all inferior processes, if there were such initially, have been

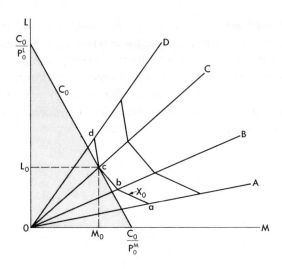

Figure 11–8

removed. It is assumed that the firm's input budget is C_0 dollars, and hence if the firm takes input prices as given, the isocost function is a straight line. When the firm is restricted by certain constraints, as in the above example, it is customary to refer to the region enclosed by the isocost and the two axes (including the isocost itself, and the appropriate segments of the axes) as the **feasible set** (shown in Fig. 11–8 as the shaded triangle). The rest of Fig. 11–8 is referred to as the **unfeasible set,** since points in the latter involve input combinations which cannot be purchased with the sum of money indicated by the isocost. The mechanism for solving the problem can therefore be thought of as finding a point in the feasible set whose output is as great as possible. In the above example this occurs at point **c** which lies on the isoquant for X_0 units of X. In these circumstances the output X_0 is obtained by operating process C at the level **c**.*

11–2.1 Changes in input prices

Changes in input prices normally affect the firm's use of inputs. For the purpose of the present analysis we shall consider a special kind of price change: We shall assume that **both** input prices change slightly, so that the new isocost line for C_0 continues to pass through point **c**. This could happen, for example,

---

* As with nonlinear isoquants, the label X_0 indicates the level of output associated with the isoquant; the latter consists in this example of the three segments **ab**, **bc**, and **cd**. Since points on the process rays also denote levels of output, we have $X_0 = a = b = c = d$.

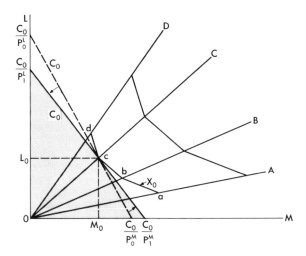

Figure 11–9

if the price of L increased slightly, while that of M decreased by a small amount.* The new isocost for C_0 dollars is shown in Fig. 11–9, which also reproduces the initial isocost as a dashed line. It is quite clear that this price change leads to no change in the firm's production plan; the firm can still produce X_0 units of X, and it will continue to do so by operating process C at the level c, using L_0 and M_0 units of the two inputs, respectively. This rigidity in the firm's production program is obviously due to the nature of the linear technology, and especially the kinked isoquants. It is in sharp contrast with the conditions of the traditional environment. If, for example, a similar change in input prices is assumed in the example in Fig. 3–10, so that the isocost C_1 in that diagram is rotated slightly around point q, then the firm will increase its output by some amount (because the isocost will form a tangency point with a higher isoquant) and, at the same time, the firm will use a different combination of inputs from that used previously.

A somewhat different result is obtained if prices are assumed to change in the same fashion as in Fig. 11–9, but by a greater magnitude, so that isocost C_0 is made to coincide with segment cb of isoquant X_0, as in Fig. 11–10. The firm can still produce X_0 units of X by operating process C at the level c, but that particular method is no longer the only choice available. It can equally well operate process B at the level b or various combinations of processes B and C.

---

* More precisely, the isoquant C_0 will pass through point c so long as the ratio of the absolute values of the changes in prices is proportional to the amounts of inputs used at c; that is, if $-\Delta P^L/\Delta P^M = M_0/L_0$.

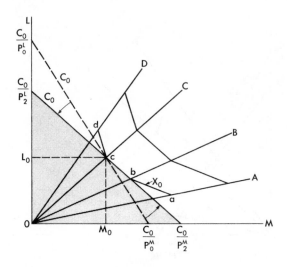

Figure 11–10

In this case the firm may use different amounts of inputs, but since the entire segment **cb** of isoquant X_0 coincides with the isocost C_0, any combination of inputs required for operating any one of the combinations of processes **B** and **C** is purchasable with C_0 dollars. Here we have an example in which the problem has more than one solution; it has, in fact, infinitely many solutions. If the isocost continues to rotate a bit more around point **c** in the same direction as in the preceding examples, then the firm will be able to produce more than X_0 units of **X**, and it will use process **B** in place of **C**. The example is illustrated in Fig. 11–11.

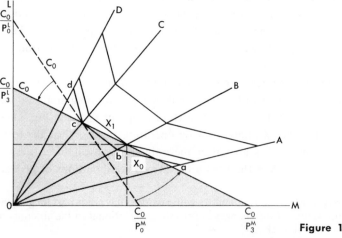

Figure 11–11

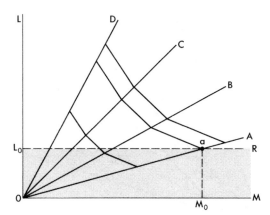

Figure 11–12

11–2.2   Restrictions on inputs

In certain circumstances the firm's choice of process and inputs may be restricted not by budgetary factors but by the availability of the inputs themselves. Such a case is shown in Fig. 11–12. It is assumed that the amount of input L is restricted to L_0 units per period of time. Hence the area below the restriction line L_0R, and the line itself, represent the feasible set, while the region above the line constitutes the unfeasible set. If the firm wishes to maximize its output, it must find a point in the feasible set which yields the highest possible output. This happens to be point a on process A, at which the firm uses all the available amount of L, and M_0 units of M.

A similar situation arises when the availability of input M is limited. In that case the feasible set consists of the restriction line M_0R and the region to the left of the line, as shown in Fig. 11–13. Output is maximized with process D

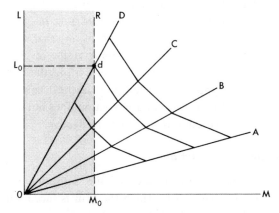

Figure 11–13

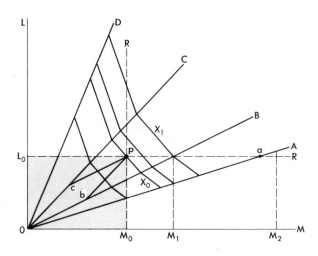

Figure 11–14

operated at level **d**, the respective amounts of the inputs being L_0 and M_0. Note that in the above two examples (Figs. 11–12 and 11–13) the highest level of output is obtained by operating that process which is **least intensive** in the **limited** input, or equivalently, the process which is **most intensive** in the **unlimited** input.

The most general case is that in which all inputs are limited in supply. For a two-input environment the situation is depicted in Fig. 11–14. The inputs are limited to L_0 and M_0, respectively, so that the feasible set is made up of the rectangle $0L_0pM_0$, including the boundary lines. The highest level of output in the feasible set is represented by point **p** on isoquant X_0. The latter is produced by a combination of processes **B** and **C** operated at the levels **b** and **c**, respectively. With this process combination the firm uses all the available amounts of the two inputs. Note that if the available amount of **M** were M_2, the firm's optimal choice would not be affected by the restriction on **M**; that is, the firm would obtain maximum output by operating process **A** at the level **a**, regardless of whether input **M** were restricted to M_2, or were altogether unrestricted. In this case the restriction of input **L** completely governs the firm's choice of production method. Whenever the removal of a restriction does not affect the optimal choice of processes, the restriction is said to be **ineffective.**

11–2.3   The nature of the solution

Let us indicate certain characteristics of the solutions to the problems examined so far. In the problem in which the firm is faced with a budgetary restriction (Figs. 11–8 through 11–11), every solution involves only one process, except in the special case shown in Fig. 11–10, in which the firm has a choice of various combinations of two processes represented by points on the line segment bc. But even in that case one single process (either B or C) can by itself produce the same level of output. In the problems in which one of the inputs is in limited supply (Figs. 11–12 and 11–13), every solution consists again of only one process.

In Fig. 11–14 there are two restrictions, one on each input, and the solution requires a combination of two processes. Two restrictions, however, need not always lead to such a combination; had the available amount of M been M_1 instead of M_0, the firm, by using process B exclusively, would have been able to produce X_1 units of X. These results are examples of the following general rule, which also holds for cases involving more than two inputs: **The number of processes (activities) in the optimal solution need never be greater than the number of effective restrictions imposed on the problem.**

11–3   PROFIT MAXIMIZATION

In the context of the theory of the firm the typical decision problem is, of course, one of profit maximization. True, to maximize output is sometimes the same as to maximize profit, but this is certainly not so if the firm produces more than one output, in which case output maximization is a meaningless objective. We shall now consider an example of a firm which wishes to maximize profit from the production of four different products. It is assumed that each

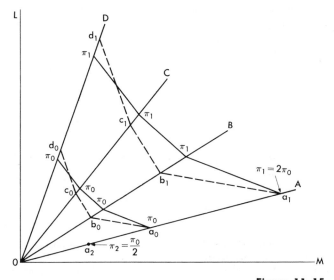

Figure 11–15

product requires the two inputs L and M, but each is produced by using these inputs in a different proportion; in other words, the production methods of these products—A, B, C, and D—are represented by four distinct processes, as shown in Fig. 11-15.

11-3.1   Profit scales and isoprofit lines

The first step toward solving this problem is to construct a profit scale on each process ray. If the firm operates under competitive conditions, and takes all prices as given, then the computation of the profit associated with various levels of output is extremely simple, as is demonstrated in Table 11-2 for product (process) A. The technological information i.e., the relationship between the inputs and the output, is given in columns 1, 3, and 5. The level of TR is obtained by multiplying the numbers in column 1 by the price of the output, assumed to be $2; the total cost of input L (TIC^L) is obtained by multiplying the numbers in column 3 by the price of L, assumed to be $1; the total cost of input M (TIC^M) is obtained by multiplying the numbers in column 5 by the price of M, assumed to be $0.50; TIC is obtained by adding the numbers in columns 4 and 6; and profit, by subtracting the numbers in column 7 from those in column 2.*

The reader may observe that the numbers in the second row are equal to the numbers in the first row in the respective columns multiplied by two, and those in the third row are obtained by multiplying the number in the first row by one-half. From this we can conclude that the proportionality property discussed earlier holds not only between inputs and output, but between any combination of the variables included in the above table. In particular, we see that profit is directly proportional to the level of output. Therefore, in order to construct a profit scale, it is necessary to compute the profit for only one arbitrarily

	X	TR $p^X = \$2$	L	TIC^L $p^L = \$1$	M	TIC^M $p^M = \$0.5$	TIC	π
	1	2	3	4	5	6	7	8
a_0	80	160	50	50	20	10	60	100
a_1	160	320	100	100	40	20	120	200
a_2	40	80	25	25	10	5	30	50

Table 11-2

* Naturally, to the extent that the production process also makes use of fixed factors, the firm will incur some fixed cost. In that case the above definition refers to gross, rather than net, profit. However, since the fixed cost is fixed, to maximize short-run gross profit is the same as to maximize net profit.

chosen level of output (other than zero), since the points which represent profit levels, like those for output levels, are proportional to their distances from the origin.

Thus let us suppose that we have computed the level of profit associated with the level of output a_0 (80), and have attached the proper label (π_0) to that point on the diagram, then the point on the ray 0A which produces $2\pi_0$ dollars of profit can be found by traveling on the ray 0A twice as far as the distance between the origin and the point π_0, and so on. The same procedure is, of course, applied to every one of the four products, so that once the construction of the profit scales is completed, points of equal profit can be joined by straight lines, such as the solid lines in Fig. 11–15. These lines are called **isoprofit lines.** Because of the proportionality relationships it is clear that isoprofit lines, like isoquants, form a set of parallel lines, but it should be noted that in general isoprofit lines do not coincide with isoquants. This is clearly shown in Fig. 11–15, in which the isoquants for output levels a_0 and a_1, respectively, are represented as dashed lines.

Since profit from any one product is proportional to the level of output, it is clear that profit can always be increased by increasing the level of output of any product, or any product combination. Formally this means that no level of profit, regardless of how high, is a maximum, and hence the problem has no solution. To make it a more realistic problem, it is customary to assume that the firm faces certain restrictions, such as a budget constraint or a limited supply of inputs. Then the problem can be solved by the same method that was used earlier in the problem of output maximization.

Profit maximization under conditions of limited inputs is illustrated with the aid of Fig. 11–16. The feasible set consists of the rectangle $0L_0pM_0$, and the highest isoprofit line in that set is the one passing through point **p**. Hence π_0

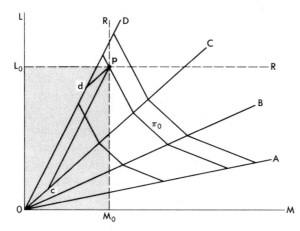

Figure 11–16

is the highest level of profit attainable, and the optimal production plan calls for operating process C at the level c and process D at the level d. Although each process in this example represents a different product, from the analytical point of view it may be convenient to think of **profit** as the final output, and to regard each process (product) as merely one method of producing profit. Then it is obvious that the above problem is formally identical with the problem of output maximization discussed earlier.

11–3.2   More than two inputs

In all the preceding examples it was assumed that the products produced by the firm require only two inputs. This assumption was made, of course, in order to make it possible to carry out the analysis with the help of fairly simple two-dimensional diagrams. In certain problems, however, it may be important, or interesting, to include more than two inputs, in which case one can use a different method of analysis. But so long as geometrical tools are used as the principal medium of analysis, it is obvious that the total number of variables must be limited; consequently in the present approach we limit the number of products to two—A and B.

Products are now measured on the two axes shown in Fig. 11–17. For expository purposes it will help if at first we assume, temporarily, that both product A and product B require for their production just one input, say L. Then it is obvious that if the supply of L is limited, the levels of output that the firm can produce must also be limited. For example, Fig. 11–17 is to be interpreted in the following manner: If L_0 is the available amount of L, and all of it is put into the production of product A, then the level of output is A_0; if all the available amount of L is used exclusively for product B, then the level of output

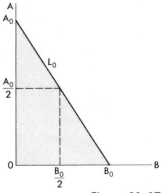

Figure 11–17

is B_0; and if the L_0 units of L are to be used for both products at the same time, then the firm can produce various combinations of products A and B, as indicated by the coordinates of the points on the line L_0.

One such combination, to give an example, is $A_0/2$ units of A and $B_0/2$ units of B. There is, of course, no explicit indication on the diagram of the amounts of L used for each level of output, but this is something which can be determined indirectly on the basis of the properties of linear processes. From the proportionality between inputs and output we know that if it takes L_0

units of L to produce A_0 units of A, it takes L_0/A_0 units of L to produce one unit of A. Hence to produce, for example, $A_0/2$ units of A, the process requires $L_0/A_0 \cdot A_0/2 = L_0/2$ units of L. Thus to produce the combination $A_0/2$ of A and $B_0/2$ of B, the L_0 units of L are divided equally between the two products. For the same reason it is also possible to say that had the available amount of L been $L_0/2$, the restriction (or iso-input) line would have intercepted the two axes at $A_0/2$ and $B_0/2$, respectively.

It should be clear that the restriction line indicates the **maximum** levels of output that can be produced with L_0 units of L. If the firm wishes, it can choose output combinations represented by points inside the triangle $0A_0B_0$, in which case it is not using all the available amount of L. The triangle $0A_0B_0$ (including the boundary lines) therefore represents the feasible set, while everything outside it belongs to the unfeasible set.

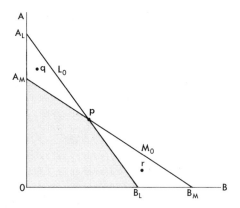

Figure 11–18

The analysis can now easily be extended to incorporate more than one input. With two inputs the situation may be described as in Fig. 11–18. The second input M is limited to M_0. The technological conditions implied by the diagram are the following: The input requirements for one unit of A are L_0/A_L units of L and M_0/A_M units of M, and one unit of B takes L_0/B_L units of L and M_0/B_M units of M. The feasible set consists of the polygon $0A_MpB_L$. This means, for instance, that points such as q and r are not within reach of the firm under the given conditions; point q represents a combination of products A and B which requires more of input M than is available, while the input requirement for the combination represented by point r exceeds the restriction on L.

Since the purpose of the present approach is to deal with cases in which the number of inputs is greater than two, we present next an example with four inputs—L, M, V, and W. The feasible set is now reduced to the polygon as shown

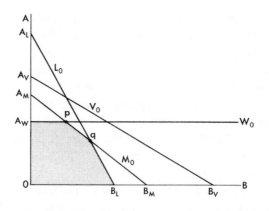

Figure 11–19

in Fig. 11–19. Note that the restriction on input V is ineffective, since it has no effect on the firm's choice; in other words, if it is removed, the feasible set remains unchanged. The fact that the restriction line of input W is horizontal implies that the production of product B makes no use of input W.

Isoprofit lines. In order to solve the profit maximization problem, we must again introduce profit scales; this time the scales are constructed on the axes. The computation of the profit at various levels of the output proceeds in a manner identical to that explained earlier (Section 11–3.1 and Table 11–2), and it is sufficient to compute only one level of profit for each product. Suppose that the profit for A_M units of A is found to be π_0 dollars, then from the proportionality between output and profit it follows that the output $A_M/2$ (halfway between the origin and A_M in Fig. 11–20) yields a profit of $\pi_0/2$ dollars, and so on. Once a profit scale is constructed for each product, points of equal profit can be joined by straight lines to form a family of isoprofit lines.

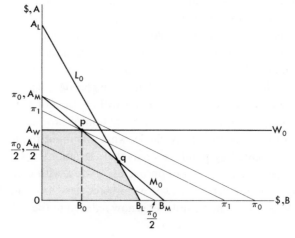

Figure 11–20

Three such isoprofit lines are shown in Fig. 11–20. Each point on the isoprofit line represents a combination of products whose combined profit is equal to the amount associated with the isoprofit line. The problem is solved by finding the highest isoprofit line in the feasible set. This turns out to be isoprofit line π_1, and hence the optimal output combination is A_W units of A and B_0 units of B. To produce that combination of outputs the firm uses the maximum amounts of inputs M and W available, but the amounts of inputs L and V used are less than their respective limits. The restriction line for input V is omitted since, as was shown earlier, the latter restriction is ineffective. It should be pointed out, however, that even though the firm is using less than L_0 units of L, the restriction on L is not ineffective, because its removal would change the feasible set. And if, for instance, the price of product B should rise enough to increase the steepness of the isoprofit lines, the firm may switch from the combination at p to that represented by point q, and thereby use all the L_0 units of L.

11–4 THE IMPUTED VALUE OF THE INPUTS

In situations in which certain inputs are limited in supply, it is interesting, and often of practical significance, to calculate the opportunity cost of these restrictions. More specifically, one may want to know, for example, by how much the firm could increase its profit if the amount of one limited input were to be increased by one unit.* In order to clarify this problem, let us look first at the single process shown in Fig. 11–21.

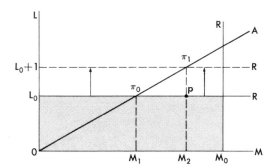

Figure 11–21

The two inputs are initially limited to L_0 and M_0, respectively. Under these conditions process A is operated at the profit level π_0 and the amounts of inputs used are L_0 and M_1, respectively. The availability of L is now increased by one

---

* A slightly different approach to this problem is to determine the *loss* in profit as the amount of one limited input is *decreased* by one unit.

unit to $L_0 + 1$. It is now possible for the firm to operate at a higher level, and to increase its profit to π_1. The increase in profit due to the fact that the availability of L has been increased by one unit, that is, $\pi_1 - \pi_0$, is called the **imputed value** of one unit of L, and we shall denote it by V^L. Note that the triangles $\pi_0\pi_1p$ and $0\pi_0M_1$ are similar triangles, so that $\overline{\pi_1p}/\overline{\pi_1\pi_0} = \overline{\pi_0M_1}/\overline{\pi_00}$. Using the corresponding numerical values instead of the line segments, this last equation can be written as $1/V^L = L_0/\pi_0$, and after suitable multiplications we get $L_0 \cdot V^L = \pi_0$. The left-hand side of this equation is the imputed value of the total amount of L used at the level π_0, and the right-hand side is the level of profit. Note also that the imputed value of one unit of M is zero, since the restriction on M is ineffective; consequently an increase in M has no effect on the firm's level of profit. Thus we can state: **At the optimal level of output the imputed value of the total amounts of inputs used is equal to the level of profit.**

▶ **The two-product case**

The above relationship holds in general, and not only for the special example of Fig. 11–21. We cannot, of course, prove it for the general case with geometrical tools, but the two-product case is still manageable, and it may be instructive to demonstrate it. The two processes are represented in Fig. 11–22, where the inputs are limited to L_0 and M_0, respectively, and the highest isoprofit line attainable is π_0. (The particular product combination associated with point p is not shown.) If the amount of L is increased by one unit, M being held constant at M_0, the firm can increase its profit to π_1 by producing the

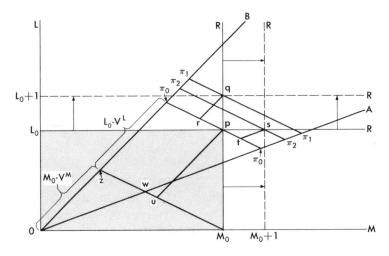

Figure 11–22

combination associated with point q. We now draw the following lines: a line through q parallel to 0B, intercepting isoprofit line π_0 at r; a line through M_0 parallel to isoprofit line π_0, intercepting 0A and 0B at w and z, respectively; and a line through p parallel to 0B, intercepting the segment M_0z at u. Then it follows that prq and M_0up are similar triangles. Thus we can write $\overline{pq}/\overline{rq} = \overline{M_0p}/\overline{up}$, and in terms of numerical values we get $1/V^L = L_0/(\pi_0 - z)$ (since up is parallel to 0B). By proper multiplications we then get $L_0 \cdot V^L = \pi_0 - z$, which is the imputed value of input L.

If input M is increased by one unit, holding input L at L_0, profit can be increased from π_0 to π_2 by producing the product combination associated with point s. A line is drawn through s parallel to 0A, intercepting isoprofit line π_0 at t. Then we get the following similar triangles: pst and $0wM_0$. Therefore $\overline{ps}/\overline{ts} = \overline{0M_0}/\overline{0w}$, and in numerical values $1/V^M = M_0/z$. (The profit level w equals z, since the line M_0z is drawn parallel to isoprofit line π_0, hence the segment wz is also an isoprofit line.) By suitable multiplication we get $M_0 \cdot V^M = z$. The imputed value of both inputs can now be obtained by addition; that is, $L_0 \cdot V^L + M_0 \cdot V^M = (\pi_0 - z) + z = \pi_0$, which is what we intended to show.

11–4.1   The dual

If the imputed values of one unit of the different inputs, that is, V^L and V^M in the two-input case, are considered as unknowns, then the value of the total imputed value function, i.e., the value of the function $L_0 \cdot V^L + M_0 \cdot V^M$, is also unknown. We can then formulate a problem in which we seek to assign numbers to V^L and V^M to **minimize** the total imputed value function, subject to certain limitations (which will not be stated here). This problem is known as the **dual** of the original profit maximization problem (the **primal**). The two problems are closely related, and, in fact, they share the same solution; that is, the maximum profit level (the solution to the primal) is equal to the minimum imputed value of the inputs (the solution to the dual). This relationship may be of practical value when, for instance, the solving of one of these problems gives rise to unusual difficulties; in that case one can obtain the value of the solution by solving the other problem instead.

SUMMARY

In this chapter we have examined the decision-making process of a firm when it operates under conditions of linear processes. In order to analyze problems with linear processes, we introduced a special technique which makes use of the concept of a process. Because of the various proportionality relationships which characterize a linear environment, a process can be described by a single point. Isoquants also play an important role in the analysis, but the isoquants in this analysis are slightly different from those which appear in the traditional models. In the course of the exposition we indicated the differences, as well as the affinities, between the traditional and the linear technology, and also suggested that linear processes can be thought of as a special case of the more general nonlinear technology. An optimization problem involving linear processes has, among other features, the following characteristics: (a) the problem has no solution (e.g., there exists no maximum level of profit) unless certain restrictions are imposed; (b) the solution is invariant to small changes in the parameters (e.g., changes in prices).

For problems with more than two inputs we introduced a somewhat different technique of analysis; however, this technique, while capable of accommodating more than two inputs, cannot handle more than two outputs. A slight disadvantage (from the instructional point of view) is that in this analytical method the underlying processes have no explicit geometrical representation.

Finally, we have shown how one may impute values to those inputs which are limited in supply. The imputed value of one unit of a limited input may be interpreted as the highest price the firm would be willing to pay to have the input increased by one unit. It was also shown that the total imputed value of all inputs is equal to the firm's maximum profit. The imputed values are also the unknown variables in the dual of the profit maximization problem.

SELECTED REFERENCES

BAUMOL, W. J., "Activity Analysis in One Lesson." *American Economic Review* **48**, 1958, pp. 837–873.

DORFMAN, R., "Mathematical, or 'Linear' Programming: A Nonmathematical Exposition." *American Economic Review* **43**, 1953, pp. 797–825.

MORTON, G., "Notes on Linear Programming." *Economica*, New Series **18**, 1951, pp. 397–411.

EXERCISES

1. Figure E11–1 shows three linear processes, A, B, and C, which a firm may make use of in the production of product X. Also shown are the three isoquants for the output level 48. The output of each process is proportional to the amounts of the inputs used. Complete the sentences given below.

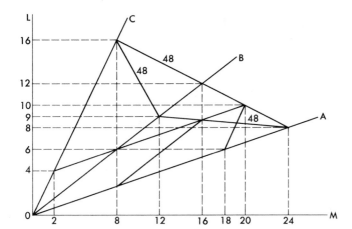

Figure E11–1

(a) The technological characteristics of each process can be specified as follows: (i) To produce one unit of X, process A requires _____ units of L and _____ units of M. (ii) To produce one unit of X process B requires _____ units of L and _____ units of M. (iii) To produce one unit of X, process C requires _____ units of L and _____ units of M.

(b) In view of (a) above, it is correct to say that process _____ is the most L-intensive of the three, and process _____ is the most M-intensive.

(c) If the firm cannot use more than 12 units of M (per period of time), its maximum level of X is _____.

(d) If the firm cannot use more than 10 units of L (per period of time), its maximum level of X is _____.

(e) If the input limits are 12 and 16 for L and M, respectively, the firm's maximum level of X is _____.

(f) If the firm operates process A at a level which requires 6 units of L and 18 units of M, and process C at a level which requires 4 units of L and 2 units of M, then the combined output of the two processes is equal to _____. Of these, _____ units are produced by process A, and _____ units by process C.

(g) The production plan given in (f) above may be described as (*optimal, inefficient*).

(h) The level of output which is obtained under the production plan stated in (f) above can also be produced by a different method; namely, operating processes A and B at levels at which each process uses 8 units of M. What is the output of each process?

(i) The production plan given in [(*f*), (*h*)] above is the better of the two.

2. A firm turns out two products, X and Y. Each is produced by a linear process Figure E11–2 shows the iso-input lines of the inputs in question, assuming that each input is limited to the amount indicated. Complete the sentences given below.

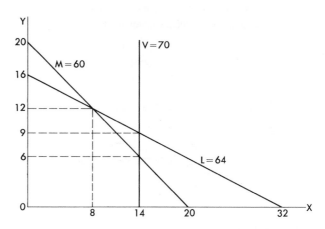

Figure E11–2

(a) The technological characteristics of each process can be specified as follows:
(i) The production of one unit of X requires _____ units of L, _____ units of M, and _____ units of V. (ii) The production of one unit of Y requires _____ units of L, _____ units of M, and _____ units of V.

(b) The maximum amount of X that the firm can produce equals _____ units.

(c) The maximum amount of Y that the firm can produce equals _____ units.

(d) The output bundle consisting of 14 units of X and 9 units of Y (*is, is not*) in the feasible set.

(e) If the firm produces 14 units of X and 6 units of Y, then it (*uses, is not using*) the maximum amount of each input available.

(f) If the available amount of input M were increased to 75, the answers to (b) and (c) above should be: (b) _____ units, (c) _____ units, and the answer to (d) above would be _____.

(g) If the available amount of L were equal to _____ units or more, the restriction on input L would be ineffective.

3. A manufacturer of kitchen utensils can produce four different products by using the following linear processes (specified in appropriate physical units):

Product	Output	Input L	Input M
Frying pans	2	3	6
Pots	1	1	1
Griddles	5	6	4
Coffee pots	1	3	1

The manufacturer is a pure competitor, and faces the following environmental conditions:

Product prices

Frying pans	$12.50 per unit
Pots	$ 6.00 per unit
Griddles	$ 6.00 per unit
Coffee pots	$13.00 per unit

Input prices

L	$3 per unit
M	$2 per unit

Input limitations

L: no more than 18 units per period of time
M: no more than 14 units per period of time

Assume that the firm wishes to maximize its profit in every period of time.

(a) How many units of each product should the firm produce?
(b) What is the firm's profit?
(c) Are there any inferior products (processes)? If so, which?
(d) What would be the answers to (a) and (b) above if the available amount of L were to decrease by 2 units, and that of M to increase by 2 units?
(e) What would be the answers to (a) and (b) above if the price of coffee pots were to increase to $15, and the firm were to be restricted to 15 units of each input?
(f) What is the imputed value of each input, respectively, under the environmental conditions stated in (e) above?

4. A pharmaceutical firm has facilities to produce aspirin pills and a certain type of sleeping pills. Each drug requires certain ingredients:

Product	Output, in units of 1000 pills	Inputs (in single units)				
		L	M	V	W	Z
Aspirin pills	1	4	2	10	0	5
Sleeping pills	1	6	1	10	1	0

The firm operates in a highly competitive market, and hence it must make its plans on the basis of the current market prices, which are:

Product prices

Aspirin pills	$5.00 per 1000 pills
Sleeping pills	$5.60 per 1000 pills

Input prices

L	25 cents per unit
M	80 cents per unit
V	6 cents per unit
W	100 cents per unit
Z	12 cents per unit

In addition, the firm must obey the following input limitations:

L	no more than	96 units per period of time
M	no more than	32 units per period of time
V	no more than	220 units per period of time
W	no more than	12 units per period of time
Z	no more than	70 units per period of time

(a) What product mix will yield the greatest profit to the firm?
(b) What is the firm's maximum profit?
(c) Are any of the input limitations ineffective? If so, which?
(d) Of which inputs, if any, is the firm using less than the respective limit stated above?
(e) What would the answers be to (a), (b), (c), and (d) above if the maximum amount of L available were 120?

12

THE DEMAND FOR
CONSUMER GOODS

We have now reached the point in the text at which we must analyze the behavior of the consuming unit—the household. Although in a sense households and businesses can be viewed as two sectors which stand at opposite poles of the economic system, there exists a strong affinity between the analysis of consumer behavior and the behavior of the firm. The similarity stems from two facts: (a) the behavior of the consumer, like that of the firm, is assumed to be goal-oriented; i.e., it is assumed that the consumer's behavior can be explained in terms of an attempt on the part of the consumer to attain an objective, subject to certain environmental conditions; (b) the formal analysis of the consumer's actions employs the same type of tools as those used in the first part of the text.

So far as his environment is concerned, we normally think of the consumer as acting like a pure competitor who takes market prices as given. This is a reasonable assumption, since in most cases the number of consumers in any market is so great as to create the conditions of pure competition. In addition it is assumed that the consumer has only a limited amount of resources at his disposal during any period of time; customarily this assumption takes the form of a budget constraint which specifies what level of income the consumer is free to spend.

The role of the consumer in the market system is to spend his income among the various commodities offered by sellers. The theory of consumer behavior attempts to explain how the allocation of the consumer's income is determined.

Broadly stated, the basic assumption of the theory is that the consumer is motivated by his desire to maximize the satisfaction he gets from the commodities purchased in the market. This assumption certainly has considerable intuitive appeal, but it raises a problem of a formal nature, since satisfaction, unlike the output of the firm, cannot be measured in any direct way.

12-1   THE UTILITY FUNCTION

In order to make the theory meaningful we shall assume that the consumer is capable of **ordering** all possible collections of goods that he might be offered. In other words, let us suppose that the consumer is confronted with any two bundles of goods, say bundle A and bundle B, where a "bundle" means a collection of various quantities of different goods. We assume that the consumer can ponder the relative desirability of each bundle, and then express his preference in one of the following statements:

(1) I prefer bundle A to bundle B;
(2) I prefer bundle B to bundle A;
(3) I like both bundles equally well.

This is by no means a trivial assumption, since situations may frequently arise in which the consumer, in fact, feels undecided about which of the two bundles he prefers.

We make the further assumption that we can assign to every possible bundle of goods a number which reflects the consumer's preference with respect to the various bundles.   More formally, we assume that there exists a functional relationship between the quantities of various goods and some artificial variable, say U, such that for any two bundles the value of U associated with the preferred bundle is higher than that for the other bundle. If there are n goods, denoted by G^1, G^2, ..., G^n, then the functional relationship between the quantities of the G's and U can be written as

$$U = f(G^1, G^2, \ldots, G^n), \qquad (12\text{-}1)$$

and this relationship is referred to as a **utility function,** with U being the **utility index.** Suppose that bundle A, consisting of various quantities of the n goods, and denoted by G_A^1, G_A^2, ..., G_A^n, is preferred by the consumer to bundle B, which is denoted by G_B^1, G_B^2, ..., G_B^n. Then the utility function assigns a higher value to bundle A than to bundle B. That is,

$$f(G_A^1, G_A^2, \ldots, G_A^n) > f(G_B^1, G_B^2, \ldots, G_B^n), \qquad (12\text{-}2)$$

or equivalently, $$U_A > U_B, \tag{12-3}$$

where U_A and U_B are the values of the utility function when evaluated for bundles A and B, respectively.

It should be pointed out that the level of the utility index (i.e., the value of U) has no meaning as such, its only function being to **rank** all possible bundles in accordance with the consumer's pattern of preferences. Thus if there exists some function which truly reflects the consumer's preferences for all possible bundles, such as $U = f(G^1, G^2, \ldots, G^n)$, then no distortion is introduced, for example, by doubling the value of U associated with every bundle. In other words, if $f(G^1, G^2, \ldots, G^n)$ is a legitimate utility function, then

$$2f(G^1, G^2, \ldots, G^n)$$

is also a utility function from which one can correctly tell which one of any two bundles the consumer prefers.

The reader should also be warned against presuming that the consumer's preferences are determined by the level of utility of the various bundles. Utility (at least as used in this theory) is not an inherent characteristic of a bundle, or of the goods which make up the bundle. The consumer's preferences are determined by strictly subjective factors with which the theory of consumer behavior does not concern itself directly. The assignment of suitable levels of utility to various bundles is merely a means of **describing** the consumer's preferences, not an attempt to **explain** them. Thus to say that "the consumer prefers bundle A to bundle B because A has more utility than B" is not a correct statement, but it is proper to say that "bundle A has a higher utility index than bundle B because the consumer prefers bundle A to bundle B."

As to the nature of the consumer's preferences, it is assumed that the consumer always prefers the "bigger" of any two bundles. "Bigger" can be illustrated as follows: Suppose that there are two bundles, A and B, such that the amounts of the various goods in bundle A are not smaller than those of the same goods in bundle B, while the quantity of at least one good in bundle A (possibly more than one, perhaps all of them) is greater than the amount of the same good(s) in bundle B, then we say that bundle A is "bigger" than bundle B, or conversely that bundle B is "smaller" than bundle A. If bundle A, in relation to bundle B, has more of some goods, but less of others, then A is neither "bigger" nor "smaller" than B, nor, of course, are the two identical. In that case the two bundles are **noncomparable.** If the consumer is assumed to prefer "bigger" bundles, then it also follows that the utility index of "bigger" bundles is higher than that of "smaller" ones. From this we can infer something about the general shape of the utility function.

12–1.1 Total utility curves

Let us take a two-good example, good X and good Y, so that the utility function can be symbolized by

$$U = g(X, Y). \tag{12–4}$$

If the quantity of one good is held constant, then it is possible to draw a total utility curve for the other good. Figure 12–1 shows the total utility (TU) curve for good X, assuming that the amount of good Y is held fixed at Y_0. The TU function must obviously be an increasing one, in view of what was said in the preceding paragraph. For example, point a may represent bundle A, consisting of X_1 units of X and Y_0 units of Y, while point b represents bundle B, with X_0 units of X and Y_0 units of Y. Then, since bundle A is "bigger" than bundle B (having more of X, but not less of Y, compared with bundle B), the utility index at a must be higher than at b, and therefore the TU curve must have a positive slope. (By the way, the TU function is the analog of the total product function introduced in Chapter 2. See Fig. 3–1.)

In line with earlier definitions, we may say that the slope of the TU function represents **marginal utility,** i.e., the increase in total utility as the amount of good X is increased by a small amount. Since the slope of the TU function in Fig. 12–1 decreases (i.e., becomes flatter) as X is increased, we can say that in the above example the marginal utility of X diminishes. However, it must be remembered that utility itself is just an arbitrary index, and hence the concept of marginal utility has no empirical meaning and plays no important role in the theory of consumer behavior.*

If the amount of good Y is varied, the TU function of good X will shift, as shown in Fig. 12–2. If the amount of Y is increased, say to Y_1 ($Y_1 > Y_0$), then total utility at every level of X is also increased. For example, bundle C, consisting of X_0 units of X and Y_1 units of Y, is "bigger" than bundle B as represented by point b, hence the utility index of bundle C is higher than that of bundle B. Similarly, if the amount of good Y is reduced to Y_2 ($Y_2 < Y_0$), then

---

* When the modern theory of consumer behavior was first developed in the late nineteenth century, economists held the view that the satisfaction the consumer derived from a bundle of goods could be measured as a quantifiable magnitude, and the utility index was defined as representing that quantity. In that theory marginal utility represented the actual amount of utility (i.e., satisfaction) which the consumer obtained from the last unit of the respective good. However, so long as we reject the idea that satisfaction is measurable, marginal utility merely indicates the increase in the utility index due to an increase in, say, commodity X. This tells us only that the consumer prefers the bundle which has more, rather than less, of commodity X, but it gives no indication whatsoever of the intensity of the consumer's preference.

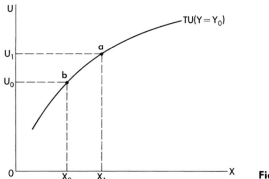

Figure 12–1

bundles such as that represented by point **d** are associated with lower levels of total utility. Figure 12–2 also indicates that the bundles represented by the points **c**, **a**, and **e** have the same level of utility, from which it follows that no one bundle is preferred by the consumer to either of the other two. In other words, in spite of the fact that the three bundles are not identical (since they contain different amounts of **X** and **Y**), the consumer likes them equally well. This could be interpreted, for instance, by saying that if the consumer were given the opportunity to choose one of these bundles as a free gift, he would be completely indifferent in his choice.*

There are, of course, many more bundles (in fact, infinitely many) which have a total utility level of U_1, each consisting of a particular combination of

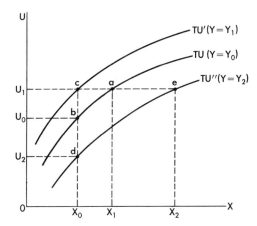

Figure 12–2

---

* This does not mean that the consumer could not make up his mind, only that he would be willing to let the choice be determined by some random process such as drawing a straw.

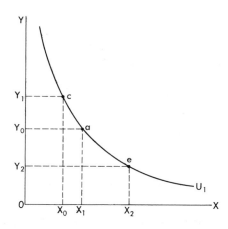

Figure 12–3

goods X and Y. All these bundles are represented by the curve drawn in Fig. 12–3. Since every bundle represented by a point on that curve is associated with the same level of utility, it is proper to call it an **iso-utility curve.** Traditionally, however, such a relationship is referred to as an **indifference curve**—a name which emphasizes the consumer's indifference between the various bundles represented by points on that curve.

12–1.2   Indifference curves

The indifference curve is the analog of the isoquant, and like the latter it has a negative slope. This means that if the quantity of one of the goods in some initial bundle is reduced, the consumer can be adequately compensated by being given more of the other good. For example, if the consumer initially possesses the bundle represented by point c, and the amount of Y in that bundle is reduced from Y_1 to Y_0, then an increase in X equal to $X_1 - X_0$ will leave the consumer just as satisfied as he was with the initial bundle. The curvature of the indifference curve is given the same interpretation as that of an isoquant. Since the slope represents the ratio at which one good can be substituted for the other and still maintain the same level of utility, the slope is referred to as the **marginal rate of substitution** (MRS) (Section 3–1.4). If the indifference curve is convex (as is the one in Fig. 12–3), then as the amount of X increases by successive units, the amounts of Y which are replaced by the successive units of X become steadily smaller. Therefore to assume that the indifference curve is convex is the same as assuming a **diminishing marginal rate of substitution.**

Needless to say, there exists an indifference curve for every level of utility, all of which make up a family of indifference curves, or, as it is sometimes called, an **indifference map.** This map represents the consumer's preference pattern

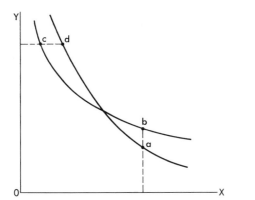

Figure 12–4

with respect to the two goods in question. Since in the short run these preferences can be taken as fixed, it is convenient to think of the indifference map as constituting the consumer's psychological environment. We should also add that indifference curves, like isoquants, do not intersect. The reason for this is explained below.

Consider the two indifference curves in Fig. 12–4. Since **b** represents a "bigger" bundle than **a** it is obvious that **b** is preferred to **a**, and for a similar reason we can say that **d** is preferred to **c**. But since **b** and **c** lie on the same indifference curve it is also true, since the consumer is indifferent between bundles **b** and **c**, that he prefers **d** to **b**. Furthermore, since he is indifferent between **a** and **d**, the consumer also prefers **a** to **b**. But this is inconsistent with our earlier observation that **b** is preferred to **a**, from which it follows that indifference curves cannot intersect.*

12–1.3   The budget line

At the beginning of the chapter we pointed out that the consumer is normally assumed to have at his disposal some fixed level of income. This necessarily puts a limit on the combinations of goods X and Y which the consumer can purchase in any period of time. Those bundles which are within the consumer's reach can be represented by a line which essentially corresponds to the isocost of which we made use in the chapters on the theory of the firm. In the context of the theory of consumer behavior, such a line is usually called a **budget line.**

---

* However, it may happen that if the consumer prefers **b** to **a** at some particular point in time, he might at some *future* point in time prefer **a** to **b**. Such a phenomenon represents a change in preferences over time, and it amounts to a shift in the entire indifference map. In the present analysis we shall not deal with such cases.

The geometrical representation of the budget line is shown in Fig. 12–5. Assuming that the consumer's income is I_0 dollars and that the price of good Y is P^Y, then we can see that if the consumer decides to spend all his income on good Y, he can purchase I_0/P^Y units of Y. Similarly, when he puts all his income into good X, he can purchase I_0/P^X units of X. Bundles which have some amount of each good are represented by the other points on the budget line. The slope of the budget line is given by

$$\frac{I_0/P^Y}{I_0/P^X} = \frac{P^X}{P^Y} .$$

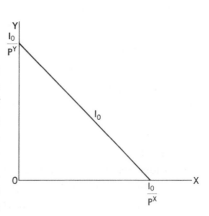

Therefore, as the price of good X rises, the budget line becomes steeper, and as the price of good Y rises, it becomes flatter. If the level of income changes, the budget line shifts in a parallel fashion; when income increases, the budget line moves away from the origin (indicating that with a larger budget the consumer can purchase "bigger" bundles), and when income falls the budget line moves toward the origin.

Figure 12–5

12–2   UTILITY MAXIMIZATION

Early in the chapter we introduced the assumption that the consumer's desire to maximize his satisfaction from any given level of income is the factor which motivates his behavior. We can now restate this objective more formally, and say that the consumer's goal is to maximize his utility function, subject to the budget constraint. Analytically, the consumer's problem is the same as the firm's problem of maximizing output while staying within a limited budget for inputs. But we wish to remind the reader once more that the consumer's satisfaction (utility), unlike the firm's output, is neither observable nor measurable. To say that the consumer maximizes his utility function is simply to say in a formal way that the consumer always attempts to choose the most preferred bundle from those which are within his budget.

The method of finding the optimal bundle is described with the help of Fig. 12–6. Since the consumer will presumably spend all his income, he will purchase some bundle which is represented by a point on the budget line (rather than inside the shaded triangle). Now the most preferred bundle is that which is associated with the highest level of utility; hence to find the optimal bundle

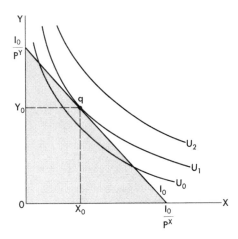

Figure 12–6

means to find a point on the budget line which lies on the highest indifference curve. This is point **q**, which indicates that the most preferred bundle consists of X_0 units of X and Y_0 units of Y. We can see that at point **q** the indifference curve U_1 is tangent to the budget line, and therefore these two functions have the same slope at that point. This leads to the following optimality rule:

(12A) If the indifference curves are convex to the origin, the consumer who wishes to maximize his utility function should choose a bundle (i.e., a combination of goods X and Y) which satisfies the condition

$$MRS = \frac{P^X}{P^Y}.$$ (12–5)

12–2.1 Some special cases

The assumption of the convexity of the indifference curves is very important. We do not claim, of course, that convex indifference curves are more realistic in terms of what is known about consumers' preferences, but the assumption helps simplify the analysis. To demonstrate this point, we shall examine a number of cases in which the convexity assumption is not fulfilled.

First let us consider the case in which the indifference curves are concave to the origin, as in Fig. 12–7. At point **q** the condition $MRS = P^X/P^Y$ holds, but it is clear that there are other bundles on the budget line which the consumer prefers to the bundle at **q**. In fact, **every** other bundle has a higher level of utility than the bundle at **q**, so that if **q** is chosen, utility is **minimized.** The highest indifference curve that can be reached with a budget of I_0 dollars is the curve labeled U_2, and the optimal bundle consists of I_0/P^Y units of Y and zero

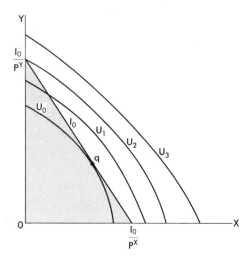

Figure 12–7

units of **X**. It is obvious that when the indifference curves are concave, the optimal bundle always involves one good only, and the desire to avoid this special case is one reason for the convexity assumption.

A similar situation may result when the **MRS** is constant, i.e., when the indifference curves are linear, as in Fig. 12–8. Here again the solution is found at a "corner," i.e., at the **X**-intercept of the budget line and indifference curve U_2. If, however, the indifference curves happen to have the same slope as the budget line, then one indifference curve coincides with the budget line, so that every point on the budget line represents an optimal bundle. In that case the problem has infinitely many solutions.

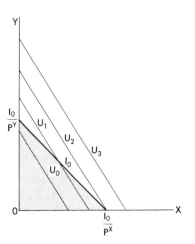

Figure 12–8

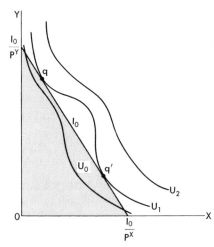

Figure 12–9

And, finally, we can conceive of a preference pattern which yields indifference curves which are partly convex and partly concave. One possible set is shown in Fig. 12–9. In these circumstances the problem of utility maximization has two solutions: One is the bundle at point q, the other is the bundle at q'. Essentially, therefore, the assumption that the indifference curves are convex at every point, and do not touch the axes, guarantees the following results: (a) For every set of prices and income there exists only one single bundle which is optimal. (b) Every optimal bundle contains some positive quantity of each good. As we pointed out earlier, the main justification for the convexity assumption is the desire to simplify the analysis without making the examples unduly un-realistic.

12–2.2 Changes in income

Our next task is to study the effects of changes in prices and income on the consumer's purchases. We begin with the simplest case, namely a change in the consumer's level of income. If we assume that income increases from I_0 to I_1, the consumer's budget line shifts to the right, as shown in Fig. 12–10. This enables the consumer to reach a higher indifference curve by moving from point q to q', and to purchase a "bigger" bundle. Hence with the increase in income the consumer increases his purchase of good X by $X_1 - X_0$, and that of good Y by $Y_1 - Y_0$.

Of course, to some extent this result depends on the position of the indifference curves. By assuming a slightly different indifference map one can change the

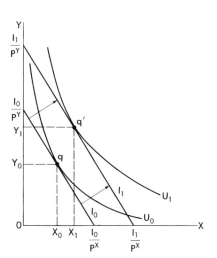

Figure 12–10

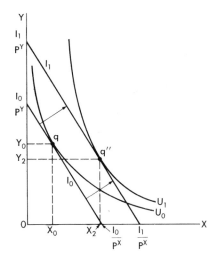

Figure 12–11

nature of the outcome. In the example shown in Fig. 12–11, the increase in income again moves the consumer to a higher indifference curve, but he does not purchase more of **both** goods. Instead we find that while his purchase of X increased by $X_2 - X_0$, his purchase of Y **decreased** by $Y_0 - Y_2$.* Whenever an increase (decrease) in income leads to an increase (decrease) in the purchase of a good, the latter is referred to as a **superior** good (sometimes also called a **normal** good). When an increase (decrease) in income leads to a decrease (increase) in the amount of the good purchased, it is called an **inferior** good. When changes in income have no effect at all on the purchase of the good, it is referred to as a **neutral** good.

12–2.3 Income demand functions

By setting the consumer's income at different levels, it is possible to generate a relationship between income and the amounts of each good purchased, assuming at the same time that prices remain constant. Figure 12–12(a) shows the consumer's budget lines for income levels I_0, I_1, and I_2, respectively, while the respective optimal bundles are represented by the points q, q', and q''. In Fig. 12–12(b), we have plotted quantities of X purchased against income. For example, the relevant information at point q in part (a) (that is, I_0, X_0) is shown as point r in part (b), point q' is shown as point r', and point q'' as

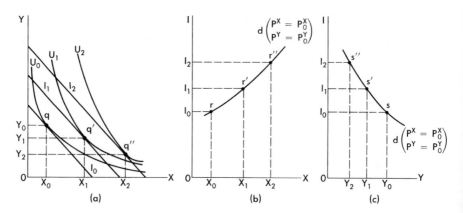

Figure 12–12

---

* Thus the bundle represented by point q'' is neither "bigger" nor "smaller" than that at q. The reader may observe that even though we assumed (in Section 12–1) that between any two bundles the consumer always prefers the "bigger" of the two, the converse may be false; i.e., it is not true, as Fig. 12–11 shows, that a preferred bundle is necessarily "bigger" than a non-preferred bundle.

r''. The same is done for good **Y** in Fig. 12–12 (c). The curves drawn through these points show quantities of the respective goods purchased at various levels of income, and hence they are appropriately referred to as demand curves. However, the curves in Fig. 12–12, unlike the more popular price demand curves, are income demand curves. It can also be observed that the income demand curve for the superior good (**X**) is positively sloped, while the inferior good (**Y**) is represented by a negatively sloped demand curve. The income demand function of a neutral good has the form of a vertical line.

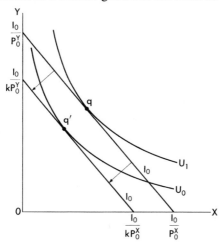

Figure 12–13

12–2.4   Price changes

Proceeding now to investigate price changes, let us assume first that all prices change in the same proportion. In particular, suppose that all prices increase by a factor of k ($k > 1$), so that if the initial prices are P_0^X and P_0^Y the new prices are kP_0^X and kP_0^Y. Higher prices obviously force the consumer to cut down some of his purchases, and this is reflected in the shift of the budget line to the left. It is also clear that the new budget line is parallel to the initial one, and hence both have the same slope. Since the slope of the budget line is given by the price ratio (Fig. 12–5, Section 12–1.3), the slope of the initial budget line is P_0^X/P_0^Y, and that of the new budget line is equal to $kP_0^X/kP_0^Y = P_0^X/P_0^Y$. The two budget lines are depicted in Fig. 12–13. Thus when both prices increase by a factor of k, the consumer moves from point q to point q'.

It is quite clear from Fig. 12–13 that the effect of a proportional increase in all prices is identical to a corresponding decrease in the consumer's income. In the example shown in Fig. 12–13, the initial budget line would have shifted to the same new position if instead of the proportional increase in prices there had been a **decrease** in the consumer's level of income by a factor of k, i.e., if the consumer's income had been decreased from I_0 to I_0/k. Another way of looking at this situation is to say that if prices increase by a factor of k, and the consumer's income increases by a factor of k at the same time, then the budget line does not move at all. This can be validated by observing that if prices and income increase by a factor of k, then the intercepts of the "new" budget line are

$$\frac{kI_0}{kP_0^Y} = \frac{I_0}{P_0^Y} \quad \text{and} \quad \frac{kI_0}{kP_0^X} = \frac{I_0}{P_0^X},$$

respectively. This fact has an important effect on the consumer's market behavior, which can be summarized in the following statement:

(12B) **If all prices and income are changed in the same proportion, the consumer's purchases remain unchanged.**

Next we shall let one price only increase, say P^X. Since the slope of the budget line is equal to P^X/P^Y, an increase in P^X means an increase in the steepness of the slope. But what about the **position** of the new budget line? The Y-intercept is obviously not affected by a change in P^X, since it is determined completely by I and P^Y. Economically speaking, if the consumer decided to spend all his income on good Y, he could purchase just as many units of Y after the increase in P^X as he did initially. From this we can conclude that an increase in P^X causes the budget line to rotate around the Y-intercept in a clockwise direction. The initial and new budget lines are shown in Fig. 12–14.

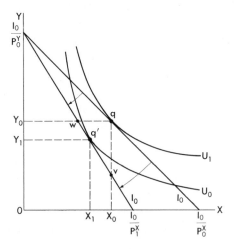

Figure 12–14

After the price of X is increased from P_0^X to P_1^X, the consumer can no longer purchase the bundle at **q**, since the highest indifference curve that he can reach is U_0. By moving from point **q** to point **q′**, the consumer cuts his purchase of X by $X_0 - X_1$ and his purchase of Y by $Y_0 - Y_1$. The consumer's response to the increase in P^X may, however, be of a different nature. If the tangency of the new budget line with the highest indifference curve occurs above point **w** instead of at **q′**, then the amount of X purchased will be smaller than X_1, while the purchase of Y will increase rather than decrease. If, on the other hand, the tangency point is below **v**, the purchase of Y is reduced below Y_1, and the amount of X purchased increases.

12–2.5 Price demand functions

Successive price changes are a convenient method for deriving the consumer's price demand functions. Figure 12–15 illustrates the procedure for changes in P^X. The optimal bundles for the price levels P_0^X, P_1^X, and P_2^X are represented by points **q**, **q′**, and **q″**, respectively, as shown in Fig. 12–15 (a). Figure 12–15 (b) shows the relationship between P^X and the quantity of X purchased, where the points **r**, **r′**, and **r″** correspond to the points **q**, **q′**, and **q″** in part (a). The relationship between P^X and purchases of Y is given in Fig. 12–15 (c); points **s**, **s′**, and **s″** represent the bundles at points **q**, **q′**, and **q″** respectively. The relationship in part (b) represents the consumer's own-price demand function for X, and that in part (c) his cross demand function for Y. These demand functions are **partial** demand functions, inasmuch as each depends on the level of income, as well as on the price of good Y.

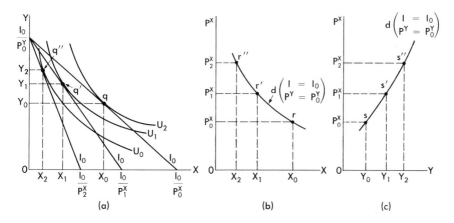

Figure 12–15

Two more demand functions can be derived by varying P^Y, while keeping income and P^X constant. The results are shown in Fig. 12–16. In this example the own-price demand function [part (b)] has a positive slope, and the cross demand function a negative slope. Positively sloped own-price demand functions are believed to be a rare phenomenon; they are not inconsistent with the principle of utility maximization, however, as this example demonstrates. There is little we can say about the slope of cross demand functions on the basis of intuition or observation. The slope of the cross demand function serves as the criterion for classifying goods as **substitutes** and **complements** for each other,* a positive slope indicating a relationship of substitution, a negative slope one of complementarity. More precisely, in Fig. 12–15 (c), good Y is a substitute for good X, while in Fig. 12–16 (c), good X is a complement to good Y.

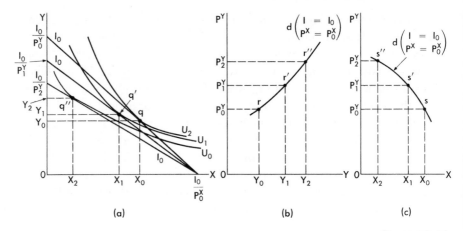

(a)   (b)   (c)

Figure 12–16

As for an economic interpretation of these classifications, we can suggest the following example. Let us suppose that goods X and Y are substitutes for each other. Except in the rare case illustrated in Fig. 12–16 (b), if the price of good X rises, the consumer will normally be induced to purchase less of good X, and (since in the case of substitutes the cross demand function has a positive slope) he will replace the amount of X given up by purchasing additional units of good Y. Thus Y may be said to be a substitute for X, in the sense that when the

*Strictly speaking, we should say *gross* substitutes and *gross* complements as distinct from *net* substitutes and *net* complements. The latter is a classification based on a slightly different criterion. It is felt that in this introductory text it is not absolutely necessary to burden the reader with both of these classificatory schemes; hence the somewhat loose use of the terms *substitutes* and *complements*.

consumer finds it necessary to reduce his purchase of X because of a rise in the price of X, additional units of Y can provide the consumer with the services originally derived from the last amount of X. (An example of substitutes is coal and firewood.) If, on the other hand, X and Y are complements, a reduction in the purchase of X (following a rise in the price of X) will at the same time cause a reduction in the purchase of Y. In this case we can say that X and Y are used hand-in-hand, so to speak, and therefore a decrease in the amount used of one of the goods also calls for a reduction in the amount used of the other. (An example is college education and textbooks.)

Thus in the two-good case one can derive six partial demand functions from the indifference map of an individual—three for each good: one income demand function and two price demand functions. These demand functions form the basis for market demand functions. The latter can be constructed by "summing" the relevant partial demand functions of all the individuals (buyers) in the market. For example, the market demand function introduced in Chapter 5 (Fig. 5–7) can be thought of as the "sum" of all the individual own-price demand functions for good X. Although Fig. 5–7 does not indicate it, the market demand function in that diagram is a partial demand function, the position of which is dependent on the incomes of the consumers, as well as on the prices of the other goods.

12–2.6 Compensated price changes

In all but one of the preceding examples of income and price changes we studied the effects of changing one variable at a time. However, changing one

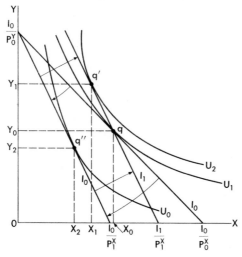

Figure 12–17

variable in our model actually results in changing **two** variables, the second being an implicit variable, i.e., one which does not appear explicitly in the model.

Let us take a closer look at the effects of changing one of the prices, say P^X. For this purpose we turn to Fig. 12–17. The consumer's income is I_0, and the initial prices are P_0^X and P_0^Y, respectively. Under these conditions the consumer purchases the bundle (X_0, Y_0), which is represented by point q on indifference curve U_1. We now increase the price of X to P_1^X, thereby moving the X-intercept of the budget line from I_0/P_0^X to I_0/P_1^X. The explicit effect of increasing P^X is, of course, to make good X more expensive relative to good Y, but in addition to this change in relative prices, the increase in P^X also lowers the consumer's **real** income.

The concept of real income can be defined in a number of different ways, but it can best be understood by interpreting it as purchasing power. It is certainly obvious that when the price of one good increases, a fixed number of dollars (that is, I_0) will not buy as much as before, unless the good whose price is increased is not included in the initial bundle. In the above example, the decrease in the consumer's real income which accompanies the increase in P^X is reflected in the fact that the budget line (except the Y-intercept) moves closer to the origin.*

Now that we have brought the consumer's real income into the picture, we may ask the following question: "What are the effects on the consumer's purchases of a change in the price of one good when real (rather than nominal) income is held constant?" To make this question meaningful we must first define the meaning of "holding real income constant." In the context of the present analysis, we shall say that the consumer's real income is constant so long as the consumer is in a position to purchase his initial bundle.

Now if P^X is increased from P_0^X to P_1^X, and nominal income is held constant at I_0, the consumer adjusts by moving from point q to point q'', indicating that he has suffered a loss in real income. To hold the consumer's real income constant, we must make it possible for him to purchase his initial bundle (represented by point q) even after P^X has increased. This can be accomplished by giving the consumer a compensatory increase in his nominal income which is just sufficient to permit him to purchase his original bundle at the new set of prices. In terms of Fig. 12–17, the consumer must be given an increase in income which will shift the new budget line back to the right until it passes through point q, his initial bundle.

---

* When prices are constant, a change in the consumer's (nominal) income always implies a change in real income by an equal amount.

The level of income which the consumer has at his disposal following the necessary compensation is denoted by l_1.* But when the consumer faces the budget line l_1, he will choose to purchase the bundle represented by point q'. Thus the movement from point q to q' is the consumer's response to an increase in P^X which is accompanied by an increase in his nominal income designed to hold his real income constant. The effects of a compensated price change on the amounts of the various goods purchased are referred to as **substitution effects.** In the case of a compensated change in P^X, the change in the quantity of X purchased may be referred to as the **own-price substitution effect,** which according to Fig. 12–17 is equal to $X_1 - X_0$. The change in the quantity of Y purchased, $Y_1 - Y_0$, is referred to as the **cross substitution effect.**

In view of the above analysis, we can view ordinary price changes (i.e., uncompensated price changes with nominal income held constant) as being effected in two stages. In the first stage the price is changed and **real** income held constant. In graphical terms this stage is represented by a rotation of the budget line around the initial bundle (point q in Fig. 12–17) until its slope is equal to the new price ratio (P_1^X/P_0^Y). This stage gives rise to the substitution effects.

The second stage consists of a decrease (increase) in the consumer's income which measures the loss (gain) in real income due to the price change. In Fig. 12–17 the second stage is represented by a parallel shift of the budget line so as to change its X-intercept from l_1/P_1^X to l_0/P_1^X. Since such a shift amounts to a change in income, the changes in purchases resulting from the second stage are referred to as **income effects.** The total effect of an uncompensated price change can, therefore, be shown to consist of two components. For the increase in P^X assumed in Fig. 12–17, we have the following.

	Total price effect		Own-price substitution effect		Income effect
Good X	$X_2 - X_0$	$=$	$X_1 - X_0$	$+$	$X_2 - X_1$

	Total price effect		Cross substitution effect		Income effect
Good Y	$Y_2 - Y_0$	$=$	$Y_1 - Y_0$	$+$	$Y_2 - Y_1$

---

* The initial level of income is just enough to pay for the initial bundle at the initial prices; that is, $l_0 = P_0^X \cdot X_0 + P_0^Y \cdot Y_0$. The new level of income must cover the cost of the same bundle at the higher price of X; that is, $l_1 = P_1^X \cdot X_0 + P_0^Y \cdot Y_0$. The graph of the first equation (assuming X and Y to be variables) is given by the line joining the intercepts l_0/P_0^Y and l_0/P_0^X in Fig. 12–17, and the graph of the second equation is given by the line labeled l_1.

We have seen earlier in the chapter that income effects and total price effects can be of either sign; i.e., an increase (decrease) in income or in one of the prices may lead to either an increase (decrease) or a decrease (increase) in quantity purchased. With respect to substitution effects, the situation is as follows: Cross substitution effects may in general be of either sign, except in two-good models, in which they are necessarily positive. Own-price substitution effects, on the other hand, are always negative (because of the convexity assumption). That is, **the quantity demanded of a commodity varies inversely with its own price whenever real income is held constant.** This latter conclusion is called the **law of demand.***

SUMMARY

This chapter has dealt with the behavior of the household. The main assumption underlying the analysis was that the consumer is motivated in his market behavior by his desire to derive the maximum satisfaction from his limited income. The formal structure of the household model leans heavily on the concept of the utility function, a relationship which assigns numerical values to all possible bundles in the order of the consumer's preference. The consumer's actions under any set of environmental conditions can then be explained (or predicted) by maximizing the utility function subject to the consumer's budget constraint. In two-good models, the maximization process can be carried out geometrically by making use of indifference curves.

A considerable part of the analysis was directed to the study of how the consumer reacts to changes in income and prices. We saw that in general the

---

* Sometimes this analysis is modified slightly by saying that real income is constant so long as the consumer is able to stay on the initial indifference curve (rather than being able to purchase the initial bundle). Under the modified method the income compensation in the example shown in Fig. 12–17 is smaller, since in order to have the consumer's budget line l_1 form a tangency with indifference curve U_1 the budget line need not be shifted by as much as is shown in Fig. 12–17. Since the total (i.e., uncompensated) price effect is the same in each case, the two methods differ only in the magnitudes of the income and substitution effects, respectively. However, in the limit (i.e., when the change in price approaches zero) the two methods yield identical results.

effects of such changes are indeterminate. A number of examples were presented to illustrate the intimate relationship between the layout of the indifference map and the nature of the effects of income and price changes. The signs of the income effect give rise to a classification system in which goods are classified as either superior, inferior, or neutral goods. Another classification which deals with the relationship between pairs of goods is based on the sign of cross price effects; in this system pairs of goods are defined as either substitutes or complements.

We have also shown how the consumer's demand functions can be derived from a series of successive price and income changes. The derivation of the consumer's demand functions can be regarded as the main goal of consumer demand theory, since these functions embody all the characteristics of the individual's market behavior. Like the signs of the price and income effects, the slopes of the various demand functions depend directly on the consumer's indifference map. The individual demand functions form the basis for the construction of market demand functions.

Finally, we introduced the idea of a compensated price change. Such a change is designed to maintain a fixed level of real income, and to isolate the effects of a change in relative prices. The changes in the consumer's purchases following a compensated price change are known as substitution effects. The introduction of substitution effects also makes it possible to view ordinary price changes as giving rise to two effects—the substitution and the income effect—the sum of which is equal to the total effect of the price change. The fact that own-price substitution effects are negative is the only determinate conclusion following directly from the maximization of the utility function which has convex indifference curves. This result is referred to by economists as the law of demand.

SELECTED REFERENCES

HICKS, J. R., *Value and Capital*. Oxford: Clarendon Press, 2nd ed., 1946, Chapters 1 and 2.

LERNER, A. P., "The Analysis of Demand." *American Economic Review* **52**, 1962, pp. 783–801.

STIGLER, G. J., *The Theory of Price*. New York: Macmillan, revised ed., 1952, Chapter 5.

EXERCISES

1. Figure E12–1 shows two indifference curves and two budget lines of a consumer. Complete the sentences given below.

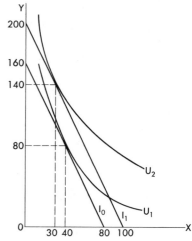

Figure E12–1

(a) If the consumer has an income of $800, and the price of Y is $4, then his optimal bundle consists of _____ units of X and _____ units of Y.

(b) Under the conditions stated in (a) above, I_0 (the value of the lower budget line) is equal to $_____.

(c) If the consumer's economic environment (i.e., prices and income) are initially as stated in (a) above, and both prices increase by 25%, the consumer (*increases, decreases*) his purchase of X and (*increases, decreases*) his purchase of Y. At his new equilibrium position the consumer spends _____ dollars on X and _____ dollars on Y.

(d) The change in prices assumed in (c) above has the same effect on the consumer as a (*25% increase, 20% increase, 25% decrease, 20% decrease*) in the consumer's income.

(e) On the basis of the information in Fig. E12–1, we can say that from the point of view of the consumer X is (*a superior, an inferior*) good and Y is (*a superior, an inferior*) good.

(f) Draw the consumer's income demand functions for X and Y, respectively, in accordance with the information available in Fig. E12–1. Locate and label as many points on each demand function as you can (i.e., two points on each demand function).

(g) Draw an indifference map and a number of budget lines illustrating an example of a consumer who considers X to be a superior good and Y a neutral good.

2. Figure E12–2 shows three indifference curves and three budget lines of a consumer. Complete the sentences given below.

(a) If the consumer's income is $300 and the price of X is $6, the consumer's optimal bundle consists of _____ units of X and _____ units of Y.

(b) If the price of X falls by 50%, the consumer responds by (*buying more of X and less of Y, buying more of both X and Y, buying less of both goods*), and his total expenditures (*increase, decrease, remain constant*).

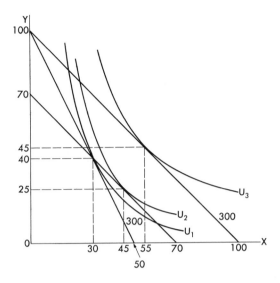

Figure E12–2

(c) The price change assumed in (b) above causes (*an increase, a decrease*) of
$_____ in the consumer's *real* income.

(d) If the price change assumed in (b) above were accompanied by a change in the
consumer's (money) income by an amount such that his real income is held
constant, then the consumer's new optimal bundle would contain _____
units of X and _____ units of Y.

(e) The total price effect of the above price change can be broken down as follows:

	Total price effect	Own-price substitution effect	Income effect
Good X	_____	_____	_____

	Total price effect	Cross substitution effect	Income effect
Good Y	_____	_____	_____

(f) On the basis of the above example we can say that, from the point of view of
the consumer, good Y is a (*substitute, complement*) for good X.

(g) Draw the consumer's partial demand functions for X and Y (as functions of
p^X) to fit the example given in Fig. E12–2. Locate and label two points on each
function.

(h) Construct a graphical example for a case in which good Y is a complement for
good X.

13

FURTHER PROBLEMS
IN DEMAND THEORY

13-1 THE CONSUMER AS A SELLER

The reader may recall that in the discussion about the behavior of the firm we pointed out a certain duality which characterizes the role of the firm in the economic system; it was shown that in the performance of its economic functions the firm acts both as seller and as buyer. A similar situation exists with respect to the household. In the preceding chapter we dealt exclusively with the behavior of the consumer as a buyer of goods. Typically, however, the consumer is also a seller, and what he offers for sale are his labor services. Our task now is to analyze the consumer's role as a seller in the labor market, using the same analytical tools we used in the preceding chapter.

Our first problem is to choose appropriate variables. For the present purpose it is convenient to let leisure time and income be the two goods of the model. These are obviously not commodities in the ordinary sense of the word, but thinking of them as such makes it possible to use the framework developed in the last chapter. It is certainly true that a typical consumer would always like to have more of either leisure or income, or both, and hence the general assumptions made in the last chapter about the nature of the consumer's preference pattern and the properties of the utility function, can be assumed to hold for the special case in which good X and good Y of Chapter 12 are interpreted as leisure time and income, respectively. In other words, we assume that the utility function which the consumer wishes to maximize is of the form

$$U = f(N, I), \tag{13-1}$$

where N denotes leisure time and I denotes income.

This approach could perhaps be criticized on the grounds that the above formulation suggests, at least by implication, that the consumer does not care **how** his income is allocated between the various commodities, but only wants the best combination of leisure and income available to him.   However, we chose this formulation in order to be able to carry out the analysis with simple two-dimensional diagrams.   We could, for instance, replace the variable I by a number of other variables representing various commodities, and thus make the model somewhat more realistic, but by doing so we would deprive ourselves of the convenience of the geometrical tools with which we are already familiar.

Even without our concern for simplicity, we can justify the above approach on more substantive grounds.   Imagine that the consumer proceeds with his decision-making in two distinct stages.   In the first stage he decides on the amount of leisure he wants to have during the time period in question.   The fact that he chooses the amount of his leisure, of course, also implies the consumer's willingness to work a certain amount of time (defining leisure as any time during which he does not work), and that choice, in turn, reflects his desire to earn a certain level of income.

The second stage of this decision-making process deals with the problem of allocating the consumer's income among various commodities.   Since the consumer faces the second problem only after he has solved the first one, the level of income is already fixed (by his own decision) when he turns to selecting the optimal bundle of goods which he is to purchase with his income.   Thus under this conception of the consumer's decision-making procedure the second stage is identical with the problem analyzed in Chapter 12, while the present discussion deals with the first stage.

13–1.1   The budget line

Before we can proceed with the actual determination of the optimal bundle of leisure and income we must introduce a suitable budget constraint.   The budget line for this particular problem is shown in Fig. 13–1.   The N-intercept

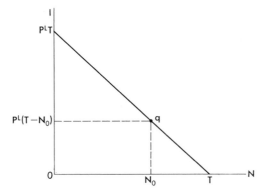

Figure 13–1

is denoted by T, where the latter denotes the length of the time period in question. (For example, if leisure time is measured in hours, and the time period is a day, then $T = 24$; if the time period is a week, then $T = 168$, etc.) Thus if the consumer wanted to have as much leisure available as possible (that is, T hours), he would not be able to work at all, and consequently his income would be zero. (We assume here that wages are the consumer's only source of income.) If, on the other hand, the consumer wanted to spend all his time working, his total income would be $P^L T$ dollars, where P^L is the price of labor; that is, the hourly wage rate. Points on the budget line between the two intercepts represent mixed bundles; for example, the bundle represented by point q consists of N_0 hours of leisure (or $T - N_0$ hours of work), and an income of $P^L(T - N_0)$ dollars. The slope of the budget line is equal to $P^L T/T = P^L$. As in the standard two-good model, the slope of the budget line can be interpreted as being equal to the price ratio. Since $P^L = P^L/1$, we see that P^L is equal to the price of leisure, and 1 equals the price of income. The latter is obvious: One can always buy a dollar for a dollar. The interpretation of the wage rate as the price of leisure may be less obvious. There is, of course, no market for leisure as such; instead, leisure is "bought" by giving up the opportunity to work. Thus the amount of income foregone by staying idle for one hour, which is equal to the hourly wage rate, may be regarded as the price of one hour of leisure. This is an example in which the price of a good is measured in terms of opportunity cost. (See definition of opportunity cost at the beginning of Chapter 2.)

Since by definition every point on the budget line represents an attainable bundle, Fig. 13–1 represents a somewhat idealized state of affairs. Normally the consumer cannot choose to work just any desired amount of time, since in most cases the agreement between employer and employee specifies some fixed number of working hours to which the employee is expected to commit himself.

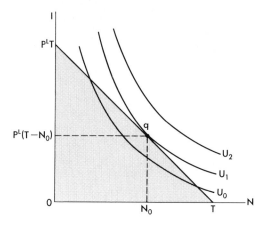

Figure 13–2

The model could, indeed, be modified to account for more realistic arrangements, but since we do not aim at more than an introductory analysis in this chapter, we shall leave it in its present form.

13–1.2 The optimal bundle

The consumer's optimal bundle can now be found by placing the indifference curves and the budget line on the same diagram, as shown in Fig. 13–2. The highest indifference curve that the consumer can reach is U_1, and his optimal bundle is represented by point q.

13–1.3 Changes in autonomous income

We now relax one of the assumptions made earlier, and permit the consumer to receive part of his income from a source other than his wage payments. We refer to these additional receipts as **autonomous income** (I^A), since their magnitude is determined by factors outside the model rather than by the consumer's own choice. If the consumer actually receives some positive amount of autonomous income in each period of time, say I_0^A dollars, then it is necessary to shift the budget line upward by a vertical distance equal to I_0^A. The consumer is then confronted by a situation such as is depicted in Fig. 13–3.

The new budget line does not extend beyond point t, since bundles which involve more than T hours of leisure are meaningless. This, incidentally, means that any optimal bundle chosen by the consumer must contain a level of income which is not less than the level of his autonomous income, that is, I_0^A. Given this particular level of autonomous income, the consumer chooses the bundle at point q' rather than that at point q. At his new position he consumes N_1 hours of leisure, and receives a total income of $I_0^A + P^L(T - N_1)$ dollars—I_0^A as autonomous income, and $P^L(T - N_1)$ in wage payments.

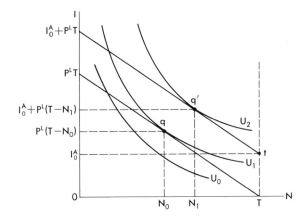

Figure 13–3

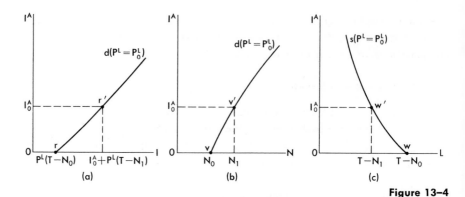

Figure 13–4

In the above example the increase in autonomous income (from 0 to I_0^A) has increased the consumer's demand for both leisure and income. By making successive changes in autonomous income it is possible to derive the relationship between autonomous income and the demand for leisure and for total income, respectively. The procedure is similar to that which was used in the preceding chapter (Section 12–2.3) and instead of repeating the entire process here, we shall show only the derived relationships.

Figure 13–4(a) shows the consumer's demand for total income as a function of autonomous income. The points r and r' correspond to the points q and q', respectively, in Fig. 13–3. Figure 13–4(b) shows the demand function for leisure, with points v and v' representing the bundles at q and q', respectively. Figure 13–4(c) represents the consumer's **supply** function of labor, which can be considered the complement of the demand function for leisure. In other words, the number of hours that the consumer is willing to work at any given level of autonomous income—denoted by L—is obtained by subtracting the amount of leisure demanded from T. That is, $L = T - N$. Note that the three functions in Fig. 13–4 depend on the wage rate, which we assumed to be fixed at P_0^L.

13–1.4   Changes in the wage rate

Perhaps of greater relevance and interest are the effects of changes in the wage rate on the consumer's choice. An increase in the wage rate, for example, means that the consumer can earn more for each hour of work. A rise in the wage rate is equivalent to an increase in the price of leisure, because the opportunity cost of an hour of leisure is thereby increased. An increase in the wage rate, therefore, increases the steepness of the budget line, as illustrated in Fig. 13–5. The N-intercept of the budget line must, of course, remain fixed at T, since the consumer can always obtain T hours of leisure (by remaining idle all the time) regardless of the wage rate.

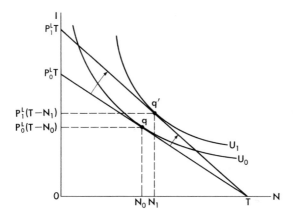

Figure 13–5

The higher wage rate permits the consumer to reach indifference curve U_1, and his new bundle has more of both leisure and income than his initial bundle. If we assume that increases in the wage rate always bring about responses on the part of the consumer in the same direction as those in Fig. 13–5, then the relevant demand and supply functions that can be derived from the consumer's indifference map are of the general form shown in Fig. 13–6. In these functions the wage rate is the independent variable, and it is assumed (as is implied by Fig. 13–5) that autonomous income is zero. Figure 13–6(a) represents the demand for income, Fig. 13–6(b) the demand for leisure, and Fig. 13–6(c) the supply of labor.

The above example represents, of course, only one out of many possible variants, and by assuming a different preference pattern one can generate demand and supply functions with different characteristics. To construct one more example, let us consider a consumer who desires to earn some **fixed** level of income, and who adjusts to changes in the wage rate to always maintain his

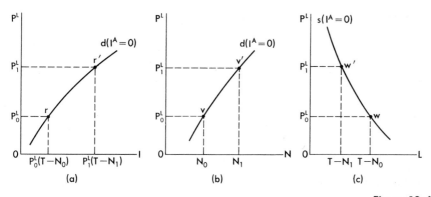

Figure 13–6

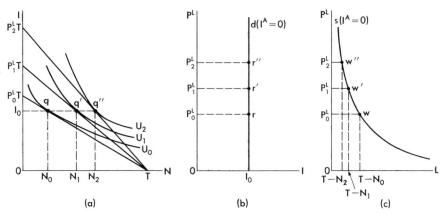

Figure 13–7

desired level of income.   This example is illustrated in Fig. 13–7, in which
part (a) shows the consumer's indifference map and the budget lines for the
wage rates P_0^L, P_1^L, and P_2^L, respectively.   The respective optimal bundles are
represented by points q, q′, and q″, and I_0 is the consumer's desired income.
Figure 13–7(b) represents the demand function for income, which is a vertical
line in accordance with the assumption of this special case. The supply function
of labor is given in Fig. 13–7(c). Since the consumer's income is equal to hours
of work times the wage rate, we have, for the wage rate P_0^L, the equation
$I_0 = P_0^L(T - N_0)$, which is represented by the area of the rectangle $0P_0^L w(T - N_0)$
in Fig. 13–7(c).   Similarly, when $P^L = P_1^L$, then $I_0 = P_1^L(T - N_1)$, which is
represented by the area of $0P_1^L w'(T - N_1)$, and so on. Since all the rectangles
under the supply function, such as the above-mentioned, have the same area,
it follows that the supply function of labor in this particular example is a rectangular hyperbola.

13–1.5 The effects of unemployment compensation

The simple model developed in this chapter lends itself easily to the analysis
of certain institutional features found in some labor markets.   One of these is
the provision for unemployment compensation (UC).   Imagine a situation in
which the individual has the choice between taking a job at the going wage
rate or collecting UC at the rate of, say, I_0 dollars per period of time.   The
individual then faces the kind of situation shown in Fig. 13–8. If the current
wage rate is P_0^L dollars, the budget line intercepts the I-axis at $P_0^L T$. Of course, in
a real situation the individual may not be entitled to collect UC unless he is
involuntarily unemployed, in which case his alternatives are described correctly
by either the budget line (if he has a job), **or** the bundle represented by point c

(if no job is available), but not both. However, whether a worker's state of unemployment is voluntary or not is not always easy to establish, so that under certain circumstances the individual's range of choices may be represented more or less faithfully by a budget line **and** point c. In the absence of UC, the individual clearly chooses the bundle represented by point q, and he works $T - N_0$ hours. However, if the current rate of UC is I_0 dollars, the individual can reach a higher indifference curve by remaining idle and collecting the UC. In doing so he foregoes a certain amount of income [that is, $P_0^L(T - N_0) - I_0$ dollars], but he gains $T - N_0$ hours of leisure which, for him, more than offsets the loss in income.

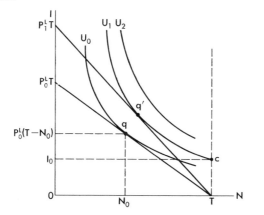

Figure 13–8

If the wage rate increases to P_1^L, the individual will either continue to collect UC, or move to point q', the two bundles being equally desirable. (In this special example the problem has two solutions in spite of the assumption of convex indifference curves. See discussion in Section 12–2.1.) But it is clear that if the wage rate increases beyond P_1^L, the individual will prefer to work rather than remain unemployed, since this would place him on a higher indifference curve than U_1. Thus in general the UC and the wage rate exert opposite effects: An increase in the former makes idleness relatively more attractive; an increase in the latter encourages the consumer to take a job.

13–2 A TWO-PERIOD MODEL

One feature shared by all the different models of consumer behavior which we have discussed so far in this chapter and in Chapter 12 is the (implicit) assumption that in planning his economic activities the consumer is concerned with only the current period of time. Another way of stating this assumption is to say that the time horizon over which the consumer plans extends over only one period. We have never specified the length of the time period underlying the various models, since in most cases it is not essential to the analysis. If the time period is relatively short, however, one month, for example, then it may be reasonable to assume that the consumer possesses enough foresight to make some provisions for the future, at least the near future, when drawing up his plans for the current period. In other words, it may in general be more correct to assume that the consumer's planning horizon is longer than just one period of time.

Some of the problems of multiperiod models can be illustrated with a very simple two-period model. In order to be able to use the same analytical technique as in the preceding models, we shall focus our attention on only two variables—the level of consumption expenditures in each of the two periods. In formal terms we assume that the consumer's utility function is of the form

$$U = f(C^1, C^2), \tag{13–2}$$

where C^1 denotes consumption expenditures in the current period of the horizon, and C^2 denotes consumption expenditures in the second period of the horizon. As in the other models presented in this chapter, the quantities of various commodities purchased by the consumer are of no concern in the present analysis. The reason for this is again our desire to keep the model simple, but it is also possible to assume once more a two-stage decision-making process, in which the first stage is designed to deal with the selection of the optimal levels of total expenditures for each period in the horizon, while the second stage is concerned with the determination of the individual purchases. (See comments on the two-stage decision-making process in Section 13–1.)

With respect to the consumer's financial position, we assume that in each time period the consumer receives a fixed level of income, say I_0 dollars. However, we no longer require that the consumer's entire income be spent in the period in which it is received, and we permit the transfer of part of the income, possibly all of it, from one period to another. Income from period 1 can be transferred to period 2 through **lending,** while the transfer of income from period 2 to period 1 is effected by **borrowing.** The cost of these transactions (excluding administrative costs such as brokerage fees) is determined by the market rate of interest, and in each case it has to be paid out of the consumer's income. (When the consumer lends, the cost is, of course, negative.)

13–2.1   The budget line

The various combinations of levels of consumption available to the consumer are indicated by the budget line in Fig. 13–9. The point in this diagram which is easiest to interpret is point q; it represents an expenditure pattern in which consumption in each period is equal to the income of the respective period. Therefore the bundle represented by point q requires neither lending nor borrowing. The C^1-intercept represents a bundle which gives the consumer the highest possible level of consumption in period 1, but at the same time it reduces consumption in period 2 to zero. The highest level of C^1, since it is greater than the income in period 1 (I_0), is attained by borrowing in period 1 a sum which can be repaid in period 2 (principal plus interest) with the income of period 2.

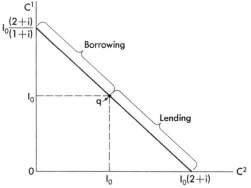

Figure 13–9

The maximum amount that the consumer can borrow in period 1 is computed as follows: Let B denote the amount to be borrowed. The cost of borrowing (i.e., the interest cost) is then equal to iB, where i is the prevailing market rate of interest, and the total amount which must be repaid in period 2 (principal plus interest) is equal to $B + iB = B(1 + i)$. The latter must be just equal to the income in period 2, that is, $B(1 + i) = I_0$, and hence $B = I_0/(1 + i)$. Thus the consumer has at his disposal in period 1 a total income of I_0 (income received in period 1) $+ I_0/(1 + i)$ (amount borrowed) $= I_0[(2 + i)/(1 + i)]$.

The C^2-intercept represents a bundle which provides no consumption in period 1, but yields maximum consumption in period 2. This bundle is realized by transferring the income of period 1 to period 2 through lending. When the consumer lends I_0 dollars in period 1, he collects in period 2 I_0 (principal) $+ iI_0$ (interest) $= I_0(1 + i)$. His total disposable income is, therefore,

$$I_0 + I_0(1 + i) = I_0(2 + i)$$

dollars. Bundles represented by points on the budget line between point q and the C^1-intercept consist of some positive levels of consumption in each period, but part of the expenditures in period 1 are financed by borrowing; points between q and the C^2-intercept also involve some consumption in each period, but these bundles require the transfer of some income from period 1 to period 2.

Note that the slope of the budget line is equal to $1/(1 + i)$, and following the usual procedure, the latter can be interpreted as the ratio of the relevant prices. In this particular case such interpretation is, of course, somewhat artificial, since the "commodities" in question (C^1 and C^2) are levels of expenditures which are already expressed in dollars. But even though it may be a bit difficult to think of this ratio as representing prices, it makes perfectly good sense to regard these quantities as measuring the true economic cost of C^1 and C^2, respectively. Thus $1 + i$ may be taken as the price of C^1, indicating that the cost of one dollar spent on consumption in the current period is equal to $1 + i$. It is true, of course, that in order to purchase one dollar's worth of consumption goods the consumer needs to spend exactly one dollar, but here the price measures not the direct expense involved, but rather the opportunity cost. In this case the opportunity cost of C^1 (in terms of C^2) is $1 + i$, because the amount of C^2 foregone by spending one dollar on C^1 is equal to $1 + i$ (since every dollar **not** spent on C^1 can be lent, and thus be turned into $1 + i$ dollars available in period 2.) The opportunity cost of C^2, on the other hand, is just equal to the actual money outlay on C^2, since the opportunity cost of a good in terms of itself is always unity (i.e., one dollar not spent on C^2 can always buy just one dollar's worth of C^2.)

13–2.2 The optimal bundle

The consumer's consumption plan can now be determined by superimposing the budget line on the consumer's indifference map, as shown in Fig. 13–10. In this example the consumer selects the plan represented by point **p** which calls for consumption levels C_0^1 and C_0^2 in the two periods, respectively. According to that plan the consumer chooses to consume in period 1 an amount which exceeds his income in that period, which implies that he is a borrower.

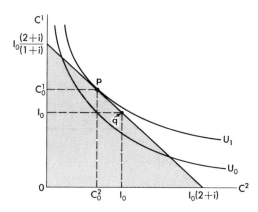

Figure 13–10

To be precise, he borrows $C_0^1 - I_0$ dollars in period 1, and the financial obligation which he incurs by doing so forces him to restrict his spending in period 2 to a level which is less than his income in that period. In other words, in order to be able to repay the principal and the interest cost, the consumer must deduct that amount from his income in period 2 when calculating his spendable income in period 2. Therefore

$$(C_0^1 - I_0)(1 + i) = I_0 - C_0^2.^*$$

13-2.3 Changes in the rate of interest

Now let the rate of interest increase. The effect of such a change is to make borrowing less attractive (since the cost of each dollar borrowed is higher), and lending more attractive (since the return from each dollar lent is higher).† The maximum level of C^1 must therefore decrease because the maximum amount that can be borrowed (with I_0 dollars available for the liquidation of the debt) falls as the rate of interest rises. The return from lending, on the other hand, rises with the rate of interest, and consequently the maximum level of C^2 increases.

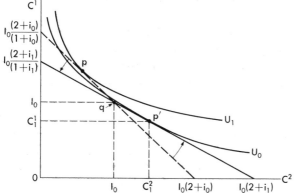

Figure 13-11

An increase in the rate of interest, therefore, causes a rotation of the budget line around point **q** in a counterclockwise direction. The case is illustrated in Fig. 13-11 in which the initial budget line is reproduced as a dashed line. After the rate of interest is increased from i_0 to i_1, the consumer moves from point **p** to point **p'**. In this case the increase in the rate of interest is sufficiently

---

* The straight line in Fig. 13-10 is the graph of this equation, c^1 and c^2 being considered as variables.

† It is assumed, of course, that the consumer can borrow and lend at the same rate of interest.

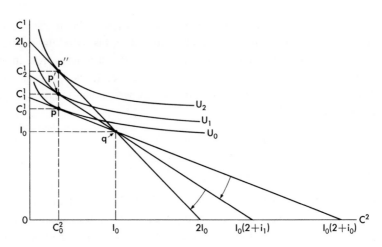

Figure 13–12

large to turn the consumer from borrower to lender. According to his new plan the consumer saves $I_0 - C_1^1$ dollars out of his income in period 1, and this enables him to spend in period 2 an amount which is greater than his income in that period.

As with most such examples, many different outcomes are possible. To take just one more, suppose that the consumer's behavior is characterized by his desire to provide himself with a certain level of consumption in the future (i.e., period 2), and to maximize his current consumption, given his fixed levels of income. The example is illustrated in Fig. 13–12, in which it is assumed that the consumer's desired level of future consumption is C_0^2. At the initial rate of interest, i_0, the consumer chooses the bundle at point **p** which provides him with his desired amount of future consumption and C_0^1 of current consumption. The portion of the income in period 2 not consumed in that period (that is, $I_0 - C_0^2$) is used to finance the borrowing of $C_0^1 - I_0$ dollars in period 1.

When the rate of interest falls to i_1, the consumer moves to point **p'**. This move involves an increase in current consumption by $C_1^1 - C_0^1$, which is made possible by the fact that with $I_0 - C_0^2$ dollars available in period 2 the consumer can borrow a larger amount in period 1 following the drop in interest. If the rate of interest drops further, the consumer adjusts in the same fashion, i.e., he increases consumption in period 1, holding future consumption constant. Of course, there is a limit to the amount of income that the consumer can make available for himself in period 1, since the rate of interest cannot drop indefinitely. Let us take the limiting case in which the rate of interest is zero. In that case the budget line intercepts each axis at $2I_0$, and the consumer chooses the bundle represented by point **p''**. Money can now be borrowed at no cost, but the consumer is still expected to repay the principal in full in period 2. Since he saves $I_0 - C_0^2$ out of his income in period 2, the consumer can borrow exactly that much in period 1, and hence $C_2^1 - I_0 = I_0 - C_0^2$.

13–3 BEHAVIOR UNDER UNCERTAINTY

Uncertainty is one of the most characteristic elements of the environment in which human actions take place; it is found in all areas of individual and collective behavior, and it is typical of economic relations as well. Uncertainty manifests itself primarily through its effect on decision-making. When uncertainty prevails with respect to some information which is required in order to plan a course of action, then the outcome that is expected to follow the action is itself uncertain.

In the context of decision problems facing the firm, especially a firm which operates under some form of monopolistic competition, a typical case of uncertainty arises with respect to the level of sales associated with any particular marketing policy of the firm. Usually the firm will have some information about the state of the market, derived primarily from historical data, on the basis of which it can estimate its sales. These estimates, however, are necessarily of a speculative nature, and they may turn out to be either right or wrong. The element of uncertainty is particularly strong when decisions are made whose outcome is expected in a relatively remote future: for example, problems of long-run planning, such as the determination of the optimal size of plant for the firm. The consumer is also subjected to various forms of uncertainty, especially as far as future market prices are concerned. Uncertainty about future prices and income is an important factor in those situations in which the consumer plans for the future, as, for instance, in the model discussed in the preceding section.

In our discussion of various problems in the theory of the firm and consumer behavior, we have not treated uncertainty in any formal manner, and for the most part have ignored it altogether. We have done so because an explicit and rigorous analysis of behavior under uncertainty requires the application of fairly advanced analytical techniques. However, for certain problems involving uncertainty, we can formulate a fairly simple decision process with the tools and concepts which have already been used earlier in the text. In the problem chosen here we think of the decision maker as a consumer, but it is quite easy, by a reinterpretation of the variables, to convert the example into an entrepreneurial problem.

For simplicity we assume that the consumer focuses his attention on one single target variable—his income. In other words, we are dealing here with an

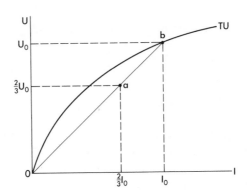

Figure 13–13

individual whose utility index depends only on his income, that is,

$$U = f(I). \tag{13-3}$$

The graph of this utility function may look like the one shown in Fig. 13–13. In line with our earlier assumption, the function must have a positive slope, since the consumer prefers higher levels of income to lower ones, and consequently higher levels of income must have a higher utility index. The choice of intercept, the origin in this case, is arbitrary, and this is justified by the fact that the value of the utility index at any particular level of income is meant only to indicate the ranking of that particular level of income in relation to others. The significance of the curvature of the TU function will be explained later.

Let us assume here that the level of income received by the consumer depends directly on the action taken by him, but the precise amount of income associated with a particular course of action is uncertain. Now the term "uncertain" or "uncertainty" is in itself somewhat obscure, and for the purpose at hand it needs to be given a more specific meaning. Perhaps the most acute case of uncertainty occurs when the decision maker has no idea whatsoever as to what a particular course of action will lead to. In many situations, however, the decision maker may at least be able to predict (he may, of course, be wrong) the range of values which the target variable may take on. A still weaker form of uncertainty is one in which the decision maker has a hunch as to which of many possible values are more likely to be realized than others, and it is this type of uncertainty which we shall assume in our example.

Specifically, we assume that every possible action (or set of actions) taken by the consumer may yield one of two levels of income. A special case is that in which one of these income levels is zero. Suppose, then, that a certain course of action yields the consumer either zero or I_0 dollars of income. The consumer believes that the likelihood of his receiving I_0 dollars is greater than that of the outcome of zero dollars; to be more specific, the consumer is assumed to have enough information to speculate that the probability of the former is, say, two-thirds, and that of the latter one-third.*

13–3.1 Expected utility

Ultimately we want to compare various actions with uncertain outcomes from the point of view of the consumer's preference, and therefore we must next find a means of attaching some sort of value, or index, to outcomes such as the one assumed above. So far as terminology is concerned, the index attached to un-certain outcomes is referred to as **expected utility,** for the simple reason that the outcome is in the nature of an expectation rather than something which the consumer can take for granted. We are, therefore, concerned now with deter-mining the expected utility of the bundle which yields zero dollars with proba-bility one-third and I_0 dollars with probability two-thirds. We can look at the problem in this way: Whenever he receives zero dollars, the consumer obtains an income whose utility is zero, and when he receives I_0 dollars, the consumer has an income which is associated with the utility index U_0. (See Fig. 13–13.) The expected utility is simply an average of the utilities of the two levels of income in the bundle, but instead of taking a simple arithmetical average we compute a **weighted** average, where the weights are the respective probabilities. Thus the expected utility of the above bundle is $\frac{1}{3} \cdot 0 + \frac{2}{3}U_0 = \frac{2}{3}U_0$.

13–3.2 Expected income

It is also possible to compute the **expected income** of the bundle under con-sideration. Expected income, like expected utility, is a weighted average in which the relevant probabilities serve as the weights. In the above example the ex-pected income is $\frac{1}{3} \cdot 0 + \frac{2}{3}I_0 = \frac{2}{3}I_0$. Now if we draw a straight line through the two points on the utility function which correspond to the two income levels of the bundle (0 and I_0), then we obtain the ray 0b in Fig. 13–13. The point a on that ray is vertically above point $\frac{2}{3}I_0$ (the expected income of the bundle), and on the same horizontal line as $\frac{2}{3}U_0$ (the expected utility of the bundle). (It follows, of course, from the law of similar triangles that since the distance between the origin and $\frac{2}{3}I_0$ is two-thirds of the distance from the origin to I_0, then the distance between the origin and $\frac{2}{3}U_0$ is two-thirds of the distance between the origin and U_0.)

---

* To say that the probability of receiving I_0 is two-thirds could be interpreted, for instance, as saying that if the consumer took the same action in a great number of successive periods of time, then, assuming no change in environmental conditions, he would receive I_0 dollars in about two-thirds of the time periods, while in the remaining one-third of the periods he would receive zero dollars.

Next we take a somewhat more general example, in which the uncertain outcome involves two positive levels of income, say I_0 and I_1, and for which the probabilities are one-fourth and three-fourths, respectively. A line is again drawn through the points on the utility function which are associated with the incomes of the outcome, that is, I_0 and I_1, shown as the line **ce** in Fig. 13–14. The expected utility of this bundle, which we shall denote as $\bar{U}$, is by definition equal to $\frac{1}{4}U_0 + \frac{3}{4}U_1$, and the expected income, denoted by $\bar{I}$, is

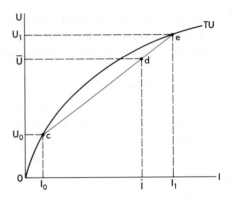

Figure 13–14

$\frac{1}{4}I_0 + \frac{3}{4}I_1$. In order to locate $\bar{I}$ on the I-axis, let us rewrite the expression for the expected income as $(1 - \frac{3}{4})I_0 + \frac{3}{4}I_1$ (substituting $1 - \frac{3}{4}$ for $\frac{1}{4}$), which in turn equals $I_0 + \frac{3}{4}(I_1 - I_0)$. Thus we can find the desired point in two steps: First, we move from the origin to point I_0, and then move three-fourths of the distance from I_0 to I_1.* The expected utility $\bar{U}$ can be located in a similar fashion, but once we know the location of $\bar{I}$, it is much simpler to find $\bar{U}$ by drawing a horizontal line from point **d** to the U-axis, where **d** is on the line **ce** and vertically above $\bar{I}$.

13–3.3 Changes in probabilities

The consumer who is considering a bundle of uncertain outcome reacts as he would in the case of complete certainty. That is, he prefers bundles with a higher index of expected utility to those with a lower index. Let us note here that the expected utility of a bundle with uncertain outcomes depends on two factors: the possible levels of income—or the **payoffs** as they are more generally known—and the probabilities of the payoffs. Changes in any of these will usually yield a different level of expected utility. For example, a change in the probabilities of the payoffs which has the effect of increasing the expected payoff (income) of the bundle† always increases the expected utility of the bundle. If the outcome involves only two payoffs, and the latter are held fixed, then the expected payoff of the bundle will increase only if the probability of the

---

* The point $\bar{I}$ divides the distance between points I_0 and I_1 into two segments whose lengths are proportional to the respective probabilities; that is, $\overline{I_0\bar{I}}/\overline{\bar{I}I_1} = \frac{3}{4}/\frac{1}{4} = \frac{3}{1}$.
† The expected income, or expected payoff, of the bundle is also known as the *actuarial value* of the bundle.

larger payoff rises. For instance, if the probability of l_1 increases to four-fifths (and that of l_0 falls to one-fifth), then the expected payoff equals $\frac{1}{5}l_0 + \frac{4}{5}l_1$, which is greater than $\frac{1}{4}l_0 + \frac{3}{4}l_1$. Locating the new expected payoff on the l-axis by the method explained in the preceding section, and denoting it by $\bar{l}'$, we find that $\bar{l}'$ lies to the right of $\bar{l}$, as shown in Fig. 13-15. (See also the footnote in Section 13-3.2.) Consequently, the expected utility of the second bundle, $\bar{U}'$, is higher than that of the first bundle. This makes good sense: Between two bundles which have identical payoffs one would always choose that for which the chance of receiving the larger payoff was higher.

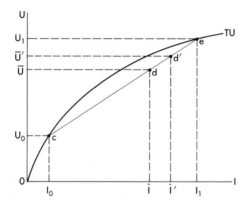

Figure 13-15

When the probability of l_1 reaches its maximum, i.e., one (and that of l_0 is zero), the expected payoff is equal to l_1, and the expected utility of the bundle is equal to U_1. Of course, to say that the probability of payoff l_1 is unity is the same as saying that the action in question yields income l_1 everytime. In that case no uncertainty exists, and therefore expected utility is the same as (ordinary) utility. Thus the approach to consumer behavior which allows for uncertain outcomes provides us with a more general model, of which a situation of complete certainty is a limiting case.

13-3.4 Changes in payoffs

Instead of changing the probability of a payoff, let us now change the payoff itself. That is, let us consider an action whose outcome involves the payoffs l_2 and l_1, with probabilities $\frac{1}{4}$ and $\frac{3}{4}$, respectively, where l_2 lies between l_0 and l_1, that is, $l_0 < l_2 < l_1$. We now wish to compare the initial bundle (call it bundle A) having payoffs l_0 and l_1 with the bundle having payoffs l_2 and l_1 (bundle B), where the probabilities of the payoffs in each bundle are one-fourth and three-fourths, respectively. The comparison is carried out with the help of Fig. 13-16.

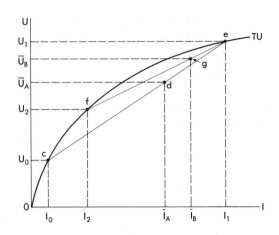

Figure 13–16

In order to determine the expected utility of bundle B, we draw a line through points e and f, which are vertically above I_1 and I_2, respectively. Now the expected payoff of bundle B, $\bar{I}_B$, is located three-fourths of the distance from I_2 to I_1 (or one-fourth of the distance from I_1 to I_2), and hence it must lie to the right of $\bar{I}_A$, the expected payoff of bundle A, since the latter is located three-fourths of the distance from I_0 to I_1. The expected utility of bundle B is then found on a horizontal line through point g, where the latter is a point on the line ef vertically above $\bar{I}_B$. We can, therefore, conclude that the consumer prefers bundle B, which differs from bundle A in that one of its payoffs is larger. A similar result obtains if we make the smaller of the two payoffs equal in each bundle, while making the larger payoff in bundle B exceed the larger payoff in bundle A; and obviously it also holds when the smaller as well as the larger payoff in bundle B is greater than the respective payoff in bundle A.

Let us briefly summarize the main points of the preceding discussion.

(1) Expected utility, which is an index ranking bundles with uncertain outcomes, depends on two factors: (a) the level of the payoffs, and (b) the probabilities of the payoffs.

(2) Given any two bundles **with identical payoffs,** the bundle with the higher expected payoff has a higher level of expected utility, and hence is preferred by the consumer. (Observe, however, that in general, i.e. when the payoffs are not identical, one cannot determine which of two bundles the consumer prefers by looking only at their expected payoffs.)

(3) Given any two bundles **in which the payoffs have the same probabilities,** if at least one payoff in one bundle is greater than the respective payoff in the other bundle, and no payoff is smaller than the respective payoff in the other bundle, then the former bundle has a higher level of expected utility,

and is therefore preferred by the consumer. (By the term "respective payoff" is meant a payoff which has the same probability as that of the original bundle.)

13–3.5 The expected utility function

Note that a line such as **ce**, as well as **ef**, in Fig. 13–16 can be thought of as a **partial expected utility function**; it indicates the expected utility of all bundles having the payoffs indicated by the points on the I-axis vertically below the end points of the line. For example, the line **ce** is the partial expected utility function for all bundles with payoffs I_0 and I_1. This is so because, if the payoffs are fixed, then the expected utility depends entirely on the expected payoff of the bundle. Therefore in order to find the expected utility one simply locates the expected payoff on the I-axis, and then reads off the expected utility on the U-axis opposite the appropriate point on the expected utility function (such as point **d**).

13–3.6 Choosing between certain and uncertain outcomes

The expected utility index serves not only as a yardstick for ranking bundles with uncertain payoffs; it also provides a means for comparing uncertain bundles with certain ones. After all, a bundle which yields I_0 dollars with certainty can be thought of as a bundle with payoffs I_0 and I_1 which have probability one and zero, respectively. It is, therefore, meaningful to compare the utility index of a bundle having a certain payoff with the expected utility index of a bundle with uncertain payoffs, and thereby determine which of the two is preferred by the consumer. Consider, for example, a consumer who can choose between two courses of actions, **A** and **B**. Action **A** yields a bundle having the uncertain payoffs I_0 and I_4 with an expected payoff of $\bar{I}$, while **B** yields I_3 dollars with

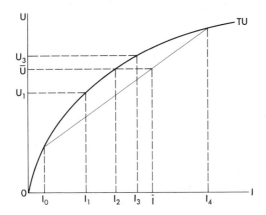

Figure 13–17

certainty. See Fig. 13–17.* Since $U_3 > \bar{U}$, it follows that the consumer prefers to receive the certain income I_3 rather than the bundle with the uncertain payoffs I_0 and I_4, and consequently he would decide on action B.

Aversion to risk. An important characteristic of the consumer's preference as reflected in this particular case is the fact that he prefers the certain income I_3 to the bundle whose expected income is greater than I_3. Had he decided on action A, then over a reasonably long period of time the consumer's average income (i.e., income per period of time) would have been $\bar{I}$ (assuming no change in the probabilities of the payoffs I_0 and I_4), while his average income from action B is only I_3. The explanation for this seemingly "irrational" behavior is to be found in the consumer's desire to avoid risky undertakings such as action A. His choice indicates that the consumer has an aversion to risk, and that he is willing to protect himself against risk by foregoing a certain amount of income. In the above example the consumer gives up $\bar{I} - I_3$ dollars in average income in return for the elimination of uncertainty from his economic environment.

If the certain income from action B is reduced to I_2, then the outcomes of the two actions are equally desirable so far as the consumer is concerned. The reason he no longer prefers the riskless outcome is the fact that he must forego a larger amount in average income in order to avoid risk; the loss of $\bar{I} - I_2$ dollars in average income exactly offsets the extra satisfaction which the consumer derives from receiving I_2 with certainty instead of the uncertain bundle. If the income from action B falls further, say to I_1, the consumer will switch to action A, since $\bar{U} > U_1$. The fact that the consumer now embarks on an uncertain course of action does not, of course, mean that he is no longer averse to risk; it simply means that the "price" of certainty has become too high, and that the consumer is unwilling to give up $\bar{I} - I_1$ dollars in average income in order to guarantee himself I_1 dollars with certainty. Thus aversion to risk is not an **absolute**, but a **relative**, property of consumer behavior. It does not mean that the consumer will **never** expose himself to risk, even if he has the choice not to do so. As the above example shows, income can become an acceptable substitute for certainty, provided the ratio of substitution is sufficiently high.

A typical example of risk aversion is the purchase of insurance. Suppose that a consumer has a regular annual income of I_4 dollars, and that in case of sickness his income drops to I_0 (Fig. 13–17). Given the consumer's general state of health, one can assign a probability to his becoming sick in any particu-

---

* The reader may replace the consumer by an entrepreneur, and reinterpret I and U as sales and profit, respectively.

lar year, and thus one can compute the level of his expected income—say $\bar{I}$.
Assume now that there is available an insurance policy which, in case of sickness, pays the consumer an amount equal to the loss in income, that is, $I_4 - I_0$
dollars. Then if the policy is not too expensive, the consumer will insure himself
against sickness by purchasing such a policy. What is the highest premium the
consumer would be willing to pay for such a policy? The consumer will pay
any premium which will leave him with a certain annual income whose utility
is not less than the expected utility of his expected income. A premium of
$I_4 - I_3$ dollars per year falls into that range. Since the insurance policy in
effect guarantees the consumer a gross income of I_4 dollars with certainty,
then after subtracting the cost of the policy ($I_4 - I_3$ dollars), the consumer
is left with a net income of I_3 dollars. Since $U_3 > \bar{U}$, the consumer prefers the
insurance to a risky situation, even though the latter has a higher expected
income.

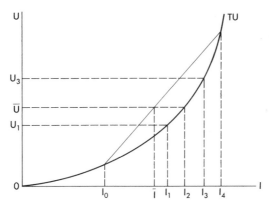

Figure 13–18

Attraction to risk. Not every consumer is averse to risk. Conditions under
which one consumer prefers an income with certainty to a bundle with uncertain payoffs may induce another consumer to choose the uncertain outcome.
Such a case is illustrated in Fig. 13–18. The consumer has a choice between
action **A**, which yields the bundle having payoffs I_0 and I_4 with expected income $\bar{I}$, and action **B**, which yields I_1 dollars with certainty. Since $\bar{U} > U_1$,
the consumer obviously prefers the bundle with the uncertain outcome, in
spite of the fact that the expected income of the latter is smaller than the expected income of the certain income. When the income of action **B** is increased
to I_2, the consumer is indifferent between the two bundles, but when action **B**
yields I_3 dollars with certainty, the latter is preferred to the uncertain bundle.

What does this type of behavior suggest? The fact that the consumer prefers
the uncertain payoffs I_0 and I_4 to I_1 with certainty clearly indicates that the
consumer is attracted to risk, and that he is, in fact, willing to give up a certain

amount of income in order to expose himself to risk. By choosing the uncertain bundle with expected income $\bar{I}$ rather than the certain income I_1, the consumer sacrifices $I_1 - \bar{I}$ dollars in average income. However, attraction to risk, like aversion to risk, is relative, and when the loss in income becomes too high (e.g., a loss of $I_3 - \bar{I}$ dollars), the consumer chooses certainty instead.

Participation in a game of chance is a manifestation of attraction to risk. By gambling, the consumer is giving up a certain amount of income (the price for participating in the game) in return for a chance of either winning an amount greater than the certain income given up, or winning an amount smaller than that (possibly zero). For instance, a lottery ticket may have payoffs I_0 and I_4, with probabilities which make the expected payoff equal to $\bar{I}$ (Fig. 13–18). Then, if the price of the lottery ticket is less than I_2, the consumer will prefer to gamble rather than hold onto the amount necessary to purchase the ticket.

The consumer's attitude toward risk can be defined in the following fashion. Consider the bundles A and B, where A has the uncertain payoffs I_0 and I_1 with an expected payoff $\bar{I}$, and B yields an income of $\bar{I}$ with certainty. Then if the consumer prefers B to A he is averse to risk, while a preference for A indicates an attraction to risk. It is easy to verify that the former occurs when the slope of the TU function in the relevant range decreases with income, and the latter when it increases. (Compare Figs. 13–17 and 13–18.) But since the slope of the TU function represents the marginal utility of income, we can say that diminishing marginal utility of income implies an aversion to risk, while increasing marginal utility of income implies attraction to risk. The nature of the marginal utility is, therefore, an important determinant of the behavior of the consumer under conditions of uncertainty. This is in sharp contrast with the insignificant role of marginal utility in making choices among riskless alternatives (Section 12–1.1).

SUMMARY

In this chapter we have examined, by way of an extension of the demand theory presented in the last chapter, a number of slightly more specialized examples, illustrating various choices with which a typical consumer may be confronted. The first of these dealt with the optimal allocation of the consumer's time between leisure and work. The problem may be viewed as one which describes and explains the consumer's role as a seller in the labor market.

As in the more general model, the consumer's choice is determined by the prevailing market prices, as well as by his income. In the income-leisure model the relevant price is the wage rate, and the consumer's income consists of autonomous receipts other than wage payments. Changing the wage rate and the autonomous income by successive steps, we derived the consumer's demand functions for income from wages as well as his supply functions of labor. It was also shown how the simple model can be used for an elementary analysis of the effects of unemployment compensation.

In the second example we generalized, in a sense, our previous approach to the theory of consumer behavior in that we extended the "vision" of the consumer beyond the current period of time, and consequently it was assumed that he plans for a horizon which includes current as well as future periods of time. An important feature of multiperiod models is the fact that the consumer can distribute his income over the entire time horizon in a way which best fits his preferences. The transfer of income from one period to another is effected either through lending or borrowing, as the case may be. In planning his consumption pattern for the horizon, the consumer is restricted not only by the income available to him in each period of the horizon, but also by the rate of interest. The latter determines the terms on which money can be lent or borrowed, and hence it determines the cost involved in the transfer of income. Thus the rate of interest directly affects the consumer's optimal distribution of income (and hence of consumption) over the horizon.

In the last part of the chapter we demonstrated how the simple model of consumer behavior can serve as a convenient framework for an elementary analysis of choice under uncertainty. When uncertainty exists the decision maker is unable to tell in advance what any particular action will lead to, but he may know that the outcome of his action may yield one of a number of possible payoffs. To explain how the consumer chooses among uncertain prospects, we assumed first that the consumer was able to rank bundles with uncertain outcomes in accordance with his preferences. Thus, in complete analogy with behavior under certainty, we assumed that we may assign an index to each possible uncertain bundle which will reflect the consumer's preference. This index, called expected utility, was defined as a weighted average of the utility of the relevant payoffs. The consumer's choice under uncertainty is then explained in terms of his desire to maximize expected utility. When studying behavior under uncertainty, one can distinguish between consumers who are averse to risk and those who are attracted to risk. Each type of behavior is characterized by a unique shape of the utility function. In terms of market behavior the two groups may be identified by their willingness to either purchase insurance or participate in a gamble, given the specifications of the relevant alternatives.

SELECTED REFERENCES

ALCHIAN, A. A., "The Meaning of Utility Measurement." *American Economic Review* **43**, 1953, pp. 26–50.

BEAR, D. V. T., "The Relationship of Saving to the Rate of Interest, Real Income, and Expected Future Prices." *Review of Economics and Statistics* **43**, 1961, pp. 27–36.

BREHM, C. T., and T. R. SAVING, "The Demand for General Assistance Payments." *American Economic Review* **54**, 1964, pp. 1002–1018.

COOPER, G., "Taxation and Incentive in Mobilization." *Quarterly Journal of Economics* **66**, 1952, pp. 43–66.

FRIEDMAN, M., and L. J. SAVAGE, "The Utility Analysis of Choices Involving Risk." *Journal of Political Economy* **56**, 1948, pp. 279–304. Reprinted in K. E. Boulding and G. J. Stigler (eds.), *Readings in Price Theory*. Chicago: Irwin, 1952, pp. 57–96.

MARKOVITZ, H., "The Utility of Wealth." *Journal of Political Economy* **60**, 1952, pp. 151–158.

OZGA, S. A., "Measurable Utility and Probability—A Simplified Rendering." *Economic Journal* **66**, 1956, pp. 419–430.

SCITOVSKY, T., "A Note on Profit Maximization and its Implications." *Review of Economic Studies* **11**, 1943–44, pp. 57–60. Reprinted in K. E. Boulding and G. J. Stigler (eds.), *Readings in Price Theory*. Chicago: Irwin, 1952, pp. 352–358.

SCITOVSKY, T., *Welfare and Competition*. Chicago: Irwin, 1951, Chapter 5.

EXERCISES

1. Figure E13–1 shows a portion of a consumer's indifference map for income and leisure, and a number of budget lines. Complete the sentences given below.
   (a) If the wage rate is $2 per hour, the consumer chooses to work _____ hours every day, and his daily income is $_____.
   (b) Suppose that an income tax is imposed, and that the tax payments are deducted directly from wages. Then if the tax rate is 25% the consumer will (*increase, decrease*) his consumption of leisure. His daily net income is $_____.
   (c) Given the above wage and tax rates, and assuming now that the consumer has the option of collecting $12 in unemployment compensation (taxfree) every day, then the consumer will choose to (*work, stay idle*).

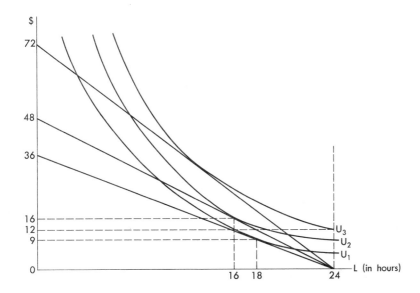

Figure E13–1

(d) What would be the answer to (c) above if the income tax on wage earnings were reduced to zero?

(e) What is the lowest net wage rate which will induce the consumer to work rather than to collect unemployment compensation?

(f) Draw the consumer's demand functions for income and leisure, and his supply function of labor (as functions of the wage rate). Locate and label two points on each function.

(g) Construct an example illustrating the case of a consumer who wishes to earn $16 every day, regardless of the going wage rate.

2. Figure E13–2 shows part of a consumer's indifference map for present and future consumption, and three budget lines. Complete the sentences given below.

(a) The consumer's fixed income in each time period is equal to $_____.

(b) If the consumer spends c_1^1 dollars on consumption in period 1 and c_3^2 dollars on consumption in period 2, then the current rate of interest is _____.

(c) Under the conditions stated in (b) above, the consumer (*borrows, lends*) $_____ in period 1. In this transaction the consumer (*incurs a cost, earns interest*) equal to $_____.

(d) From the information given in Fig. E13–2, it is correct to deduce that a rise in the rate of interest leads to (*an increase, a decrease*) in the consumer's satisfaction.

(e) It is also true that as the rate of interest rises, the consumer [*borrows more* (*lends less*), *borrows less* (*lends more*)].

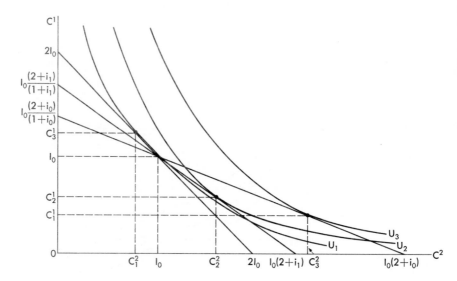

Figure E13-2

(f) When the rate of interest is zero, the consumer is (*a borrower, a lender, neither a borrower nor a lender*).

(g) The maximum amount the consumer could ever spend in period 1 (given his fixed income) is equal to $_____.

(h) Construct an example in which an increase in the rate of interest leads to a decrease in the consumer's satisfaction.

3. Figure E13–3 shows a consumer's utility function with respect to income. Complete the sentences given below.

(a) Suppose the consumer is offered job A, which yields an uncertain income: $10 with a probability of $\frac{1}{4}$, and $90 with a probability of $\frac{3}{4}$. What is the actuarial value (expected income) of the offer? What is the expected utility of the offer?

(b) Suppose the consumer is offered another job—job B—which yields $55 with certainty. Which job will the consumer take?

(c) Assume that the conditions of job A change, and consequently the probability of the $10 payoff falls to $\frac{1}{8}$. Which job will the consumer choose?

(d) Which level of certain income has the same level of utility as job A as modified in (c) above?

(e) Suppose that the consumer is offered a lottery ticket which carries the prizes $10 and $90, and in which the probability of the larger payoff is $\frac{1}{8}$. The price of the ticket is $11. Will the consumer purchase the ticket? What is the highest price the consumer would be willing to pay for the above lottery ticket?

(f) What is the expected utility of the above lottery ticket if the probability of each payoff is $\frac{1}{2}$?

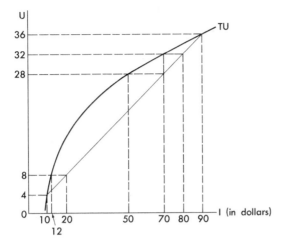

Figure E13–3

4. (a) Suppose that a consumer's utility function is such that the utility of zero dollars is zero, and the utility of $60 is 12. What is the expected utility to the consumer of a lottery ticket offering $60 with a probability of $\frac{2}{3}$, and zero dollars with a probability of $\frac{1}{3}$?

(b) Suppose that $30 is the highest price the consumer is willing to pay for the above lottery ticket. What is the expected utility of a lottery ticket having payoffs of $30 and $60, each with a probability of $\frac{1}{2}$?

(c) Suppose that the above consumer is indifferent as to the choice between a lottery ticket offering payoffs of $30 and $90 with probabilities of $\frac{1}{3}$ and $\frac{2}{3}$, respectively, and an income of $60 with certainty. What is the utility of an income of $90 with certainty?

5. (a) A consumer expresses his preference for a lottery ticket paying $4 with a probability of $\frac{1}{4}$ and $12 with a probability of $\frac{3}{4}$ over an income of $6 with certainty. What can you infer about the consumer's attitude toward risk?

(b) What would be the answer to (a) above if the consumer preferred the certain income over the lottery ticket?

14

WELFARE ECONOMICS

14-1 THE NATURE OF WELFARE ECONOMICS

Any part of the subject matter which constitutes the general body of economic theory may be said to belong to an area of either (a) **positive** economics or (b) **normative** economics. The greater part of economic theory and all the preceding chapters of this text (except for a few isolated references) may be classified as positive economics, since it is concerned exclusively with cause-and-effect relationships. The essence of positive economics is concerned with the following general type of conditional statements: "If A (a set of assumptions) holds, then C (a set of conclusions) follows."

If the reader will reflect for a moment on the discussions in the preceding chapters, he will find the same logical thread running through the presentation of most of the material in the text. For example, with respect to the firm, we started out by making various assumptions about the environment, technological as well as economic, in which the firm was said to operate, and about the objectives it wanted to pursue. These assumptions in turn led to certain conclusions as to the firm's choice of price and output, and the level of profit which it would attain in any particular set of circumstances. And indeed a great deal of our investigation, such as the study of the firm's adjustment to environmental changes, was designed to emphasize the dependence of the conclusions on the assumptions.

Normative economics also deals with cause-and-effect relationships, but it has a more ambitious goal: In addition to deriving conclusions from sets of assumptions, it seeks to **evaluate** various results and to distinguish between them from a normative point of view. Normative economics attempts to evaluate the workings, or organization, of an economic system from the point of view of society as a whole, and not from the viewpoint of any particular individual. It is concerned, therefore, primarily with statements of the general type: "X (a particular economic program) is good, Y (some other economic program) is bad"; or statements like "X is better than Y." Utterances of this kind are not admitted in the framework of positive economics, which can be thought of as taking a completely neutral position with respect to problems of social well-being. Positive economics may therefore be defined as any discourse in economics which is devoid of normative content.

Welfare economics is normative economics, since it is concerned with the examination of various economic states from the point of view of society's well-being. Some economists (and perhaps other people as well) argue that the study of economics should be restricted to purely positive aspects of economic relationships, because the problems to which welfare economics addresses itself are essentially political in nature. (Other economists, to be sure, hold exactly the opposite view.) This is a valid argument which should not be dismissed offhand, because to say that one social state is better than another is obviously a value judgment, and there is no reason why the economist's opinion should weigh more than anyone else's. After all, when it comes to value judgments, one man's is as good as the next man's. But to the extent that economists do study problems of economic welfare, they do so not because of a belief in the superiority of their own value judgments, but because they believe that once society has defined certain economic goals as desirable—and it is of no concern to the economist **how** such goals are chosen—the economist is best equipped to propose a course of action that will lead toward the fulfillment of these objectives.

The choice of an acceptable criterion for the evaluation of economic states is, therefore, the crux of welfare economics. Once a suitable standard is selected, the problem assumes a purely positive character. The difficulty in making this choice stems from the fact that in any society which consists of more than one individual and which also believes in certain fundamental democratic principles, the goals of society must to some extent accommodate the desires and the wishes of all its members. The trouble is, of course, that almost any kind of economic change will most certainly benefit some individuals and hurt others, and, as we saw in Chapter 12, an individual's preference for a certain economic state (e.g., a bundle of commodities placed at his disposal) is a highly subjective matter which defies quantitative measurement. There is, therefore, no way of quantitatively comparing the effects of a certain economic change on different members of society, and hence no obvious formula by which one can tell whether the change is good for society as a whole, or not.

However, the situation is not quite hopeless. Some headway can be made with problems in which a measurement of individual gains and losses can be dispensed with. Such a possibility arises in those cases in which an economic reorganization leads to changes in individual welfare which do not cause opposite reactions. That is, we may consider reorganizations in which all members of society, or some of them, are either made better off, or remain as well off as before, but no one is made worse off; or similarly, those changes in which some, or all, members are either made worse off, or remain as well off as before, and no one is made better off. In such situations one may not need to obtain a quantitative measurement of the individual gains and losses if, for instance, one is willing to say that society as a whole is better off whenever some individuals, or all of them, are made better off, and no one is made worse off. But even this criterion, with all its apparent reasonableness, is essentially just a value judgment, which may be acceptable to some members of society but not to others.

14–1.1   The welfare criterion

Modern welfare economics makes use of precisely such a criterion. In order to define it more rigorously a few preliminary remarks are in order. We shall be concerned here primarily with the comparison of various economic states. By "economic state" we mean a particular organization of the economic system which specifies the actions to be performed by each member of society, as well as his share of the final output. We shall assume that each consumer maximizes a utility function, and that each producer maximizes his profit. We shall also assume that the individual objective functions are independent, which means that the level of utility attained by each consumer depends only on the quantities of goods which he **himself** consumes (and not on the amounts consumed by other consumers), and the profit of each producer depends only on the level of his own output. Finally, an individual is said to be "better off" whenever he attains a higher level of utility or profit, as the case may be, and a reverse interpretation applies to the term "worse off."

Consider now any two economic states, S and S'. Then we define the following:

Definition 14–1. If under S at least one individual is better off, and no one is worse off, than under S', then S is said to be Pareto-superior.

The last term in the above definition is a technical term identifying an economic state which is preferred by society to some other state (i.e., it is a synonym for "better"). It is coined after the nineteenth-century Italian economist (and political scientist) who first proposed the above welfare criterion. The above definition can also be stated in reverse, so to speak:

Definition 14–2. If under S′ at least one individual is worse off, and no one is better off, than under S, then S′ is said to be Pareto-inferior.

Obviously, if one of two states is Pareto-superior, then the other must be Pareto-inferior, and vice versa. And finally we have the following:

Definition 14–3. If an economic state S is such that no other state is Pareto-superior to it, then S is said to be Pareto-optimal.

An alternative way of defining a Pareto-optimal state is to say that it is a state from which it is impossible to move without making at least one individual worse off.

In the framework of modern welfare economics the goal of a welfare-maximizing society is defined as the attainment of a Pareto-optimal state. One should be careful, however, not to interpret the attainment of Pareto-optimality as welfare maximization in the same sense in which we talk about utility maximization. So long as there exists no meaningful method of comparing the gains and losses experienced by different members of society under any given economic change, it is impossible to find a numerical index which will rank all possible economic states in accordance with society's preference. Consequently, certain economic states (those in which some individuals are better off and others worse off) cannot be compared at all, so that, with the Pareto welfare criterion, society can evaluate only those changes that lead either to superior states or to inferior states. By choosing as its goal the attainment of a Pareto-optimal state, society can be said to maximize its welfare in the sense that no opportunity for improvement remains unexplored, and that once the chosen state is reached, no individual can be made better off without causing some other individual to suffer a loss.

14–2 THE DISTRIBUTION PROBLEM

Concrete examples will clarify the meaning of these concepts. Therefore let us consider a society of two individuals, A and B, who have at their disposal fixed quantities of two commodities, X and Y. Here we are concerned with the distribution of the available quantities among the members of society, i.e.,

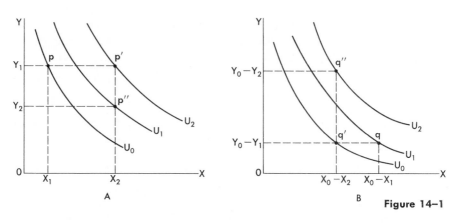

Figure 14–1

individuals **A** and **B**. Thus an economic state in the present problem simply means a particular distribution of the two commodities. Any such distribution can be represented by points in the indifference maps of the two individuals, as shown in Fig. 14–1. The total quantities available are X_0 and Y_0, respectively. Under the initial distribution, individual **A** receives X_1 and Y_1, respectively, while **B** receives the remainder, $X_0 - X_1$ and $Y_0 - Y_1$, respectively. The initial distribution is therefore represented by points **p** and **q** in the respective diagrams.

In considering this problem from the welfare standpoint, we are interested in determining whether the initial distribution is Pareto-optimal or not; in other words, whether or not there exists some other distribution which is Pareto-superior to the initial distribution. Consider the distribution which obtains when $X_2 - X_1$ units of **X** are transferred from individual **B** to individual **A**; this will move **B** from **q** to **q′**, and **A** from **p** to **p′**. Compared with the initial distribution, this redistribution makes **A** better off and **B** worse off. Now since the Pareto welfare criteria do not apply to changes which make some individuals better off, and others worse off (see Definitions 14–1 and 14–2), it follows that the second distribution (that is, **p′**, **q′**) is neither Pareto-superior nor Pareto-inferior to the initial distribution (**p**, **q**). The above two distributions are therefore said to be **noncomparable.**

Next let us consider a change in the initial distribution which calls for increasing **A**'s amount of **X** to X_2 while decreasing his amount of **Y** to Y_2, thus moving him to point **p″**, and **B** to **q″**. This redistribution has the effect of making both individuals better off, and hence the new distribution (**p″**, **q″**) is clearly Pareto-superior. Hence the initial distribution is not Pareto-optimal. (See Definition 14–3.) There are, of course, other possible ways of changing the initial distribution, and hence we cannot yet render a complete evaluation of the welfare situation in the above example, let alone make a recommendation as to how the initial distribution should be changed. In particular, although we can say that the distribution (p″, q″) is Pareto-superior to (p, q), we have not established whether (p″, q″) itself is Pareto-optimal.

To get a better view of the situation, let us use a slightly different geometrical presentation. Instead of placing B's diagram next to that of A, we impose B's diagram on A's after rotating B's indifference map 180 degrees. The result is the box diagram shown in Fig. 14–2. The origin of A is at the corner labeled A, and the quantities of X and Y at A's disposal are measured in the conventional manner. The origin of B is at the opposite corner, and the amounts of the goods in his bundle are measured from his origin to the left and downward, respectively. The indifference curves can be identified by the labels. The size of the box indicates the **total** quantities of the two goods available; X_0 units of X (the length of the box), and Y_0 units of Y (the height of the box). A point in the box represents a certain distribution of the two goods between the two individuals, such that the total amounts available are exactly exhausted. Thus the initial distribution is given by point p, and the distribution which was found to be superior to it is represented by point p″. The shaded area represents all those distributions which can be compared with the initial distribution, while the unshaded area represents the set of those distributions which are non-comparable with the distribution at p.

To determine whether the initial distribution is optimal, we need concern ourselves only with the shaded portion of Fig. 14–2. We can see that the shaded area consists of three distinct regions which are interconnected at the points

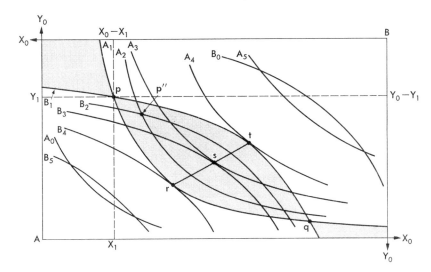

Figure 14–2

p and q. In the regions northwest of p and southeast of q, respectively, all distributions are inferior to the initial distribution (since any distribution in those regions puts either A or B, or both, on lower indifference curves), whereas the center region represents superior distributions. The distribution at q is just as good as that at p. Hence in our search for a Pareto-optimal distribution we can simplify our task by examining only the center region. For example, the distribution at r is superior to the initial distribution, since it makes B better off without hurting A. Moreover, if the move from p to r were actually carried out, no further change would be possible without putting at least one of the two individuals on a lower indifference curve. Therefore, the distribution at r is Pareto-optimal; that is, there exists no other distribution in the entire box which is Pareto-superior to r. Note, however, that the same can be said about distributions s and t; both are superior to p, and both are Pareto-optimal.

14–2.1 The condition for Pareto-optimality

It should be clear now that a distribution is Pareto-optimal if at the respective point the indifference curves of the two individuals are tangent to each other. There are, of course, other distributions in the center region besides r, s, and t which are Pareto-optimal. Since there are infinitely many indifference curves passing through the center region, there are infinitely many tangency points in that region, whose locus is shown by the curve connecting points r, s, and t. Thus the evaluation of the initial distribution p from the point of view of social welfare produces the following conclusions:

(1) There exist distributions which are Pareto-superior to p, which are represented by points in the center region other than points p and q. This means that there are various ways (infinitely many, in fact) of redistributing the available amounts of X and Y between individuals A and B without making either one worse off, and making at least one of them better off, than he is at p.

(2) Among the distributions which are Pareto-superior to p, some are Pareto-optimal; these are the distributions on the curve rst.

If Pareto-optimality is the accepted welfare criterion, then the society in the above example, in order to maximize its welfare, should redistribute its wealth, and move from the initial distribution to one of the distributions on the curve rst. However, the Pareto-optimality criterion can be of no help in choosing a particular distribution among those represented by rst, because a movement from one Pareto-optimal distribution to another always places one individual on a higher indifference curve and the other on a lower one. Thus Pareto-optimal distributions are noncomparable. In a sense one might say that in the absence of any additional criteria, society is indifferent as to the choice of one among all distributions which are Pareto-optimal, although it is quite obvious that each individual is able to rank Pareto-optimal distributions from the point of view of his own preferences. The failure of Pareto-optimality to pick out one particular distribution as being the best one stems from the conflict between individual preferences. Thus in the example shown in Fig. 14–2, given the choice of the Pareto-optimal distributions represented by rst, individual A prefers to move from point p to t, while B prefers to move to point r.

14–2.2 The contract curve

If we view the box in its entirety, then every point at which a tangency occurs between two indifference curves of the two individuals, respectively, represents a Pareto-optimal distribution. These will normally lie on a curve such as that shown in Fig. 14–3. This curve is frequently called the **contract curve** (sometimes also referred to as the **conflict curve,** since moving along it gives rise to a conflict between the two individuals in question). We can now say that society's goal (from the point of view of welfare) is to reach a point on the contract curve.

Suppose that such a point, say point p in Fig. 14–3, is chosen as the initial distribution. Then all other distributions fall into one of two classes: those

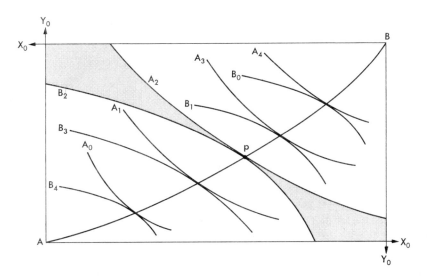

Figure 14–3

which are inferior to the initial distribution (the shaded region); and those which are noncomparable to it (the rest of the box).* Thus, once point p is attained, society cannot improve its welfare by moving away from it, since such a move will either make everyone worse off (moving into the shaded region), or yield a distribution that cannot be compared with the initial distribution. The reader should remember, however, that this is true not only about point p, but about **every** point on the contract curve. It also holds, for instance, at A's origin; the latter is a distribution which gives everything to B and nothing to A. But this distribution is Pareto-optimal since (given the fixed amounts of X and Y) it is impossible to move away from it without inflicting a loss on individual B. This extreme example clearly emphasizes one of the weaknesses of the Pareto-optimality criterion.

14–3 THE PRODUCTION PROBLEM

So far we have limited our discussion to a pure distribution problem—that of allocating to each individual a certain share of some fixed amounts of two goods. We now wish to broaden the setting of the problem by removing the assumption that the amounts of the goods are fixed. Consequently we turn our attention to the producing sector of the economy. To simplify matters, it is assumed that there are two producers, E and F, the former specializing in the

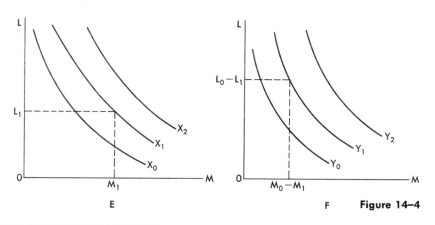

E   F   **Figure 14–4**

---

* The reader should realize that superiority, inferiority, and noncomparability are not inherent characteristics of a distribution, but rather relative terms which describe a distribution when it is compared with some other distribution. A particular distribution may turn out to be either Pareto-superior, Pareto-inferior, or noncomparable, depending on the distribution to which it is compared. This explains why the regions in Figs. 14–2 and 14–3 representing superior, inferior, and noncomparable distributions, respectively, have different shapes in each case.

production of X, the latter in the production of Y. Each good requires for its production inputs L and M, of which the economy is endowed with fixed quantities L_0 and M_0, respectively. The production possibilities facing each producer can then be represented (in part, at least) by the respective families of isoquants shown in Fig. 14–4. If producer E is given L_1 and M_1 of the two inputs, respectively, he will be able to produce X_1 units of X. This will leave F with quantities $L_0 - L_1$ and $M_0 - M_1$, respectively, making it possible for him to produce Y_1 units of Y. It is clear that if some quantity of one or both of the inputs is transferred from one producer to another, the amounts of X and Y produced will be different. Thus for any particular distribution of inputs between the two producers, society obtains a particular combination of outputs.

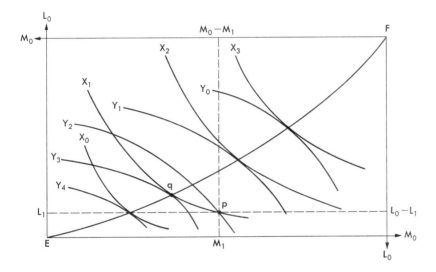

Figure 14–5

To clarify this relationship we shall use the same geometrical device applied to the preceding problem. When we superimpose the two isoquant maps in a suitable fashion, we obtain the box shown in Fig. 14–5. The size of this box is determined by the quantities of the available inputs. A point inside the box represents a particular distribution of the two resources between the two producers, and also a particular output combination. For example, the distribution indicated in Fig. 14–4 is represented in Fig. 14–5 by point p, and the amounts of the two goods produced by that input distribution are indicated by the labels of the two isoquants intersecting at p. In evaluating the optimality, or efficiency, of a particular input distribution we use a criterion similar to the concept of Pareto-optimality. Accordingly, for any two input distributions

D and D', we say:

Definition 14–4. If under D the output of at least one good is greater than and the output of no good is less than under D', then D is said to be a more efficient distribution.

Or likewise:

Definition 14–5. If under D' the output of at least one good is less than and the output of no good is greater than under D, then D' is said to be a less efficient distribution.

The criterion of efficiency, like the criterion for comparing individual welfare, does not apply to distributions which lead to an increased output of one good and a reduced output of another. The reason we do not compare such distributions is that one cannot compare the quantities of different commodities. Therefore, just as in the case of social welfare, the various distributions cannot be ranked numerically, because some distributions are noncomparable. Thus to achieve maximum efficiency in production means to reallocate the resources between the different goods whenever such redistribution leads to higher output of some good, without a loss in the output of some other good. When it is impossible to redistribute the resources any further without bringing about a reduction in the output of some good, then the distribution is efficient. Hence the following definition holds:

Definition 14–6. If a distribution D is such that no other distribution is more efficient than D, the latter is said to be efficient, or optimal.

14–3.1   The condition for efficiency in production

The goal of the production sector of the economy is the attainment of an optimal input distribution. It can easily be shown, using the same reasoning as in the preceding section, that an input distribution is optimal if at the respective point there occurs a tangency between two isoquants of the respective producers. For example, the distribution given by point p in Fig. 14–5 is not optimal, because by redistributing the inputs one can reach more efficient distributions. Clearly, the distribution represented by point q is more efficient than that at p because it yields the same output of X, and more of Y, than does distribution p. The distribution at q is also an optimal distribution, because moving away from q always reduces the output of at least one good.

The locus of all optimal input distributions forms a curve which is the analog of the contract curve in Fig. 14–3; we may call it simply the **efficiency curve.** And input distributions represented by points on this efficiency curve, like points on the contract curve, are noncomparable. Thus, in order to ensure efficiency in production, the best one can do is select an input distribution which is located on the efficiency curve. Each point on the efficiency curve does, of course, give rise to a particular output combination. For instance, the output combination associated with the input distribution at point q consists of X_1 units of X and Y_3 units of Y. Moving along the efficiency curve to the right of q yields higher quantities of X but lower quantities of Y, while moving to the left of q leads to opposite changes.

14–3.2   The transformation curve

The output combinations associated with the points on the efficiency curve can conveniently be plotted on a separate diagram. Such a diagram can be constructed by "mapping" the points on the efficiency curve onto an XY plane (i.e., a diagram with an X-axis and a Y-axis), as shown in Fig. 14–6. The curve thus obtained is called, for obvious reasons, a **production possibility curve** (sometimes, for less obvious reasons, also called a **transformation curve**). The production possibility curve indicates all the combinations of goods X and Y that

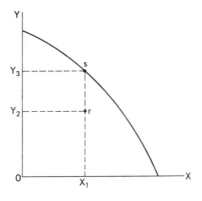

Figure 14–6

can be produced with the fixed amounts L_0 and M_0 of the two inputs, respectively, provided that all input distributions are optimal.* Point p in Fig. 14–5 is shown as point r in Fig. 14–6, and point q as point s.

The production possibility curve has a negative slope because with fixed amounts of inputs it is impossible to increase the output of one good without reducing that of the other. The intercepts of the curve indicate the maximum amount of each good that can be produced when all available inputs are put into the production of either one good or the other. Points above or to the right of the curve represent output combinations which cannot be attained with the available inputs. Points below or to the left of the curve represent output combinations which are forthcoming when the inputs are not distributed in an optimal manner, or when some of them are not used at all. Thus the region enclosed by the production possibility curve and the relevant parts of the two axes constitutes the feasible set. It is obvious, however, that an economy which is interested in maximizing its welfare will always choose a point on the outer boundary of the feasible set, i.e., on the production possibility curve.

---

* It may help, perhaps, to think of the production possibility curve as the "budget line" for the economy as a whole.

14-4   THE PRODUCTION-DISTRIBUTION PLAN

Which product combination should the economy produce? That is, which point on the production possibility curve is optimal? If efficiency in production and optimality in the distribution of the output are the only accepted criteria, then the above question has no answer. The welfare criteria which we have adopted in this analysis fail to distinguish between the different points on the production possibility curve, since all the points on that curve are equally satisfactory from the point of view of social welfare. Later in the chapter we shall point to a possible escape from this situation, but first we must reexamine the problem of the distribution of the final output.

The reader will recall that the main conclusion of our earlier discussion was that the distribution chosen should lie on the contract curve (see Fig. 14-3), but no particular point on the contract curve was found to be better than any other. This conclusion holds so long as the quantities of the goods in question are fixed (as was assumed in the above discussion), but it does not hold when the quantities of the goods can be varied through a change in production. In other words, the distribution problem discussed in Section 14-2 can be conceived of as being based on the assumption that the economy is anchored (for reasons irrelevant to this analysis) to one particular point on the production possibility curve. This assumption caused us to consider the amounts of the goods to be distributed as fixed. We now remove this restriction, and assume instead that the economy can move freely from one point on the production possibility curve to another. We shall show that, whenever the amounts of each good produced can be changed, it is no longer true that every distribution on the contract curve is as good as any other.

We select an arbitrary point on the production possibility curve, say point p, which yields X_0 units of X and Y_0 units of Y. Given this point (or any other point, for that matter) we can construct the corresponding commodity box. In Fig. 14-7, the box associated with point p is AY_0pX_0. Next we choose a distribution on the contract curve, say the distribution which allocates X_A and Y_A of the two goods, respectively, to individual A, and $X_0 - X_A$ and $Y_0 - Y_A$, respectively, to individual B. (Note that the contract curve itself is not shown.) Now let us change the construction of the commodity box slightly; instead of placing the origin of individual B's indifference map opposite to that of A (as was done in Fig. 14-2), we place it on the point which represents A's bundle. This does not change the dimensions of the box. Also, since at any point on the contract curve the respective indifference curves are tangent to each other, it follows that at point p the slope of indifference curve B_1 is the same as the slope of indifference curve A_1 at point B. (If the origin of individual B had

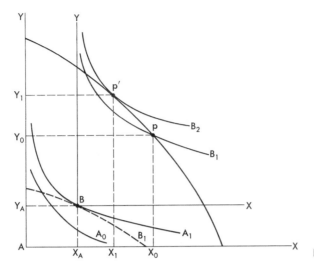

Figure 14–7

been placed at **p**, indifference curve B_1 would have been in the position shown by the dashed curve B_1.)

14–4.1 Testing for optimality

We now wish to investigate whether the economic state described in Fig. 14–7 is optimal or not, or, in other words, whether the choice of the production point **p** and the distribution represented by point **B** are consistent with welfare maximization. To test the optimality of the above production-distribution plan, we must determine whether or not it is possible, through a slight change in the plan, to make some individual better off without making anyone worse off. Consider the move from point **p** to point **p'**. This move has the effect of making the commodity box slightly higher, as well as narrower. Suppose that **A** receives the same bundle as before, then the amounts given to **B** are $X_1 - X_A$ and $Y_1 - Y_A$, respectively. But the latter bundle lies on indifference curve B_2, and hence the move to **p'** makes **B** better off. Thus the initial production-distribution plan is not optimal.* It seems equally obvious that if indifference curve B_1 were tangent to the production possibility curve at **p** (instead of intersecting it), then it would not have been possible to improve the position

---

* In considering the optimality of this plan we have ignored the two producers—individuals **E** and **F** (Section 14–3). This was done in order to confine the analysis to a two-individual case. In a more general model, the producers may be included among the consumers, in which case their individual welfare positions are evaluated (as are those of other consumers) on the basis of the amounts of final goods allocated to them.

of individual B, since in that case a movement away from point p would have put B on a lower indifference curve.

The conclusion stated in the last sentence is quite correct, but the matter is not quite so simple as it may seem, because a movement away from point p changes not only the size of the commodity box, but also the location of the contract curve. Therefore in order to make sure that the new output (as given by point p′ on the transformation curve) is distributed in accordance with the optimality condition, the movement away from point p must be accompanied by a movement from point B to some point on the new contract curve. It is not enough to examine only the effects of the move from p on individual B; one must at the same time take into account the effects of such a move on individual A. Thus in order to prove that a production-distribution plan is optimal whenever the slope of the respective indifference curves at the distribution under consideration is equal to the slope of the production possibility curve at the production point, we must show that when such a plan is changed by moving to a different point on the production possibility curve, **and** to the corresponding new distribution, then at least one of the two individuals will be made worse off. This is proved in the following section.

▶ A more formal test

In Fig. 14–8 the initial production-distribution plan consists of the production point p, and the distribution is defined by point B, which also represents the origin of B's indifference map. Indifference curve B_1 is tangent to the production possibility curve at p, and the line labeled T is the tangent line at p. The line T′ is tangent to indifference curve A_1 at B, and since, by assumption, indifference curves A_1 and B_1 have the same slope at points B and p, respectively, it follows that the lines T and T′ are parallel.

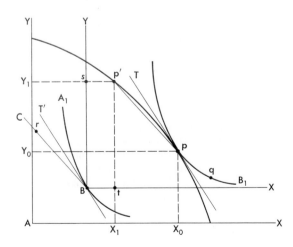

Figure 14–8

The initial plan is to be compared with the production point p′ and the corresponding distribution. Now, since we do not know where the new distribution is located (except that it must lie on the new contract curve), we must simply examine the different regions of the new commodity box. Consider all the points in a northeast direction from the initial distribution at point B, that is, all points in the rectangle Bsp′t. If the new distribution lies in that region, then individual B must be worse off, because when B's origin is moved into that region (maintaining the convention of placing B's origin at the chosen distribution), indifference curve B_1 will no longer touch the production possibility curve, and consequently a lower indifference curve will go through point p′. Let us therefore assume that the new distribution leaves individual B on the same indifference curve as at p. That is, let us assume that after we have shifted B's origin to the new distribution, indifference curve B_1 is tangent to p′. If that assumption holds, then it is clear that the origin of B's indifference map lies somewhere in a northwest direction from its initial position.

Suppose that we shift B's indifference map to make point p on indifference curve B_1 coincide with point p′. This can be accomplished by shifting the indifference map in such a way as to slide point p on indifference curve B_1 along the chord from p to p′. At the same time B's origin will slide along the line BC (which is drawn parallel to pp′) to point r, where the distance from B to r is the same as that from p to p′. It must be clear, however, that indifference curve B_1 cannot yet be tangent to the production possibility curve at p′, because the slope of the production possibility curve at p′ is less steep than at p. The tangency must, therefore, occur at a point on B_1 which has a flatter slope, say at q.

To form the desired tangency, we must shift the indifference map some more, and again in a northwest direction. The exact heading depends, of course, on the curvature of the indifference curve between points p and q, but it is clear that the heading (expressed in degrees) must be less (i.e., more westerly) than the direction of the line T′ [because the line going through points q and p has a slope which is flatter than that of the line T (or T′)]. We can therefore be sure that B's origin (which also indicates A's bundle), after the required shift is completed, must lie below or to the left of the line T′, and consequently it must also lie below indifference curve A_1. That means, of course, that although individual B is as well off as at the initial position, A is worse off. And it should be easy to see that A's position must also deteriorate if it is assumed that the new distribution puts individual B on a higher indifference curve than B_1. We can therefore conclude that a movement away from p to any other point on the production possibility curve necessarily means that at least one individual will be less well off, regardless of the location of the new product distribution. Thus the initial production-distribution plan is optimal.

14–4.2 The condition for an optimal production-distribution plan

The slope of the production possibility curve is referred to as the **marginal rate of transformation** (MRT). The term suggests that the production possibility curve can be thought of as a functional relationship which indicates how product Y can be transformed into product X, and vice versa (not directly, of course, but indirectly by a reallocation of inputs from the production of one good to that of the other), and hence the occasional reference to the above relationship as a transformation curve. The slope of an indifference curve has already been defined as the marginal rate of substitution (MRS) (Chapter 12), so that the optimality conditions for a production-distribution plan can be stated as

$$\text{MRS}^A = \text{MRS}^B = \text{MRT}^{XY}, \tag{14–1}$$

where the superscripts identify the respective individuals and commodities.

Let us recapitulate briefly. In a pure distribution problem, which can be thought of as one in which the size of the commodity box is fixed, all the distributions represented by points on the contract curve are optimal, but since all such distributions are noncomparable, it is not possible to rank these on the basis of Pareto-optimality alone. When, on the other hand, the size of the commodity box can be changed by moving along the production possibility curve, then for any one commodity box (i.e., for one particular point on the production possibility curve) there exists in general only one distribution which is optimal, namely, that for which the relevant MRS's are equal to MRT. However, even that condition does not present us with a unique solution, since the set of all optimal alternatives still comprises infinitely many production-distribution plans, all of which are noncomparable. This result is further illustrated in Fig. 14–9.

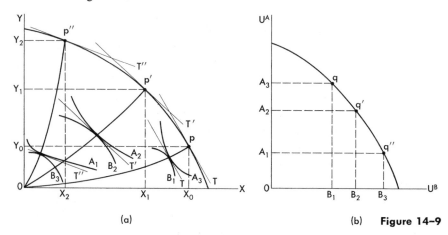

(a)   (b)   **Figure 14–9**

14–4.3 The utility boundary

Figure 14–9(a) shows the production possibility curve and three selected production-distribution plans. For each of the three production points, p, p′, and p″, we have indicated the corresponding commodity box, as well as the respective contract curves, and the indifference curves at the optimal distribution. The pairs of lines labeled T, T′, and T″ are the tangent lines at the respective production and distribution points, and from the optimality conditions it follows, of course, that each pair is a set of parallel lines. In order to emphasize the fact that each of these plans is optimal, we have shown in Fig. 14–9(b) the levels of utility attained by the two individuals under each plan. For example, the plan which calls for producing at point p on the production possibility curve puts individual A on indifference curve A_3 and individual B on indifference curve B_1. If we let A_3 and B_1 denote the values of the respective utility indices, then this particular distribution can be represented by point q in Fig. 14–9(b), where the axes measure the utility of the respective individuals. Similarly, points q′ and q″ indicate the levels of utility attained by the two individuals under the other two production-distribution plans, respectively. When this mapping is carried out for all points on the production possibility curve, we obtain the curve shown in Fig. 14–9(b). This curve is called the **utility boundary.** It shows all combinations of the individual levels of utility that can be attained when all the optimality conditions are satisfied; i.e., providing that there exist efficiency in production and optimality in distribution. Since the utility boundary has a negative slope, it is obvious that it represents a set of noncomparable combinations, none of which can be said to be the best.

This is as far as the analysis of our example can be carried with the Pareto-optimality welfare criterion. It is, admittedly, somewhat disappointing that we were unable to find a unique solution, i.e., a particular production-distribution plan which could be said to be better than any other. This is not really surprising, in view of the nature of the Pareto-optimality criterion; after all, a great number of economic states (i.e., those under which some individuals are made better off and others worse off, compared with some initial state) cannot be evaluated at all in this approach. Thus the application of the Pareto-optimality criterion to the problem of social welfare reduces the set of all **feasible** alternatives to a narrower set of **optimal** choices (by eliminating all the Pareto-inferior states), but this reduction still leaves society with infinitely many plans to choose from.

14–4.4 The social welfare function

There is obviously no way of overcoming this indeterminateness unless one devises a method for comparing gains made by one individual with the losses suffered by another. Suppose, for instance, that society is able to express a preference between any two economic states, where the latter are described in terms of the levels of utility attained by each individual. In other words, assume that for any two states S and S', each consisting of a pair of values (U^A, U^B), society either prefers S to S', S' to S, or is indifferent as to the choice between them. If these preferences can be described by some numerical function, then this function is called a **social welfare function,** and in the two-individual case can be symbolically represented by

$$W = f(U^A, U^B), \tag{14-2}$$

·where W denotes the welfare index. The welfare index, like the utility index, is designed merely to rank the various economic states, and the numerical value of W has no meaning as such.

The general properties of the social welfare function are similar to those of an individual utility function. In particular, the value of the welfare index increases whenever the utility level of one individual is increased without lowering that of the other individual. Thus the social welfare function is consistent with the Pareto-optimality criterion, but, it goes much farther, since it assigns a value to **every** economic state, including those which according to the Pareto criterion are regarded as noncomparable. The existence of a social welfare function, therefore, implies a comparison of the welfare positions of the individual members of society.

Given a particular social welfare function, we can then state the welfare problem as an attempt to maximize the social welfare function, subject to certain environmental restrictions. These restrictions include the limited quantities of the resources with which the economy is endowed, the technology which governs the productive processes, and the tastes (preferences) of the individuals in the society. But since the social welfare function is defined in terms of individual utility levels (rather than, for instance, in terms of levels of output), the restrictions which must be obeyed can be imposed on the problem in the form of the utility boundary (Fig. 14-9b), since that relationship embodies all the above-mentioned constraints. The region enclosed by the utility boundary and the relevant segments of the axes can therefore be thought of as the feasible set for this problem.

Thus solving this problem means finding a point in the feasible set which is associated with the highest level of social welfare. We can do this by deriving social indifference curves from the social welfare function and superimposing them on the utility boundary, as shown in Fig. 14-10. Assuming that the social indifference curves are convex, we can easily find a unique solution, such as point q' in the above diagram. In order to determine the actual program associated with point q', we must first find the distribution which yields the utility combination (A_2, B_2), and then locate the corresponding point on the production possibility curve.   In the above example, this turns out to be point p' in Fig. 14–9(a).   In order to find the proper allocation of inputs to the two producers we must go back to the input box (Fig. 14–5), and locate the point on the efficiency curve which yields the output combination (X_1, Y_1).

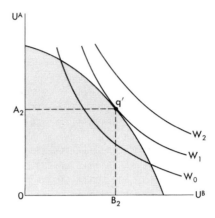

Figure 14–10

14–5 WELFARE AND THE PRICE MECHANISM

In our discussion up to this point we have approached the question of social welfare more or less from the planner's point of view.   That is, we have posed during the discussion a number of questions of the kind which a central planning board might ask itself (or be asked), and thus the various conclusions which we derived from the analysis can be interpreted as guiding lines for those who are in charge of planning the economic organization.   The degree to which any particular economy is governed by public planning varies, of course, from one society to another, but there is no doubt that some form of government control is to be found in almost every modern society.   However, in certain situations it may not be feasible, or desirable, to subject the economy to extensive planning, and it is therefore of considerable interest to study the optimality of the performance of an economy when it is left to operate without any direct controls. If we exclude direct planning from the simple model which we have used in this chapter, then the allocation of inputs, as well as the distribution of the output, will be determined by the forces of the market.

14–5.1 The competitive mechanism

Let us first examine the question of input allocation.   Figure 14–11 shows an input box like the one in Fig. 14–5.   The total input endowment consists of L_0 and M_0 of the two inputs, respectively, and the initial allocation is represented by point p.   Now, instead of having a planning board decide on how the inputs should be allocated between the two producers, we introduce a market mechanism and permit the two producers to trade with each other.   The question, therefore, is: Given the opportunity, will the two producers trade inputs among

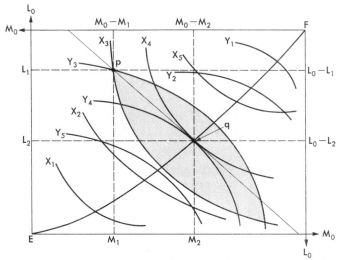

Figure 14–11

themselves, and if so, what will be the final allocation? It is clear that trade will take place only if it does not make any producer worse off than he is at the initial position. In the present example the welfare position of each producer is measured in terms of the level of output he is able to produce, as indicated by the respective isoquant. Thus producer **E** will refuse to take part in any exchange that will move him to a point in the input box below or to the left of isoquant X_3, while producer **F** will reject any trade offer that puts him on an isoquant lower than Y_3. However, both producers can benefit, or at least remain as well off as at **p**, if they agree on a trade which will move them to a point inside the shaded region of Fig. 14–11.

For example, if **E** offered $L_1 - L_2$ units of L to F in exchange for $M_2 - M_1$ units of M, and F accepted the offer, the allocation of inputs after the trade took place would be given by point **q**, and each producer would be able to produce a higher level of output.

The terms of this particular transaction are defined by the ratio of the quantities exchanged, that is $(L_1 - L_2)/(M_2 - M_1)$, which in geometrical terms is given by the slope of the straight line passing through points **p** and **q**. Since the ratio of the quantities exchanged is equal to the price ratio, the above-mentioned line also represents the budget line facing each producer.* We can therefore conclude that if the two producers were operating under conditions of pure competition, and if the ratio of the prevailing market prices were equal

---

* Note that the slope of that line is the same regardless of which of the two origins serves as the point of reference.

to the slope of the line passing through p and q, then producer E would sell $L_1 - L_2$ units of L and purchase $M_2 - M_1$ units of M, while producer F would purchase and sell these quantities, respectively.

Suppose, however, that the ratio of the market prices is different from the slope of the above line, what then? Let us look at Fig. 14–12, which shows part of the input box in greater detail. Let the initial price ratio be given by the slope of the line through points p, r, and s, a line which now serves as the budget line for the respective producers. Under these conditions producer E will want to reach isoquant X', and he will consequently offer to sell $L_1 - L_3$ units of L and to purchase $M_3 - M_1$ units of M. Producer F, on the other hand, will plan to place himself on isoquant Y', and thus will offer to purchase $L_1 - L_4$ units of L and to sell $M_4 - M_1$ units of M. Clearly, the quantities offered for sale do not match the quantities demanded; specifically, there is an excess demand $(L_3 - L_4)$ for L, and an excess supply $(M_4 - M_3)$ of M. The two markets cannot be in equilibrium, and the prices can be expected to change in response to the forces of the market. Under the above conditions of excess demand and supply, we would expect the price of L to rise relative to that of M, or, what amounts to the same thing, the price of M to fall relative to that of L. The budget line will therefore rotate around point p counterclockwise.

It is clear from what we have just said in reference to the initial price ratio that the two markets will be in equilibrium only if both producers want to move to the same point in the input box, and that, in turn, will occur only if the budget line is tangent to the respective isoquants at the same point, such as q in Fig. 14–12. The market price can therefore be expected to continue to change until such an equilibrium is reached.

Thus we see that if buyers and sellers in each input market behave as pure competitors (i.e., take market prices as given), and if market prices respond

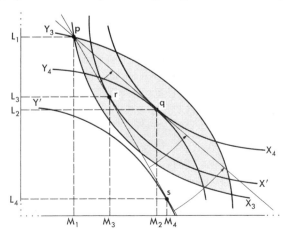

Figure 14–12

freely to the forces of demand and supply, then an equilibrium price ratio will be reached for which the corresponding budget line is tangent to two isoquants. Since such a point lies on the efficiency curve (see Fig. 14–11), we can say that the purely competitive market mechanism tends to bring about an efficient allocation of resources. It is because such an allocation is a necessary condition for the attainment of a Pareto-optimal production-distribution plan that we can describe the competitive mechanism as being socially desirable.*

Once the input markets are in equilibrium and a particular input allocation is obtained, the economy will produce a particular combination of outputs. It remains to be seen how the market mechanism distributes the given output between consumers. The answer can now be anticipated, since the problem is analogous to that of the input allocation. Each consumer is assumed to have at his disposal an initial share of the total output, and hence the initial distribution is simply described by a point in the commodity box. Consumers are then given the opportunity to trade in the various commodity markets, which are assumed to operate under purely competitive conditions. The mechanism by which each market is cleared is the same as that which equilibrates the input markets (as described in the preceding discussion, and Fig. 14–12), and therefore the final distribution when all commodity markets are in equilibrium is Pareto-optimal, since it is located somewhere on the contract curve. Thus we can conclude that when pure competition prevails in all markets, the equilibrium production-distribution plan is Pareto-optimal.

14–5.2   An imperfectly competitive mechanism

It is equally true that lack of competition is inconsistent with Pareto-optimality. This has already been demonstrated in Chapters 7, 9, and 10 in a somewhat different context. Let us repeat this demonstration in the framework of our two-individual model. Suppose that individual A acts like a monopolist and B like a pure competitor; A is, therefore, free to set prices, while B considers them given. The monopolist also possesses the relevant information about market demand and supply, which we assume he obtains by having the pure competitor make trade offers for different price ratios (Fig. 14–13).

The initial product distribution is at point p_0. For any particular price ratio set by the monopolist, the competitor will be faced with a particular budget line passing through p_0, and the tangency point of each such line with the respective indifference curve indicates the position to which the competitor is

---

* A competitive market presupposes, of course, that the number of buyers and sellers is large. The above analysis can easily be extended (using mathematical, rather than geometrical, tools) to markets with more than two individuals, in which case the above condition is applied to every possible pair of individuals.

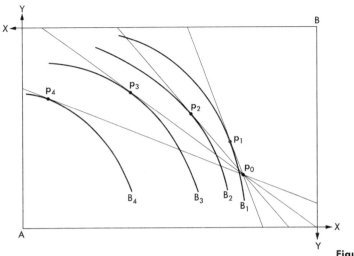

Figure 14–13

willing to move in each case. When this is done for all possible price ratios, then the locus of all such tangency points may be a curve such as curve C in Fig. 14–14. Given this information, the monopolist chooses that price ratio which places him on his highest indifference curve. In the above example the highest indifference curve that the monopolist can reach is A_1, which is tangent to the curve C at p_2. The competitor B at the same time reaches indifference curve B_2, which is tangent to the budget line at p_2. It is therefore obvious that at p_2 indifference curves A_1 and B_2 intersect each other (since at p_2 curve C has a different slope from that of the budget line), and consequently the distribution at p_2 does not lie on the contract curve and is not Pareto-optimal.

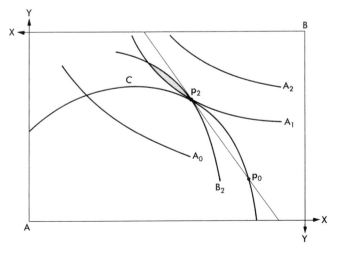

Figure 14–14

SUMMARY

This chapter has dealt with an area of economic theory whose primary objective is to evaluate economic states from the point of view of social welfare. In contrast to topics in positive economics, welfare economics derives its conclusions from value judgments, and consequently its subject matter is of normative nature. While ethical values and social goals are not the exclusive domain of the economist, nevertheless the economist is called on to formulate economic programs which will help realize the chosen objectives.

Modern welfare economics relies heavily on the concept of Pareto-optimality, a welfare criterion which avoids any comparison of individual preferences (utilities), and consequently fails to distinguish between a great number of possible economic states. In this approach welfare is said to be maximized whenever society reaches a position from which it is impossible to move without inflicting a loss on at least one of its members. One of the characteristics of these optimal positions is their lack of uniqueness, and that makes it necessary for society to adopt additional criteria in order to make a choice of a particular position from among all those which are Pareto-optimal.

The first phase of our analysis dealt with the pure distribution problem. We saw that the set of Pareto-optimal distributions consisted of those points at which the MRS's of the respective individuals were equal. Geometrically these distributions form the contract curve. When the scope of the problem is broadened to include production, welfare maximization imposes certain efficiency conditions on the producing sector. These require that inputs be allocated in a way which will equate the MRT's of the respective producers, and we defined the set of all such points as the efficiency curve. We found that a production-distribution plan is Pareto-optimal if the production and distribution points of such a plan equate the respective MRS's with the relevant MRT. The set of optimal production-distribution plans, like the solution to the distribution problem, contains infinitely many choices which cannot be ranked on the basis of Pareto-optimality alone.

One method of making a choice among Pareto-optimal plans is to make use of a social welfare function. Such a function admits of an interpersonal comparison of utility, and therefore it provides a complete ranking of all possible states. A unique solution to the welfare problem can then be obtained by maximizing the social welfare function, subject to certain restrictions.

Finally we saw that if all markets in the economy operate under conditions of pure competition, then the final production-distribution plan is Pareto-optimal. If, on the other hand, there exists an imperfection in the competitive mechanism, the performance of the economy is no longer consistent with Pareto-optimality.

SELECTED REFERENCES

BATOR, F. M., "The Simple Analytics of Welfare Economics." *American Economic Review* **47**, 1957, pp. 22–59.

BOULDING, K. E., "Welfare Economics." *A Survey of Contemporary Economics* **II**, B. F. Haley (ed.). Homewood, Ill.: Irwin, 1952, pp. 1–38.

KENEN, P. B., "On the Geometry of Welfare Economics." *Quarterly Journal of Economics* **71**, 1957, pp. 426–447.

MISHAN, E. J., "A Reappraisal of the Principle of Resource Allocation." *Economica*, New Series **24**, 1957, pp. 324–342.

SCITOVSKY, T., "A Note on Welfare Propositions in Economics." *Review of Economic Studies* **9**, 1941–42, pp. 77–88.

SCITOVSKY, T., *Welfare and Competition.* Chicago: Irwin, 1951, Chapter 4.

STREETEN, P., "Economics and Value Judgments." *Quarterly Journal of Economics* **64**, 1950, pp. 583–595.

EXERCISES

1. A society of two individuals—A and B—has at its disposal 100 units of good X and 80 units of good Y. Figure E14–1 shows part of the indifference maps of the two individuals. Complete the sentences given below.

   (a) Suppose that initially A has 40 units of X and 60 units of Y, while B has the remaining amounts. Then a redistribution which transfers 10 units of X from

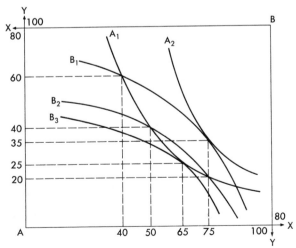

Figure E14–1

B to A and 20 units of Y from A to B, so that each individual will have one-half of the available amount of each good, will make (**A, B,** *both individuals, neither individual*) better off.

(b) The distribution which obtains if the equalizing redistribution mentioned in (a) above is carried out (*is Pareto-optimal, is not Pareto-optimal*).

(c) The distribution mentioned in (b) above is just as good, from the point of view of social welfare, as that which gives individual B _____ units of X and _____ units of Y.

(d) Denote the initial distribution [see (a) above] by D_1, and denote by D_2 the distribution which gives individual B 35 units of X and 55 units of Y. Then it is correct to say that (*D_2 is Pareto-superior to D_1, D_2 is Pareto-inferior to D_1, D_2 and D_1 are noncomparable*).

(e) Let D_3 be the distribution which puts A on indifference curve A_2, and B on indifference curve B_1. Then it is true that (*D_2 and D_3 are equally good, D_2 is Pareto-superior to D_3, D_2 is Pareto-inferior to D_3, D_2 and D_3 are noncomparable*).

(f) A movement away from D_3 must necessarily (*make at least one individual better off, make both individuals better off, hurt at least one individual, hurt both individuals*). Therefore D_3 is said to be (*a nonoptimal distribution, a Pareto-optimal distribution, the best distribution in the diagram*).

(g) Shade that part of Fig. E14–1 which represents all the distributions that are Pareto-superior to the initial distribution (D_1).

2. An economy has at its disposal 400 units of input L and 500 units of input M. Its production sector consists of two industries: one, in the charge of manager E, produces good X; the other, in the charge of manager F, produces good Y. Figure E14–2 represents a partial picture of the technological conditions under which each industry operates. Complete the sentences given below.

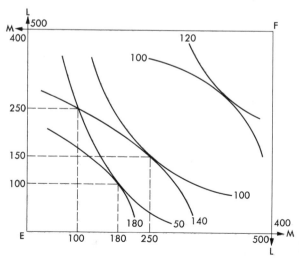

Figure E14–2

(a) If 150 units of L and 400 units of M are allocated to the Y industry and the remaining quantities are allocated to the X industry, then the economy will produce _____ units of X and _____ units of Y. This distribution of inputs is (*efficient, inefficient*).

(b) If the allocation mentioned in (a) above is changed by transferring 50 units of L from producer E to producer F, then the economy will produce (*more of X and less of Y, more of Y and less of X, less of both goods*).

(c) If the planning board decides to produce 50 units of X, then the maximum amount of Y that can be produced is _____ units. To carry out this production plan producer E requires _____ units of L and _____ units of M.

(d) A production plan which calls for the production of 100 units of each good can be said to be an (*efficient, inefficient, unfeasible*) plan.

(e) Draw (on a separate diagram) the production possibility curve for the above economy. Locate and label three points on that curve.

(f) Locate on your diagram the points associated with the following input distributions: (i) the distribution described in (a) above; (ii) the distribution which is required for the production plan in (d) above; (iii) the distribution under which all available inputs are put at the disposal of producer F.

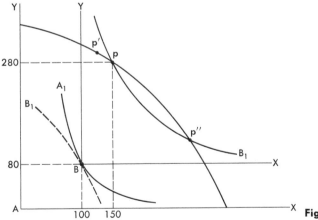

Figure E14–3

3. An economy with two individuals, A and B, faces the production possibility curve shown in Fig. E14–3. The initial production point is at p and the initial product distribution is represented by point B, which is also the origin of B's indifference map. The dashed curve indicates the position of indifference curve B_1 if B's indifference map is drawn with its origin at p rather than at B. Complete the sentences given below.

(a) Under the initial distribution A receives _____ units of X and _____ units of Y, while B receives _____ units of X and _____ units of Y.

(b) If production is moved from point **p** to point **p′**, and **A** receives the same bundle as in the initial distribution [your answer to (a) above], then **B** will be made (*better off, worse off*).

(c) If the economy produces at point **p″** and the origin of **B**'s indifference map were placed at **p″**, then at point **B** indifference curves A_1 and B_1 (*are tangent to each other, intersect each other*). Therefore, given the production point **p″**, the distribution represented by point **B** is (*Pareto-optimal, not Pareto-optimal*).

(d) If production takes place at **p″**, the contract curve passes (*above, through, below*) point **B**.

(e) If production takes place at a point on the production possibility curve between points **p** and **p″**, and if individual **B** receives a bundle which leaves him on indifference curve B_1, then individual **A** will be made (*better off, worse off*). Therefore the above production-distribution plan is (*Pareto-superior, Pareto-inferior, noncomparable*) to the initial plan (i.e., production at point **p** and distribution at point **B**).

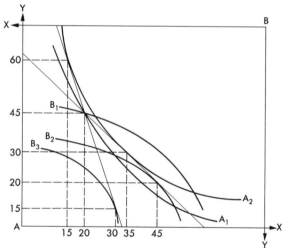

Figure E14–4

4. Figure E14–4 shows the commodity box of an economy consisting of individuals **A** and **B**. Initially **A** has 20 units of X and 45 units of Y. Complete the sentences given below.

(a) The initial distribution is (*Pareto-optimal, not Pareto-optimal*). Thus if the two individuals were to meet in the market place, it is (*likely, not likely*) that they would find it mutually advantageous to engage in trade.

(b) If $P^X/P^Y = 3$, **A** will be a (*buyer, seller*) of X and **B** will be a (*buyer, seller*) of X. Thus there will be an excess (*demand for, supply of*) X equal to _____ units and an excess (*demand for, supply of*) Y equal to _____ units. Consequently the price ratio P^X/P^Y is likely to (*rise, fall*).

(c) If $P^X/P^Y =$ _____, A will offer to buy 15 units of X. At this price ratio B will offer to (*buy, sell*) _____ units of X. There will therefore be an excess (*demand for, supply of*) Y equal to _____ units.

(d) Suppose that A is a monopolist who is in a position to choose one of two values for the price ratio P^X/P^Y, either 3 or 1. Individual B acts like a pure competitor. In that case A will set the price ratio at _____. At that price ratio B will buy from A _____ units of _____ and sell him _____ units of _____. Following this exchange A will be (*better off than, as well off as*) he was before the trade, and B will find himself (*better off, worse off*) than prior to the exchange.

15

GENERAL EQUILIBRIUM

Models dealing with the behavior of economic units, such as the firm and the household, are interesting and useful to the economist for two reasons primarily: (a) They provide a means for learning, or hypothesizing, about how an economic unit formulates its economic problems and the process by which it attempts to solve them; and (b) they provide a basis for studying the behavior and performance of the economy as a whole, or parts of it. This text is designed to deal almost exclusively with the first of these needs, but in order to provide the student with a broader perspective and to illustrate the relationship between different areas of economic theory, we shall show in this last chapter how the models of individual behavior we have developed can be used in the construction of models designed to describe the workings of an entire economic system. Models of the latter type are usually referred to as **general equilibrium** models.

15–1 THE CONSTRUCTION OF THE MODEL

It is possible to distinguish between two types of general equilibrium models: (a) aggregated models, and (b) disaggregated models. In the former types of models the entire system is described by relatively few functional relationships connecting several crucial variables. These variables represent aggregated quantities such as the total amount of expenditures on consumption goods, the total amount expended on capital goods (investment), total employment, aggregate output, and the like. The attraction of aggregate models lies in their simplicity, as well as in the availability of empirical data necessary for the testing of these models.

On the other hand, many important variables and relationships tend to disappear in the process of aggregation, and thus aggregated models are not applicable to a great number of problems which are of interest to economists as well as policy makers. Moreover, viewed from the methodological vantage point, aggregated models lose a great deal of their appeal since their basic behavioral assumptions are not derived directly from models of individual behavior, such as models of consumer behavior or the firm.

Disaggregated models, on the other hand, are characterized by their atomistic nature. In its most extreme, or pure, form a disaggregated model represents every single economic decision maker and every economic good in the system. Since this text was devoted to the study of individual behavior, it is only natural that we should have chosen as our example a disaggregated general equilibrium model. However, to keep the exposition within manageable bounds we shall limit the number of markets to be considered. Accordingly, we shall first construct a model with only two markets—a factor market and a product market. The individuals who trade in these markets are either consumers or producers.

15–1.1 The consuming sector

Beginning with the consumers, let us assume that each consumer maximizes a utility function which depends on leisure and on product X. This model differs only slightly from that which we considered in Section 13–1, in that we have replaced the variable I (income) by the variable X. We can then derive for each consumer a supply function of labor and a demand function for product X, as shown in Fig. 15–1. Part (a) shows the representative consumer's indifference

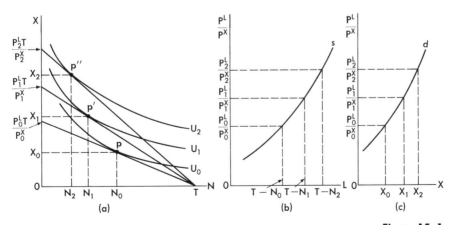

Figure 15–1

map and three budget lines for three different price ratios. The X-intercept of the budget line is now equal to $P^L T/P^X$ (rather than $P^L T$, as it was, for example, in Fig. 13–1), since the vertical axis measures units of product X and not the consumer's level of income. Note also that the position of the budget line, and hence the quantities demanded, depends only on **relative** prices, i.e., the ratio P^L/P^X. This is so because if the wage rate increases by, say, a factor of k, the consumer's earned income from a given number of hours worked will increase by the same proportion, while an increase in the price of X by a factor of k increases the consumer's expenditure on any fixed amount of X by that proportion. Therefore a proportionate change in both P^L and P^X leaves the consumer's purchasing power, as shown by the position of the budget line, unchanged.

The invariance of quantities demanded in this model to proportionate changes in P^L and P^X is analogous to the invariance of quantities demanded to proportionate changes in prices and income in the standard consumer model. (See statement 12B, Section 12–2.4.). The consumer's supply function of labor (where $L = T - N$) is shown in Fig. 15–1(b), and his demand function for X in Fig. 15–1(c). The demand function has a positive slope because it is plotted against P^L/P^X; when plotted against P^X/P^L it has a negative slope.*

To obtain the respective **market** supply and demand functions we simply "sum" the respective functions of all the consumers in the market. If it is assumed that all consumers have indifference maps of the type shown in Fig. 15–1(a) (although not necessarily identical ones), then the supply and demand functions of all individuals have positive slopes, and consequently the market functions have similar shapes, as shown in Fig. 15–2. Capital letters denote market supply and demand functions, respectively.

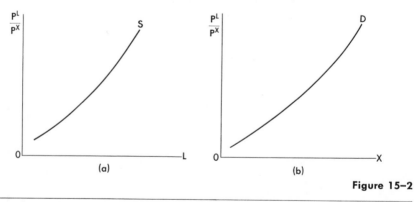

Figure 15–2

---

* Actually, there also exists money in the economy which serves as the medium of exchange. However, it is assumed here that consumers have no desire for cash balances as such; hence the amount of cash available has no effect on the demand (or prices) of the real goods in the model.

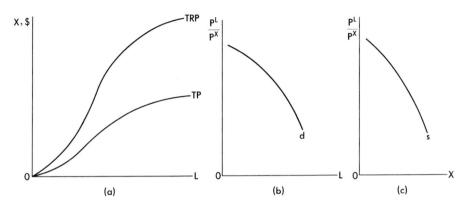

Figure 15–3

15–1.2 The producing sector

Turning now to the production sector, we assume that each producer is confronted with a certain technology which can be described by a conventional production function. In the two-good model used here, labor is the only factor of production.* We shall further assume that producers behave like pure competitors in both the factor and the product market, and that they are profit maximizers. In addition we want the model to be "closed," which means that every flow of payments must be accounted for. Therefore we also impose on each producer a budget constraint which equates his expenditures with his receipts. Since the producer's expenditures consist entirely of his wage payments (which make up his cost of production), and since his receipts are his sales revenues, the imposition of the above budget constraint is tantamount to assuming that each producer earns zero profit.†

We can now derive for each producer a demand function for labor and a supply function of X. Figure 15–3(a) shows the producer's TP (production) function and his TRP function. The demand function for labor is given in Fig. 15–3(b), which shows that the amount of labor demanded depends on the ratio P^L/P^X. Recall that the optimal amount of labor used by the producer is that which satisfies the condition

$$MRP = P^L \tag{15–1}$$

or, since $MRP = MP \cdot P^X$,

$$MP \cdot P^X = P^L. \tag{15–2}$$

---

* To make the model applicable to somewhat more realistic situations, one may assume that there exist other inputs besides labor which are used in production, but that for some reason they are not traded in any market.
† Therefore this model can be thought of as dealing with a long-run situation.

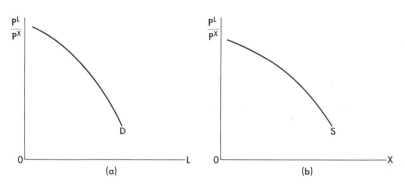

Figure 15–4

Dividing both sides of Eq. (15–2) by P^X, we obtain

$$MP = P^L/P^X. \qquad\qquad (15\text{–}3)$$

Thus, for example, when P^L/P^X falls, MP must also decline. Since the producer always operates in the range in which the slope of the production function (that is, MP) decreases as L is increased, it follows that when P^L/P^X falls the producer demands more labor. Hence the negative slope of the demand function for labor. Furthermore, since more (less) labor means more (less) output, the level of output produced (and supplied) also varies inversely with P^L/P^X, as shown in Fig. 15–3(c). Here again the supply function appears to have the "wrong" slope, because it is plotted against P^L/P^X rather than P^X/P^L. Finally we "sum" these functions over all producers to obtain the respective market functions shown in Fig. 15–4.

15–1.3   The integrated model

Now that we have the different components of our model, we can complete the construction by putting the parts together. We do this by superimposing Fig. 15–2 on Fig. 15–4, thereby obtaining a complete picture of the whole system, as shown in Fig. 15–5. The main purpose of this analysis is, of course, to learn something about the nature of the general equilibrium of the economy; i.e., the state of affairs which prevails when both markets are in equilibrium at the same time.

Since quantities offered and demanded in each market depend on relative prices, the first question we shall want to answer is: What set of prices (i.e., what values of P^L/P^X) will bring about general equilibrium? An inspection of the labor market, for instance, indicates quite clearly that the pair (P_0^L, P_0^X) clears that market, since at these prices both quantity demanded and quantity offered are equal to L_0. What about the product market? Figure 15–5(b) indicates

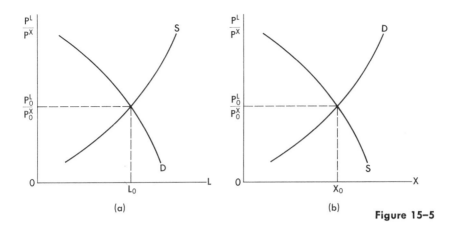

Figure 15–5

that the product market is cleared at the same price ratio which clears the labor market.

Now this is not a graphical coincidence, but an important feature of general equilibrium models. If the labor market is in equilibrium, then the amount paid out in wages by all producers is exactly equal to the incomes of all consumers. But since each producer, and each consumer, must obey his budget constraint, it also follows that the amount received by all producers in sales receipts must be equal to what all consumers pay out in expenditures on X. Since all transactions take place at some fixed price (P_0^X), the quantity of X sold is equal to the quantity of X purchased. We see, therefore, that if the labor market is in equilibrium in this model, the product market must also be in equilibrium at the same price ratio, and vice versa. This result is called **Walras' law,** after the nineteenth-century Swiss economist who was a pioneer in general equilibrium analysis.

15–2 THE WORKINGS OF THE MODEL

Let us now study the reactions of the two markets to a disturbance which jolts the system out of equilibrium. Suppose that an increase takes place in consumers' preference for leisure, which means, of course, a diminished willingness to work at any given set of relative wages. This change manifests itself in a shift to the left of the supply function of labor as shown in Fig. 15–6(a). However, if consumers offer less labor at each value of P^L/P^X, they will also receive a smaller income, and hence will not be able to spend as much on product X as they did prior to the change. Therefore it is also necessary to shift the demand function for X to the left, as shown in Fig. 15–6(b). In fact, since Fig. 15–6(a) tells us that the labor market is in equilibrium at the ratio P_1^L/P_1^X,

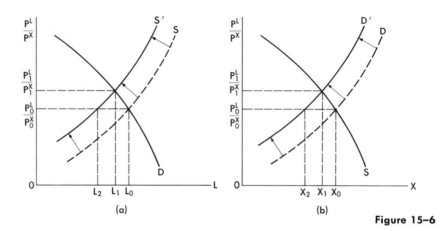

Figure 15–6

the new demand function (D′) must intersect the supply function at the same price ratio.

What causes the economy to move from its initial equilibrium to the new equilibrium? As soon as the consumers' supply and demand functions shift, the labor market is confronted with an excess demand $(L_0 - L_2)$, while the product market faces a state of excess supply $(X_0 - X_2)$. This situation will induce producers to raise the wage rate in an attempt to increase the availability of labor, and to lower the price of X in order to stimulate sales. The effect of these changes in P^L and P^X is to raise the value of P^L/P^X, thus moving each market toward the new equilibrium. The reader may note, however, that it is not necessary that both prices should change in order to have the excess demand and supply removed from the two markets. Suppose, for example, that producers raise the wage rate, while leaving the price of X unchanged. This, too, has the effect of increasing P^L/P^X, and it is therefore possible to reach the new equilibrium by placing the burden of the adjustment entirely on the wage rate (or the price of good X, for that matter). Thus in the absence of additional information we cannot tell whether both prices change during the adjustment process, nor can we determine the direction and magnitude by which they change. In other words, all we know is that $P_1^L/P_1^X > P_0^L/P_0^X$, but this by itself gives us no indication of the actual change in each of the two prices; we may have $P_1^X < P_0^X$ and $P_1^L \gtrless P_0^L$, or $P_1^L > P_0^L$ and $P_1^X \gtrless P_0^X$.

There is one problem, essentially methodological in nature, to which we must draw the reader's attention. In the preceding paragraph we have said that in response to the excess demand and supply in the two markets, respectively, producers raise the price of labor, and lower the price of X. On the other hand, in Section 15–1.2 we have assumed that producers behave like pure competitors. We are thus confronted with an inconsistency! We could have easily avoided this by replacing in the preceding paragraph the phrase "will induce producers to raise the wage rate" with the phrase "will induce a rise in the wage rate," and a similar substitution in the second part of the same sentence. Had we done so the reader would have been entitled to ask: **Who** changes the prices?

This is a legitimate question since prices are, after all, the outcome of decisions made by human beings. In the study of individual behavior under purely competitive conditions this question may be dismissed as irrelevant; the model of the individual competitor merely postulates that a set of market prices exists which gives rise to a choice of output, or inputs, on the part of the competitor, but the model is not concerned at all with the determination of prices, or the reason for changes in them. In the framework of a general equilibrium model, however, this question can no longer be ignored.

One approach to this question suggested by some economists is to think of trade in purely competitive markets as an auction. (This is by no means a far-fetched idea, in view of the fact that some of the staples are marketed through organized exchanges.) In this scheme the auctioneer sets the prices, and the traders make their bids and offers accordingly. However, prices and contracts are not final until a set of equilibrium prices is reached. If for some set of prices there exists excess demand of some commodity, then the auctioneer raises the price of that commodity by some amount, and he lowers the price in the case of excess supply. If the demand and supply functions have the "right" slopes, then such price changes (provided they are of sufficiently small magnitude) tend to eliminate excess demand and supply, and will lead to a set of general equilibrium prices. Thus if the reader is willing to accept the conception of competitive trade as a particular type of auction, then he should replace the word "producers" by the words "the auctioneer" in the above-mentioned sentence.

15–2.1 A three-good model

Since the above two-good model is apt to leave the misleading impression that general equilibrium models are by and large simple affairs, we shall present now an example of a three-good model. We introduce a second product, product Y, and assume, for simplicity, that some producers produce only product X and others only product Y. The demand and supply functions depend again on relative prices, and for the sake of symmetry we have chosen to define all functions in terms of the ratios P^X/P^L and P^Y/P^L. The production side of the economy is represented by Fig. 15–7, with part (a) showing the demand function for labor. This relation is represented by a family of partial demand functions because the total quantity demanded depends on both price ratios—the quantity demanded by producers of product X depends on P^X/P^L, and the

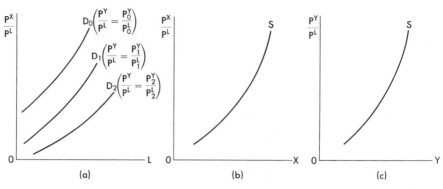

Figure 15–7

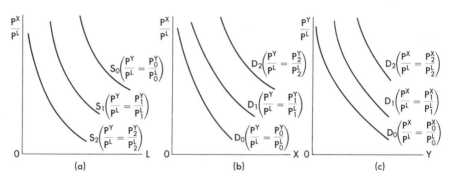

Figure 15–8

quantity demanded by producers of product Y depends on P^Y/P^L. It is assumed in the diagram that

$$\frac{P_0^Y}{P_0^L} < \frac{P_1^Y}{P_1^L} < \frac{P_2^Y}{P_2^L}.$$

Figures 15–7(b) and (c) show the two supply functions, respectively; each of these functions is represented by a single relationship due to the simplifying assumption that every producer produces either product X or product Y, but not both.

The consumer sector is represented by Fig. 15–8. It is assumed that all goods are substitutes for one another; i.e., an increase in the price of one good always increases the demand for each of the other goods. (See the definition of substitutes in Section 12–2.5.) Note that the supply and demand functions of the product markets now have the "right" slopes, since we have defined relative prices in a fashion slightly different from that used in the one-good example.

We now superimpose Fig. 15–7 on Fig. 15–8 to obtain the presentation of the complete model, as shown in Fig. 15–9. (The notation in parentheses is

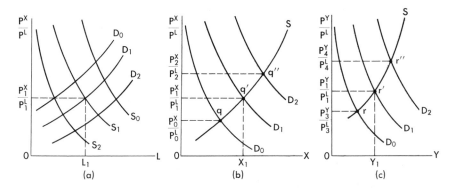

Figure 15–9

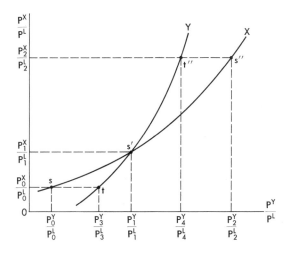

Figure 15–10

omitted to preserve clarity.) The diagram shows quite clearly that the set $(P_1^X/P_1^L, P_1^Y/P_1^L)$ is an equilibrium price set, since it clears all markets simultaneously. Note that, in each market, equilibrium obtains at the intersection of the correct members of the various families of demand and supply curves, i.e., the curves for the relative prices P_1^X/P_1^L and P_1^Y/P_1^L, respectively. The equilibrium quantities exchanged in each market are L_1, X_1, and Y_1, respectively.

Since in the three-good model the functions in each market depend on two price ratios, Fig. 15–9 is a somewhat awkward tool for studying the adjustment of the system during disequilibrium. Let us, therefore, make use of a more convenient geometrical presentation. First, we "map" the points q, q', and q'' from Fig. 15–9(b) into Fig. 15–10, in which they are represented as points s, s', and s''. Note that both axes of Fig. 15–10 measure price ratios. These points, as well as the other points on the curve labeled X, indicate pairs of the two price ratios which maintain equilibrium in market X. For example, point q in Fig. 15–9(b) represents an equilibrium point if the relative prices are P_0^X/P_0^L and P_0^Y/P_0^L; therefore the coordinates of point s in Fig. 15–10 are P_0^X/P_0^L and P_0^Y/P_0^L. It should also be obvious that points in Fig. 15–10 **off** the equilibrium curve represent pairs of price ratios at which the market is in disequilibrium; that is, in a state of either excess demand or excess supply.

Next, we carry out a similar "mapping" for the points r, r', and r'' in Fig. 15–9(c) and show them as points t, s', and t'' on curve Y in Fig. 15–10. It is obvious that the two equilibrium curves must intersect at s', since we know (from Fig. 15–9) that the set $(P_1^X/P_1^L, P_1^Y/P_1^L)$ is consistent with equilibrium in both markets. And if we were to derive a similar curve for the labor market, it is clear that that curve would also have to pass through point s', since if the two product markets are in equilibrium, then the labor market must also be in equilibrium. Thus Walras' law, when applied to a model with n markets (n = 3 in the present example), states that any set of relative prices which establishes equilibrium in n − 1 markets also maintains equilibrium in the nth market. (See discussion in Section 15–1.3.) It is for this reason that we can leave out one of the markets, and it makes no difference which one, when examining the equilibrium of the model.

15–2.2 The stability properties

We now let the equilibrium be disrupted through a disturbance in market X, such as an increase in the demand for X due to a change in consumers' tastes. This has the effect of shifting the equilibrium curve of market X to the left, as shown in Fig. 15–11. An increase in the demand for X shifts the demand functions in Fig. 15–9(b) to the right, from which it follows that for any given level of P^Y/P^L the level of P^X/P^L which clears the market is higher than it was

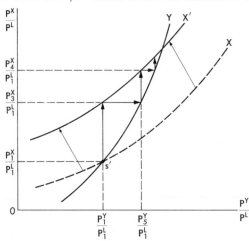

Figure 15–11

prior to the increase in demand. Hence the **upward** shift in the equilibrium curve in Fig. 15–11. (Actually, the equilibrium curve of market Y is also likely to shift, but for the problem at hand this latter shift can be ignored.)

To simplify matters, we shall assume that the adjustments in the two markets take place sequentially, rather than simultaneously, starting, for example, with market X. Market X experiences an increase in demand; therefore it now faces a situation of excess demand, and consequently the price of X will rise. We shall also assume that the magnitude of each change in price in any market is just sufficient to reestablish equilibrium in the respective market. Thus the new price ratio in market X is set at P_3^X/P_1^L. (Since we have left out the labor market, we can ignore changes in the wage rate. It is quite permissible to assume that the wage rate remains unchanged during the adjustment, and hence the identical subscripts on the P^L's.)

Now, however, market Y is out of equilibrium, since the increase in P^X/P^L, given the prevailing level of P^Y/P^L, increases the demand for product Y. (See Fig. 15–8c.) The excess demand in market Y results in an increase in P^Y/P^L to P_5^Y/P_1^L. As soon as the price of Y rises, market X is again in disequilibrium, because the increase in P^Y further raises the demand for X. The price of X, therefore, rises once more. And so on. It is clear from the few steps we have outlined that the changes in the price ratios become steadily smaller, and that both markets converge to the new equilibrium at the intersection of the two equilibrium curves. When a system behaves in this fashion we refer to it as being **stable.**

Of course, a system may not possess stability, and whether it does or not depends on the nature of the demand and supply functions, as well as on the manner in which markets react to states of disequilibrium. In the example just presented the stability derives directly from the assumptions that (a) all goods are substitutes, and (b) each market succeeds, through variations in its price, in reestablishing its own equilibrium.

Assumption (b) is clearly a very strong one, because if we "permitted" prices to either "undershoot" or "overshoot" their equilibrium targets, they could behave very erratically during the adjustment period, and thus fail to converge toward a general equilibrium point. But assumption (a) is equally important, although its relationship to the stability of the system may be less obvious. To demonstrate the role of assumption (a), we shall show that the violation of that assumption can make the system unstable.

Let us suppose that good Y is a complement for good X; in other words, assume that when the price of Y rises, the quantity of X demanded falls. To introduce this assumption into the above model we must interchange the numbers P_0^Y/P_0^L and P_2^Y/P_2^L in the labels of the demand functions in Fig. 15–8(b).

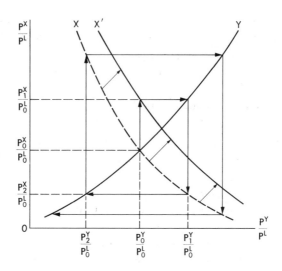

Figure 15–12

As a result of this change, the slope of the equilibrium curve of market X turns negative, as shown in Fig. 15–12. We assume an initial equilibrium at $(P_0^X/P_0^L, P_0^Y/P_0^L)$, followed by an increase in the preference for good X, and hence an upward shift in the equilibrium curve of X, as Fig. 15–12 shows. This shift creates an excess demand in market X, and consequently the price ratio rises to P_1^X/P_0^L, reestablishing equilibrium in that market. Now there is excess demand in market Y, and therefore P^Y/P^L is increased to P_1^Y/P_0^L. This time the increase in P^Y/P^L creates excess supply in market X, because of the assumption about the complementarity between goods Y and X. Consequently the price of X must be lowered, and equilibrium is reached at the ratio P_2^X/P_0^L. The fall in P^X/P^L, in turn, creates excess supply in market Y, so that P^Y/P^L falls to P_2^Y/P_0^L, and so on. As Fig. 15–12 shows, the magnitude of the changes in relative prices increases steadily, and the "cobweb" pattern traced out by the changes in prices pulls the system away from equilibrium. This system is, therefore, unstable.

15–3 CONCLUDING REMARKS

Even though the foregoing discussion presented no more than a bare outline of a disaggregated, or Walrasian, general equilibrium model, it was designed to throw at least some light on the more characteristic features of such models. In particular, we demonstrated that the basic ingredients of a Walrasian model—the market demand and supply functions—can be derived directly from our models of consumer behavior and the theory of the firm. The significance of this lies in the fact that the properties of the market functions, and hence the properties of the entire model, can be traced directly to the preferences of consumers and the technology confronting the producers. This enables us to study the effects of changes in preferences and technology on the equilibrium prices, and on the levels of output and consumption. But at the same time it must be remembered that if the number of goods and individuals in the system is large, the relationships of the model will necessarily be quite complex, and consequently the effects of given changes in preferences and technology will be determinate only if one makes rather restrictive assumptions about the nature of the utility and production functions. This may be unfortunate, but it is a fact of life: the more refined or "realistic" a model is, the greater its complexity.

We have also said a few words about the adjustment process of the model. This topic belongs in the general area of **dynamics** which is concerned with the behavior of variables over time. The Walrasian model may give rise to a variety of adjustment processes, one of which we have analyzed in the preceding section. In that discussion we were concerned primarily with the question of stability (or lack of it). The two examples we have chosen were meant to demonstrate the existence of a direct link between the properties of the demand functions, and the stability properties.

But the study of dynamics is useful also for purposes other than the analysis of stability properties. Some economists hold the view that even if the demand and supply functions are such as to yield a set of equilibrium prices, the equilibrium is never reached because at any moment, or in any interval of time, some of the functions are bound to shift. Under these conditions the equilibrium point itself is constantly (or at least intermittently) in motion. If such a model is stable, prices may be said to be "chasing" the equilibrium point, although they may in fact never reach it. In this case the study of the dynamical properties of the model may reveal the **direction** in which certain prices are likely to move at any particular point of time, as well as the **speed** of their movement. This information is not only interesting from the theoretical point of view, but also useful for policy purposes.

Whatever view one takes about the nature of the economic system and the manner of its workings, it is clear that general equilibrium models are powerful tools of analysis, which provide a convenient framework for formulating hypotheses concerning the behavior of different variables which make up the entire system, and the outcome of the interactions between them. In a sense, this text was designed to give the reader a basic understanding of the elements which constitute the building blocks of such models.

SUMMARY

This final chapter was meant to be a brief introduction to general equilibrium analysis. It was designed to illustrate one of the uses of the theory of individual behavior and at the same time to emphasize the intimate relationship between different areas of economic theory. For our example we chose a general equilibrium model, consisting of a number of different markets, in which the demand and supply functions were derived directly from the conventional models of consumer behavior and the theory of the firm, respectively. The analysis concerned itself primarily with the question of equilibrium. We called attention to an important property of general equilibrium models known as Walras' law. We also showed how the general equilibrium may be affected by changes in the behavior of the individuals in the model. The last part of the discussion was devoted to the study of the adjustment process and an examination of the stability of the system. We concluded with some remarks about the place and role of general equilibrium models in economic theory.

SELECTED REFERENCES

HAYEK, F. A., "The Use of Knowledge in Society." *American Economic Review* **35,** 1945, pp. 519–530.

HICKS, J. R., *Value and Capital*. Oxford: Clarendon Press, 2nd ed., 1946, Chapters 4, 5, and 8.

LANGE, O., and F. M. TAYLOR, *On the Economic Theory of Socialism*, B. E. Lippincott (ed.). Minneapolis: University of Minnesota Press, 1938.

SCHNEIDER, E., *Pricing and Equilibrium*. New York: Macmillan, 1952, Chapter 4.

EXERCISES

1. Consider an economy with two markets: a labor market and a market for product X. Assume that all traders observe a budget constraint which equates expenditures with receipts. The labor market can be described by the following linear functions. *Demand:* (i) If the relative wage rate (that is, P^L/P^X) is $12, then quantity demanded

is zero. (ii) Whenever the relative wage rate falls by one dollar, quantity demanded increases by one unit. *Supply:* (i) If the relative wage rate is $2, quantity supplied is zero. (ii) Whenever the relative wage rate rises by one dollar, quantity supplied increases by one.

(a) Plot the demand and supply functions on one diagram.
(b) Determine the relative wage rate which clears the labor market. What is the quantity of labor traded?
(c) What is the general equilibrium relative wage rate, i.e., what value of P^L/P^X clears both markets simultaneously?
(d) Suppose there occurs a shift in the demand function for labor which can be described by a shift in the functions' intercept from $12 to $14. Plot the new demand function.
(e) What effect will the above shift have on the functions of the product market?
(f) Determine the new general equilibrium relative wage rate.
(g) What is the effect of the above shift on the quantity of X produced?

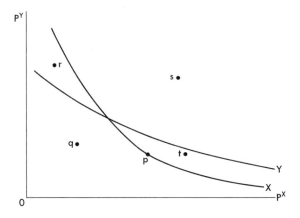

Figure E15–1

2. Consider an economy with three markets, X, Y, and Z. For simplicity we shall assume that the price of good Z is fixed (like money, the price of which is always equal to unity), and that P^X and P^Y denote the relative prices (in terms of the price of Z) of goods X and Y, respectively. Figure E15–1 shows the equilibrium relations for markets X and Y, respectively; i.e., each curve indicates the pairs of values of P^X and P^Y which maintain equilibrium in the respective market.

(a) What is the state of excess demand (supply), and what is likely to happen to the price in each market under the conditions represented by the following points: (i) p, (ii) q, (iii) r, (iv) s, (v) t?
(b) Assume that the current prices are given by point p. Trace out on the diagram the movement of the prices over time, assuming a sequential adjustment process according to which the relative price in each market adjusts by an amount which is just sufficient to clear the respective market.
(c) Is the above adjustment process stable or unstable?

(d) Copy Fig. E15–1 on a sheet of paper, but interchange the labels on the equilibrium curves. (This means that we are now dealing with an economy different from that described by Fig. E15–1.) Answer questions (a), (b), and (c) above under the new specifications.

3. Consider a three-market economy of the general type described in Question 2 above. Assume the following specifications for the equilibrium functions in markets X and Y. *Market* X: The function is linear with a P^Y-intercept at \$2 and a positive slope equal to unity. (It is assumed that P^Y is measured on the vertical axis.) *Market* Y: The function is linear with a P^Y-intercept at \$8 and a negative slope whose numerical value is unity.

(a) Plot (on graph paper, for greater accuracy) the two equilibrium functions.

(b) Determine the set of general equilibrium prices.

(c) Assume the following initial prices: P^X = \$2, P^Y = \$6. Trace out the changes in prices over time under the assumptions stated in Question 2 (b) above.

(d) Comment on the stability of the model.

(e) Assume the following change in the specifications of the model: the slope of the equilibrium relation of market X changes from one to $\frac{3}{5}$. Answer questions (a), (b), (c), and (d) for the modified model.

INDEX

INDEX

Activity (in linear programming), 198
Actuarial value, 266 n
Advertising, 129 ff
  its direct effects, 129 ff
  optimal level of, 131 ff
  secondary effects, 133 ff
Alchian, A. A., 274
Attraction to risk, 271–272
Auction, 315
Average fixed cost; *see* Cost, average
  fixed
Average product
  defined, 29
  illustrated graphically, 29
Average profit, 62, 110
Average revenue product
  defined, 166
  illustrated graphically, 167, 184, 186
Average total cost; *see* Cost, average total
Average variable cost; *see* Cost, average
  variable
Average variable input cost
  defined, 168
  illustrated graphically, 167, 184, 186
Aversion to risk, 270–271

Bator, F. M., 303
Baumol, W. J., 154, 222
Bear, D. V. T., 274
Behavior under uncertainty
  in the context of utility maximization,
    263 ff
  in an oligopolistic market, 141

Bilateral monopoly, 189 ff
Black market
  in an input market, 193
  in a product market, 111
Boulding, K. E., 118, 303
Brand demand function, 124
Brands (of commodities), 123
Break-even point, 57, 92, 129, 165, 182
Brehm, C. T., 274
Budget line, 233, 289 n
  illustrated graphically, 234, 251 ff,
    258 ff, 298–299, 301, 309
  rotation of, 240, 245, 261, 299
  shifts of, 234, 237, 239
  its slope, 234

Carlson, S., 40
Cartels, 143 ff
Cassels, J. M., 40
Chamberlin, E. H., 154
Change in demand
  compared with change in quantity
    demanded, 75
Clark, J. M., 154
Collusion, 144 ff
Compensated price change, 243 ff
Competition; *see* Pure competition,
    Monopolistic competition
Competitive fringe, 138
Complements, 171, 242, 319
Constant-cost industry, 79
Contract curve, 285, 290 ff
Convexity of indifference curves, 235 ff

Cooper, G., 274
Cost
  average fixed (short-run)
    defined, 15
    illustrated graphically, 17
    illustrated numerically, 15
  average total (short-run)
    as affected by changes in size of
      plant, 45–46
    defined, 15
    illustrated graphically, 17, 45–46
    illustrated numerically, 15
    represented as the slope of a ray, 18
    its shape explained, 21–22
  average variable (short-run)
    defined, 15
    illustrated graphically, 17
    illustrated numerically, 15
  direct, 9–10
  of inputs; *see* Input cost
  long-run average
    defined, 47
    illustrated graphically, 46
  long-run marginal
    defined, 48
    illustrated graphically, 48
    its relation to short-run marginal
      cost, 48–49
  long-run total
    defined, 48
    illustrated graphically, 49
  marginal (short-run)
    defined, 15, 20
    illustrated graphically, 17
    illustrated numerically, 15
    its independence of fixed cost, 23–24
    [Exercise 1. (e)], 113
  minimization of, 36–37
  opportunity, 9–10, 219, 254, 260
  related schematically to other
    variables, 4
  total (short-run)
    defined, 10
    illustrated graphically, 13
    illustrated numerically, 12, 15
    represented as an area of a
      rectangle, 21
  total fixed (short-run)
    defined, 10
    illustrated graphically, 13
    illustrated numerically, 12, 15

  total variable (short-run)
    defined, 11
    illustrated graphically, 13
    illustrated numerically, 12, 15

Decreasing-cost industry, 79
Demand function
  for income, 254 ff
  for an input
    effective, 169, 172, 175, 311, 315
    partial, 168, 172
  for leisure, 254 ff
  for an output
    effective, 141 ff, 151 ff, 309
    of the form of a rectangular
      hyperbola, 83, 94–95
    its inverse, 87
    kinked, 99, 139 ff
    of a market leader, 150
    of a monopolistic competitor, 124
    partial, 140 ff, 150 ff, 238–239, 241 ff
    its properties, 85 ff
Diminishing marginal rate of substitution,
    32, 232
Diminishing marginal utility, 272
Diminishing returns, law of, 30
Diseconomies of scale, 48
Distribution of commodities
  illustrated graphically, 282–283
  noncomparable, 282 ff
  Pareto-inferior, 281 ff
  Pareto-optimal, 281 ff
  Pareto-superior, 280 ff
Distribution of inputs (resources)
  efficient, 288
  illustrated graphically, 287
  noncomparable, 288
Division of labor, 47
Dorfman, R., 222
Dual (of a problem in linear
    programming), 221
Duopoly, 122
Dynamics, 321

Economics
  positive, 107
  normative, 107
  welfare, 278 ff
Economies of scale, 47
Efficiency
  defined, 34

condition for, 36
criterion for social welfare, 287–288
Efficiency curve, 288, 300, 302
Elasticity
arc, 85
of nonlinear demand functions, 88
point, 85
of a rectangular hyperbola, 94
in relation to prices under conditions
of discrimination, 103
its relationship to marginal revenue,
89
its relationship to total revenue, 90
unitary, 88, 94
Encarnación, J., 154
Entry of firms (into a competitive
market), 75 ff
Environment
economic, 3, 5
psychological, 4–5, 233
technological, 3
Equilibrium
adjustment to long-run—the firm,
71–72
adjustment to long-run—the market,
72 ff
equivalence between firm and market,
96
general, 308 ff
long-run, 71, 75
in monopolistic competition, 127, 128
short-run, 64–65
in an input market, 169
in monopolistic competition, 127
in oligopoly, 145
in a two-person exchange model, 299
quasi long-run, 75, 78–79
Excess demand, 299, 314–315, 318 ff
Excess supply, 299, 314–315, 318, 320
Excise tax, 114
Expected income, 265 ff
Expected utility, 265 ff
Expected utility function, 269

Factors of production; *see* Inputs
Feasible set, 208, 211–212, 215, 217, 289,
296
Fellner, W., 194
Foldes, L., 194
Friedman, M., 8, 274
Frisch, R., 40

Gabor, A., 81
General equilibrium
aggregated models, 308
disaggregated models, 308, 320
Grunberg, E., 65

Hall, R. L., 154
Harberger, A. C., 118
Hayek, F. A., 322
Hicks, J. R., 40, 247, 322
Hirschleifer, J., 178
Hitch, C. J., 154
Horizon, time, 257

Imputed value of inputs (in linear
programming), 219 ff.
Income
autonomous, 251
expected, 265 ff
real, 244–245
redistribution of, 116
Income effect, 245, 246 n
Increasing-cost industry, 79
Increasing marginal utility, 272
Indifference curve
illustrated graphically, 232–233
slope of, 232
social, 296
Indifference map, 232, 309
Inferior good, 238
Inferior process, 207
Inferior process combination, 206–207
Inferior state, 281
Input combinations
least-cost (efficient), 34 ff
Input cost; *see* Average variable input
cost, Marginal input cost, Total
input cost
Input restriction (in linear programming)
illustrated graphically, 211–212, 216 ff
ineffective, 212
Inputs
effects of changes in their prices, 38–39
fixed, 10–11
their imputed value (in linear
programming), 219 ff
substitution of, 32
transformation of, 26
Interdependence between firms, 138 ff
Isocost
defined, 34

in linear programming, 208
slope of, 34–35
Isoelastic, 88
Isoprofit line, 215, 218, 220
Isoquant
defined, 31
in linear programming, 201 ff
slope of, 32–33
Iso-utility curve, 232

Kenen, P. B., 303
Koopmans, T. C., 8
Koplin, H. T., 65

Lange, O., 8, 322
Law of demand, 246
Law of diminishing returns, 30
Leadership,
market, 149 ff
price, 138–139
Lerner, A. P., 247
Level (of a linear process), 199
Linear programming, 198 ff
Long-run cost; *see* Cost, long-run
average, long-run marginal,
long-run total
Loss minimization, 59

McKenzie, L. W., 23
Marginal cost; *see* Cost, marginal
Marginal input cost, 163, 184, 186
Marginal product
defined, 29
illustrated graphically, 29
illustrated numerically, 162, 175
Marginal rate of substitution
between inputs, 32–33
between products, 294
Marginal rate of transformation, 294
Marginal revenue; *see* Revenue, marginal
Marginal revenue product
defined, 161
illustrated graphically, 167, 184, 186
illustrated numerically, 162, 175
interdependence in the two-input case,
170–171
Marginal utility, 230, 272
Margolis, J., 154
Market leadership, 149 ff
Market-sharing, 149 ff
Markowitz, H., 274
Mark-up, 62
Methodology (of the text), 5 ff

Mishan, E. J., 303
Model (economic)
defined and characterized, 6
its nature alluded to allegorically, 6 ff
Monopolistic competition
compared with pure competition and
pure monopoly, 151–152
its nature, 122 ff
Monopoly (pure)
compared to pure and monopolistic
competition, 151–152
compared to pure competition, 105 ff,
176–177
defined, 84
its effect on the revenue product
functions, 173–174
under regulation, 108 ff
as a result of collusion, 145
in a two-person exchange model,
300–301
Monopsonistic competition, 181
Monopsony (pure)
compared to pure competition, 185
defined, 181
Morton, G., 222

Nagel, E., 8
Neutral good, 238
Noncomparable distributions, 282 ff
Normal good, 238
Normative economics, 278

Objective
of consuming units, 3
of producing units, 2
of the text, 2, 7
Oligopolistic markets, 138 ff
Oligopoly, 123
Oligopsony, 181
Opportunity cost, 9–10, 219, 254, 260
Optimal distribution
of inputs, 108, 288
obtained through price control, 110
of products, 281 ff
Optimal state, 281
Output
as affected by regulation, 115–116
maximization of (in linear
programming), 207 ff
maximization of (in a nonlinear
problem), 36–37
Ozga, S. A., 274

Pareto-inferior, 281 ff
Pareto-optimal, 281 ff
Pareto-superior, 280 ff
Pay-off, 266
  changes in, 267 ff
Pearce, I. F., 81
Positive economics, 278, 302
Price ceiling, 109
Price control
  in an input market, 192–193
  in a product market, 109 ff
Price discrimination
  in an input market, 187 ff
  in a product market, 96 ff
Price floor, 192
Price index, 101
Price leadership, 138–139
Probability (of an uncertain pay-off),
  265
  changes in, 266–267
Process (linear)
  defined, 198
  inferior, 207
Process combination
  inferior, 206–207
  its relation to an isoquant, 202
Product differentiation, 123, 147 ff, 152
Production-distribution plan, 291 ff
  condition for optimality of, 294
Production function, 26 ff, 33, 311
Production possibility curve, 289–290
  slope of, 294
Profit
  as affected by regulation, 116–117
  average, 62, 110
  defined, 56, 163
  gross, 168, 184, 214 n
  illustrated graphically, 56, 58, 61, 163,
    182
  related schematically to other
    variables, 4
Profit maximization
  by a cartel, 148
  choice of inputs, 163 ff
  choice of optimal product mix in
    linear programming, 213 ff
  under conditions of market leadership,
    138–139
  under conditions of market-sharing,
    149 ff
  its equivalence to cost minimization, 94
  its equivalence to loss minimization, 59

equivalence between optimal choice
    of output and optimal choice of
    inputs, 163 ff
  as producers' objective, 2–3
  relation between short-run and
    long-run, 71
  rule for its attainment under price
    discrimination
    in input markets, 189
    in product markets, 103
  rule for its attainment under pure
    competition
    in the long run, 70
    in the short run, 66
  rule for its attainment under pure
    monopoly
    in the long run, 96
    in the short run, 92
  rule for choosing the optimal level
    of inputs
    under pure competition, 167, 172
    under pure monopsony, 184, 186
  voluntary deviation from by a
    monopolist, 115
Pure competition
  among buyers, 163
  compared to pure monopoly, 105 ff,
    176–177
  compared to pure monopoly and
    monopolistic competition, 151–152
  compared to pure monopsony, 185
  the nature of, 53 ff
Pure monopoly; *see* Monopoly

Quasi long-run market equilibrium, 75,
  78–79

Rationing, 111
Real income, 244–245
Redistribution of commodities, 282
Redistribution of income, 116
Regulated monopoly, 108 ff
Returns to scale, 47–48
Revenue
  average
    defined, 62
    illustrated graphically, 62, 89
  marginal
    defined, 57
    illustrated graphically, 62, 89
    illustrated numerically, 175
    its relationship to a downward
      sloping demand function, 89

marginal, net, 133
marginal, total, 148
total
   defined, 56
   illustrated graphically, 56, 90
Revenue product; *see* Average revenue
   product, Marginal revenue
   product, Total revenue product
Risk
   attraction to, 271–272
   aversion to, 270–271
Robinson, J., 23, 118, 154, 178, 194
Rothschild, K. W., 154

Satisfaction
   related schematically to other
      variables, 5
Satisfaction maximization, 3
Savage, L. J., 274
Saving, T. R., 274
Schneider, E., 322
Scitovsky, T., 274, 303
Short run
   defined, 11
   cost; *see* Cost
Simon, H. A., 66
Slope (of a line or curve)
   measurement of, 19–20, 87
   positive, 14
Social indifference curve, 296
Social welfare function, 295 ff
Stable (system), 319, 321
Stigler, G. J., 40, 51, 66, 81, 154, 247
Streeten, P., 303
Substitutes, 123, 125, 171, 242, 316
Substitution effect, 245, 246 n
Superior good, 238
Superior state, 280
Supply function, 63, 311
   of labor, 254 ff, 309
   long-run market, 76, 79–80
Sweezy, P. M., 154

Tax shifting, 114
Taxation (of a monopoly), 112 ff
Taylor, F. M., 322

Technological change, 50
Time horizon, 257
Total cost; *see* Cost
Total input cost
   defined, 162
   illustrated graphically, 163 ff, 182 ff
   shifts in, 182
Total product
   defined, 28
   illustrated graphically, 28
   illustrated numerically, 162, 175
Total product curve, 27 ff
   shifts of, 30–31
Total revenue product
   defined, 160–161
   illustrated graphically, 160 ff, 182
   illustrated numerically, 162, 175
Total utility curve, 230–231
Total variable input cost
   defined, 162
   illustrated graphically, 166, 182 ff
   shifts of, 182
Transformation curve, 289

Uncertainty; *see* Behavior under
   uncertainty
Unemployment compensation, 256–257
Unfeasible set, 208, 211, 217
Unstable (system), 319
Utility boundary, 295–296
Utility curve (total), 230–231
Utility function
   defined, 228
   expected, 269
Utility index, 228, 264
Utility maximization (*see also*
   Satisfaction maximization)
   rule for its attainment, 235
   under uncertainty, 263 ff

Viner, J., 23, 51, 66, 81

Walras' law, 313, 318
Welfare economics, 278 ff
Welfare index, 296
Wootton, B., 8

Date Due